Synthesis Lectures on Computer Science

The series publishes short books on general computer science topics that will appeal to advanced students, researchers, and practitioners in a variety of areas within computer science.

Stijn Van Hijfte

Blockchain Platforms

A Look at the Underbelly of Distributed Platforms

Second Edition

 Springer

Stijn Van Hijfte
Howest University of Applied Sciences
Zottegem, Belgium

ISSN 1932-1228   ISSN 1932-1686 (electronic)
Synthesis Lectures on Computer Science
ISBN 978-3-032-00978-4   ISBN 978-3-032-00979-1 (eBook)
https://doi.org/10.1007/978-3-032-00979-1

This Springer imprint is published by the registered company Springer Nature Switzerland AG
The registered company address is: Gewerbestrasse 11, 6330 Cham, Switzerland

If disposing of this product, please recycle the paper.

Preface to the Second Edition

For this 2nd edition, I once again started the search: what information was out there and how I could try to create a clear picture on how the world has changed since the 1st edition. It is still a rich and amazing world out there, deserving of a good book explaining both old and new concepts.

In this book you can find explanations for new concepts such as Verkle trees, LayerZero, modular architecture, but also more details on zero knowledge proofs. The chapters on Bitcoin and Ethereum were adapted to reflect the current state of these blockchain networks. Similarly, other items were updated to reflect the reality of 2025, some items which are now outdated are either removed or received some more context. We introduce Avalanche, Solana and Polkadot amongst others. Other items remained unchanged, as they still offer key info which is interesting to the avid researcher.

This is once again not a simple training manual but rather a guide to help you understand key concepts, meet different solutions and networks, and of course, give you the tools to start discovering completely new things on your own. Good luck out there!

Zottegem, Belgium   Stijn Van Hijfte

Acknowledgements For all the people close to me, who know I always work too much. To my parents, who made me the person I am today, to my brother, who is always there for me. To my friends, who support me despite the fact that I am always busy.

But most importantly to my wife and 2 beautiful daughters Ella-June and Eleonore, you are always in my heart and my mind even when I seem far away.

Competing Interests The author has no competing interests to declare that are relevant to the content of this manuscript.

Preface to the First Edition

Why another book on blockchain? I asked myself the same question when I started to write this very line. The reason is actually quite simple. By this point, everyone seems to have heard of blockchain in one way or another. But it is clear to me that, on average, not one person really understands the core concepts or really knows what it was all about. Others had deep knowledge but either only of the core concepts or of one specific platform. Theory and personal perception are the core of the information and many of the sources I scoured from all over the world all seemed to be limited. Not bad, just limited. They all brought only a small piece of the puzzle that I had to try to form myself. This book attempts to give an extensive explanation of the core concepts and explain several platforms. Do I want to create a training manual that explains each platform in excruciating detail? No. However, this book should at least show you how these platforms generally work and, upon your choosing, allow you to investigate certain platforms in more detail on your own. All of the information is out there; it is up to you to go out and explore.

Zottegem, Belgium   Stijn Van Hijfte

Contents

The Past, The Present and The Future

While we are looking towards the present and the future in this book, it is still crucial for you to understand the past. It is this past that paved the way to the entire cryptospace as we know it today. There had been some 'experiments' in the past, such as B-money, which was a kind of 'cryptocurrency' that was released in 1998 by Wei Dai (Bitcoin was even named after B-money so its importance cannot be underestimated). Even before the emergence of B-money there was the creation of ecash by David Chaum as early as 1983. People often have the idea that the search for a real 'digital' currency is something new but since the advent of the internet, people have been searching for possibilities to implement digital currencies in a secure manner and it is in this field that blockchain finds its initial roots. However, also technologies that were used in security (such as hashcash) and the idea of peer-to-peer networks (which we know from file sharing application such as Napster or Bittorrent) all were crucial parts that eventually led to blockchain technology.

The real name of the person that started the entire blockchain revolution remains to this date unknown. All we know is that she/he/they called themselves 'Satoshi Nakamoto'. It was in 2008 that this Satoshi Nakamoto published a white paper titled: "Bitcoin: A Peer-to-Peer Electronic Cash System". In this paper an alternative solution was proposed to solve the well-known Byzantine General's problem in computer science and double spending problem more known in economic fields. The Byzantine General's problem refers to the issue of how one can know if a certain message is real when several parties are sending messages, and one or more have become corrupted. Who do we trust and how do we know who the liar is? The double spending problem is a classic case surrounding digital currency. Physical money can only be spent once, but how do you prevent digital money to be spent twice?

© The Author(s), under exclusive license to Springer Nature Switzerland AG 2026
S. Van Hijfte, *Blockchain Platforms*, Synthesis Lectures on Computer Science,
https://doi.org/10.1007/978-3-032-00979-1_1

In combination with earlier technologies, Satoshi Nakamoto introduced a new concept: a Proof-of-Work algorithm that would allow a distributed computer system to accept transactions in contrast to all earlier solutions, which needed in some way or another, a central authority to accept transactions or create currency. Consensus is at the core of the paper, consensus between the members of the network. The main idea that you should consider when you think about the advent of blockchain is that of distrust. Bitcoin was created in a time of political and financial unrest as the crisis of 2008 was unfolding all over the world. This distrust towards any central entity that could be corrupted or become some entity that would eventually become 'too big to fail'. Blockchain could fix this very problem as the entire system is built on not trusting the other party. You don't have to and you don't need some third 'impartial' party to validate the other participants. The network itself makes sure that each participants has to fall in line, or eventually be destroyed by the network. That last statement might be a little bit harsh but it is the core concept to understand.

It was a year later that the bitcoin network saw the light of day. The first block was mined (the so-called genesis block which meant the start of the network. The first 50 Bitcoin were created with this block but were completely unspendable!) and a secret message was hidden in the block by its creator: "The Times 03/Jan/2009 Chancellor on brink of second bailout for banks." Hereby confirming the underlying ideas to the technology and the entire cryptocurrency network. Of course the implementation has been revised by many programmers over the years. Satoshi Nakamoto was only involved with the development until 2011, after which he withdrew from the public scene and it was up to the community to not only up-hold the network, but also update it regularly. This meant that consensus was not only something that was used within the algorithm of the network but also by the people surrounding it. As you will find out later, the consensus within the technology proved to be more reliable that the one in the community. Over the years the bitcoin network grew (as you without a doubt know to a huge market). This could not last alone and other competitors joined the market.

In the years that followed, 'altcoins' or alternative cryptocurrencies started to emerge such as Litecoin, Namecoin and others. All of these had the same codebase as Bitcoin but tried to give their own twist to how a cryptocurrency should look like. Some tried to increase privacy, others tried to increase the amount of cryptocurrencies that were created with each new block, increase the number of transactions and so on. But the underlying model, basically stayed the same. Even though governments all over the world were well-aware of the evolution in the world of cryptocurrencies, it was waiting until 2013 when the first action was taken by one of these governments. The US authorities seized all accounts associated with Mt. Gox, which was a cryptocurrency exchange, as it wasn't registered as a money transmitter. It was the beginning of a lot of misunderstanding concerning the legal context of blockchain technology and cryptocurrencies. Research would follow, but it would still take years before real action was taken to provide a legal framework and to this day, many governments keep on struggling to create a real framework that can be used by both individuals and businesses.

One of the issues that Bitcoin and other altcoins started to struggle with, was the relation with drug trafficking and terrorism. As early as 2013, Bitcoins were seized during a drug investigation and to this day there are suspicions that some altcoins (certainly those focused on privacy), are used in the funding of criminal activities. Nowadays, crypto-exchanges need to adhere to similar laws as any other financial institution such as KYC (know your customer) legislation and AML (anti-money laundering) legislation.

Apart from the association with criminal activity, there was one main issue with Bitcoin and similar networks. There was a lot of computing power and interactions across the network. However, developing applications on top of the Bitcoin network proved to be (extremely) difficult and to this day, developers are trying to work out new ways to make use of the computing power to make powerful and trustworthy decentralized applications. One of the developers that was working on Bitcoin application was a 19-year old programmer, named Vitalik Buterin, and he was about to change the world. He saw the potential of blockchain technology and realized that its potential could go much broader than cryptocurrencies and financial services alone.

It was late 2013 when Vitalik Buterin published his white paper ("A next generation smart contract and decentralized application platform") describing a new way of working and a new open source protocol. The main issue he wanted to solve was that Bitcoin did not have a scripting language to help with the creation of decentralized applications. Because it proved too difficult to come to a general consensus within the Bitcoin community, he proposed an entirely new platform: Ethereum. It would be officially announced at the North American Bitcoin Conference in Miami, in January 2014. Quite quickly the founders decided to put the platform and its development in a non-profit. The development would be funded by a crowd sale of the new cryptocurrency called 'ether'. The idea of putting smart contracts in the blockchain was specified by Gavin Wood in the Ethereum yellow paper that describes the Ethereum virtual machine.

In July 2014, the Ethereum Foundation held an ether crowd sale which sold over 60 million tokens and about 12 million tokens were created so that the Foundation could fund future development and marketing efforts. A first version of the network was released a year later and was called 'frontier'. Any future developments came with new names and releases, proving the evolution that the network made.

Over time more and more players entered the field with their own implementations of blockchain technology or distributed ledger platforms focusing on specific target groups (i.e. developers or even business professionals) or industries (i.e. financial services and others). The popularity increased over the coming years and reached its highest moment around 2018, after which a massive crash followed. In the meantime, around 2015, the Hyperledger project was created, which has arguably incorporated some of the most famous development frameworks for enterprise blockchain today. Over 6000 altcoins have been created and are (more or less) functioning today.

1.1   The First Major Crash

We must offer some specific explanation on the cryptocurrency crash (also known as the Bitcoin crash or the great crypto crash). A huge sell-off took place in January 2018, leading to a crash in the value of Bitcoin for about 65 percent. A lot of other cryptocurrencies crashed even harder and in some cases completely disappeared from the map. Of course to have a crash, there first has to be some kind of boom. In the years leading up to 2017 there had been a steady increase in the value of Bitcoin and other cryptocurrencies. It was in 2017 that there was an unprecedented boom in cryptocurrencies and their values. All major institutions and investors seemed to be involved into the cryptocurrency markets, leading to results such as that of Bitcoin, which had grown with 2,700% in value in 2017!

This lead to the interest of a lot of small investors that also wished to enter the cryptocurrency market and took great risks. Starting to invest in unknown cryptocurrencies, either not understanding how the altcoin worked, not knowing what projects they were supporting (which in some cases was completely unrealistic) but even worse, had attracted a lot of con artists that wished to take advantage of gullible investors or those that wished to get 'rich quick' as some others had done in the beginning of the cryptocurrency markets. As there was no clear legal framework, a lot of initial coin offerings (ICOs) were launched, rounding up bigger and smaller investors, which eventually led to abuse and theft of funds. For those of you who aren't familiar with the term 'ICO', it is a type of funding where cryptocurrencies are used. These cryptocurrencies can become functional units of currency in the case the funding goal is met and eventually the project is successful (which is a big 'if'). To give you an idea, only about half of all ICOs tended to survive longer than four months in the years 2017 and 2018, and still over seven billion US dollar was raised via ICOs in the first half of 2018 alone! Other schemes involved 'pump-and-dump' scenario's where a couple of people would create transactions between one another, to give the impression of market interest and value. Other investors would invest in the altcoin as well, after which the original participants started dumping their holdings, leaving the investors with worthless coins.

A final important aspect that one should take into account is that most of the altcoins being launched are grounded in start-ups. And as anyone knows, start-ups also tend to fail and with it the cryptocurrency they launched. All of this created a very volatile market in which investors thought they were outsmarting the others or could hold out just a bit longer. Even though warnings kept on increasing that there was a major bubble in place, this didn't stop most of the investors.

To give you an idea of the timeline, on December 17th, 2017, Bitcoin reached a price of $19,783.06. A couple of days later, on the 22th of December, the price fell below $11,000 which was only one of the many cryptocurrencies dropping to all time lows. Here the bad news didn't stop, as rumors regarding possible bans of trading in cryptocurrencies in South-Korea, even led to more sell-offs and on January 28th, 2018, there was a major hack of CoinChck which was at the time Japan's largest cryptocurrency OTC market (over the counter market where seller and buyer interact directly), which led to a loss of 530 million USD of NEM (where NEM is a blockchain development platform written in Java). Also other cryptocurrency exchanges were dealing with hacks and irregular trades, leading to even more distrust in the market and investors seeking refuge from the highly volatile cryptocurrency markets. By September 2018, the cryptocurrency market had crashed for over 80% in value, making it worse than the Dot-com bubble that had led to a drop in market value of internet-related companies from their peak in March 2000, to their low in October 2002, which was about 78% lower in value.

Now you know the story, or at least a part of it. Because a story like this one has many different perspectives that one needs to take into account. The most important aspect that I would like you to remember is that none of these reasons has anything to do with blockchain technology itself. Some projects might have failed with certain start-ups because of wrong implementations. As with any technology and with any application, mistakes can be made. Again, this doesn't mean that there is an issue with the underlying technology. Rather, people not understanding the technology or how they should implement a blockchain project.

The reasons for the crash were to a large extent financial, as with any bubble, but the scrutiny regarding blockchain technology has remained. This means that people have become very skeptical towards distributed ledgers and rather than looking into the possibilities of the technology, they rather declare that they have lost 'faith' and wonder why you 'still believe'. As I stated before, there are enough reasons to wonder why you should or should not implement a blockchain platform but believing in the underlying concepts shouldn't be one of those.

Although the cryptocurrency crash has led to major distrust and since that major crash, other crashes have happened over the last couple of years. Other scandals also have risen in the field of cryptocurrencies (the stablecoin Tether is a prime example. Over a long period there have been scandals regarding the parity with USD. There have been problems with audits, independence, allegations of price manipulation and more. We go in more detail in the final chapter of the book on this topic). Still, those that really wanted to do something with blockchain haven't been waiting around and have made major steps forward in the development of new and exciting implementations. All of this has led to an entire industry of its own, with new developers and architects taking a more prominent position in the new IT-landscape. Facebook has tried to launch its own coin with the creation of Libra and other major payment providers have tried and succeeded as well. As Ripple and others are transforming entire industries, blockchain and cryptocurrencies are here to stay, for better or for worse.

But in the last couple of also other exciting and less exciting events have taken place. ByBit reported the theft of 1.5 billion USD in ether on February 21, 2025 estimated to be the largest crypto heist in history (or at least so far). Hackers have stolen hundreds of millions worth of cryptocurrencies but also "smaller" crimes have taken place, such as the pump-and-dump scheme performed by the now notorious "Hawktua" girl. We witnessed the rise and fall of the bored ape yacht club and saw different crypto CEOs go to jail such as Bankman-Fried and Alex Mashinsky. But despite all these facts, the technology remains fascinating and worth exploring!

1.2   Now

The world of 'blockchain' has become much broader than we have ever seen, and keeps on increasing. You have the 'traditional open implementations such as Bitcoin and Ethereum, while there are currently also closed implementations such as Hyperledger Fabric and Hyperledger Sawtooth which allow you to create consortiums between a selected group of partners that work together. However, don't be surprised if you are confronted with terms such as DAGs (directed acyclic graphs), MerkleDAGs, BlockDAGs and others. These are all exciting ways of implementing decentralized networks but all want to achieve the same as the "original" blockchain technology.

Underlying Concepts and Technologies

2

To understand blockchain and distributed ledger solutions, one should also understand the underlying technologies and concepts that make up, or at least have influenced, the creation of blockchain technology. Only that way we can hope to understand how the idea of Bitcoin and blockchain saw the light of day. You can simply pass through this section, but you will see that if you are willing to take the time to understand what underlying principles have helped to define blockchain, it will give you an edge once we start to dive deeper into blockchain itself.

2.1   Hash Functions

The use of hash functions or "hashing" is the use of a certain algorithm to map an input of variable-length arbitrary input data to a unique fixed-length output. This output is what we generally also call a "hash". Important to understand is that these are one-way functions, meaning that you shouldn't be able to reverse the output data back to the original input data. We can often make the link between these hashes with 'hash tables' which are simply tables containing a number of hashes to speed up the look up of a certain hash in computer software. So here are some of the most important characteristics of cryptographic hash functions:

- Pre-image resistance: for a certain hash value a it should be difficult to find any other message m so that hash(m) = a
- Second pre-image resistance: when we consider a message m_1, it should be difficult to find a second message m_2 so that hash(m_1) = hash(m_2)

© The Author(s), under exclusive license to Springer Nature Switzerland AG 2026   7
S. Van Hijfte, *Blockchain Platforms*, Synthesis Lectures on Computer Science,
https://doi.org/10.1007/978-3-032-00979-1_2

- Collision resistance: it should be difficult to find to different values that lead to the same hash value.

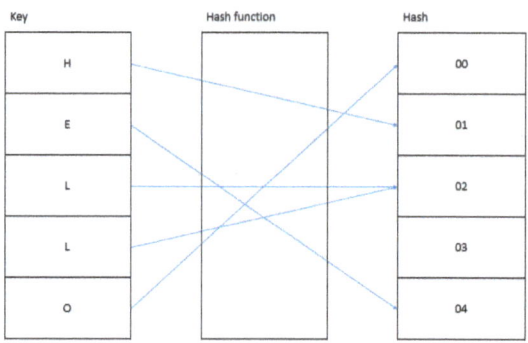

Hashing

Hash functions have some specific characteristics which make them so useful in todays' world, both for cryptography and for blockchain platforms. One of these relations is that a specific input in the function will always lead to a specific output. If you only change one letter, number or symbol, the entire output will change; this has three valuable properties. First of all, it allows us to check the integrity of what you have received. For example, if you download certain software on your pc, you can often check if the hash of your download matches the hash of the website. When this is not the case, you know there is a possibility that you have downloaded malware or at least not the application you were originally looking for. Secondly, when you receive the hash, you have no way of knowing what the input was. As we said before, only changing one letter will lead to a completely different outcome. In the world of cybersecurity there is something called "rainbow table attack". In this case the attacker has a table of hashes of which he knows the input and the specific hash function that has been used and he compares these with the hash of a password he was able to steal. If he finds a match, he knows your password. So if an attacker knows which hashing algorithm was used, he can try to guess what the input was but normally the hash itself will not help him with this (some hashing algorithms have been 'broken' in the past so that attackers can much faster and easier guess what the original input was). The final positive outcome we are looking for is a function that is collision-resistant, leading to a situation where you cannot find two inputs that have the same output. Ultimately, every hashing function is not completely collision resistant because there is a variable input and only a limited fixed output. At least it should take a long time to find such a collision, otherwise the function loses its value. Over time several hash functions have commonly been in use within software. The reason why these have been developing over time is because with increasing computer power, several of the 'older' standards have been broken, while others contain vulnerabilities that have been exploited. Such attacks include the 'collision attack' where the attacker will try to find two inputs which lead to the same output. No hash function is really 'collision-free' but it should normally take an extremely long time to find such a collision. Other attacks are the 'birthday attack' and the 'pre-image attack'. There are even competitions that aim at breaking current hash functions such as SHA-256. Why? When vulnerabilities are discovered, better hash functions are created that overcome these vulnerabilities. Wouldn't you rather have that an attacker breaks the function 'legitimately' than using his newfound knowledge for malicious activities?

2.2   eCash

ECash was an idea of David Chaum back in 1983.[1] It was meant as an anonymous cryptographic way of spending money where the money would be stored on the computer of the user and signed by the software of the bank. There was a public key system but the bank was in control as a central authority. Eventually in 1990 DigiCash implemented the system with Mark Twain Bank in Saint Louis where over three years about 5000 people made use of the system. It would remain in use until 1998 (even though DigiCash went broke in 1993). ECash did know some use in Europe at several institutions as electronic payments started to become more and more popular and organizations were looking for new ways of performing transactions. The reason why David Chaum deserves specific credit here, is that his paper from 1982 "Computer Systems Established, Maintained, and Trusted by Mutually Suspicious Groups" had all elements that we would see in the first blockchain implementation, except for the proof of work algorithm.[2]

2.3   Hashcash

The second of the earlier technologies that preceded Bitcoin and other blockchain platforms we would like to reference is hashcash which is a proof of work algorithm which has been used as a counter measure for denial-of-service attacks in several systems. It has been invented by Adam Back in 1997 and is to this day widely used all over the world as it is being used as the bitcoin mining function.[3] The cost-function must be efficiently verifiable, but parameterisably expensive to compute. In human words this means it must be easy to verify if a found solution is also the correct solution, while it should be sufficiently hard to find such a solution in the first place.

---

[1] Edwin (November 15, 2017). 1983: eCash door David Chaum. https://www.bitcoinsaltcoins.nl/1983-ecash-david-chaum/. Accessed May 17, 2020.

[2] Wat is de geschiedenis van blockchain? https://btcdirect.eu/nl-nl/geschiedenis-blockchain. Accessed June 3, 2019.

[3] The paper on Hashcash can be found here: http://www.hashcash.org/papers/hashcash.pdf.

2.3.1   The Hashcash Cost-Function

The hashcash cost-function is used in the Bitcoin network to this day. It is a non-interactive, publicly auditable, trapdoor-free cost function with unbounded probabilistic cost. What does this actually mean? Publicly auditable means that the cost-function can easily be verified without making use of any secret information or trapdoors.[4] There should be no trapdoors within the cost-function we are using, otherwise the protocol itself could be broken with anyone who has knowledge about the function and one could no longer rely on the fact if one actually did the work or achieved the result by making use of this trapdoor. It would attack the trust that exists within the network and be detrimental to the willingness of the miners to invest time and energy to solve the challenge. As we noted earlier, the result of a cost-function of any kind should be easy to verify but difficult to create in the first place.[5] But we can understand that there are different types of cost functions. A first difference can be made between fixed cost and probabilistic cost functions. The fixed cost-function, as you could have guessed makes use of a fixed amount of resources to compute, with the fastest possible algorithm a deterministic one. A probabilistic cost-function on, the other hand, has a predictable expected time to compute but in reality has a random actual time because the client is trying to compute the cost-function by making use of a randomly selected start value.[6] Within the probabilistic cost-functions we can again make a distinction between two groups: the unbounded and bounded probabilistic cost-function. An unbounded cost-function can in theory take forever to compute, although one should note that the probability of taking longer than expected quickly decreases towards zero. With a bounded cost-function, one should know and realize that there is a limited space within the result can be calculated (rings a bell?), a specific key space needs to be searched so there is always an upper bound to the cost of finding a solution.

$$\begin{cases} \mathcal{C} \leftarrow \text{CHAL}(s, w) & \text{server challenge function} \\ \mathcal{T} \leftarrow \text{MINT}(\mathcal{C}) & \text{mint token based on challenge} \\ \mathcal{V} \leftarrow \text{VALUE}(\mathcal{T}) & \text{token evaluation function} \end{cases}$$

We see above a challenge c called by the server towards the client, computed by the server by making use of the CHAL() function where the service-name bitstring s and the amount of work w are the key parameters. The client then has to compute a token $\mathcal{T}$

---

[4] We do not mean literally 'auditable' by an auditor that would repeat the work in any sense. It means that we can efficiently verify the result of a cost-function without the cost of repeating the work to come to this final result.

[5] Back, A. (August 1, 2002) Hashcash—A denial of Service Counter-Measure.

[6] You can sense that 'luck' is also an important factor here, as it is almost a lottery to find the right starting value within the cost-function. This is also the case for the challenge put forward by the Bitcoin protocol.

using a cost-function MINT()[7] and with the work difficulty w as part of the challenge. Finally, the server will check the token by making use of an evaluation VALUE(). There is also a possibility for a non-interactive cost function (so without the interaction between the server and the client) where the client can choose a challenge or a random start value in the MINT() function.

$$\begin{cases} \mathcal{T} \leftarrow \text{MINT}(s, w) \text{ mint token} \\ \mathcal{V} \leftarrow \text{VALUE}(\mathcal{T}) \text{ token evaluation function} \end{cases}$$

For the hashcash cost function, you should take some consideration for the following notation, introduced by Adam Back. Considering a bit string $s = \{0,1\}^*$, we can define $[s]_1$ so that this is the left-most bit while $[s]_{|s|}$ is the right-most bit so that $s = [s]_{1...|s|}$. There is also the binary infix comparison operator $x \overset{\text{left}}{\underset{b}{=}} y$ where b is the length of the common left-substring of the two bitstrings.

$$x \overset{\text{left}}{\underset{0}{=}} y \ [x]_1 \neq [y]_1$$
$$x \overset{\text{left}}{\underset{b}{=}} y \ \forall_{i=1...b}[x]_i = [y]_i$$

We see that the hashcash cost-function is computed relative to a service-name s to prevent tokens minted from another server being used on another. This service-name s can be any bit-string which is used to uniquely identify the service (such as the host name or an email address). The basis of the cost-function is finding partial hash collisions on all 0 bits k-bit string 0^k and the fastest way to do this is by making use of brute force. To make sure there is no double spending the server (or network) needs to keep a ledger of all transactions so that it is clear that all actors remain true. There should also be a time constrain to take into account clock inaccuracy, computation time and transmission delays.

$$\begin{cases} \text{PUBLIC:} \qquad\quad \text{hash function } \mathcal{H}(\cdot)\text{with output size } k \text{ bits} \\ \mathcal{T} \leftarrow \text{MINT}(s, w) \ \textbf{find } x \in_R \{0, 1\}^* \textbf{st} \mathcal{H}(s\|x) \overset{\text{left}}{\underset{w}{=}} 0^k \\ \qquad\qquad\qquad\quad \textbf{return } (s, w) \\ \mathcal{V} \leftarrow \text{VALUE}(\mathcal{T}) \ \mathcal{H}(s\|x) \overset{\text{left}}{\underset{v}{=}} 0^k \\ \qquad\qquad\qquad\quad \textbf{return } v \end{cases}$$

In practice the value of |x| could be chosen large enough (around 128 bits could suffice depending on the use case) to reduce the probability that a previously used value us reused by the client. The server can retain a double spending database with a timestamp to discard entries from the spent database after they have expired. The interactive hashcash

---

[7] The "mint" refers to the analogy between creating a cost token, or cryptocurrency, and actually minting physical money.

cost-function is used in interactive settings where we see TCP, TLS, SSH, etc. In the original implementation it was used as a challenge chosen by the server to defend its resources against DoS-attacks.

$$
\begin{cases}
\mathcal{C} \leftarrow \text{CHAL}(s, w) & \textbf{choose } c \in_R \{0, 1\}^k \\
& \textbf{return } (s, w, c) \\
\mathcal{T} \leftarrow \text{MINT}(\mathcal{C}) & \textbf{find } x \in_R \{0, 1\}^* \textbf{st } \mathcal{H}(s \| c \| x) \overset{\text{left}}{\underset{w}{=}} 0^k \\
& \textbf{return } (s, w) \\
\mathcal{V} \leftarrow \text{VALUE}(\mathcal{T}) & \mathcal{H}(s \| c \| x) \overset{\text{left}}{\underset{v}{=}} 0^k \\
& \textbf{return } v
\end{cases}
$$

Several improvements were proposed over the years, where i.e. the target string to find the hash collision against a fixed output string as it is simpler and reduces verification cost. Even though it is used in Bitcoin, several important aspects have been changed: the hashing algorithm (SHA-1 versus SHA-256, 20 to 160 hash bits 0 versus at least first 32 of 256 hash bits zero, Bitcoin periodically resets difficulty level as explained later).

2.4   B-money

B-money was created by Wei Dai in an effort to create an anonymous, distributed electronic cash system in a paper that was published on the cypherpunks mailing list in 1998. He proposed two separate protocols to come to his solution. The first was a symmetric proof of work function to create his digital currency. The reason why this protocol wouldn't be deemed acceptable was because that it required a broadcast channel that could not be jammed and remained synchronous. The B-money is being transferred by broadcasting all transactions to all participants. All the participants are hereby forced to keep accounts on all other participants. When there are conflicts on the network, each party can broadcast the evidence over the network and each participant needs to determine the effect and outcome for themselves within the accounts they keep. As you can sense this is not something that would be sustainable over time both from a technical standpoint (broadcasting, unjammable, synchronous) as from a business standpoint (determination by each participant of what the eventual outcome is of a dispute within accounts). A second approach was based on a small set of participants in the network would keep the accounts ('servers'). They would have to lock a certain amount of money to become a server and lose it if they proved to be dishonest. Important was that the other participants had to keep on checking the accounts to make sure the servers remained honest and to verify that the money supply was not being affected by this small group of participants. The importance of B-money and the ideas behind it cannot be underestimated. Satoshi Nakamoto, the writer of the Bitcoin paper, even made a reference to B-money.[8]

2.5   Peer-To-Peer

A peer-to-peer network is a different way of working when it comes to the 'classic' internet. In the usual way of accessing the internet, when a person tries to access a webpage, a request is sent from your computer to a central server where the webpage resides. The server responds and you see the webpage on your client. Every person on the planet that tries to access the same webpage, will send a request to the same central webserver (more or less, but we want to keep the example as simple as possible).

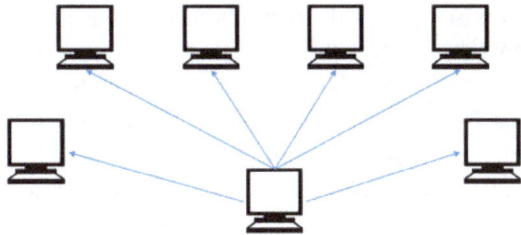

Server–client environment

In a peer-to-peer environment, the clients are connecting directly to each other and transfer data between one and another without a central server taking any part in the process. P2P is very similar to how humans communicate in real life: several nodes need to identify each other directly (making use of the IP-address of the partner) and check if communication over the correct port is possible. Only if this is the case, communication can begin. Peer-to-peer networks are different from other distributed systems on the following aspects[9]:

- **Symmetric role**: each participant typically acts as a client and a server
- **Scalability**: there is no all-to-all communication in the network necessary, allowing for scaling
- **Heterogeneity**: node software can run on different hardware
- **Distributed control**: control in the network is shared by all participants
- **Dynamism**: P2P applications are often functional in a very dynamic environment.

---

[8] If you would like to know more, please do not hesitate to read the paper written by Wei Dai http://www.weidai.com/bmoney.txt.

[9] Vu, Q.H., Lupu, M., Ooi, B.C. (2010) Peer-to-peer Computing: Principles and Applications. 1st ed. U.S.: Springer, p. 35.

There are centralized possibilities for P2P systems but these systems lack the robustness and scalability one can expect from an actual decentralized P2P system. Other specifications that one needs to take into account for decentralized systems are the following: the network can either be hierarchical or flat, and the overlaying network can either be structured or unstructured. The first concept relays to the fact that there can be a network where certain nodes have more responsibilities than other nodes in the network (often called 'supernodes' or 'masternodes'). We will see several blockchain network where this is actually the case. This can deliver several advantages to a network, such as faster synchronization, better message throughput and increased scalability. These special nodes can become responsible for voting on events in the network or carry other key responsibilities which help determine the future of the network. Secondly, there is the choice between structured and unstructured data. In case we are working with unstructured data, each of the peers is responsible for its dataset and the queries on how it can forward this information. This comes with several disadvantages because it makes it very difficult to return data from such a network, which will often be incomplete and you are never sure that you will find back the correct data. Structured networks on the other hand, work with a predefined data format (specific JSON-format, XML-format, etc.). This allows for better information transferring and you can predict how the data will look like, once queried from the network. These types of networks come also with a set of challenges. The system can be very unpredictable as all nodes in the network control their own actions and can decide to enter or leave the network whenever they want. This, in turn, has an effect on the performance of the network. Depending on the nodes, the same query for data can be answered by multiple nodes or not at all, but also at different cost vectors. As data is copied over multiple nodes, there is the possibility that some of the nodes have conflicting data sets or even outdated data. There is no central point of a single truth, which can bring problems of its own. The networking aspect of a P2P system can also provide challenges as queries need (in some cases) to be broadcasted throughout the network, leading to congestion when there are a lot of these requests. Furthermore, the network cannot always support complex queries (as this means that nodes need to process more information on the data they are storing), security is often in question as the network is often open to all participants, privacy is a concern as there is accountability for the actions of a node in the network, there is the need for incentives so that participants will actually follow the rules of the network and support it. Finally, there is the need of a parallel programming model (which such networks sadly often lack). Routing in such networks (as stated before) often poses a challenging task. Certainly, the scalability of unstructured P2P networks often poses a challenge because of network congestion. This is the trade off one has to make for high autonomy and low maintenance costs of the nodes. Often these networks make use of TTL (time-to-live) to determine the validity of queries that are being propagated throughout the network. Several techniques for routing have been defined over time. First, we are going to give a short overview of the techniques used in unstructured networks: breadth-first search (BFS) and depth-first search (DFS). The first has a predefined parameter D that determines the maximum TTL of a query. It forwards the query to all nodes and the message keeps on propagating until D is reached. The second technique on the other hand also uses the same parameter D but only sends the query to the most promising nodes in the network. There are also heuristic-based routing strategies such as iterative deepening. Iterative deepening is a technique that has been derived from AI research and basically comes down to several breadth-first searches that are been scaled over time until the TTL is reached (or the result is returned). Another technique is directed BFS, where the message is first propagated to a subset of the neighboring nodes, after which 'classic' BFS takes over. A third technique is called 'local indices search' where the node not only creates an index for its local data but also for the data stored at neighboring nodes. Routing indices-based search takes it up a notch by making nodes store topics and the number of documents stored by their neighbors. There are several techniques that fall under routing indices-based search (RI) called compound RI, hop-count RI and exponential aggregated RI. Next, there is the random walk where the query is forwarded to one or more random neighbors until the result is found or TTL is reached. The sixth technique is adaptive probabilistic search which is a random walk query with some probabilities added. The node sending the message will choose its neighbor based on some indicators. Next is the bloom filter based search which will make use of bloom filters (explained later) to determine which information is stored at which (neighboring) node. Structured peer-to-peer networks also have a number of routing options. These can be divided in three groups: networks using distributed hash tables, skip list systems and tree based systems. The first uses distributed hash tables (explained below), the second will make use of Skip graph or something similar which are lists and the nodes participate at each level of the lists. The tree based systems make use of a tree-based structure to index the data. The first routing technique used is called 'chord' and makes use of hashes to map nodes and data items in a single-dimensional identifier space. Another is 'CAN' or 'content addressable network' which is built on a virtual d-dimensional Cartesian coordinate space. A third type is called 'PRR trees' of which 'Pastry' and 'Tapestry' are 2 implementations. Each node constructs a routing table based on node-IDs and these IDs indicate which of them are closest. A third technique is called 'Viceroy' which is a multi-level DHT-based system while a fourth called 'Crescendo' takes a hierarchical DHT approach. Skip Graph, as described above, makes use of multiple lists at a level. There is also SkipNet, P-Grid, P-Tree and BATON. There are of course also hybrid P2P systems which makes use of techniques such as 'ultrapeers'. In this technique there are two types of nodes: ultrapeers and leaf peers. The first will forward queries to other ultrapeers while these ultrapeers will also search its leaf peers based on indexing to locate the node with the desired data. There is also the system of structured supernodes and edutella. The concept of 'trust' is also an important one to consider when we talk about P2P systems. How do you trust the other nodes in the network? In a world without servers there are 2 techniques that can be used to manage trust: a gossip protocol to exchange knowledge amongst the all the nodes in the network while the second techniques only focuses on 'local' reputation. One of the first P2P networks was Napster (a centralized peer-to-peer network) which allowed file sharing over the internet. If we are really looking at fully decentralized peer-to-peer networks, we know examples such as FreeNet, Gnutella, Free-Haven and others. The BitTorrent protocol is another such a specific implementation of a peer-to-peer network that is still in use today.

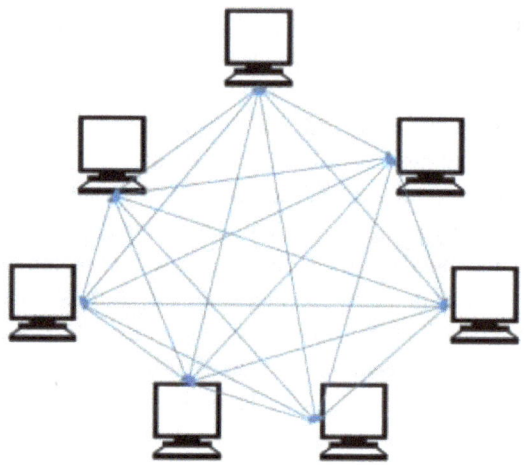

Peer-to-peer

In the BitTorrent world, a computer joins a 'swarm' when it starts loading a .torrent file. Based on this file, the client contacts a tracker, which is a server that keeps track of all the connected clients. The clients start to share IP-addresses based on this information, after which data can be shared. From the second you have downloaded a specific bit of a file, you start to upload it as well in the network, speeding up every participants download speed without stressing a single machine. This tracker system is more and more being replaced by a traceless system so that a central server can be completely avoided. This is done by making use of a distributed hash table. From the second you start using a 'magnet link' more and more nodes in the network are contacted until the information on the file requested is found.

2.6   Distributed Hash Table

A distributed hash table or 'DHT' is a hash table in a decentralized distributed system. This means that key-value pairs are stored in a table and each node in the network can make use of the key to look up a certain value in the table. The nodes in the network are responsible to keep up the table with unique keys so that there are no double values and hence issues in the network. These DHTs came into live by P2P networks such as Napster, Freenet, Gnutella and BitTorrent. These DHTs are easily scalable with any number of nodes in the network. They are also fault tolerant and are easily maintained as it doesn't matter as new nodes join or leave the network. When we go into more detail, we already know that the DHT consists out of a key. This keyspace partitioning scheme is divided among all the participating nodes. There is also an overlay network that is responsible for connecting all the nodes (structured). The final component is the actual hashing of the values in the table. There is either consistent hashing or rendezvous hashing that helps to map keys to nodes. The advantage here is that only neighboring nodes are influenced when a node enters or leaves the network.

2.7   Decentralized Versus Distributed

We often talk about a distributed network versus a decentralized network but what is the difference between these two and how do they differ from classic centralized solutions? One can easily imagine a centralized structure. As in the example with the server and the clients in the paragraph before, you have one point of failure and one point of control. This is the central power in the network that determines everything. Decentralized is the next step. Here there isn't a single central power, but you can find several of these 'central' clusters within the network. So the network has moved away from a central, single point of failure but we haven't reached the stage of a 'distributed' network just yet. In a distributed network no central point(s) can be discovered in the network, so taking out a node will not lead to information loss as there is no single point of failure (nor four points of failure i.e.).

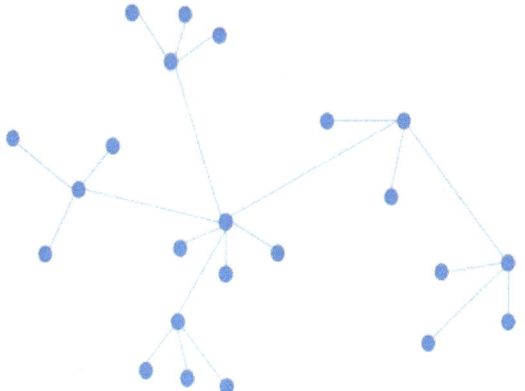

Decentralized structure

This structure can be seen as a subset of the distributed network where power between all the nodes is even more divided throughout the network. There is no longer a real point of failure as any node can leave or enter the network without impacting the overall functionality (up to a certain point depending on the replication rate of date throughout the network).

2.7.1   SHA-256

SHA or secure hashing algorithms are a specific family of cryptographic functions which were specifically designed to deal with the security of data. And as you guessed it, it does so by making use of hashing. What is hashing? Easily explained it is a mathematical algorithm to come to a fixed-size output.[10] No matter how long the input is, the output will always have the same size! Change one letter, one number or even something as small as a dot (.) and the output will be completely transformed. Or at least that is how a good functioning hashing algorithm works. It will make use of Boolean operations such as AND ($\wedge$), XOR ($\oplus$) and OR ($\vee$), bitwise complements ($^-$) and integer addition modulo 2^{32} (at least for SHA-256). Several attacks are imaginable on these hashing algorithms. The first is a brute force attack where the attacker tries every possible input to find the output. The harder it is for the attacker to find the original message, the better the so called 'pre-image resistance'. A second type of attack is the collision attack. Here the attacker tries to find two possible inputs that lead to the same kind of hashing output. If this happens, and an application compares the hashes rather than the passwords, an attacker could gain access without actually knowing the correct password. A third type of attack is the birthday attack which is based on the 'birthday paradox'. This paradox states that, if you are in a given room with for example 30 people, and you ask for everyone their birthday, you have about 70% chance that 2 of them will share the same birthday. Not to go too deeply into any explanation[11] the birthday attack the attacker will try to create the same hash as the correct one but with incorrect input. This can be done when the output string isn't large enough. Then there are only a limited amount of possibilities of how input is transformed to output. Of course you could say that this is also impossible, because the output of a hashing function is always limited. This is true, but the larger the output becomes, the more difficult it will be for the attacker to perform this kind of attack. A final attack that could take place is the rainbow table attack. A rainbow table is a table that simply contains a list of inputs with their hashed outputs. All the attacker does is trying to match a certain hash to a specific input. There are several types and families of hashing algorithms but the focus here lies on the SHA-family. Over time there has been SHA-0, SHA-1, SHA-2 and SHA-3. SHA-0 and SHA-1 were proven to be vulnerable to several types of attacks in the past. SHA-2 produces 224 or 256 sized digests where

---

[10] Important to note is that the output of a hashing algorithm is also one-way, which means it is impossible to transform the output back to the original input data. Or at least that is the theory...

[11] The formula behind the paradox is the following: $1 - 365!((365 - n)! * 365^n)$ with n the number of participants in a room.

SHA-1 only produced 160-bit digests. SHA-256 has a digest length of 256 bits and is a keyless hash function. Its algorithm operates on 32-bit words and makes use of the following functions (just to give you a general idea):

$$ch(X, Y, Z) = (X \wedge Y) \oplus (\overline{X} \wedge Z),$$

$$\mathrm{Maj}(X, Y, Z) = (X \wedge Y) \oplus (X \wedge Z) \oplus (Y \wedge Z),$$

$$\sum_0 (X) = RotR(X, 2) \oplus RotR(X, 13) \oplus RotR(X, 22),$$

$$\sum_1 (X) = RotR(X, 6) \oplus RotR(X, 11) \oplus RotR(X, 25),$$

$$\sigma_0(X) = RotR(X, 7) \oplus RotR(X, 18) \oplus ShR(X, 3),$$

$$\sigma_1(X) = RotR(X, 17) \oplus RotR(X, 19) \oplus ShR(X, 10),$$

where RotR(A, n) stands for the circular right shift, ShR(A, n) stands for the right shift of the binary word A. A∥B stands for the concatenation of both the binary words A and B. it also makes us of the 64 binary words K_i given by the first 32 bits of the fractional parts of the cube roots of the first 64 prime numbers:

0x428a2f98	0x71374491	0xb5c0fbcf	0xe9b5dba5	0x3956c25b	0x59f111f1	0x923f82a4	0xab1c5ed5
0xd807aa98	0x12835b01	0x243185be	0x550c7dc3	0x72be5d74	0x80deb1fe	0x9bdc06a7	0xc19bf174
0xe49b69c1	0xefbe4786	0x0fc19dc6	0x240ca1cc	0x2de92c6f	0x4a7484aa	0x5cb0a9dc	0x76f988da
0x983e5152	0xa831c66d	0xb00327c8	0xbf597fc7	0xc6e00bf3	0xd5a79147	0x06ca6351	0x14292967
0x27b70a85	0x2e1b2138	0x4d2c6dfc	0x53380d13	0x650a7354	0x766a0abb	0x81c2c92e	0x92722c85
0xa2bfe8a1	0xa81a664b	0xc24b8b70	0xc76c51a3	0xd192e819	0xd6990624	0xf40e3585	0x106aa070
0x19a4c116	0x1e376c08	0x2748774c	0x34b0bcb5	0x391c0cb3	0x4ed8aa4a	0x5b9cca4f	0x682e6ff3
0x748f82ee	0x78a5636f	0x84c87814	0x8cc70208	0x90befffa	0xa4506ceb	0xbef9a3f7	0xc67178f2

The algorithm also makes use of padding to make sure that the input has a length that is an exact multiple of 512 bits. It always follows a specific procedure whereby a bit 1 is appended, k bits 0 are appended[12] and the length $l < 2^{64}$ of the input is represented by exactly 64 bits. These are all added to the end of the message. For each block $M \in \{0,1\}^{512}$, 64 words of 32 bits are constructed with the first 16 being created by splitting M in 32-bit blocks $M = W_1\|W_2\|...\|W_{16}$ and the remaining 48 are created by: $W_i = \sigma_1(W_i - 2) + W_i - 7 + \sigma_0(W_i - 15) + W_i - 16$, $17 \leq i \leq 64$. The initial step of the hash computation is done by setting 8 variables to their initial values, which are given by the first 32 bits of the fractional part of the square root of the first 8 prime numbers:

$$H_1^{(0)} = 0x6a09e667 \quad H_2^{(0)} = 0xbb67ae85 \quad H_3^{(0)} = 0x3c6ef372 \quad H_4^{(0)} = 0xa54ff53a$$
$$H_5^{(0)} = 0x510e527f \quad H_6^{(0)} = 0x9b05688c \quad H_7^{(0)} = 0x1f83d9ab \quad H_8^{(0)} = 0x5be0cd19$$

The initial formula is set to the following:

---

[12] With k the smallest positive integer so that $l + 1 + k = 448 \bmod 512$ with $l =$ length in bits of the input.

$$(a,b,c,d,e,f,g,h) = \left(H_1^{(t-1)}, H_2^{(t-1)}, H_3^{(t-1)}, H_4^{(t-1)}, H_5^{(t-1)}, H_6^{(t-1)}, H_7^{(t-1)}, H_8^{(t-1)} \right)$$

What follows is the processing of each of the 64 blocks M_I and do the following 64 times:

$$T_1 = h + \sum_1 (e) + Ch(e,f,g) + K_i + W_i$$

$$T_2 = \sum_0 (a) + Maj(a,b,c)$$

$$h = g$$

$$g = f$$

$$f = e$$

$$e = d + T_1$$

$$d = c$$

$$c = b$$

$$b = a$$

$$a = T_1 + T_2$$

Out of which we can compute the new hashed values by:

$$H_1^{(t)} = H_1^{(t+1)} + a$$
$$H_2^{(t)} = H_2^{(t+1)} + b$$
$$H_3^{(t)} = H_3^{(t+1)} + c$$
$$H_4^{(t)} = H_4^{(t+1)} + d$$
$$H_5^{(t)} = H_5^{(t+1)} + e$$
$$H_6^{(t)} = H_6^{(t+1)} + f$$
$$H_7^{(t)} = H_7^{(t+1)} + g$$
$$H_8^{(t)} = H_8^{(t+1)} + h$$

The final step is the following:

$$H = H_1^{(N)} \| H_2^{(N)} \| H_3^{(N)} \| H_4^{(N)} \| H_5^{(N)} \| H_6^{(N)} \| H_7^{(N)} \| H_8^{(N)}$$

and we end up with the results from the SHA256-algorithm. To give you an idea: abc translates to ba7816bf8f01cfea414140de5dae2223b00361a396177a9cb410ff61f20015ad. To give you an idea of how it works, I also added the entire process in Python[13]:

---

[13] Smith, N.T. SHA 256 pseuedocode? *Stackoverflow*. https://stackoverflow.com/questions/119 37192/sha-256-pseuedocode/46916317#46916317. Accessed May 26, 2020.

```
W = 32           #Number of bits in word
M = 1 << W
FF = M - 1       #0xFFFFFFFF (for performing addition mod 2**32)


K = (0x428a2f98, 0x71374491, 0xb5c0fbcf, 0xe9b5dba5,
     0x3956c25b, 0x59f111f1, 0x923f82a4, 0xab1c5ed5,
     0xd807aa98, 0x12835b01, 0x243185be, 0x550c7dc3,
     0x72be5d74, 0x80deb1fe, 0x9bdc06a7, 0xc19bf174,
     0xe49b69c1, 0xefbe4786, 0x0fc19dc6, 0x240ca1cc,
     0x2de92c6f, 0x4a7484aa, 0x5cb0a9dc, 0x76f988da,
     0x983e5152, 0xa831c66d, 0xb00327c8, 0xbf597fc7,
     0xc6e00bf3, 0xd5a79147, 0x06ca6351, 0x14292967,
     0x27b70a85, 0x2e1b2138, 0x4d2c6dfc, 0x53380d13,
     0x650a7354, 0x766a0abb, 0x81c2c92e, 0x92722c85,
     0xa2bfe8a1, 0xa81a664b, 0xc24b8b70, 0xc76c51a3,
     0xd192e819, 0xd6990624, 0xf40e3585, 0x106aa070,
     0x19a4c116, 0x1e376c08, 0x2748774c, 0x34b0bcb5,
     0x391c0cb3, 0x4ed8aa4a, 0x5b9cca4f, 0x682e6ff3,
     0x748f82ee, 0x78a5636f, 0x84c87814, 0x8cc70208,
     0x90befffa, 0xa4506ceb, 0xbef9a3f7, 0xc67178f2)

#Initial values for compression function
I = (0x6a09e667, 0xbb67ae85, 0x3c6ef372, 0xa54ff53a,
     0x510e527f, 0x9b05688c, 0x1f83d9ab, 0x5be0cd19)

def RR(x, b):
    '''
    32-bit bitwise rotate right
    '''
    return ((x >> b) | (x << (W - b))) & FF

def Pad(W):
    '''
    Pad & convert
    '''
    mdi = len(W) % 64
    L = (len(W) << 3).to_bytes(8, 'big')        #Binary of len(W) in bits
    npad = 55 - mdi if mdi < 56 else 119 - mdi  #Pad so 64 | len; add 1 block if
needed
    return bytes(W, 'ascii') + b'\x80' + (b'\x00' * npad) + L    #64 | 1 + npad + 8
+ len(W)

def Sha256CF(Wt, Kt, A, B, C, D, E, F, G, H):
    '''
    SHA256 Compression Function
    '''
    Ch = (E & F) ^ (~E & G)
    Ma = (A & B) ^ (A & C) ^ (B & C)        #Major
    S0 = RR(A, 2) ^ RR(A, 13) ^ RR(A, 22)   #Sigma_0
    S1 = RR(E, 6) ^ RR(E, 11) ^ RR(E, 25)   #Sigma_1
    T1 = H + S1 + Ch + Wt + Kt
    return (T1 + S0 + Ma) & FF, A, B, C, (D + T1) & FF, E, F, G

def Sha256(M):
    '''
```

```
Performs SHA256 on an input string
M: The string to process
return: A 32 byte array of the binary digest
'''

M = Pad(M)              #Pad message so that length is divisible by 64
DG = list(I)            #Digest as 8 32-bit words (A-H)
for j in range(0, len(M), 64):  #Iterate over message in chunks of 64
    S = M[j:j + 64]             #Current chunk
    W = [0] * 64
    W[0:16] = [int.from_bytes(S[i:i + 4], 'big') for i in range(0, 64, 4)]
    for i in range(16, 64):
        s0 = RR(W[i - 15], 7) ^ RR(W[i - 15], 18) ^ (W[i - 15] >> 3)
        s1 = RR(W[i - 2], 17) ^ RR(W[i - 2], 19) ^ (W[i - 2] >> 10)
        W[i] = (W[i - 16] + s0 + W[i-7] + s1) & FF
    A, B, C, D, E, F, G, H = DG #State of the compression function
    for i in range(64):
        A, B, C, D, E, F, G, H = Sha256CF(W[i], K[i], A, B, C, D, E, F, G, H)
    DG = [(X + Y) & FF for X, Y in zip(DG, (A, B, C, D, E, F, G, H))]
return b''.join(Di.to_bytes(4, 'big') for Di in DG)   #Convert to byte array

if __name__ == "__main__":
    bd = Sha256('Hello World')
    print(''.join('{:02x}'.format(i) for i in bd))
```

2.8   Merkle Tree

A Merkle[14] tree or binary hash tree is a way of summarizing a large set of data on a sufficient manner because it will form a generalization of a hash chain. You could imagine an upside down tree, we are dealing with a branching data structure, where every leaf node is labelled with the hash of a data block and every non-leaf node is labeled with the hash of the labels of its child nodes. The root of the tree can be found on the top, while the leave nodes will spread out underneath the structure. When we are dealing with a number of n data elements, you can check if a certain data element is part of the root with at most $2 + \log_z(n)$ calculations, which proves that it is a very effective way of reducing data.

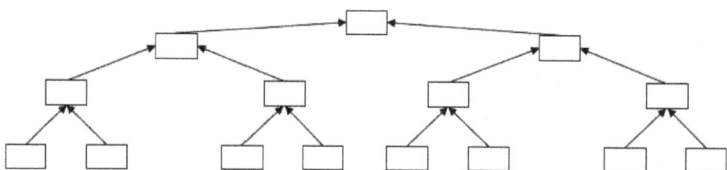

Simple example of a Merkle tree structure

This technology can be found in peer-to-peer networks where it can be used to verify if data is being received undamaged. We can also find this within both the Bitcoin and the Ethereum networks. The Merkle trees help to summarize information in a sufficient

---

[14] The hash trees were created by Ralph Merkle who patented it in 1979.

manner, in the case of Bitcoin and Ethereum, it are the transactions which are being summarized. Hashes of transactions are being hashed together until there is only one hash left, the root, which will be included in the block header. When we are dealing with Bitcoin, the hashing algorithm used is double-SHA256. To verify if a transaction is included in a specific block, all that is needed for the node to identify this, is the block header, from which it can extract the Merkle root and consequently retrieve a Merkle path from the full node, without actually storing the entire blockchain. This is something we can find back in simplified payment verification systems or SPV's.

2.8.1   Merkle Patricia Tree

When we talk about the Ethereum network, we make use of the Patricia Merkle Tree. This is a combination of the Merkle tree (described above) and the Patricia Trie. A Patricia Trie,[15] also called a Prefix Tree, Redix tree or simple trie, is a data structure that uses a key as a path so that nodes that share the same key, can share the same path. This means that this structure is the fastest for finding common prefixes and requires small memory at the same time.[16] When we make the step to the Merkle Patricia Tree, we see that each node receives a hash value which is decided by the SHA3 hash value of its contents. At the same time, this hash is used as the key that refers to this node. For example, Go-Ethereum uses levelDB while parity uses rocksDB to store states as key-value storages.[17] These key-values of the Ethereum state are used as paths on the Merkle Patricia Tree. We express the unit to distinguish between the key values in 'nibble'. From this we know that each node can have up to 16 branches. When a node does not have a child, we call this a 'leaf node'. This node consists of 2 items: its path and its value. Next to the branch nodes and the leaf nodes we can also distinguish a third type of node: the extension node. This is an optimized node of the branch node. Within the Ethereum state, there are often branch nodes with 1 leaf node, which are than compressed to extension nodes which contain the path and the hash of the child. To be able to distinguish between leaf nodes and extension nodes, there is a prefix being added. If we are dealing with a leaf node which has an even number of nibbles, the prefix 0x20 is added, in the event of an uneven number of nibbles, the prefix 0x30 is added. For extension nodes, in the case of an even number of nibbles, we add 0x00 while in the case of an uneven number of nibbles, we add 0x10.

---

[15] Check out Medium.com for more information regarding the Patricia Merkle Trie or blockchain in general.

[16] Commonly used for routing tables.

[17] Keys and values saved in the storage are not the key-values of the Ethereum state.

2.8.2   Bloom Filters

A final concept within the world of Merkle trees, is the concept of Bloom filters. It is a probabilistic data structure that can tell with certainty if an item is not in the dataset while it can otherwise only state with a certain probability that a data item 'might' be present in the dataset. This creates a situation where false negatives aren't possible while false positives can occur. What does this structure look like? It basically consists of a bit field and a set of hashing functions that eventually return a number with an index that corresponds with a bit in the bit field. So if the Bloom filter is tested with an input, it can be sure if it has seen the input before when the bit within the bit field is 1, otherwise it will be 0. How? The starting position of the bit field, is with all the bits turned to 0. When it is introduced to new data, certain bits are set to 1.

Starting position	Introduce elements	New position
Bit field	X and Y	**Bit field**
0		1
0	X	0
0		0
0	Y	0
0		1
0		1
0		0
0		0
0		1
0		1
0		0

Bloom filter set-up

Next, if you send data to the filter, it will know for sure that it has never seen the data before if not all the bits are equal to 1.

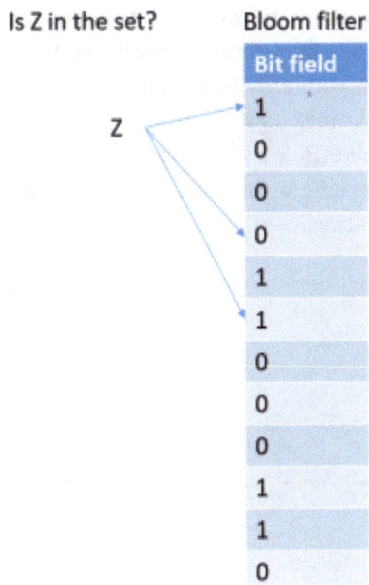

Z is not in the set

This is an interesting feature as Bloom filters are way more advantageous when it comes to space efficiency than other data structures because the data itself is not actually stored, only the results of the hashing of a data item is stored. In the world of blockchain this is sometimes used in wallet technology to speed up convergence (light clients).

2.9   State Machine

The concept of the 'state machine' is an important one within computer science. It is a mathematical abstraction that is used to design algorithms.[18] The state machine reads in a series of inputs and with each input it will switch to a different state. Depending on the input, the state machine can tell you about the sequence of the input. Even though this might not sound very interesting at first, several problems within computer science can be solved with this concept. An example is the rendering of web pages. Even if you are not a programmer, you can imagine that a webpage needs to be rendered in a certain order. Otherwise there will be an error and you will receive nothing. The state machine can move the state over the several tags of a webpage html-file and make sure that everything is at least in the right order. A deterministic state machine, is a state machine where that

---

[18] Shead, M. (February 14, 2011) State Machines – Basics of Computer Science. *Blog.markshead.com* https://blog.markshead.com/869/state-machines-computer-science/. Accessed June 5, 2019.

for each input there is only one transition, with the output being its final state. There is also the possibility of non-deterministic state machines. So this means that several inputs come to the same transition within the state machine. This is possible because only the output is important when it comes down to a state machine. It is only at this moment that an external action is triggered. Below you can find an example of a finite state machine regarding you entering or exiting a car. There are only a certain set of possibilities that can lead to a certain set of states.

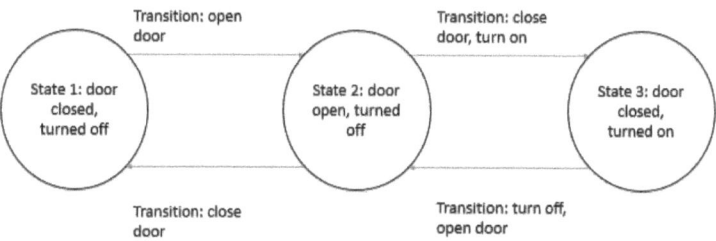

Finite state machine

2.9.1 Turing Machine

A Turing machine is a hypothetical machine, namely one that is capable of recognizing non-regular patterns. It is computationally complete and anything that can be computed, can be computed on a Turing machine. It is not limited to a finite number of states, as it is able to make changes to the input it receives. We should also understand that it operates on an infinite amount of memory. The machine has a finite table with user-specified instructions which leave the machine to enter a symbol and move on to the next input and instruction until it halts the computation.[19] A system of data-manipulation rules is called Turing complete, if it is capable of simulating a Turing machine. The system is able to recognize other data-manipulation rule sets. This way it shows the power of such a data-manipulation rule set.[20]

---

[19] Mullins, R. (2012) What is a Turing machine?. *Department of Computer Science and Technology—University of Cambridge.* https://www.cl.cam.ac.uk/projects/raspberrypi/tutorials/turing-machine/one.html. Accessed on June 5, 2019.

[20] Invented by the well-known mathematician Alan Turing.

2.10   Elliptical Curve Cryptography

While the previous concepts and technological implementations might have been quite straightforward to understand, this is certainly not the case for elliptical curve cryptography. I will try to explain the best way I possibly can, considering the many pitfalls one can face when trying to do so. First, I will have to explain in short what public key cryptography is. Public key cryptography (or asymmetric cryptography) is generally used to produce two types of keys: a private key and a public key. The public key can in some sense be shared with the public while the private key has to remain private (shocking, I know). To generate these keys a one-way function is used and came into practice to solve an age old problem when it comes to secure communication. We all know symmetric key cryptography: you just produce a private key and use this as a password or passphrase for an account, lock, or anything else. Easy right? Imagine we want to send messages to one another, which we would like to encrypt so that we are the only people that can read it. Solution: we just share the same password, problem solved! Well, not really, because first of all we need to find a secure manner to share those keys with each other. This can already pose quite a problem. The second problem is the one of numbers. You might want to send secure messages to me, but I can imagine you would like to do the same with all your friends, family and colleagues. That are a lot of private keys to send and store! And you haven't even started changing passwords or anything else. This would mean complete mayhem in the real world. Public key cryptography found the solution here. You can just share your public key with everyone, leave it in a public database and transmit it over insecure networks. It is meant to be shared and known by everyone. If you now use my public key to encrypt a message, I am the only person that can decrypt it with my private key.

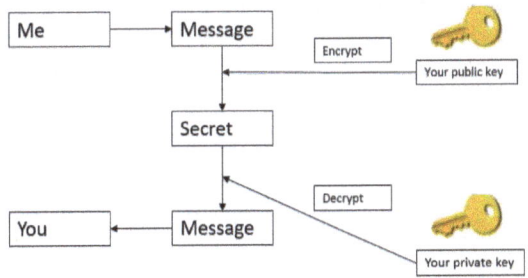

Public key cryptography

Some of you might have already made the link to blockchain and cryptocurrencies: your wallet address and the private key you use to access it. Of course there are many more uses for public key cryptography, think about digital signatures that are used to verify the sender of a message. The way these keys are generated is more often than not based on hashing algorithms that produce a certain outcome based on entropy. There is a reason why you can no longer access your wallet when you lose your private key, these are meant to be unbreakable. Of course when the algorithm can be broken, your keys can be broken as well. Depending on the blockchain platform you are using, different types of hashing are being used to generate these keys. This is also the reason why some coins can be stored together and others cannot. Often there is also some added procedures: this is why i.e. the addresses for Ethereum and Bitcoin look so different, but more about that in the related sections. Now we can return to our original topic: elliptic key cryptography. This will bring us a bit out of our comfort zone (certainly if cryptography is completely new for you). To start with we have to talk about finite fields which can be defined as a finite set of numbers and two operations (addition and multiplication) that satisfy a specific set of rules.[21] These are:

- **Closed**: if a and b are in the set, so are $a + b$ and $a . b$
- **Additive identity**: $a + 0 = a$
- **Multiplicative identity**: $a . 1 = a$
- **Additive inverse**: if a is in the set, so is $- a$ with $a + (- a) = 0$
- **Multiplicative inverse**: if a is in the set and is not $= 0$, so is a^{-1} with $a . a^{-1} = 1$.

We can define a finite field the following way: $F_p = \{0, 1, 2, 3, ... p - 1\}$ where p stands for the order of the finite field F. The order will always be the power of a prime and this is because all the rules we have defined can only apply if the order is in fact a prime. If we want to remain consistent with the rules we have previously defined, we know that i.e. addition will take on another form than regular addition if we wish to maintain the 'closed' parameter. In finite fields, addition takes on the form of modulo arithmetic.

$$a +_f b \in F_p \Rightarrow a +_f b = (a + b)\%p \text{ with } a, b \in F_p$$

Similarly we know that (where f denotes finite field operations such as subtraction, addition or multiplication):

$$a -_f b \in F_p \Rightarrow a -_f b = (a - b)\%p \text{ with } a, b \in F_p$$
$$-_f a = (-a)\%p$$
$$a._f b = a +_f a +_f a (b \text{ times})$$
$$a^b = a._f a._f a (b \text{ times})$$
$$n^{(p-1)}\%p = 1 (\text{Fermat's Little Theorem})$$
$$a/b = a._f(1/b) = a._f b^{-1}$$

---

[21] Song, J. (2019). *Programming Bitcoin: Learn How to Program Bitcoin from Scratch*. 1st ed. Boston, MA: O'reilly, p. 123.

The next step are elliptical curves. These are of the form: $y^2 = x^3 + ax + b$.

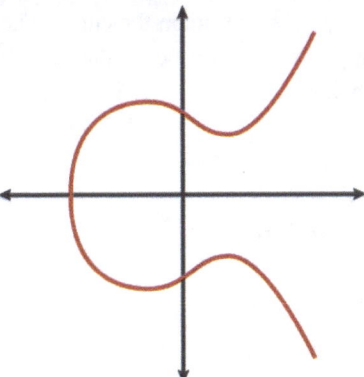

Secp256k1

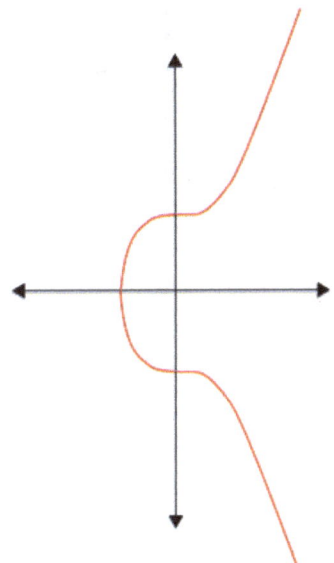

Continuous elliptic curve

These elliptical curves are used in cryptography and in blockchain implementations. For Bitcoin it is $y^2 = x^3 + 7$ or secp256k1. It is often said that this specific implementation was picked because it has the lowest probability of kleptographic backdoors being implanted by the NSA. This is why many other blockchain platforms make use of the same elliptical curve. But now towards the why: why do we need elliptical curves? Elliptical curves are used for something very specific: point addition. Point addition is actually just as it sounds. We add two points that lie on the curve. The weird thing is that the outcome of this addition, a 3th point, will also be on the curve![22] This is a very interesting property that is thankfully being put to use. Also here there are severable properties that need to be respected:

- **Identity**: if $I = 0 \Rightarrow I + A = A$
- **Commutativity**: $A + B = B + A$
- **Associativity**: $(A + B) + C = A + (B + C)$
- **Invertibility**: $A + (- A) = I$.

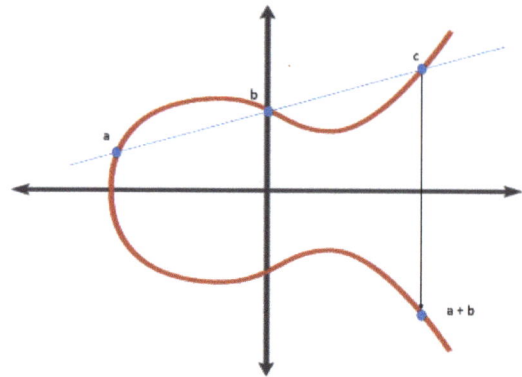

Point addition

There is the case where $X_1 \neq X_2$. Here we have to base ourselves on the slope s of the curve to calculate (X_3, Y_3) where Y_3 is the reflection over the x-axis.

$$s = (Y_2 - Y_1)/(X_2 - X_1)$$
$$X_3 = s^2 - X_1 - X_2$$
$$Y_3 = s(X_1 - X_2) - Y_1$$

when $X_1 = X_2$ but $Y_1 \neq Y_2$ we have the situation where $P_1 + P_2 = I$.

The reason behind this is because when $P_1 = P_2$ we will be dealing with the slope of the tangent when we start to do calculations and point addition will fail. Now we have come to the end of our journey: we will combine finite fields with elliptical curves. Most of the assumptions that we have defined for both finite fields and elliptical curves seem to

---

[22] Exceptions are when the intersecting line with the curve is perfectly vertical or when it is the tangent of the curve.

work together without much of a problem. Only point division isn't that easy and is also called 'the discrete log problem'. It is this 'problem' that is the foundation of elliptical curve cryptography.

$$P^a = Q \Rightarrow \log_p Q = a$$

The problem is that '$\log_p Q$' is no analytically calculable algorithm. Another aspect of elliptical curves over finite fields is that it gives us scalar multiplication which has an asymmetric problem as it is easy to calculate in one direction but hard to reverse. All of this is finally combined to come to the actual core of the business: elliptical curve cryptography for which we need finite cyclic groups. So what are groups? Groups are finite fields with only 1 operation, which in this case is point addition. We have to respect the following properties, with G being the generator point that helps us generate the group:

- **Identity**: $0 + A = A$
- **Closure**: $(a + b)G = ((a + b) \%)G$ with n the order
- **Invertibility**: if aG is in the group, so is $(n - a)G$
- **Commutativity**: $aG + bG = bG + aG$
- **Associativity**: $aG + (bG + cG) = (aG + bG) + cG$.

Now, if we wish to define the elliptical curve for public key cryptography, we will need to define the following information:

- What are a and b in $y^3 = x^3 + ax + b$
- What is the prime p of the finite field
- What is the generator point G
- What is the order n of the group.

If you have all of this information, you can start creating your cryptographic curve which can be used in elliptical curve public key cryptography. It has many uses, but in the world of blockchain it is used for signing and verifying transactions. You can clearly see that it is crucial that these underlying curves cannot be broken by attackers, otherwise the security of the entire system would be at stake. Again, as mentioned before, secp256k1 was chosen by many blockchain platforms because it had the least chance of a backdoor being built in by the NSA. The parameters of this are the following:

- $a = 0$, $b = 7$, making the equation $y^2 = x^3 + 7$
- $p = 2256 - 232 - 977$
- $G_x = 0 \times 79be667ef9dcbbac55a06295ce870b07029bfcdb2dce28d959f2815b16f81798$
- $G_y = 0 \times 483ada7726a3c4655da4fbfc0e1108a8fd17b448a68554199c47d08ffb10d4b8$
- $n = 0xfffffffffffffffffffffffffffffffebaaedce6af48a03bbfd25e8cd0364141$.

It is here that once again the discrete log problem shows himself. The equation that we need to solve is the following:

$$P = eG$$

Not that hard is it? When we know e and G, it is easy as hell to compute P. However, if we know P and G, we cannot compute e! Welcome to the world of blockchain, where P is also better known as your public key and e is known as your private key.

2.11   Byzantine Generals' Problem

The byzantine generals' problem[23] is a famous problem in computer science that was solved by Satoshi Nakamoto. Important to note is that he was not the first person to solve the problem at hand, rather he gave another solution which proved to be successful. The original allegory is a thought experiment which tries to clearly explain the issues and challenges when you try to communicate in a distributed manner over unsecure or unreliable links. It refers to the Byzantine Empire where several armies try to coordinate an attack. The attack must happen simultaneously or the attack will fail and the armies will be defeated. The generals of these armies try to communicate with each other by sending messengers to one another. The problem is of course that a messenger can be killed, captured or bought. Even a general can turn on his comrades. They must both decide the time of attack and agree on this time. How will they reach consensus and succeed? And more importantly: How will they safely agree on this?[24] When we make the switch to computer science, the generals can be replaced by computers and the messengers are digital communication messages. We achieve 'Byzantine fault tolerance' if we are able to solve the problem. Until this point the more "general" explanation (no pun intended). What follows next is the more technical and in-depth explanation. The first sections cover the proof of the Byzantine generals' problem while the second part goes into the several solutions that have been given for allegory.

---

[23] Also known under other names, such as the 'interactive consistency problem' which was coined by Robert Shostak. The Two Generals Problem was published in "Some constraints and Trade-offs in the Design of Network Communications" (1975) by Akkoyunlu, Ekanadham and Huber.

[24] One can imagine sending an infinite number of messages and messengers or just gamble on the chance that one of a number of messengers might succeed. This is of course not the goal of the exercise.

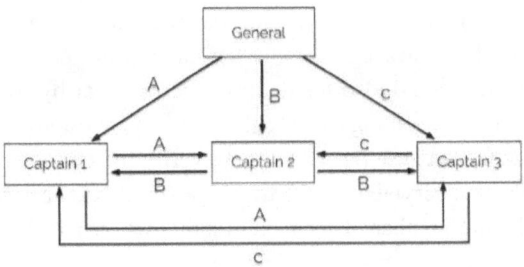

The Byzantine generals' problem

Several scenarios can be devised in which this allegory can take place. First of all, there are the deterministic protocols with a fixed number of messages. The problem here can quite quickly be spotted. Because we have a fixed number of messages, we can assume that some will be delivered while others are not. The last message received by the receiver will probably not be the last message send by the sender. The other factor that is in play here, is that we are using a deterministic protocol. Therefore, the sender will stick with his original decision. The receiver, on the other hand, will not follow this decision because the final message was not received. We end up with one attacker and one holding off, and the overall attack fails. The second possibility is given by non-deterministic and variable-length protocols.[25] Here we will have to imagine a tree, with its roots all the possible starting messages that can be send out. The branches of the tree are all the following messages with the leaves, or nodes, with all the possible ending messages. We also have the so called 'null trees' which are protocols that end before sending any messages at all. So far so good? Okay, now suppose that we could discover some kind of non-deterministic protocol that solves the problem, by a similar argument as before in the deterministic example, one could derive from the non-deterministic protocol a deterministic one by removing all the ending messages or leave nodes. We are left with a deterministic protocol to solve the problem. We also know that the non-deterministic protocol is finite. We therefore know that the solution would be a null tree. There is only one possible conclusion: a non-deterministic protocol that solves the problem simply doesn't exist. Before the paper from Satoshi Nakamoto, already several solutions were coined for this specific problem.[26] One of these early solutions is based on simple mathematics. Instead of looking at the messages being sent, one takes into account the number of generals. As long as the number of traitors among the generals is not equal or less than one third of the total number of generals, we still achieve Byzantine fault tolerance. It starts at a number of three: one general and two lieutenants. If the general sends conflicting messages to the two lieutenants, and they have to check with each other before attacking,

---

[25] More detail can be found in 'Thought Experiments: Popular thought experiments in philosophy physics, ethics, computer science and mathematics' by Kennard (2015).

[26] For more details on these solutions, refer to 'The Byzantine generals problem' by Lamport, Shostak, Pease (1982).

one can easily see that none of them can find out who the traitor is. If we increase the numbers, we come to the following formula: the number of generals (nodes) n > 3* the number of traitors t. You could also try to solve the problem by working with unforgeable message signatures. By making use of public key cryptography one can try to achieve Byzantine fault tolerance because one can always verify the true sender of a message and the message can only be decrypted by the true receiver. A message might still not arrive but when sending a finite number of messages, some will arrive showing the true sender and receiver. A traitor can eventually be identified based on identity and message information. The problem here is that it is not a good solution for safety–critical systems.[27] Several technical implementations were developed over time.[28] A more comprehensive approach was developed by Miguel Castro and Barbara Liskov called 'Practical Byzantine Fault Tolerance' or PBFT in short. Also this protocol was introduced in many different technical implementations, either addressing robustness (such as Aardvark) while others focusses on performance (such as Q/U).

2.11.1 Double Spend Problem

Double spending is the problem of spending a digital currency more than once. One can easily imagine that this is impossible with physical money, while with digital money, something that one can't hold in their hand and barely see on a screen, information can easily be reproduced. The classic way of preventing double spending is by making use of a centralized authority that, as a trusted third party, is responsible for accepting transactions and the creation of new currency. This way one can verify that no double spending has occurred. One can see several problems with this solution: if one values his or her privacy, a third party might not be the best solution. Certainly because you have to trust this third party to do as intended. The control over the network is also performed by this third party, thereby leaving the other nodes in the network as mere 'participants in payments'. The most important issue that one could identify is that there is a single point of failure within the network: the central authority. The central power could be compromised or deceived after which the double spending could take place once again. Cryptocurrencies resolve the double spending problem in a decentralized manner. This way the single point of failure can be removed from the network and one can focus on the participants themselves. To solve this issue there have been created several consensus algorithms which we can divide

---

[27] Security versus safety critical systems. While the first focuses on the intelligence, the second focusses on the mission or action itself. Safety wants to make sure that the action itself occurs as it should while security will focus on keeping the messages themselves hidden. Based on this logic one might think that these enhance each other but this is not always the case. Security measures might undermine safety and vice versa. This is certainly the case for public key encryption.

[28] Hopkins et al. (1984) *'The evolution of fault tolerant computing'* Springer.

in two main groups: the proof of work mechanisms and the proof of stake mechanisms. Each deal on their own way with consensus and the double spending problem.

2.11.2 CAP Theorem

The CAP theorem or Brewer's theorem (named after Eric Brewer) is a theory that has its foundations in computer science and refers to an impossibility that exists in distributed data stores (such as blockchains). It comes down to the fact that when one is working with a distributed data store, you can only provide two out of three of the following:

- Consistency (every read consists out of the most recent write / error)
- Availability (every request receives a response)
- Partition tolerance (the network continues to operate despite a number of messages being dropped).

Network partitioning is one of the essences of a distributed system (network failures and nodes falling out) thus this seems to be implied when we want to set up a network, which leaves the choice between consistency and availability. The blockchain implementation opts for partition tolerance and availability with a lesser focus on the actual consistency. The consistency is being supported by making use of a consensus algorithm such as proof of work but a transaction can only be called 'confirmed' not after it has been mined in a block, but after several others have followed so that the transaction is not being contested on a later moment.[29]

2.11.3 SPECTRE and the Condorcet Paradox

This paradox is related to specific to the SPECTRE-protocol (explained later) and similar protocols implemented in blockDAG structures. If this first sentence looks like something from a science-fiction novel it might be better to read on and return when you have read both the explanations on SPECTRE and blockDAGs. The Condorcet paradox (or voting paradox) was created by the Marquis de Condorcet and is in essence a social choice theory. The paradox can be found in the fact that voters don't have cyclic views while this might occur in groups. Easily explained: there are three candidates we have to vote on. When we look at the group preference, we see that there is a preference of A over B, B over C and C over A. It is clear that this wouldn't make sense from an individual standpoint but within groups we can find different majorities, made up out of different

---

[29] Nelaturi, K. (February 5, 2018) Understanding blockchain tech—CAP theorem. *Mangosearch.com.* https://www.mangoresearch.co/understanding-blockchain-tech-cap-theorem/. Accessed June 27, 2019.

individuals. This also means that there cannot be no Condorcet winner. Each candidate finds himself in the same symmetrical situation and only if one of the candidates were to leave the election, a majority could be found to elect a winner out of the remaining two candidates.

2.11.4 Fermat's Little Theorem

Fermat's little theorem isn't really a thought experiment but rather a mathematical theory regarding prime numbers. It states that when there is a prime number p, then for any integer a, the number $a^p - a$ is equal to a multiple of p. You can also state this as $a^p =$ a (mod p).

2.11.5 Pedersen Commitments

In several blockchain technologies, one makes use of Pedersen commitments. This is used to increase privacy but also to introduce implementations that are able to reduce overhead. We will find this in several platforms such as Monero, Bitcoin and Ethereum. But what is it? The story begins with a sender that wants to send a secret 'm' in some public messaging space with at least two elements. The second element is a random secret 'r'. The sender has to combine 'm' and 'r' to produce a commitment c by making use of a commitment algorithm C so that c = C (m, r). Next, c is made public and later also m and r are revealed. It is up to the receiver (or verifier) to check that the combination of the commitment algorithm with m and r really leads to the commitment c. In more detail, Pedersen commitments make use of a public group (G, ·) of a large order q in which the discrete algorithm is hard and with 2 random public generators g and h. The random secret r is chosen in Zq and the actual secret m is a subset of that. This leads to the following equations:

$$C(m, r) = g^m \cdot h^r$$

It is of crucial importance that the commitment c does not give any indication of m before m is actually revealed. Another condition is that the commitment algorithm should lead to a different outcome when m or r are changed. Also a different combination of m and r shouldn't lead to the same result. All of this is necessary to prevent specific attacks within the blockchain world (such as double spending).

2.11.6 Fungibility and Liveness

When we talk about blockchain and distributed networks, fungibility and liveness are some core concepts that you need to understand as these are crucial success factors that need to be addressed for the future of any blockchain platform. Fungibility simply means that something that you use, can easily be replaced by something else that has the same and identical function. We generally expect for any currency to be fungible. If I loan someone 20 euro, I really don't care if that person gives me back 4 bills of 5 euro, 1 bill of 20 euro or any other combination. The value is the same. With this we have immediately landed on another key concept that is tied to fungibility: divisibility. If I have to pay 15 euro, and I pay with a 20 euro bill, I expect 5 euro back. The same rules apply for cryptocurrencies. If we want the general population to make use of cryptocurrencies, we also want to be able to receive change and when I am being paid back, I don't care how many outputs are used to create my input, as long as I get my money. However, there are also non-fungible tokens in place. These are indivisible, cannot be interchanged and have unique properties. What can be the purpose? Well, you are able to create unique assets with rich metadata so that these assets can be traded among participants. These non-fungible tokens cannot be used as a currency but have other interesting applications. There was the cryptokitties craze in 2017. These had unique properties and could (and still can) be traded amongst the participants. A more serious implementation of non-fungible tokens is the creation of unique proofs of identity and unique digital certificates. This can be used for property deeds, academic qualifications, voting (and eliminate election fraud), licensing and the management of the exchange of personal data.[30] Another concept that is connected with distributed networks and blockchain is 'liveness'. This idea is strongly connected with 'safety' as a consensus algorithm in a network can never guarantee both safety and liveness. Consensus in a network is reached by the nodes that exchange messages and eventually these nodes have to reach a final state. Safety is the guarantee that nothing bad will happen during the search for consensus, while liveness guarantees that eventually something good will happen. Each network has chosen either of safety or liveness as their main priority. The Bitcoin network with Nakamoto consensus has chosen for liveness over safety. An example for an implementation that emphasizes safety is Tendermint that makes use of Byzantine Fault Tolerance style consensus algorithm to achieve consensus. Problem is that BFT-style consensus protocols in the worst case never achieve consensus as the voting on a block could keep on going on. HotStuff is a protocol that was announced early 2018 that wants to deal with the liveness problem of BFT-style algorithms. This is done by creating blocks that contain the validators votes (or commit-certificates). Blocks without votes can also be created with this protocol, with the risk that finality isn't guaranteed. These blocks reach consensus when other blocks

---

[30] Chandraker, A., Kachhela, J. and Wright, A. (2019) Digital identity, cats and why fungibility is key to blockchain's future, *PA Consulting.* https://www.paconsulting.com/insights/blockchain-fungibility-future/. Accessed June 26, 2019.

with votes have their finality guaranteed. This is the sacrifice of safety for liveness.[31] This protocol is proposed by Facebook as the consensus protocol for its LIBRA coin (they call it LibraBFT, but it is a protocol that has been derived from HotStuff).

2.11.7 Transaction and Settlement Finality

Transaction (or operational) finality is another major concept that one needs to understand when they want to discuss the future and acceptance of blockchain and cryptocurrencies. Finality is a concept well-known in the financial world and probably with all of you. It is the general understanding that when you perform an operation, that operation is completed for good and doesn't change in some moment in the future. You also have settlement finality which is a statutory, regulatory and contractual construct in which you agree on a moment in time when a party has discharged an obligation or to have transferred an asset or financial instrument to another party, and this becomes unconditional and irrevocable despite insolvency or bankruptcy.[32] Based on the nature of the blockchain network, transaction finality can be provided, is probabilistic or can't be provided at all, which in turn influences how the network can actually be used. You can understand that when it comes to financial transactions this is quite important to the participants. If I can know in a quick and concise manner that a transaction is final, I can provide goods and services for this transaction. But what if you weren't able to get this certainty? Would you still be willing to perform services for that transaction? No, of course you wouldn't. But are the current financial systems we rely on that secure? Well, Vitalik Buterin argues that you can never be 100% certain that a transaction is final.[33] There could be corruption at the central bank, systems can fail, hackers can change information, paper ledgers can be stolen or burn and I am sure that you can think of some other examples. This means that you rely on probability when it comes to the concept of finality. In blockchain networks, one can imagine attackers taking certain assets or cryptocurrencies from other participants. As it is with any case of theft, it is up to the court system to determine the real ownership of a certain asset when it comes to theft or malicious intent. In the past, there have been some reversals in blockchain networks, which leads to the reversal of other transactions or to splits that have to be resolved over time. So when do you accept a transaction as final when you look at a decentralized network? Well, when several nodes start accepting the transaction and want to mine it. So, if you really want

---

[31] Woo Kim, S. (May 28, 2018) Safety and Liveness—Blockchain in the Point of View of FLP Impossibility. *Medium.* https://medium.com/codechain/safety-and-liveness-blockchain-in-the-point-of-view-of-flp-impossibility-182e33927ce6. Accessed June 28, 2019.

[32] Liao, N. (June 9, 2017) On Settlement Finality and Distributed Ledger Technology. *Yale Journal on Regulation.* yalejreg.com/nc/on-settlement-finality-and-distributed-ledger-technology-by-nancy-liao/. Accessed June 30, 2019.

[33] Buterin, V. (May 9, 2016) On Settlement Finality. *Ethereum blog.* https://blog.ethereum.org/2016/05/09/on-settlement-finality/. Accessed on July 2, 2019.

to be certain that a transaction is valid, run multiple nodes and look if they all accept the transaction (whether you are making use of a public chain or a consortium is beside the point in this case). When we look at proof of work blockchains, a transaction is never truly finalized as one can create a chain with more mining power and overcome the main chain. However, in general 6 confirmations are accepted for a transaction to be final. If you assume that an attacker has less than 25% of the hashing power in a network, there is a probability of an attacker succeeding to overcome your transaction of 0.00137. If you wait 13 transactions, this is even reduced to 1 in a million. However, one can still imagine certain attacks on the network such as the P + epsilon attack or the Maginot line attack (explained later). Proof of stake protocols can offer even more security when they make use of predefined voters that have to put their stake behind their vote. Voters voting the other way, and losing, lose their entire stake. This means that a transaction can still be reverted but only at enormous cost of the voters, leading to an incentive to act honestly. And a final point is that in a proof of stake network, a participant cannot be forced to follow a certain chain, but can choose in case of a fork which transactions he believes to be true. As you can see, transaction finality can be guaranteed to a certain point in a distributed network, similar to what you expect from a central authority. Settlement finality is something different. The 'problem' is that settlement finality refers to a point in time while blockchain networks reach consensus over time. Settlement finality is in the end a concept that is clearly defined by legal frameworks and as it is a legal construct, this differs from jurisdiction to jurisdiction. This means that some jurisdictions and countries can easily accept the probabilistic finality that is offered by a distributed network while others will see a blockchain network as never truly 'final'. Important is that permissioned networks will find acceptance much quicker within the existing frameworks as it relates to a defined number of participants that can interact with each other and exchange i.e. fiat currencies. However, permissionless ledgers are something novel when it comes to legal frameworks and with the current definitions, it might be more difficult to reach settlement finality. This because such networks operate cross-border, make use of cryptocurrencies (which have properties of both fiat currencies and assets) and the current legal framework isn't prepared for the issuance and transferring of cryptocurrencies, leading to uncertainty when we talk about settlement finality. However, this doesn't mean that it will never happen. The technology is ready, now we just need the legal frameworks to support it.

2.11.8 Censorship Resistance

When you read up on public blockchain platforms, you will almost certainly run into the concept of censorship resistance, something that cannot be offered by any permissioned blockchain network. So what is it? Censorship-resistance means that anyone can transact with the network on the same terms, regardless of their identity, status or any other criteria. The only rules that need to be adhered to, are the rules of the network. You can imagine that networks that completely secure the privacy of their participants, are more censorship resistant than others. However, there is always a 'but'. Public ledgers are also able to exclude participants of making use of certain decentralized applications that are built on top of them. This seems to be counter to what you would like to hear. The reason why Bitcoin became popular in the first place, was the fact that it was censorship resistant. Even to this day, it is very popular all over the world. In countries where the fiat currency experiences hyperinflation or where people live under international sanctions, such as Venezuela and Iran, Bitcoin offers a means of payment (and even stability to a sense). Again, there is a 'but'. To increase acceptation of public networks, decentralized applications on top of them can be blocked for certain participants. There is the case of the Tron network that works together with the Japanese government to prevent citizens to excessively use gambling applications.[34] This introduces censorship in an otherwise open network! Also Ethereum allows decentralized applications to exclude participants, as i.e. financial institutions have to be able to exclude participants based on certain criteria, and this way they can also create applications on top of the network. So public blockchain platforms can be censorship resistant, to a point.

2.11.9 Winternitz One-Time Signatures

Winternitz one-time signatures or 'W-OTS' are used in several schemes within blockchain networks to increase security and prepare for the age of quantum computing. An example of a network that has already implemented the scheme is IOTA. In 1979 the concept of one time signature was introduced by Leslie Lamport. It relied completely on hash functions for the security proof. You could use these once to keep the security of your messaging scheme (public–private).

Your public key looks like: $h(x_0)|h(y_0)|h(x_1)|h(y_1)|...$
Your private key looks like: $(x_0, y_0, x_1, y_1, ...)$

After only a few months, Robert Winternitz proposed a different scheme where $h^w(x)$ is used instead of $h(x)|h(y)$. There is also a short checksum added to prevent attackers from guessing the secret x when they figure out w.

---

[34] Sedgwick, K. (April 4, 2019) Decentralized Networks Aren't Censorship-Resistant as You Think. *News.Bitcoin.com.* https://news.bitcoin.com/decentralized-networks-arent-as-censorship-res istant-as-you-think/. Accessed on July 2, 2019.

2.12 What is Blockchain?

2.12.1 Foundations

When we talk about blockchain, we need to talk about the foundations. If you already have a general understanding of blockchain and distributed ledger technology, feel free to skip this part. If not, I will try to remain as general as possible in these sections, as deeper explanations will follow later on in this book. When we talk about blockchain, we talk about ledgers. In the classic way of working there is a third-party necessary to verify payments, notarize transactions, make use of escrow, allow voting and registration. With the advent of blockchains, we move away from these third parties which centralize power. In itself centralization isn't necessarily bad but it often leads to inefficiency, high cost, loss of privacy and control, corruption and more. With a distributed network this is no longer possible, as the participants decide the outcome and validity of transactions. There is a single truth that must be supported by the majority, and not by a single power in the network. People often forget what this technology actually is, and instantly start looking at the implementations. But to understand the possibilities, you first need to truly know and realize what this technology represents. One important part is the existence of a peer-to-peer network, which we explained before. We remove any centralized servers and allow the participant nodes to directly communicate with each other. A second important technology to understand is asymmetric cryptography. Explained in a bit more detail in the glossary, it basically exists out of 2 keys: a public key and a private key. As you could guess, the public key can be shared with the public, the private key should remain private. In many blockchain implementations, the public key is better known as the 'account' address where you can send cryptocurrencies such as bitcoin or ether to. The private key is the 'password' to the account. The final part to understand the technology is the concept of hashing. When you hash a certain dataset, you receive a unique identifier of that dataset. If you only change 1 number, letter or symbol, the resulting hash will look completely different. And when I say completely, I mean COMPLETELY. This way you have an assurance that the data has not been modified. As you can see below, the difference between the hashes of the word 'apple' and the word 'apples' is clear.

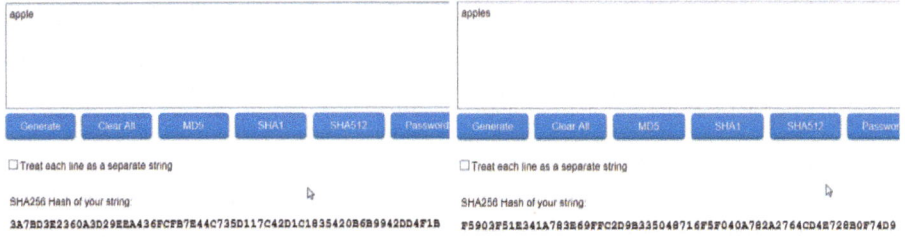

In blockchain this technique is used so that resulting datasets can rather fast be compared with each other. It uses a technique called the 'Merkle tree' (details above) which allows to create a hashing structure based on other hashes, which again refer to datasets (transactions). These are afterwards used in the mined blocks. All of these blocks are sets of transactions that are chained together in 1 huge ledger. The blockchain, in fact, represents nothing more than a historical overview of the transactions that have taken place in the network. All these techniques together help us create an append-only ledger of transactions which is distributed over all the nodes in the network. These transactions are contained in a linked list of blocks.

2.12.2 Building 'Blocks'

The term 'blockchain' refers to the very core of the technology.[35] The data structure underlying is an ordered back-linked list of blocks which consist out of transactions. These transactions are exactly what you would think they are. They represent payments between all the participants taking part in the blockchain network. You could store this data in several ways, as a database or even as a flat file. The way the blocks are linked to each other, is by making use of the hash of the previous block that was last added to the chain. If you think about it, the blockchain with the transaction data is nothing more than a ledger where the data has been structured in a new way.

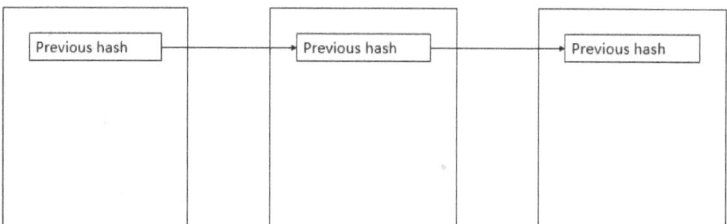

Linking together of blocks

This hash is used in the calculation of the hash of the next block, therefore linking this information to the core of the system. Because we know that each hash is a unique fingerprint, we can always know for sure that the block is part of the chain (i.e. when we try to look up a certain transaction with a block explorer). Important to note here is that a parent block (the most recently added block) can have more than 1 child blocks, while a child will always have 1 parent. When there is more than 1 child, we are dealing with a fork in the system. Normally these forks will be resolved and only one of the children is used to continue the chain. In some cases however, as we will see later, some of these

---

[35] Van Hijfte, S. (2020) *Decoding blockchain for business*. 1st ed. New York, NY: Apress.

forks stay on and we will deal with separate chains that all once had the same parent. We always need to have a starting point, a first block, which is conveniently called the 'genesis block'. Because we could visually understand that blocks are being stacked upon each other, we refer to the most recent block as the 'tip' or 'top' and the distance to the genesis block as the 'height'.[36] The greater this 'height' becomes, the more difficult it will be to make a change to one of these earlier blocks. The longer the chain becomes from a certain block, the more computer power it will require to recalculate the information contained in all the blocks. This is also immediately the most important security that is offered by the technology. As we mentioned before, the blocks are linked to each other by making use of the hash of the previous block. But what else is stored in the blocks? We have two main parts between which we have to distinguish: the block itself and the block header. The hash of the previous block is one of the items that is stored in the block header. That is not the only thing though, depending on the blockchain platform you can also find the Merkle root, timestamp and nonce in there with a couple of other parameters (i.e. difficulty target, version, …). Below you can find the example for the Bitcoin blockchain.

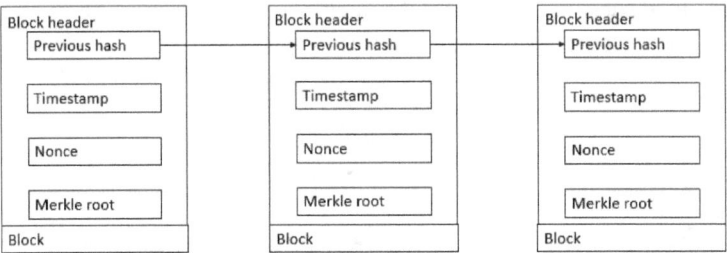

Block header information Bitcoin

Not all this information might be clear for now but no worries, we will explain as we go on in the book. Important for now is that you still remember what a Merkle root is. It is this Merkle root that gives us the digital fingerprint of the transactions that are stored in the block itself. As we explained before, the Merkle root is a 'hash of hashes' based on the transaction IDs of TXIDs. This hash is unique for the transactions in the block itself.

---

[36] One could try to use this height to try to identify a block but this is error prone, as the height is not a unique identifier. The hash on the other hand, will give you this unique identifier.

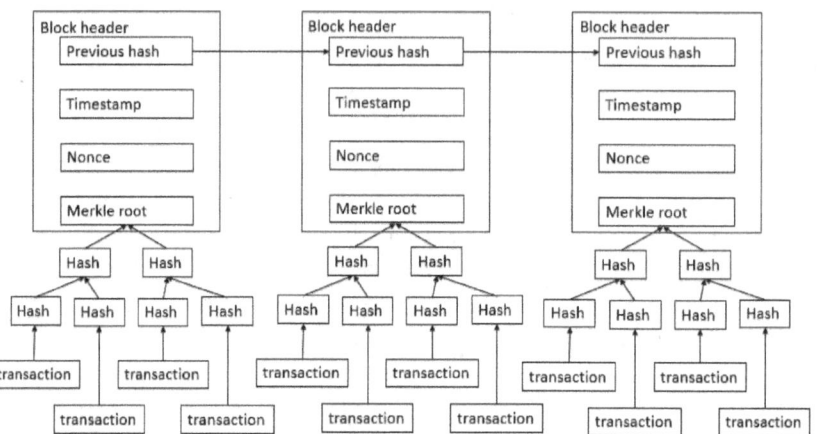

What can be found in the Merkle root for Bitcoin

Again, this is a simplified view of what can be found in the block headers but for now it can give you at least a first understanding of what you can find in a block header. Of course, the block consists out of more than only the block header. The 'bulk' of a block is made up out of the transactions themselves.

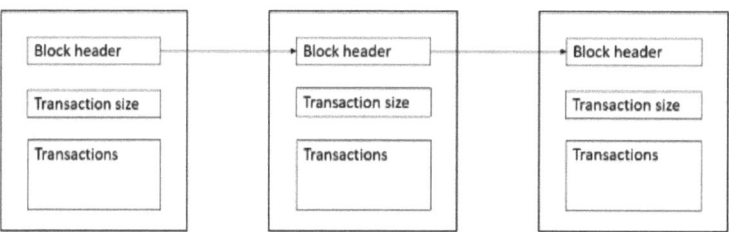

The entire chain

As you can see, there is a lot of data, not only in the blocks, but also in the block header. The header is crucial for creating the link between all the blocks as we contain in this header the hash of the previous block. It is the hash that is ultimately calculated that can correctly and uniquely identify a block within the entire blockchain.[37] For Bitcoin, the SHA-256 algorithm combined with RIPEMD-160 is used to calculate these hashes. Now we have an idea of how transactions are put into blocks and how everything is linking together, the main question remains: how do we perform transactions? The 'how' in technical detail will be shown later on in the section, as this differs from one platform to another, but the idea is that you can sign your transactions with your personal key in such a way that it is not only clear that you are the person that are spending it, but also that

---

[37] The hash of the genesis block within the Bitcoin network is 000000000019d6689c085ae165831e 934ff763ae46a2a6c172b3f1b60a8ce26f.

you have the right to spend it and that you didn't spend the currency before. So if we look back at the story so far, we have a peer-to-peer network of nodes which communicate with one another by means of a 'gossip' protocol. (We will explain later on) Transactions are broadcast through the network and mined into blocks. These transactions represent state transitions that need to be processed by the state machine of the blockchain network. These will only be processed if these transactions are performed based on the consensus rules that all participants agree on. So in short the lifecycle of a transaction is as follows: a transaction is created and signed by the creator. This transaction should immediately contain all information necessary to verify and execute the transaction. These proposed transactions are shared with other nodes in the network which verify them. If accepted, they are propagated throughout the network, otherwise they are disgarded. Mining nodes can include these transactions into blocks that can be mined and eventually added to the chain of earlier accepted transactions.

2.12.3 Blockchain or Distributed Ledger?

An important note that I immediately want to make here is the distinction between blockchain and distributed ledger technology (or DLT). Often is said that each blockchain is a distributed ledger but not every distributed ledger is a blockchain. So you can see that there are some similarities in concept and what they try to achieve. Distributed ledgers are databases that try to share data among geographical different locations without a central actor having control over the entire network. A major difference between the 2 is how new data is appended to the platform. While in blockchain technology one makes use of a consensus algorithm to add new information, distributed ledgers don't always have such an algorithm in place. The application of DLT's differ in many forms as you will see in this book, just as the application of blockchain platforms. The use of name "blockchain" or "distributed ledger" has many implications. Not only is the technology different but also the perception of the 2 names. While the first is well-known and hyped all over the world, the second remains more hidden in the shadows and seems to be more known among IT specialists. So why use one name or the other? Some companies want to ride the hype and use "blockchain" while others want to step away from the hype and show that they are really focusing on the technology itself and use "distributed ledger". Another point one should take into account is the "types" of blockchain that currently exist. There are the public, permissionless blockchains (such as Bitcoin and Ethereum) which have no restrictions when it comes to either access or participation. We can also call them the "true" blockchains. We also have private, permissioned blockchains where only a certain group of people can gain access and participate (such as Rubix and Hyperledger platforms). You also have some platforms that exist in-between these 2 'extremes'. The first are the public but permissioned blockchains which allow everyone to transact and see the transaction log while only a few can participate in the consensus mechanism (such as Ripple and private versions of Ethereum). Finally, there are also the private but permissionless blockchains where the consensus algorithm is open to everyone while transactions are limited to a specific number of participants. There is no real example available of a network that fully achieves this (the one that comes closest currently might be the Exonum network). Next to these examples there are also the DAGs or directed acyclic graphs that have also entered the blockchain space with their own solutions and networks. To not further complicate the progress in this book, I will use the term blockchain and distributed ledger as synonyms (I know you might not agree with this approach), and will specifically refer to DAGs in case we are discussing them in more detail.

2.12.4 Blockchain Address

The next step in understanding the world of blockchain, is the blockchain address. A blockchain address[38] is one of the main concepts within blockchain and cryptocurrencies to understand. It is based on public key cryptography (also known as asymmetric cryptography) where one makes use of a private key and a public key. As you could infer from the name, public keys are keys that can be known by the public. They are mainly used to identify you, while private keys should always be kept private. Imagine that I would like to send a message to you, the reader, and I wouldn't want anyone else to read it, and I could make use of public key cryptography. By encrypting a message with your public key, I make sure that you are the only person that is able to read it. You would need your private key to decrypt the message. Similarly, if you would like to reply on the message, you would encrypt it using my public key, after which I would use my private key to decrypt the message. There is a wide arrange of algorithms that is able to create such public and private keys using one-way functions. You should be aware that public key cryptography has a lot of uses in computer science.[39] The same way public key cryptography can be used in blockchain networks. If payments are being send over the network to blockchain addresses (which are hashed public keys) and these can only be unlocked by making use of private keys. In the Bitcoin network for example,[40] you have several possible addresses which can be used.[41] One of these is the P2PKH address, also known as the "Pay to public key hash" address. The wallet creates an address by using ECDSA (elliptic curve digital signature algorithm) and entropy to generate the private

---

[38] In the early days of the Bitcoin network, you could pay directly to an IP address. You can imagine several problems with this, such as 'man in the middle'-attacks. This is why this system was abandoned in favor of more secure options.

[39] Think about PGP, S/MIME, GPG, SSH, SRTP, ...

[40] Hoogendoorn, R. (December 3, 2019) Easypaysy makes Bitcoin addresses much easier. *Medium.* https://medium.com/@nederob/easypaysy-makes-bitcoin-addresses-much-easier-faf40988614. Accessed on June 4, 2020.

[41] P2PK or 'Pay To Public Key' is where you would send funds directly to the public key without concealing it with an hash. This seems to be inherently unsafe.

key. From this private key the public key is derived. This public key is then hashed[42] with SHA256 and afterwards with RIPEMD-160. Afterwards, the prefix bytes of '00' is added to the result which is the reason why a Bitcoin address starts with a '1' and why there are 4 checksum bytes on the end. These checksum bytes are generated by double SHA256 hashing and taking the first 4 bytes of the result. Finally, the result is converted into a base58 string. A more advanced example is the 'P2SH address' or "pay to script hash" address.[43] Instead of paying to the hash of a public key, you pay to the hash of a script. Here you need to provide a script to unlock the account linked to the hash. These addresses add the byte prefix '05' and this is the reason why they start with a '3'. Finally, you also have the 'P2WPKH' or 'Pay to witness public key hash' in the Bitcoin network. This was introduced with segregated witness.[44] Based on the manner that these addresses are derived, it can be possible to store altcoins on the same address. Coins such as Litecoin, Dash and Dogecoin are all derived in a similar manner as Bitcoin. The main difference is the prefix that is added. They each use their own prefix to identify the altcoin ("D" for Dogecoin, "X" for Dash and "L" for Litecoin). This means that you can use the same public and private keys to store these coins. Litecoin uses the same prefix for P2SH addresses and this way you can store the coin on the same address. However, you could identify a whole number of cryptocurrencies which use different algorithms to calculate the address. Such an example is Monero,[45] where the cryptonote algorithm is used. Not only is edDSA is used here, there is also the use of 'ring signatures' to provide more privacy and therefore you need 2 public keys, a view and a spend key. It also uses Keccak-256 instead of a double SHA256. Because it is quite hard to remember these addresses, several alternatives have been thought of and a more recent one for Bitcoin is called Easypaysy where Bitcoin addresses are transformed to something that looks like an email address.

Ethereum takes another approach to the generation of blockchain addresses. Here you also start with a private key and ECDSA to derive the 64-byte public key. Next, the public key is hashed with Keccak-256 which results in a 32-byte string. The first 12 bytes are dropped and to the remaining 20 bytes, the prefix '0x' is added. This doesn't seem very secure if you compare it to address generation on other blockchain networks. In the beginning, Ethereum developers didn't really care as much about the security because their main focus was the development and possibilities of the platform. There is also another reason why this isn't as important: by making use of smart contracts, one can adapt and transform the addresses as needed, there will always be a reference to the original address. The ICAP-format, or 'Inter Exchange Client Address Protocol' is gaining

---

[42] This to increase the security with quantum computing on the rise.

[43] https://bitcoin.stackexchange.com/questions/64733/what-is-p2pk-p2pkh-p2sh-p2wpkh-eli5.

[44] The scriptSig with its parameter is replaced with 'witness' in the transaction to verify the validity.

[45] Rosic, A. (2017) Blockchain Address 101: What Are Addresses on Blockchains? *Blockgeeks*. https://blockgeeks.com/guides/blockchain-address-101/. Accessed on July 4, 2019.

more and more support in the community.[46] This new design uses the IBAN format which is widely used in banks (or BBAN in the UK).[47] In the ICAP-format, the country code is replaced by 'XE' after which the BBAN can be split in 3 possibilities: direct, basic or indirect. The BBAN for the code when 'direct' will consist out of 30 characters and this will be interpreted as a big-endian encoded base-36 integer representing the least significant bits of an Ethereum address. The 'basic' option will be non-compliant for IBAN as it will consist out of 31 characters instead of the 30 characters mentioned before in the 'direct' option. Finally, there is the 'indirect' option and here there will be 16 characters and will comprise out of 3 fields: an asset identifier of 3 characters, institution identifier of 4 characters and institution client identifier of 9 characters.

2.12.5 Blockchain Wallet

Closely related to addresses is the concept of blockchain wallets. These wallets aren't used to store cryptocurrencies but are used to interact with the network. They are used to generate the information necessary to send and receive cryptocurrency and to do this they make use of public and private keys. The public key, or address (as explained before) is used to receive transactions. The private key is used to sign transactions.[48] Depending on how you make use of a wallet, they can be defined as either 'cold' or 'hot'. A hot wallet is the easiest to understand, as it is a wallet that is connected to the internet. There are several providers out there that will allow you to make a wallet. Hot wallets are also called software wallets and they come in several different kinds. There are the web wallets which can be created in a browser, another type is the desktop wallet. This can be downloaded on your machine and are therefore considered safer than web wallets. Still, you will have to keep your wallet safe and take backups if possible. Another type of software wallet is the mobile wallet, which is an implementation specifically for your smartphone. Again backups seem to be necessary to make sure you don't lose your wallet with your phone and encrypt the phone to prevent cyberattacks or at least mitigate them to a certain level. A cold wallet on the other hand has no connection to the internet, and are used to store cryptocurrencies offline. This is a much safer way of storing (keeping in mind you don't lose your cold wallet) as hot wallets can be prone to cyberattacks. A hardware wallet is a first form of cold wallet. These are physical devices that are used to store tokens for a longer time. There are also implementations that can be used similar to perform transactions. Problem here can be the firmware implementation of the wallet,

---

[46] Chen, M. (April 13, 2019) Inter exchange Client Address Protocol (ICAP). *Github—Ethereum* https://github.com/ethereum/wiki/wiki/Inter-exchange-Client-Address-Protocol-(ICAP). Accessed on July 3, 2019.

[47] The IBAN contains 3 pieces of information: the country code, error detection code and the basic bank account number.

[48] Or seed phrase, depending on the wallet you are using.

which is not always as secure as it should be. A smartphone permanently kept offline can be seen as a hardware wallet with similar security. Another interesting example is the ZERO developed by NGRAVE which is a hardware, cold wallet with extreme security measures in place. Finally, there are also paper wallets. As you might have imagined, this is simply a piece of paper with QR codes that contain the public and private keys. Paper wallets are very dangerous, as a piece of paper is clearly open to specific dangers. On top of that, these types of wallets can only be used once, to send the entire amount to another address.

2.12.6 Node

When we talk about blockchain and the network it represents, we also speak about nodes. Nodes are the lifeblood of the network as they are always responsible for a given set of tasks. Without the nodes, the network would no longer exist, even if the software would still be up to date. These nodes are distributed all over the world, across a widespread network. So what is a node? A node is any electronic device that is connected to the network and has an IP address. One of the main purposes of the network is to maintain a copy of the blockchain and process transactions (depending on the type of node). The owners of these nodes willingly use their hardware, computer power and energy to maintain the network. To be rewarded for this, miners have the chance to collect a reward, based on the transaction fees within a block and new coins being minted. This is known as mining or forging. Depending on the type of blockchain network, this can require huge amounts of computer power and linked with this, a huge cost of electricity. We should also make a distinction between two types of nodes. It can either be a communication endpoint or a point of communication redistribution. Even though they are equal throughout the network, each type supports the network in a different manner. First of all, there is the full node which downloads a complete copy of the blockchain and checks for any new transactions based on the consensus protocol that is in use. A light node on the other hand is referencing the copy of the blockchain on a full node.

The network nodes have a tree like structure so that we can also identify the following terms:

- Root node: this is the highest node in a binary tree
- Leaf node: a node with no children
- Tree: a structure of nodes
- Forest: a set of tree
- Parent node: node that has other nodes extending
- Child node: linked to a parent
- Sibling node: node connected to the same parent
- Edge: the connection between the nodes

- Degree: the number of children of the node.

Important to know and understand that the security and strength of a blockchain network originates in a large extent from the number of nodes. The more nodes in the network, the more distributed the power is in the network and the lower the chance that a malicious actor will try to take advantage of the network.

2.12.7 Mining

Mining is one of the key concepts within blockchain technology. It is the way new transactions are being accepted within new blocks[49] that are added to the existing chain, as well as how new currency is being created. It is always used as a countermeasure against fraud and makes sure that all participants within the network remain true. The mining itself is quite costly, as it requires hardware to be used for the mining process, energy to power the mining itself and time. For this, the miner should be rewarded and this is done in two ways: the miner receives the transaction fees of the transactions that are included in the block and the new coins that are being created when a new block is added. The miner can receive this reward based on the algorithm that is being used within the network, either proof of work or proof of stake. The mining process is not only the key to the creation of new cryptocurrency, it is also the mechanism that helps create decentralized consensus in a trustless environment. All nodes over the network receive the blocks and can consequently check its validity. This means that consensus is will emerge over time as there is not an election at a specific time but by an asynchronous interaction of all the nodes in the network. You must realize that in networks such as Bitcoin, the computer power necessary to compete and mine for the next block has increased exponentially over time. This is because of the increase of entrants in the market space but also because of evolutions in hardware solutions.[50] Over time mining pools saw the light of day. By working together, the pool has a higher chance to find the next winning block so that the rewards can be shared among the participants. The infrastructure of mining installations has evolved greatly over time and depending on the blockchain platform, we will go deeper into the when and why of these developments. For some of these platforms one needs quite advanced infrastructure, while others are still open for everyone. So what infrastructure is actually necessary to perform mining? Depending on the network and consensus protocol in place, the least you need is a CPU (Central processing unit). In 2009 and early 2010 this was still in use for the Bitcoin network, but was later replaced with GPU (Graphical processing unit) mining. These GPUs were eventually replaced end 2011 by FGPA (Field Programmable Gate array) mining. Eventually, in 2013 the rise of

---

[49] In the case of Bitcoin, a new block is being added every 10 min.

[50] There was the shift from CPU to GPU and FPGA mining. Later there was the introduction of ASIC mining.

ASIC or Application specific integrated circuits made sure that network specific mining infrastructure could be created. This is very expensive mining hardware and in the case of Bitcoin, this even gave rise to specific Bitcoin mining startups. This immediately leads to a lot of criticism. First of all, it makes sure that the network no longer is really distributed and accessible to everyone when it comes to earning cryptocurrency and power comes in the hand of mighty corporations who do have the cash to buy such infrastructures. Also the power consumption is enormous, certainly when you know that a network such as Bitcoin, on itself, already consumes the power of a small country! Certainly if the network wants to keep the same block time, this increase in participants willing to mine, leads to more difficult computations, which leads to more need for computing power (an endless cycle). On top of that, the cost for transactions also increases, making the network even less desirable for day to day use. This has led to several reactions by other networks. Some of them change to other consensus protocols such as proof of stake. Here the energy consumption is much lower and the mining is based on reputation. The stake might still be high but can be adjusted based on the needs of the network participants. Another reaction has been to implement alternative proof of work consensus protocols which are ASIC resistant. This means it is very difficult to build a specific mining infrastructure if these protocols are in place, so that participants have to rely on, i.e. FPGA mining which is open for a lot more participants.

2.12.8 Merge-Mining

Merge-mining is a special case where the miner is actually capable of mining more than 1 chain.[51] This does not mean that the chains have to be related in any way or that they have to contain data of one another. You once again create hashes based on the transactions you are trying to mine. If you finally find a solution, it is up to you to provide the solution to both chains. If it is correct for the first chain, you receive tokens of this chain, if it is correct for the second chain you subsequently receive tokens of the second chain. If it is correct for none, you simply receive nothing. The extra security that is being built into the system is because of the link that can be created between 2 or more chains. An example is the relation between Bitcoin and Namecoin. When a Namecoin block is created, this is hashed and included in a Bitcoin block as a transaction hash, therefore effectively linking the Namecoin block to a Bitcoin block. While on the other hand, in a Namecoin block you can also find a Bitcoin block header. This way the Bitcoin chain is linked to the Namecoin chain. This block header is used to as a proof of work. It clearly shows that only the mining is linked, improving the security (against for example a 51% attack).[52]

---

[51] Roberts, D. (January 9, 2014) Mergen-Mining.mediawiki. *Github—Namecoin*. https://github.com/namecoin/wiki/blob/master/Merged-Mining.mediawiki. Accessed on July 6, 2019.

[52] Schwartz, D. (August 31, 2011) How does merged mining work? *Stackexchange* https://bitcoin.stackexchange.com/questions/273/how-does-merged-mining-work. Accessed on July 10, 2019.

2.13   Block Time

Block time is an important concept that one needs to understand. Vitalik Buterin has published several blog posts on the concept and why it is important. Bitcoin has a block time of 10 min on average while the Ethereum network has a block time that varies between 12 and 17 s (the white paper states 12 s while the reality, due to a specific difficulty, is around 17 s). The block time, as you might have guessed, is the time necessary for a new block to be accepted on the blockchain. Each network has its own time because of the choices that were made by the creators. A long block time can create frustration for its users. Certainly if sellers are careful for certain attacks such as the Finney attack or the double spend attack (explained later), it can be better to wait a couple of blocks before the transaction is actually accepted.[53] So why not immediately go for a high block acceptance speed? Well, here is the problem: blocks are mined based on the score that they are given. This score depends on the distance between a certain block and the genesis, or first block, in the chain. The block with the highest score is seen as the correct one and mined. But there is a problem, stated by Decker and Wattenhoffer in their paper 'Information propagation in the Bitcoin network' where they state that it takes 6.5 s for a block to reach 50% of the nodes and 40 s to reach 95% of the nodes. At a rate of 10 min per block there isn't a problem but at a rate of 12 s per block, you can easily understand that the frequency of miners finding a block only seconds apart from each other increases. The first miner always wins, leading to more stale blocks in the network. This again leads to insecurities such as the 51%-attack that no longer requires 51% of the network and the problem of mining centralization (there is an efficiency gain for mining pools versus single miners in this situation, leading to centralization, the very thing one would want to avoid in a public, permissionless blockchain ecosystem). Decker and Wattenhoffer did offer some possible solutions to speed up the transmission time of the blocks through the network, such as broadcasting the header first, and only the block itself after or simply cutting the block size (because the transmission time is linked to the size of the block). Another blog post by Vitalik Buterin ('On slow and fast block times'), in which he concludes that faster block times can be beneficial because they provide granularity of information throughout the network. In case of a fork, the network can quicker decide on the right path to continue on. He also clearly states that it is a balancing act between user experience, scalability and usability versus security concerns such as centralization risk and higher stale rates. The trade-off between slower or faster is not perfect and completely relies on the mechanisms that are built into the network. You will soon learn that each platform has made their own choices based on whether they are private or public, permissioned or permissionless.

---

[53] Buterin, V. (July 11, 2014) Toward a 12-s block time. *Ethereum blog.* https://blog.ethereum.org/2014/07/11/toward-a-12-second-block-time/#:~:text=At%2012%20seconds%20per%20block,a%20stale%20rate%20of%2050%25. Accessed on July 11, 2019.

2.14   The Consensus Protocol

We quite often talk about protocols when we talk about blockchain technology. This is of course not something that is only limited to blockchain but can be found in any implementation of telecommunication technology. When we are talking about a protocol, we are talking about an entire set of rules which decide how you can connect to a system and interact with it. These rules can be really extensive as they can determine which hardware you have to use, which software is allowed and what the parameters are of messages that are being transmitted over a network. Same as with other telecommunication services, this is the same for blockchain. When we talk about open-source blockchain implementations, like Bitcoin or Ethereum, there are no restrictions on hardware and the software needed is completely free. Even though, now this is also still the case for private blockchain (or rather distributed ledger) implementations, one could see future developments where this would no longer be the case.

2.15   Round Robin

More suitable for a private blockchain than a public one, round robin allows the participant adding the block to sign the transaction. This system works when the participants actually know each other and there is a certain level of trust. Within selected time-frames specific participants are allowed to create new blocks which can be added to the chain, making sure that not a single participant can take over the network.

2.16   Proof of Work

Proof of work was the first consensus protocol to be used within a blockchain network. The first network to implement this type of consensus protocol was the Bitcoin network and which was afterwards used by many other networks. The idea is that miners have to use their nodes to solve a mathematical problem. It will require a lot of work and computer power to solve, but verifying the result should be easy. This way of consensus is designed to be difficult and to require a lot of fire power. A target hash will be set by the network and the nodes have to try to compute a hash based on the block and the nonce that will be below this target number. The lower the target is set, the more difficult it will be for the participants to find a correct and acceptable hash. The proof of work protocol can help to address the issue of Byzantine fault tolerance by making use of the before mentioned nonce and by combining messages into blocks. To prevent precomputation, the nonce is unique for each node and can only be used once. An important point of criticism on this type of protocol is the amount of energy that is being consumed by networks that apply this type of protocol. In times of climate change, scarce resources and economic crisis this is an important point to consider. There are a lot of different proof of work consensus protocols that are currently in use by several networks and several of these will be described here. It is only a limited list as any number of protocols can be created and put into use based on the use case you are working on.

2.17 Nakamoto Consensus

Nakamoto consensus is a term you will often see re-appear with blockchain platforms and their consensus protocols. For Nakamoto consensus to take place we need proof of work consensus, block selection, scarcity and an incentive structure.[54] It are all the rules that govern the Bitcoin network and have been used by a lot of other platforms since. The proof of work algorithm makes sure that computational power is needed to come to the correct consensus and no 51%—attacks can take place in the network. These miners are mining a lottery-type of algorithm in the hopes of mining the correct outcome and therefore select the next block for the blockchain. The only way of wining is contributing enough power in the hope of making a good chance to mine the block. The third concept, scarcity, is created by the limited amount of Bitcoin that can be mined. Only 21 million can ever be mined. The final part, the incentive structure, has been set up by rewarding the miners when they mine the winning block. This way the network remains socially scalable while the participants are encouraged to stay honest and invest their time and power to keep up the entire blockchain structure.

2.18 Proof of Stake

Proof of stake was developed after the proof of work protocol and is more and more being used within blockchain networks. The first network to implement this kind of protocol was Peercoin in 2012. In the proof of stake network the miner of the next block is selected pseudo randomly as the amount of cryptocurrency held by the node influences the chances of being chosen. The probability of being chosen is thus directly linked to the stake you have in the network. It is clearly more cost effective than the proof of work consensus protocol as miners don't have to use energy to solve a mathematical problem. Secondly, it has proven to be more secure. It helps prevent the 51% attack. This might seems contradictory, but the stakeholders with the highest stakes are motivated to maintain the network, because if an attack would occur, this would damage the reputation of the network and hurt these participants as the value of their stakes would diminish. There is also a downside to this protocol, called the 'nothing at stake'-problem. When there is

---

[54] Curran, B. (June 26, 2018) What is Nakamoto Consensus? Complete Beginner's Guide. *Blockonomi*. https://blockonomi.com/nakamoto-consensus/. Accessed on July 12, 2019.

a consensus failure in the network, and the participants in the network have nothing to lose, there is nothing to stop these participants of supporting different side chains.

2.19 Delegated Proof of Stake

The delegated proof of stake protocol maintains an irrefutable agreement on the truth across the network. The protocol makes use of real-time voting combined with reputation to achieve consensus. This allows every holder of cryptocurrency to influence the network. This network makes use of delegates which are elected in their roles and have to put a certain amount of cryptocurrency within a base account. The larger this amount is, the more influence the delegate can exert over the network. In case of malicious behavior, the money in the base account is lost. We can also call this deposit-based proof of stake. While the delegates are responsible for the validation of transaction, it is up to the participants to request regularly if the blocks mined contain all the correct transactions. This makes sure that the network is self-governed and policed. You can immediately sense that this is more democratic than the other consensus protocols.

2.20 Proof of Authority

Proof of authority (or PoA) is an alternative that is often used by private blockchain[55] networks (more related towards distributed ledger networks) where proof of work is replaced by the 'identity' of the nodes as a stake in the network. It are only these selected nodes that are allowed to mine new blocks. It are only these 'validator' nodes that are allowed to add transactions to the blocks that are consequently added to the blockchain. With proof of authority and validators, there is also the new concept of 'reputation'. The reputation of the validators is crucial for the existence of the network. It requires validators to invest money and to confirm their real identities. This reduces the risk of malicious activity. If the reputation of one of the validators or the 'validator authority' is damaged, the other participants might leave the network or challenge the newly created blocks and its transactions. This protocol brings both advantages and disadvantages if you compare this to the other protocol implementations. The main risk with PoA is that if there is only 1 validator node, you centralize the risk to a single point of failure. This is a main risk to take into consideration when we talk about distributed networks. However, it does not require the massive computing power that is necessary for networks that make use of proof of work. PoA also has an advantage over proof of stake. With PoA the entire identity of a node is put forward. If it act maliciously it stands to lose his entire stake into the network. With proof of stake, the participant only stands to lose his current stake that he put forward.

---

[55] There are also certain public networks that make use of this protocol.

Which means that someone who has a lower overall participation in the network stands to lose less than someone who has invested heavily in the network.

2.21   PBFT

PBFT or 'practical Byzantine Fault Tolerance' is a consensus protocol that is being used in consortiums where the members in the network can at least be partially trusted. It was introduced already in 1999 by Miguel Castro and Barbara Liskov in their paper that carried the same name. The network relies on a 'primary' node and all the other nodes act as backups.[56] They are all in communication with one another in order to achieve consensus. There is a lot of communication in the network as nodes not only communicate all with one another but also want to confirm that the message really came from the node claiming to have sent it but also wants to verify that the message wasn't altered during transmission. This protocol can withstand 1/3 malicious nodes (also see the Byzantine's Generals problem) before becoming faulty so a larger network brings with it more security. The main concern of this protocol is that it isn't seen as very scalable because of the huge amount of messages that has to be sent out. It is also a consensus algorithm that might be vulnerable for the Sybil attack. Again, this is why this consensus algorithm only seems to work for a small group of participants which trust each other to a certain level. Positive note is that there is a major reduction in the computational cost of this consensus algorithm (compared to for example proof of work).

2.22   The Cuckoo Cycle[57]

The cuckoo cycle is a proof of work algorithm that is aimed to be ASIC-resistant. This specific algorithm was designed when the cryptocurrency craze (2018) was at a height and a lot of companies and people were investing in ASIC-miners and pushing other participants out. Blockchain was always intended to leave space for all participants who have general purpose computers but with all these participants, they were pushed out for those specializing in miners. So there was the rise of ASIC-resistant protocols such as the cuckoo cycle. It was created by John Tromp and is fit for GPU-mining while it focuses on memory use, rather than drawing out the GPU speed. This makes it also an energy efficient algorithm to use. It is based on a graph theory-based algorithm where it tries to find a fixed length L ring in the cuckoo cycle bipartite graph randomly generated by

---

[56] Curran, B. (April 18, 2020) What is Practical Byzantine Fault Tolerance? Complete Beginner's Guide. *Blockonomi.* https://blockonomi.com/practical-byzantine-fault-tolerance/. Accessed on July 18, 2019.

[57] Tromp, J. (November, 2019) Cuck(at)oo Cycle. *Github—cuckoo.* https://github.com/tromp/cuckoo. Accessed on July 22, 2019.

siphash.[58] As the scale of the graph increases, the L value increases and becomes more difficult to find. There are also 2 alternative proof of work algorithms based on the Cuckoo cycle called CuckAToo and CuckARoo. The first is designed to be more ASIC-friendly while the second is made to be even more ASIC-resistant.

2.23   Proof of Space/Proof of Capacity

Proof of Space (PoSpace), also referred to in certain implementations as Proof of Capacity (PoC), is a consensus mechanism premised on the allocation of disk storage rather than computational work, as seen in classical Proof of Work (PoW). It represents a paradigm shift in blockchain consensus by transforming unused storage resources into a source of network security, thereby mitigating the energy consumption concerns endemic to PoW. In PoSpace, the process bifurcates into two distinct phases: *plotting* and *challenge-response*. During the plotting phase, a participant, henceforth termed a miner, commits a substantial amount of storage by generating a large dataset of precomputed cryptographic elements, typically in the form of hash chains derived from a challenge string and bound to the miner's public key. This operation is computationally intensive but only occurs once per plotting cycle. The resultant data structure is written to disk in what are called *plot files*. These files act as a commitment to the availability of space and are static until replotting is required, which lends the protocol a degree of stability and predictability. Upon initiation of a new block round, the network issues a cryptographic challenge. Each miner examines their precomputed plot files for the solution which minimizes a hash function applied to a subset of their stored data. The participant whose plot yields the most optimal result, defined typically as the closest hash output to the challenge, gains the right to append the next block. The solution must then be publicly verifiable by the network, demonstrating both the integrity of the stored data and its binding to the challenge. Unlike PoW, where the work is continuously redone, PoSpace relies on random access to stored data, allowing rapid response with minimal energy expenditure. From a security-theoretic standpoint, the fundamental proof rests on the non-reusability of space and the binding of plot data to unique identities through public keys. Since a participant cannot re-derive valid solutions without possessing the original plotted data, and since plots are non-transferable across nodes, Sybil resistance and storage-based security are achieved. This consensus type has been effectively implemented in networks such as Chia, which exemplify the time–space trade-off model: increased disk space yields higher probability of block production, while CPU and energy costs remain bounded.

---

[58] Oscar, W. (March 22, 2019) WTF is Cuckoo Cycle PoW algorithm that attract projects like Cortex and Grin? *Hackernoon*. https://hackernoon.com/wtf-is-cuckoo-cycle-pow-algorithm-that-attract-pro jects-like-cortex-and-grin-ad1ff96effa9. Accessed on July 25, 2019.

2.24   Proof or Replication/Proof of Space–Time

While Proof of Space offers a compelling alternative to computational work, it does not inherently prove that a participant is storing unique or replicated data, nor that this storage persists over time. This limitation is addressed by two complementary primitives: Proof of Replication (PoRep) and Proof of Space–Time (PoSt). These are foundational to storage-based cryptocurrencies such as Filecoin, where participants must convincingly demonstrate not only that they possess sufficient space, but that they have replicated a particular dataset and retained it over a specified duration. Proof of Replication formalizes a mechanism whereby a storage provider proves that a unique copy of data has been stored. The protocol mandates the transformation of client data via a miner-specific encoding process using randomization and encryption. This transformation is computationally costly and intentionally non-deterministic, ensuring that different participants cannot collude by storing a shared copy. Once the data is encoded, the miner generates a cryptographic proof asserting the presence of this uniquely encoded dataset in their local storage. The verification of such a proof relies on the infeasibility of reconstructing the encoded state without prior possession of the full dataset, thereby affirming the act of replication. Proof of Space–Time extends this commitment longitudinally. It obliges the miner to furnish ongoing evidence that the data remains in storage across discrete time intervals. This is typically achieved through random challenge issuance, wherein the network compels the miner to respond with cryptographic commitments—often zero-knowledge proofs such as zk-SNARKs, that validate the presence and availability of the data during those moments. The unpredictability of the challenges precludes precomputation or response caching, ensuring that the data must reside in local storage continuously. Together, PoRep and PoSt constitute a framework for decentralized storage markets. They prevent dishonest actors from faking data possession or compressing storage obligations. By encoding temporal continuity and spatial uniqueness into their proofs, they elevate the cryptoeconomic trust assumptions of storage networks to parity with those of energy-based systems.

2.25   Proof of Burn/Proof of Elapsed Time

Proof of Burn (PoB) departs from hardware or temporal resource commitment and instead employs economic destruction as the basis for consensus participation. The central tenet of PoB is that participants prove their commitment to the network by *irreversibly destroying value*. This is executed by sending tokens to verifiably unspendable addresses, known as *eater addresses*, whose private keys are unknown or non-existent. The logic underpinning PoB is predicated on cost-bearing signaling: a participant who is willing to destroy scarce assets demonstrates long-term alignment with the network's success. In exchange for this economic sacrifice, the network may grant block creation rights, governance privileges, or newly issued tokens in a subsequent or parallel blockchain. The approach thus mirrors investment behavior: a sunk cost incurred upfront provides an avenue for future influence or returns, contingent on network participation and rule adherence. From a formal perspective, PoB achieves Sybil resistance not through hardware constraints but via economic disincentives. Since the act of burning is immutable and publicly visible on-chain, the proof can be trivially validated. Furthermore, because burned coins are removed from circulating supply, PoB mechanisms can also function as deflationary instruments or bootstrapping mechanisms for new chains, as was the case with Counterparty and Slimcoin.

Proof of Elapsed Time (PoET) is a consensus protocol that leverages trusted execution environments (TEEs) to emulate the fairness properties of random leader election without incurring the computational expense of PoW. PoET was developed under the Hyperledger Sawtooth framework and utilizes TEEs, most notably Intel SGX, to execute randomized waiting periods in a verifiable and tamper-proof manner. The protocol operates as follows: each validator requests a random wait time from the TEE, during which it remains idle. The first validator whose TEE concludes the waiting period is authorized to propose the next block. Crucially, the TEE provides a cryptographic attestation that the validator (a) genuinely waited the specified duration, and (b) did not manipulate or parallelize the process. This attestation is broadcast alongside the block proposal and verified by the rest of the network. The proof provided by PoET is thus a hardware-enforced temporal commitment, ensuring that the block leader was selected in a fair and unpredictable fashion. The efficiency of the protocol is notable: it consumes virtually no energy beyond the maintenance of the TEE and circumvents the need for extensive message-passing protocols seen in classical BFT consensus systems. PoET's security model is contingent on the integrity of the underlying hardware enclave. A successful compromise of the TEE, or collusion among TEE-equipped nodes, could enable protocol subversion. Hence, while PoET offers scalability and energy efficiency, it introduces trust assumptions that diverge from the permissionless ethos of most blockchain networks.

2.26   DECOR + HOP

Proposed by Sergio Demian Lerner, DECOR + HOP is a protocol designed to help the blockchain to easily scale while still being Byzantine fault tolerant.[59] We can split this approach in 2 different parts: DÉCOR + or 'Deterministic Conflict Resolution' and HOP or 'Header Only Propagation'. The first is a reward sharing strategy while the second (you might have guessed it) combines several elements such as propagating the headers first but also mining on unverified parents (SPV mining, later explained in the Bitcoin chapter). The main changes that DECOR + brings to the existing, 'classic' proof of

---

[59] Lerner, S.D. (November, 2014) DECOR + HOP: A Scalable Blockchain Protocol. *Semantic scholar.* https://pdfs.semanticscholar.org/141e/d5f15e791ec7a9537a7b3250f4b7524ce302.pdf. Accessed on July 27, 2019.

work consensus protocol is the way it wants to resolve conflicts. In the classic approach, there is a determination of which block is correct in case of conflict and the miner that mined the correct block will consequently receive the reward. With this new approach there is a much wider field being considered. The resolution that is being achieved should maximize the revenue of all miners involved, both for the conflicting miners and the rest. In combination with HOP this can be done with a high speed as it is not block size dependent but it evolves with the logarithm of the network diameter.

2.27   Ghost—Spectre—Phantom

An important protocol that we will often see in 'modern' implementations is the GHOST-protocol or 'Greedy Heaviest Observed Subtree'. The concept was introduced in 2013 by Zohar and Sompolinsky and put forward in their paper 'Secure High-Rate Transaction Processing in Bitcoin' as an answer to some of the problems that are created when a blockchain platform makes use of a higher block time. It combats both the high number of stale blocks that are propagated through the network and the centralization bias. How does it achieve this? By actually adopting the stale or 'orphaned' blocks as 'uncle' blocks. This way the miners that mined such a block still receive a partial reward and selfish mining can be prevented. The uncle blocks can be included in the main chain, increasing its security. Therefore the longest chain is no longer the most important one, it is the chain that has the most computational effort that becomes the main chain. You can see that here we still have the added value of faster block time while it does not affect the security of the blockchain itself. In case of conflict, the main chain thus becomes the one with the heaviest subtree rooted at the fork.[60] In its core it is still a proof of work consensus protocol that wishes to increase the security when you want to increase the scalability and speed of the network.

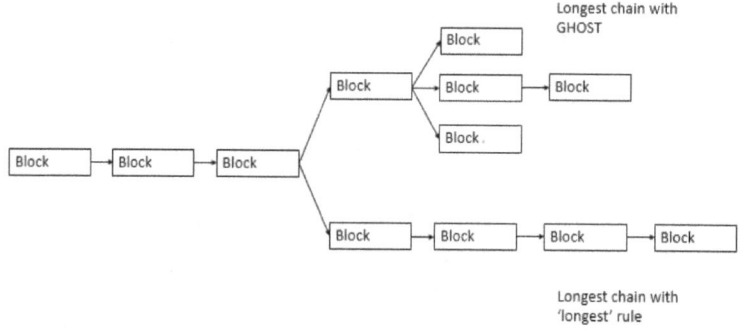

GHOST

---

[60] Sompolinsky, Y. and Zohar, A. (August, 2013) Secure High-Rate Transaction Processing in Bitcoin. *IACR*. https://eprint.iacr.org/2013/881.pdf. Accessed on July 30, 2019.

When we start to move to BlockDAG structures (explained below), other consensus protocols can be used to achieve consensus in the network. SPECTRE or 'Serialization of Proof-of-work Events: Confirming Transactions via Recursive Elections' is proposed by Sompolinsky, Lewenberg and Zohar.[61] With this implementation, the concepts of mining and consensus are partially split from one another. On the mining-level we still work with a proof of work protocol that makes no assumptions about the transactions that are actually included in the blocks. This way we can create new blocks at a high speed (the network speed). To achieve consensus SPECTRE looks at the transaction level completely separate from the mining of the blocks. There is a recursive voting system in place based on the precedence of the blocks where every block submits a vote for every pair of blocks. While looking at the pair, every block votes either − 1, 0 or 1 depending on which block they prefer. In example, if there are 2 blocks A and B, and block C has to vote. It will vote 1 if C prefers A, vote − 1 if C prefers B and simply 0 if there is no preference. This creates an additional ordering on top of the topological ordering of the blockDAG structure and gives us an idea of which transactions can be seen as confirmed and verified within the network.[62] This voting occurs based on the vision that block C has of the network. If block C only exists in the future of block A (it has been built on top of A), of course it will vote for A. If C exists both in the future of A and B, it will look at the past and determine which block has the most support in the network. And even if C doesn't exist in the future of either A and B, it will cast a vote according to the entire blockDAG structure. One of the most important aspects that one needs to consider is time. Transactions are bound to a certain timing and attackers often try to hide a certain block that they propagate later through the network. With SPECTRE this leads to no profit whatsoever because in case of conflicting transactions, the oldest one receives precedence. When blocks become visible they connect to other blocks within the blockDAG in such a way to other honest block will quickly be able to determine which block has the truthful transactions. With SPECTRE we get also the introduction of the 'weak-liveness' concept because every non-faulty node their transactions are being accepted (assuming no conflicts). So we have a non-linear network of blocks in the DAG-structure. A limitation of the SPECTRE protocol is that it can only be used with cryptocurrencies or networks where a strict ordering of the transactions is not a necessity (we refer to Condorcet's paradox explained in the beginning). PHANTOM is very similar to SPECTRE but it assumes a strict ordering of blocks and transactions in the overall system. This comes with both advantages and disadvantages. We lose here the risk of Condorcet's paradox and we achieve a system that can be used for smart contracts but on the other hand we have to give in on the

---

[61] Sompolinsky, Y., Lewenberg, Y. and Zohar, A. (2016) SPECTRE: Serialization of Proof-of-work Events: Confirming Transactions via Recursive Elections. *HUJI.* www.cs.huji.ac.il/~yoni_sompo/pubs/17/SPECTRE.pdf. Accessed on August 1, 2019.

[62] Stone, D. (March 26, 2018) An overview of SPECTRE—a blockDAG consensus protocol (part 2). *Medium.* https://medium.com/@drstone/an-overview-of-spectre-a-blockdag-consensus-protocol-part-2-36d3d2bd33fc. Accessed on August 3, 2019.

speed that can be achieved by a consensus protocol such as SPECTRE. So, while mining remains similar to the SPECTRE-system in place, PHANTOM will take another approach when it comes to consensus because it will look for a correct blockchain inside the entire blockDAG. Within the blockchain the ordering of the transactions is enforced by the recursive algorithm being used.[63]

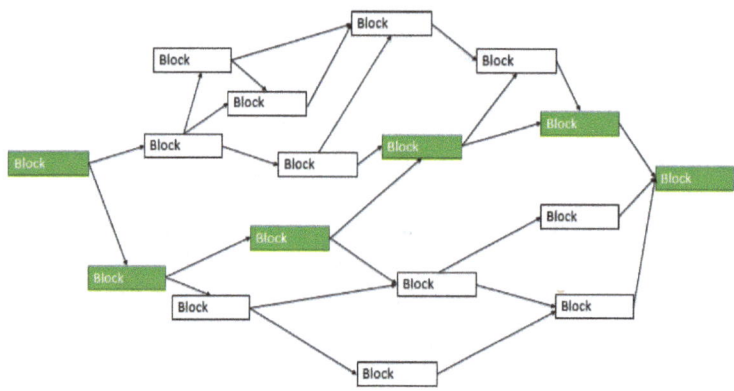

Blockchain in the blockDAG

Attackers are diverted in two important ways. Again, withholding a block from the network is not beneficial as the network continuously keeps on building interrelated blocks and a block that has been kept from the entire network for too long simply can no longer wreak real damage because the 'honest' blockchain will clearly have the longest structure. The attacker could also try to build the longest chain by mining faster than the other miners in the network but to achieve this, the attacker should have at least 50% of all computational power in the network.[64]

2.28   LMD-GHOST

In the domain of blockchain consensus protocols, the fork choice rule determines which chain, or more generally, which branch of a block tree, should be regarded as canonical by honest participants. While proof-of-work (PoW) networks such as Bitcoin and Ethereum 1.0 adopt the longest chain rule, where the chain with the highest cumulative work is

---

[63] Sompolinsky, Y., Wyborski, S. and Zohar, A. (February 2, 2020) PHANTOM and GHOSTDAG. A scalable generalization of Nakamoto Consensus. *IACR.* https://eprint.iacr.org/2018/104.pdf. Accessed on February 27, 2020.

[64] Stone, D. (March 29, 2018) An overview of PHANTOM: A blockDAG consensus protocol (part 3). *Medium.* https://medium.com/@drstone/an-overview-of-phantom-a-blockdag-consensus-protocol-part-3-f28fa5d76ef7. Accessed on August 4, 2019.

selected, proof-of-stake (PoS) systems lack an objective external resource like computational work to measure chain validity. As such, the design of secure, incentive-compatible, and fork-resilient fork choice rules is critical in PoS-based networks. The LMD-GHOST (Latest Message Driven—Greediest Heaviest Observed SubTree) protocol represents a refined and adversary-aware solution tailored to these requirements. LMD-GHOST builds upon the original GHOST protocol (introduced by Sompolinsky and Zohar), which was developed to address the inefficiencies of the longest-chain rule in high block frequency networks. GHOST selects the head of the chain by recursively choosing the child node of the current block with the largest subtree weight, where weight is defined in terms of descendant blocks or votes. While GHOST operates over block trees and is better suited to high-throughput environments, it does not scale efficiently in PoS systems, where thousands of validators cast votes continuously. The LMD-GHOST protocol, introduced in the context of Ethereum 2.0's Beacon Chain, adapts GHOST by introducing a latest message optimization that makes the algorithm tractable under the high validator churn of a PoS network. Rather than counting all messages or votes recursively across the block tree, LMD-GHOST considers only the most recent message (or vote) from each validator, significantly reducing computational complexity and improving responsiveness. LMD-GHOST then proceeds from the genesis block and at each step chooses the child of the current block with the greatest vote weight—i.e., the "heaviest observed subtree" as derived from the set of latest validator votes. The protocol is thus "greedy": it chooses the path that is most strongly supported by the most recent observable consensus signals, rather than re-evaluating historical votes. This "latest message driven" approach significantly improves scalability because the protocol only needs to process one vote per validator, not an unbounded sequence of prior messages.

From a consensus-theoretic perspective, LMD-GHOST satisfies several crucial properties:

- Safety under honest supermajority: As long as more than two-thirds of validators follow the protocol and their latest votes are available, honest nodes will converge on the same head block.
- Liveness under dynamic participation: The fork choice adapts as validator activity evolves, enabling reorganization if required (e.g., when nodes recover after downtime).
- Resilience to long-range attacks: Because only recent votes are considered, stale or historic messages lose influence over time, which defends against long-range forks by slashed or exited validators.

LMD-GHOST is particularly relevant in finality-driven PoS systems like Ethereum 2.0, where it is used in tandem with Casper FFG (Friendly Finality Gadget). While Casper finalizes blocks via two-thirds supermajority attestations over checkpoints, LMD-GHOST selects the head of the chain on a finer-grained, block-by-block basis between finality checkpoints. This hybrid design allows the protocol to achieve fast chain selection (via

LMD-GHOST) while ensuring irreversibility (via FFG), balancing responsiveness with finality guarantees. The use of validator balances as weights, rather than simple vote counts, preserves proportional stake influence, aligning the fork choice with economic incentives and enabling sybil-resilience under the assumption of stake-based trust.

2.29   Ethash Algorithm and Dagger Hashimoto[65]

Dagger Hashimoto was the first research implementation of the proof of work mining algorithm used in Ethereum 1.0. The goal of this protocol was double: on the one hand it aimed to be ASIC-resistant so that the benefit of using specialized hardware was reduced to a minimum. Ethereum aimed to be a network that was accessible for all users, also those that couldn't afford expensive hardware. On the other hand, a light client should have been able to verify the mined blocks with relative ease.[66] It was based on 2 previous algorithms, called Hashimoto and Dagger. The first was developed by Thaddeus Dryja and its goal was ASIC-resistance. Dagger was the algorithm that wanted to achieve memory-hard computation but memory-easy validation. Several approaches were tried such as "Blockchain-based proof of work"[67] and "random circuit".[68] The advantage of adding Dagger Hashimoto over Hashimoto is that a custom-generated 1 GB data set is used as data source instead of the blockchain itself. This data source is updated based on block data every N blocks by making use of the Dagger algorithm. Eventually it would be overtaken by Ethash which originated from the Dagger Hashimoto protocol but was changed drastically. This protocols starts with a seed which can be computed for each block by scanning the block headers, from this seed a 16 MB pseudorandom cache can be computed. From this cache, a 1 GB dataset is generated with each item in the dataset depending on only a small number of items in the dataset. When you are mining, you grab random slices of the dataset and hash them together, where verification can be done by using the cache to generate the pieces of the dataset you need. The large dataset is updated once every 30,000 blocks.

---

[65] Ray, J. (April 2, 2019) Welcome to the Ethereum Wiki! *Github—Ethereum.* https://github.com/ethereum/wiki/wiki/Ethash and https://github.com/ethereum/wiki/wiki/Dagger-Hashimoto. Accessed on August 6, 2019.

[66] A third goal was that miners should store a full copy of the blockchain but for this, some modification tot he algorithm were necessary.

[67] Based on running contracts on the blockchain but proved to be vulnerable to long-range attacks (think trapdoors).

[68] Developed by Vlad Zamfir and its goal was to generate a new program every 1000 nonces, choosing a new hashing function each time, faster than FPGAs can reconfigure. Difficulty is to generate random programs general enough so that there are no gains from specialized hardware.

2.30   Keccak256/SHA3[69]

Keccak-256 was the hashing algorithm that won the competition of NIST to become the SHA3 algorithm. There is one important difference though, NIST changed the padding, so that SHA3-256 and Keccak-256 have different outcomes even though the underlying algorithm is the same. To this day Keccak is being used in the Ethash proof of work protocol in the Ethereum network but it is also used by other networks such as Monero where it is not used as a proof of work protocol but rather helps with random number generation, block hashing, transaction hashing and much more. Keccak is based on the sponge construction, which is a mode of operation where a fixed-length permutation and a padding rule is used so that a variable-length input can be translated to a variable-length output. This translation consists out of XORing of the message blocks that are being used as input, into a subset of the state which is then transformed as a whole by making use of a permutation function f (this is also called the 'absorbing' phase). The next phase, called the 'squeeze' phase, output blocks are read from the subset of the state and alternated with the transformation function f.[70]

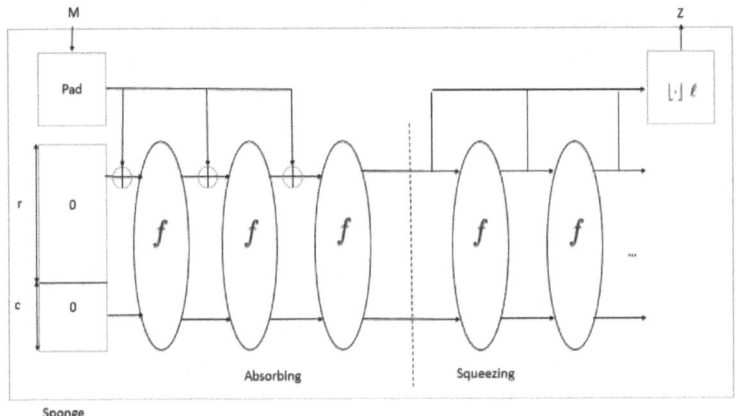

The sponge construction

---

[69] Bertoni, G., Joan, D., Hoffert, S. Peeters, M., Van Assche, G. and Van Keer, R. Keccak specifications summary. https://keccak.team/keccak_specs_summary.html. Accessed on August 7, 2019.

[70] The size of the part of the state that is written and read is called the 'rate' while the size of the part that remains untouched is called the 'capacity'. It is this capacity that determines the security of the algorithm.

2.30.1 Other Protocols Used in Blockchain Platforms

Several other types of protocols can be used in blockchain platforms so that one can come to a consensus. One of these protocols, strongly related to proof of stake is proof of importance. The difference with proof of stake is that in the PoI environment, also the transactions of the user are taken into account. This way the protocol tries to measure the level of trust and importance of the node in the entire network.[71] Another interesting protocol is the Proof of Activity protocol, related to both proof of work and proof of stake. It's more energy efficient than proof of work as only in the first phase this is used, as in the second the protocol makes use of proof of stake. There is also proof of capacity, where the main driver is the hard disk space that is still available (instead of CPU as we find with the proof of work protocol).[72] Other protocols that you might encounter are: proof of replication, proof of burn, proof of space, proof of space–time, proof of deposit, proof of data possession and so on. You can clearly see that that a lot of different blockchain platforms are experimenting with different solutions to provide consensus in a distributed and decentralized environment, in a secure and efficient way. For each of these protocols you can give both advantages and disadvantages, depending on the goal you are trying to achieve and the way you are working with your organization. In the following chapters we will meet several of these protocols and others and we will go into more detail on how these work.

2.31   Nonce

The nonce is a term that finds its source in cryptography. It is an arbitrary number that can only be used once to be used in cryptographic communication. The source of this number is more often than not a (pseudo-)random number generator and is used within communication to prevent for example replay attacks.[73] When we speak about blockchain, we often speak about the nonce. In Bitcoin and its proof of work algorithm where it plays an important role for the miners involved in the network. While the serialized block headers in Bitcoin are in an 80-byte format, the nonce is a 4-byte field. The number in the nonce can be modified as needed so that the header hash is lower than or equal to the value set by the network difficulty. When there is a solution found that is acceptable, we say that the 'golden nonce' has been found. In practice, this often means that mining applications will look for a nonce that results in a block hash with 32 leading zeroes. Important to

---

[71] Used by the NEM blockchain.

[72] It is also called hard drive mining and can be found, i.e. with the Burstcoin cryptocurrency.

[73] A replay attack is an attack where the attacker has found his way within the network. There he waits for a data transmission and tries to delay or repeat it. If there is no way of knowing that a communication already took place, the attacker is successful. A nonce is a possible way to help prevent this attack, as it can be used only once.

know is that the nonce shifts the workload to the searching of the correct hashing value and makes it much easier to verify a found hash. Because the output of a hashing function cannot be easily predicted based on the input, mining involves a lot of trial and error until an acceptable hash can be found. The nonce used within the Bitcoin network has changed over time. In the beginning, a miner could iterate through the nonce until he found the correct solution. With the increasing difficulty, it happened that miners went through all values of the nonce without finding a solution so that they had to update the timestamp in the block header to account for the elapsed time, which again let to different results among the miners. With the increasing computer power, also this approach became difficult as the nonce values were exhausted in less than a second.[74] A new source of chance was thus necessary to make sure that mining could continue within the Bitcoin network. The solution that was brought forward focused on the coinbase transaction and to use this space as a source of extra nonce values. This allows the miners to explore 8 bytes of extra nonce on top of the 4 bytes of standard nonce. If in the future the miners are able to completely cover this space as well, we could once again work with adjusted time stamps and even use the coinbase script to allow for more nonce space. Now one important question remains: how is this nonce propagated through the network? The answer is: by making use of a gossip protocol. A gossip protocol works like a virus would in an epidemic, or how gossip spreads. Person A tells person B a gossip, both A and B tell it to C and D, and so on. You can see how gossip, or in this case the nonce spreads through the network. It is used by Bitcoin, Hyperledger implementations and Hashgraph to spread information through the network (not always the nonce!).

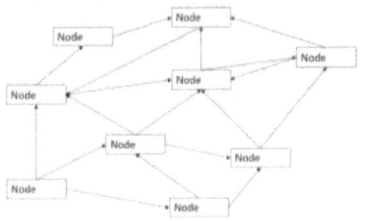

Gossip protocol at work

2.32   Blockchain Forks

Blockchain forks are an important subject within the world of blockchain. It refers to competing or coexisting side chains within the same network. Simply because of the decentralized structure of the network, the occurrence of forks seem to be natural. Blocks

---

[74] The hardware mining computer power started to exceed GH/s and with ASIC mining, we even entered the TH/s hash rate.

are propagated through the network and arrive at different nodes at different times. This is can also be the cause of the so-called orphan blocks. Normally, the nodes will try to extent the chain with the largest cumulative difficulty.[75] We can talk about a fork when there are 2 or more candidate blocks that are competing with one another to form the longest chain. If a miner discovers a 'correct' block, it is immediately sent to its neighbors. Several nodes can in time discover a different solution and broadcast this through the network. The nodes closest to the original miners of the block will start building their chain based on this block and continue working on next blocks. If a fork comes into existence this way, the issue is normally resolved within 1 block. The reason is that one group of miners will find a next solution first, even if the computer power within the network is evenly distributed among the several competing groups. The next solution will be shared among the network nodes, accepted and spread through the network. The competing nodes will receive this next solution, accept it and stop working on the competing solution, thereby resolving the fork.[76]

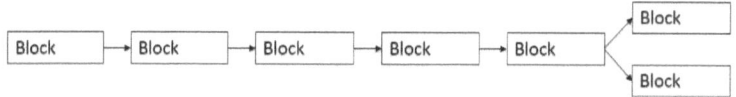

Blockchain fork

There is also the occurrence of hard forks. This is when there is a software update over the network where protocols or mining procedures are upgraded. Once the upgrade has happened, transactions that are being mined by making use of the older software, will no longer be accepted by the upgraded nodes. This way a new and persistent branch comes into being. There comes a parallel set of transactions into being that take place on the different chains. A soft fork is a change in the software where only previous blocks and transactions are made invalid while still being backward-compatible going forward. Another difference between a hard and a soft fork is that for a soft fork only a majority of the miners need to upgrade while a hard fork requires all nodes to upgrade to the new version.

2.33   Sidechains

With the explanation of forks, you can start to imagine the existence of sidechains. These are blockchains attached to another (the 'parent' and the 'child') by making use of a 2-way peg. Because of this connection, assets are interchangeable over the network at a fixed

---

[75] The chain that contains the most proof of work.

[76] A fork like this might happen once a week while a fork that extends to 2 blocks is extremely rare (because of the explanation above).

deterministic exchange rate while the sidechain can operate completely independently of the parent and make use of its own consensus protocol.

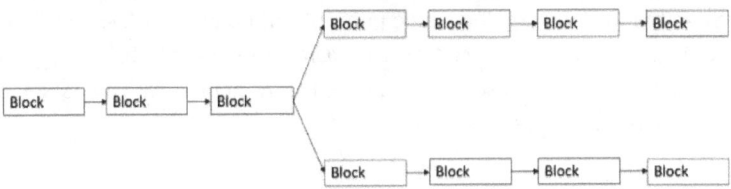

Sidechains

This transfer is in fact nothing more than an illusion. Tokens are locked in the parent chain and the equivalent amount of tokens are unlocked in the child chain. If you want to transfer, the tokens in the child are locked while the cryptocoins in the parent are once again unlocked. For this to be possible, there are several assumptions that are made. The most important underlying principle that we want to reach and understand is the point of something called 'settlement finality' (which we explain in more detail in section II). Its practical implications mean that we have to trust in the honesty of the participants in both chains and that they are both censorship resistant. All of this requires that the participants are honest, including those participants holding the locked tokens. Otherwise you enter a situation where locked tokens can be spent and we create a situation where double spending is once again possible. There also exists the possibility where the child chain doesn't have settlement finality. In this case one could make use of so-called custodians that have to vote when to lock or unlock a certain amount of tokens. This voting system can be adapted to any form which suites the blockchains that are being linked the best which makes this quite a flexible system to work with. There are several ways that this system can be implemented. The first is by making use of a central exchange that enforces the 2-way peg between the 2 chains by only unlocking coins of chain 1 when an equivalent amount of tokens belonging to chain 2 are locked.

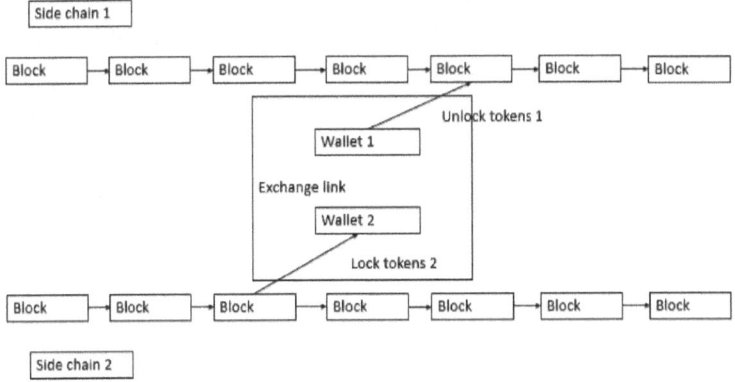

Central exchange

You can clearly see that using this system goes against the very nature of blockchain. This way you are reintroducing the single point of failure and you are once again making use of centralization. You could try to set up a form of decentralization by making use of multiple parties that make use of a multi-signature approach. This is something that could perfectly work in a private setting.

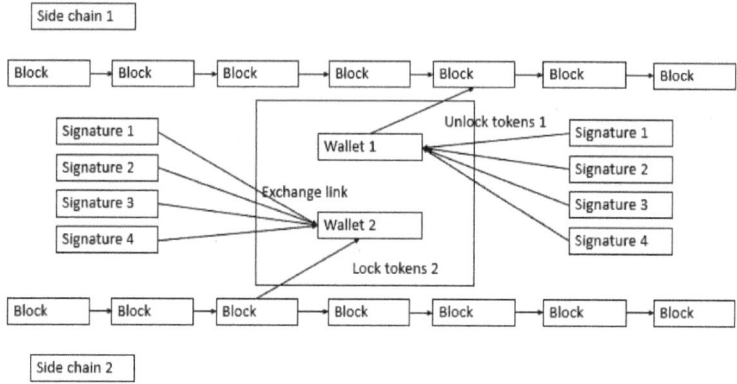

Multi-signature approach

A second approach is stepping away from any centralization and linking the 2 chains by implementing an understanding of each chains consensus system. This way the tokens can be unlocked from the second the chain is able to verify that there has been a locking transaction. This brings several insecurities with it when you are working with a system where one of the chains doesn't have settlement finality. This is something that again could be applied in a private blockchain/distributed ledger setting, but not in the public world considering the risks that this set-up would bring in what is essentially a trustless environment. You could make use of several ways to create this specific set-up, but it would have to come down to a simplified way of acknowledging transactions and therefore make use of the Merkle root that is so often used in one way or another in the blockchain world.

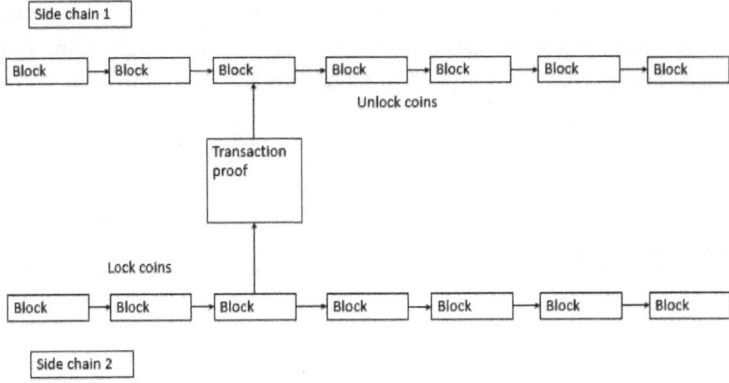

Linked by consensus

Another approach that is related to the previous example is called 'entangled blockchains'. Here the relationship between the 2 separate chains is brought to the next level. When coins are locked in one chain, this immediately means that the equivalent amount in the other chain are released and vice versa. There are several ways to achieve this. The easiest might be to lock this in metadata within the transactions themselves (this is what we will see later on in the link between Counterparty and Bitcoin as the OP_RETURN opcode is used to lock in certain information). Other ways exist out of using multiple parents for each block in the second chain or anchoring by cryptographic means in the transactions.[77]

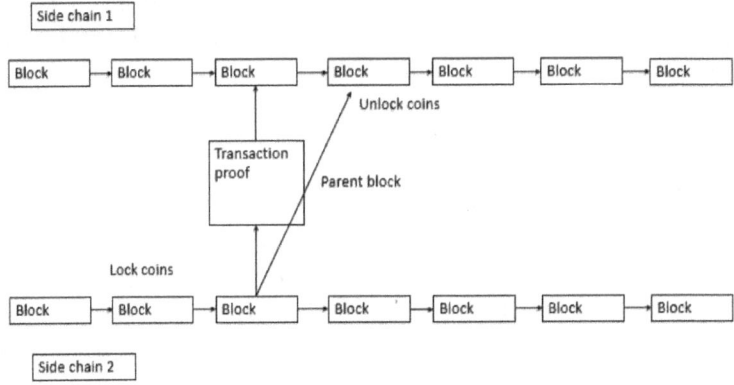

Entangled chains

The final example we are going to give is that of 'drivechains'. Here the participants are allowed to vote on when to release the locked coins and when to send these to another

---

[77] (2015) Sidechains, Drivechains, and RSK 2-Way peg Design. *Rootstock*. https://www.rsk.co/noticia/sidechains-drivechains-and-rsk-2-way-peg-design/. Accessed August 12, 2019.

chain. These votes can be locked within a certain section of the transaction information. These voters are more often than not linked to one of the chains, determining the actions that take place for the other chain as well. You can clearly see that trust in the participants is the main concern here.

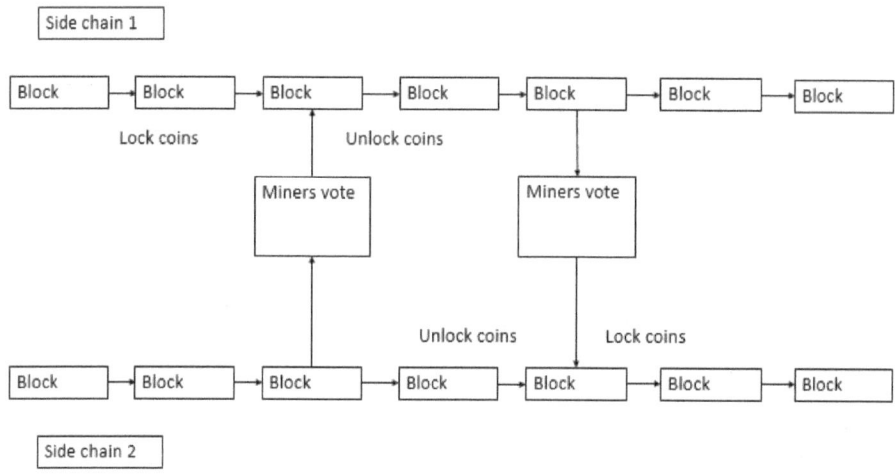

Drivechain

Of course these are all just clear-cut examples that can be used independently but in reality a number of combinations between these approaches is a real possibility. Depending on the use case you are working on, splitting or combining these approaches can fit your solution best. A lot depends on the private–public and permissioned—permissionless approach, combined with the expected trust in the participants.

2.34 Blockchain Execution Engine

First, before we go into the explanation of the blockchain execution engine, you should understand two concepts: the state machine and the virtual machine. In short, a state machine records every state and will process changes to this state. Explained with a simple example: if you have 10 euro in your wallet, this is the 'starting' state. You decide to spend 2 euro, there is a new state. To be able to process the transactions taking place, a blockchain makes use of a virtual machine which is capable of executing the instructions which are encoded within these transactions. The Bitcoin transaction validation engine is quite simple as it relies on 2 types of scripts: a locking script and an unlocking script). This locking script (or scriptPubKey) specifies the conditions that must be met so that the output can be spend in the future. The unlocking script (or scriptSig) satisfies the conditions specified by the locking script so that the output can be spend. The Ethereum virtual machine on the other hand aims to be a runtime for executing general-purpose smart contracts. There are currently 140 unique opcodes that can be used to execute a specific set of instructions. With the Serenity update, a new EVM will be implemented which is based on WebAssembly.[78] Currently the perception is that this will be EWASM (Ethereum flavored WebAssembly) because it leverages improved hardware features and can be built on a wide ecosystem of tooling and language support. It is 'Ethereum-flavored' because it has to be deterministic and includes several smart contracts that provide access to specific Ethereum platform features.

2.35   Serialization

A concept that you will get familiar with later on in the book is 'serialization'. In the world of computer science and networking, serialization helps you a lot to get ahead. It basically refers to how you are going to store certain data structures and how you are going to transmit these over the network. Certainly in distributed networks this is of importance (refer back to the concept of block time). You need an efficient and secure way to transmit the data. Over time this might change and new formats can be used to help improve security, accuracy or other implementations in the network. Sometimes these new formats can be backward compatible, at other times the new format is forces through the network (and here we have hard and soft forks again). Of main importance to remember for now, is that there is a structured way in each network to store and transmit the data. These can differ significantly between the different platforms based on the choices that were made by the developers.

2.36   The Blockchain Technology Stack

We are going to talk about the blockchain technology stack in way more detail as we progress in this book but it might be good that you already have a general idea of how new applications are being built when we talk about blockchain and how the architecture (in a very general sense) might look like. Opposite to other technology implementations, you have to consider the entire 'stack' of the technology when you would like to work with it within your organization. At the core there is decentralization and consensus that you would like to consider and so you have to look at your very infrastructure and ask yourself the question: are you currently prepared to step into a new way of working? You have to, in a sense, let the classic view of centralization and control go to make room for an interconnected system that no longer has a single point of failure.

---

[78] WebAssembly is an open standard which provides an optimized binary format which is supported by several runtime environments so that it is executable in most modern web browsers.

Layer	Description	Examples
Application	User interface	dApp, …
Services	Interconnection of applications	Oracles, wallets, smart contracts, …
Protocol	Consensus protocol	Algorithms and side chains
Network	Transportation of information	P2P, RPLx, …
Infrastructure	Node infrastructure	Mining tokens, nodes, storage, …

It comes with both advantages and challenges but each of these 'layers' has to be taken into consideration when you are thinking about applying blockchain. It is much more than cryptocurrencies alone, as you will soon discover. So keep this image somewhere in the back of your head as we are starting our journey.

2.37 DAG—Directed Acyclic Graph

I was in doubt when I was writing this chapter if I should already add a chapter on DAG or not. I decided to do it because, even though it might seem a little confusing, soon you will clearly understand what this technology can do and a discussion about DAG never seems to be far away in the current IT landscape. So what are we talking about? DAGs are another form of distributed ledger technology, just as blockchain is. The main difference lies in the fact that in the world of DAG there are no more blocks. This might seems confusing as I just try to tell you that everything in the world of blockchains is basically 'chained blocks' but of course, as with everything in life, things just aren't that simple. With DAGs the transactions are directly linked to each other. Not in a neat little row, more in a cloud of transactions that link to a couple of new transactions and so on. It actually just tells you everything that you need to know in the name of the technology itself. It is directed, which means that (as you can see in the image below) that all links point in the same direction and because of this there will be no loops possible within the network. It is therefore 'acyclic'.

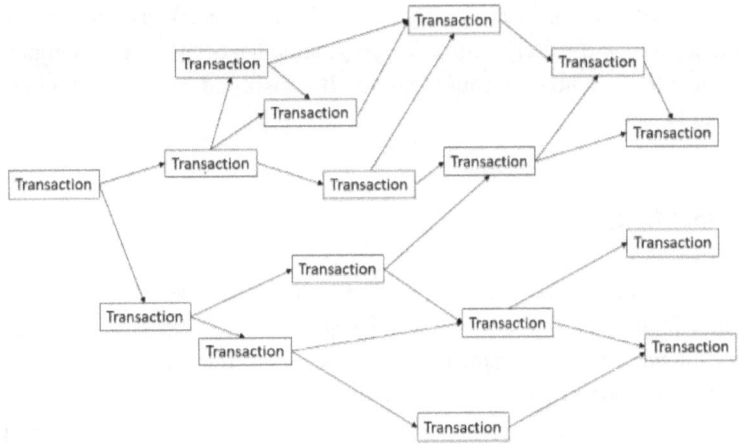

DAG at work

It basically tries to offer the same functionalities of blockchain but with a better performance.[79] It offers on top of that better scalability and lower transaction fees (because there are no miners in the network). Contrary to what you have learned from blockchain technology, here the network will start to work faster as the number of transactions that wait to be validated starts to increase (minimizing the possibility of congestion of the network). The main concern that currently people are working on is the best manner to reach a secure decentralized consensus within the network. When the answer is found on this question, DAGs might pose a 'threat' to the current blockchain landscape because of the advantages they bring. It is also often called 'blockchain 3.0' as it is seen as the next natural step in the world of decentralized applications and the future way of working. As always, this was just a very broad base on what DAGs are, while in reality, each and every implementation differs greatly and comes with its own advantages and disadvantages. Later on in the section, we will look in more detail in what is currently already there and what will be possible in the near future.

2.37.1 MerkleDAG

And while we have entered the world of DAGs, why not immediately explain what MerkleDAGs are. This is a Merkle Directed acyclic graph, which has a similar structure as a Merkle tree with that difference that it does not need to be balanced and the non-leaf nodes are also allowed to contain data. The edges are constructed as Merkle-links

---

[79] Thake, M. (November 9, 2018) What is DAG Distributed Ledger Technology? *Medium.* https://medium.com/nakamo-to/what-is-dag-distributed-ledger-technology-8b182a858e19. Accessed on August 14, 2019.

which means that these links can be used to identify the objects that they are linking to.[80] This way it allows for uniquely defined cryptographic hashes which are tamper proof and makes sure that there is no duplication of data. It transferred, you can send huge amounts of data to another person.

2.37.2 BlockDAG

We also have the blockDAG paradigm. When you understand how blockchains and DAGs function on a high level, this concept will be quite clear. We still work with blocks but there is no longer a single parent. Instead, each block references all tips of the graph that the miner can observe locally. You might immediately see the issue here. As there are many blocks and many branches of blocks referencing to each other, the possibility certainly exists that there are conflicting transactions that are part of the same chain. Therefore it needs specific consensus protocols to achieve some sense of security over the entire network. There have been some protocols that already have been developed (such as SPECTRE, PHANTOM and Inclusive).

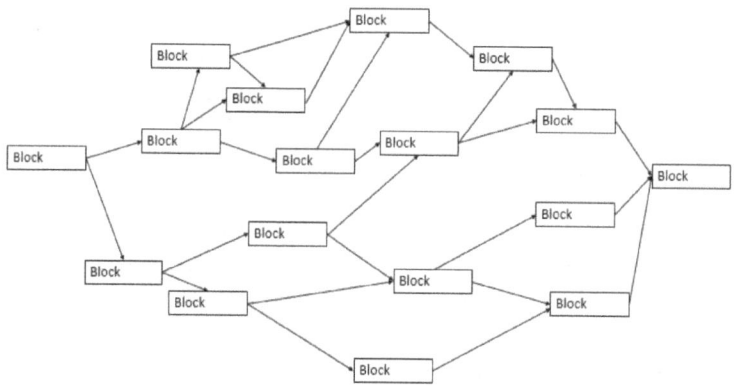

BlockDAG structure

With a functioning blockDAG network, you could speed up transactions to seconds, reduce fees to a minimum, support decentralization of your network (because a lot more blocks can be mined), there are less orphaned blocks and the incentive for selfish mining is strongly reduced.[81] BlockDAG based networks try to find a suitable relationship between

---

[80] Batiz-Benet J. (2018) go-merkledag. *Github—ipfs.* https://github.com/ipfs/specs/tree/master/mer kledag. Accessed on August 14, 2019.

[81] Tran, A. (May 23, 2018) An Introduction to the BlockDAG Paradigm. *Daglabs.* https://blog.dag labs.com/an-introduction-to-the-blockdag-paradigm-50027f44facb. Accessed on August 28, 2019.

the networks that were devised by Satoshi Nakamoto, Vitalik Buterin and others and DAGs. An example of a network that implements this technology is Soteria.

2.38 Blockchain Specific Attacks

While the Bitcoin network and other blockchain implementations (or distributed ledger implementations for the purists among you) try to solve the Byzantine general's problem, still other attacks are possible on these types of networks.

The 51% attack
A famous one is the 51% attack. The principle behind this is simple: if you are able to gain control over at least 51% of the nodes on the network, you could drive the consensus needed to a lie. The network would accept the lie that you initiated but this would also mean that you need to retain control over at least 51% at all time. From the moment that you lose control over the majority, the network will be able to push out the lie. You can easily see that such an attack in a large network such as Bitcoin or Ethereum is virtually impossible, this is why this type of attack is mainly used on the smaller cryptocurrencies where it is easier to gain a majority in computer power within the network. In practice of course at this time the attacker(s) have already left the network with their profits. It has happened in the past that attackers have used the 51% attack to start double spending coins or completely stop the acceptance of new payments. Several of these attacks have happened in the past and while the damage in terms of monetary value lead to numbers often in millions, the real damage is the loss of trust in the network. It can not only damage the network but also completely destroy a cryptocurrency. One of the more recent attacks was the attack on Litecoin cash, in June 2018. The damage was limited due to the early detection of the attack on the network.[82] It is important to note that one cannot push out old blocks, unless the networks abandons a part of the chain or fork.

Race attack
This is another type of attack which focusses on anyone accepting payments on a blockchain network. Here speed is the key for the attack taking place[83] as the attacker will first make a payment to one receiver, for example a merchant, and a second to another merchant or even himself. If the first receiver accepts the payment with 0 block confirmations, the possibility exists that the second transaction is being mined and accepted in the next block while the first remains unmined, which leaves the first without payment for the delivered services.

---

[82] Several other attacks have happened in the past with as famous examples: Krypton, Verge, Bitcoin gold, Monacoin, Zencash and others.
[83] This type of attack would not occur for example on a Bitcoin network where mining takes about 10 min per block.

Finney attack

The Finney attack is quite an ingenious attack whereby the focus also lies on receivers of payments, specifically (once again) on those that accept payment for a good or a service at 0 block confirmations. The attacker himself is a miner that has a mined block but did not yet broadcast it to the other nodes within the network. He includes within this block a false payment between 2 addresses that he both owns. Next, he sends a payment to a merchant which accepts the payment before it is confirmed and provides the good or service demanded. In the final stage the attacker finally broadcasts the block with the false payment and this payment would be accepted before the payment to the merchant ever has a chance, thereby leaving him unpaid.

Vector76 attack

The vector76 attack is a combination of the Finney and Race attacks. There are two nodes in this attack: 1 connected to the exchange node and 1 connected to several peers in the network. After this, the attacker has a high-value and a low-value transaction, pre-mines and withholds the high-value transaction block from the exchange service. After a block announcement, he quickly sends the pre-mined block to the exchange service. Part of the network will accept this block, while another part of the network doesn't see this transaction. Once the high-value transaction is confirmed by the exchange service, the attacker sends the low-value transaction to the main network that finally rejects the high-value transaction. This will end in the attacker's account being deposited the high-value amount.

Sybil attack

Here the attacker fills the network with his nodes. When new nodes connect to the network, the chance exist that they are only connected to the nodes of the attacker. In the next phase, the attacker stops blocks and transactions that are otherwise shared through the network. Instead, he only shares what he wants and fills the blocks with false information, thereby putting the new node on a separate network.

Eclipse attack

The eclipse attack differs from the Sybil attack in that sense it does not aim to attack the entire network. Instead, it focuses on specific user/users which the attacker wants to isolate and attack. This allows the attacker to make sure that the user no longer has a clear view of the network and the ledger state. This in turn can lead to double spend attacks or other types of attacks on the victims.

Selfish mining

A selfish mining attack (or block withholding attack) is an attack where the miners try to earn more cryptocurrency than they would normally be able to.[84] By hiding newly mined blocks from the other miners and the blockchain, they create a separate fork. This way they create a private fork and by timing when other miners get to see the new fork, they will abandon their own work to join this new fork. This process continues until the private chain is greater than the public chain, showing that it becomes more lucrative to join this separate chain. If the majority would join this private chain, this could lead to the collapse of the decentralized nature of the public blockchain as a whole.

Cryptocurrency mining malware

Not really an attack on a blockchain network, but still it deserves being mentioned here. Mining malware is a type of malware that uses the resources of computer systems (any device connected to the internet) to generate revenue for criminals. There are examples of browser-based mining malware since 2011 but they are gaining more and more popularity in recent years.

Outsourcing Attacks

Malicious miners could commit to store more data than the amount they can physically store, relying on quickly fetching data from other storage providers.[85] This is a form of cyber criminality specifically linked to blockchain networks or DApps that focus on the storage of data and / or files.

Generation Attacks

Malicious miners could claim to be storing a large amount of data which they are instead efficiently generating on-demand using a small program. If the program is smaller than the purportedly stored data, this inflates the malicious miner's likelihood of winning a block reward in Filecoin, which is proportional to the miner's storage currently in use.

Maginot line attack

This name was coined by Tim Swanson and basically means that if an actor has enough hashing power within the network, he would be able to block transactions or rewrite them as they would like.

P + epsilon attack

---

[84] Eyal, I. and Sirer, E.G. Majroity is not Enough: Bitcoin Mining is Vulnerable. *Cornell.* https://www.cs.cornell.edu/~ie53/publications/btcProcFC.pdf. Accessed August 20, 2019.

[85] Protocol labs (July 19, 2017) Filecoin: A Decentralized Storage Network. *Protocol Labs.* https://filecoin.io/filecoin.pdf. Accessed on August 28, 2019.

The p + epsilon attack is a bribery attack.[86] The basic underlying assumption is that the attacker offers a slightly higher reward than the honest participants would normally obtain for participation in the network. These bribes can be locked in a smart contracts in which the additional reward 'epsilon' is available for those proving to have voted for the bribe. However, there is an important catch: if the consensus of the votes is in favor of the attacker, no bribe is being paid out! Only if the briber loses, the bribe is actually paid.

Transaction malleability attack
Transaction malleability tries to trick the victim to pay a certain transaction twice. Depending on the blockchain network, attackers can try to change transaction IDs or otherwise to trick the victim into thinking that the first transaction has failed. This can lead to the victim trying to send a second transaction, making him pay twice.

DDoS
Even though not a specific attack for blockchain networks, it is the most common type that these networks are dealing with. By bringing down certain mining pools, wallet providers, crypto exchanges and so on, they can inflict damage on the network.

Time jacking
Time jacking is an attack where the attacker tries to alter the network time counter on a certain node by making use of fake peers in the network with inaccurate timestamps. If the attacker is able to convince the node to adjust its network time counter, he can force the node to accept a different blockchain.

Single shard takeover attack
The 1% shard attack is an attack that becomes a possibility in a sharded network environment. In this case an attacker is focusing on a single shard of the network and he uses his hashing power to take over this shard. The idea is that an attacker has 1% of the hashing power of the network, and if there are 100 shards, the attacker can take over 100% of a single shard. With a proof of stake implementation, this attack vector is taken away from the possibilities.[87]

---

[86] Buterin, V. (January 28, 2015) The P + epsilon Attack. *Ethereum blog.* https://blog.ethereum.org/2015/01/28/p-epsilon-attack/. Accessed on September 2, 2019.

[87] Dexter, S. (March 11, 2018) 1% Shard Attack Explained—Ethereum Sharding (Contd..) *Mango research.*   https://www.mangoresearch.co/1-shard-attack-explained-ethereum-sharding-contd/. Accessed September 5, 2019.

2.38.1 Virtual Machines

There are many blockchain networks nowadays that make use of virtual machines.[88] Also these aren't free from possible attacks. A common issue is the loss of tokens when they are sent to an address that no longer exists or when a smart contracts runs but cannot complete its execution. Some platforms have started mitigating action against such flaws but not all of these platforms are already proof against such losses. A second issue is the fact of immutability. Once a smart contract is deployed, it can no longer be changed, meaning that an attacker can make use of the discovered vulnerabilities within a smart contract without the developers being able to protect their users or change their code. Another possibility is access control where attackers can try to get access to sensitive functionalities of smart contracts when a bug is discovered.[89] Finally, there are the short-address attacks. If the virtual machine accepts incorrectly padded arguments, an attacker could use this vulnerability to send crafted addresses to potential victims.

2.38.2 Smart Contracts

One of the most famous examples of vulnerabilities in smart contracts is the attack on the DAO in 2016. Commonly, the vulnerabilities are related to the source code of the smart contract language but developers using i.e. Solidity are also quite capable of building in vulnerabilities in their smart contracts themselves quite easily. This means that users always have to be aware that smart contracts aren't flawless and developers always have to review their code time and again to prevent abuse of their code.

2.38.3 Wallets

Wallets can fall victim to several types of attacks. There are the classic attacks such as phishing where an attacker attempts to gain access to the wallet by stealing the user information of the victim. This type of attack is a classic attack vector where the attacker tries to gain control over the victim his assets. In the same line, there are dictionary attacks where the attacker attempts to guess the victim his password and break the cryptographic hash of the victim. More specific attacks on the wallet of a victim can be related to the signature algorithm used by the wallet software. If there isn't enough entropy, the same value can be generated multiple times to create a private key, leading to a vulnerability in

---

[88] Bryk, A. (November 1, 2018) Blockchain Attack Vectors: Vulnerabilities of the Most Secure Technology. *Apriorit.* https://www.apriorit.com/dev-blog/578-blockchain-attack-vectors; Accessed on September 7, 2019.

[89] Monahan, T. (2017) Unprotected function. *Github—Crytic.* https://github.com/crytic/not-so-smart-contracts/tree/master/unprotected_function. Accessed on September 14, 2019.

the signature itself. Similarly, if the key generation has a vulnerability, an attacker can try to gain access to the wallet of the victim. Even cold wallets aren't completely safe. There is for example the Nano S Ledger wallet (which is quite popular) where researchers were able to perform an Evil Maid attack on the bugs in the software in the wallet and obtain user information based on this attack.[90]

2.38.4 Other Attacks

This list is certainly not definitive and will change and increase over time. Cyber security is more than ever a living subject and the cyber war has never been waged so massively as in recent years. There are certainly more attacks to come but this doesn't mean that there is no value in blockchain technology, it just means that it is vulnerable to attacks just as any other technology.

2.38.5 Zero-Knowledge Proofs

Zero-knowledge proof or ZKP is a technology in which a person wants to prove something without sharing any other knowledge.[91] This means that the prover wants to prove the fact that he knows the knowledge without sharing any other knowledge with the person who wants to verify that fact (the verifier). While in reality, in a standard conversation, you proof your knowledge by sharing information, in an online environment, where you aren't sure you can really trust the other person, this is far from ideal. For this very reason, zero-knowledge proofs were developed.

To be able to be used, a zero-knowledge proof must satisfy three different properties:

- Completeness: if the prover is in fact correct, it will be determined to be correct by the verifier
- Soundness: if the prover is incorrect, it must be determined to be incorrect by the verifier with a high probability
- Zero-knowledge: the verifier cannot obtain any knowledge other than the fact that the prover wants to prove.

A great explanation on zero-knowledge proofs is given by Jean-Jacques Quisquater et al., in their paper 'How to Explain Zero-Knowledge Protocols to Your Children' which dates

---

[90] Mihov, D. (February 6, 2018) All Ledger wallets have a flaw that lets hackers steal your cryptocurrency. *The next web.* https://thenextweb.com/hardfork/2018/02/06/cryptocurrency-wallet-ledget-hardware/. Accessed September 26, 2019.

[91] What is Zero-Knowledge Proof—a hot technology bringing trustworthiness to Web3 privacy?|NTT DATA Group.

back to 1989! Later on in this book (in the chapter on Zcash) you will find more details on how they explained zero-knowledge proofs, and also some explanations on zk-SNARK and zk-STARK.

2.38.6 ZKRP

Zero-knowledge range proofs were developed by ING (a major Dutch bank) back in 2017.[92] This application can prove that a numerical value (in the case of the bank an amount of money) is within a certain range, without actually sharing the actual numerical value with the verifier.

2.38.7 (N)IZKPs

(Non-)interactive zero-knowledge proofs are two major groups of zero-knowledge proofs. Non-interactive zero-knowledge proofs include zk-SNARKs and zk-STARKs as they require only a single proof coming from the prover, which the verifier can independently verify. These types of zero-knowledge proofs are more efficient and scalable than their counterparts, and as such make them more interesting for blockchain applications. As you might have guessed, interactive zero-knowledge proofs require multiple rounds of communication between the prover and the verifier. This becomes more computationally intensive and as such they are less practical for larger applications.

2.38.8 ZK-SNARK

zk-SNARK stands for *Zero-Knowledge Succinct Non-interactive Argument of Knowledge.* It is one of the earliest and most widely used forms of zero-knowledge proofs. At its core, zk-SNARK allows someone to prove that they know a certain piece of information (like a solution to a puzzle or a valid transaction) without revealing the information itself and in a way that the proof is very small and fast to verify. What makes zk-SNARKs powerful is their succinctness and efficiency. The proofs are just a few hundred bytes in size, regardless of how complex the underlying computation is. Verification time is nearly instantaneous, which makes zk-SNARKs ideal for high-performance blockchain applications such as Zcash, Ethereum rollups, and private smart contracts.

However, zk-SNARKs come with a significant caveat: they require a trusted setup. This is a one-time process where cryptographic parameters are generated—if this setup is compromised, it could allow malicious users to forge proofs. Many zk-SNARK implementations include rigorous ceremonies involving multiple participants to ensure the setup

---

[92] Idem.

remains secure, but it remains a potential point of vulnerability. From a technical perspective, zk-SNARKs rely on advanced mathematics such as elliptic curve pairings and quadratic arithmetic programs (QAPs). These contribute to their efficiency but also make the implementation complex and less transparent for the average developer.

Despite these challenges, zk-SNARKs have been extensively battle-tested and remain a cornerstone of privacy and scalability solutions in the blockchain space. Their combination of compact proofs, quick verification, and real-world adoption make them a proven and powerful tool—albeit with the caveat of needing trust in the setup phase.

2.38.9 ZK-STARK

zk-STARK, short for *Zero-Knowledge Scalable Transparent Argument of Knowledge*, is a newer and more robust kind of zero-knowledge proof system. What sets zk-STARKs apart is their transparency—they do not require a trusted setup—and their scalability, making them highly suited for verifying large and complex computations. STARKs were developed in response to the limitations of SNARKs, particularly the dependence on trusted setups and the complexity of the cryptographic assumptions. STARKs use hash-based cryptography, which is simpler and believed to be resistant to quantum attacks, giving them an edge in long-term security. Instead of relying on elliptic curves, STARKs leverage Merkle trees and low-degree polynomial testing, which, while increasing proof size, offer much greater transparency and trustlessness.

One of the standout features of zk-STARKs is their scalability. They can efficiently prove computations involving massive datasets, making them ideal for applications like blockchain rollups, verifiable computation, and off-chain data integrity proofs. For example, platforms like StarkNet and Immutable X are already leveraging zk-STARKs to power high-throughput, low-cost decentralized applications. The trade-off, however, is that zk-STARK proofs are larger and slower to verify compared to zk-SNARKs. While this makes them less suitable for scenarios where bandwidth or on-chain storage is limited, ongoing research and compression techniques are helping to close the gap.

2.38.10 ZKRP, SNARK and SPLONK

As we explained earlier, zero-Knowledge Proofs (ZKPs) allow one party, the Prover, to convince another, the Verifier, that a statement is true—without revealing why it's true. A particular kind of ZKP, called a SNARK (Succinct Non-interactive Argument of Knowledge), aims to make this process not only private but also efficient: the proof should be short, quick to verify, and convey nothing beyond the validity of the claim. For example, imagine you wanted to prove that you know a message M such that the SHA256 hash of M equals zero, without ever revealing the message. A SNARK makes this possible by allowing the Prover to convince the Verifier of this claim with a tiny proof, without disclosing M, and in such a way that the Verifier doesn't even need to re-run the hash function.[93]

To construct such a SNARK, we need to translate the underlying computation—like a hash function—into a mathematical structure. This is done using *arithmetic circuits*, which model computations in terms of algebraic operations over finite fields. These circuits act like blueprints, capturing a program's logic as sequences of additions and multiplications. Once we have this representation, the challenge becomes proving that we know inputs (known as the *witness*) that satisfy the circuit's constraints without revealing the inputs themselves.

At the heart of a modern SNARK lies the combination of two powerful constructs: an *Interactive Oracle Proof* (IOP) and a *Polynomial Commitment Scheme* (PCS). The IOP is a protocol where the Prover and Verifier interact by exchanging pieces of information called oracles. These oracles are essentially functions the Verifier can query to test specific aspects of the Prover's claim. However, oracles are abstract—information-theoretic in nature—and must be grounded in actual cryptographic constructs to be useful in practice. This is where the PCS comes in.

The PCS allows the Prover to commit to a polynomial (a mathematical expression derived from the arithmetic circuit) and later prove properties about that polynomial without ever sending its full description. Instead, the Prover sends a concise commitment—think of it like a cryptographic summary—and responds to the Verifier's challenge by revealing the value of the polynomial at randomly chosen points, along with a proof that these values are accurate. This mechanism enables succinctness: the Prover need not send the whole polynomial, and the Verifier can still be confident in the validity of the computation.

Different PCS designs offer trade-offs in terms of efficiency, transparency, and cryptographic assumptions. For example, KZG commitments require a trusted setup but offer very short proofs, while hash-based schemes like FRI are post-quantum secure but produce larger proof sizes. These schemes also differ in their structural properties— some allow batching (verifying multiple statements efficiently) due to their *homomorphic* nature, while others do not.

Meanwhile, the IOP governs the interactive portion of the SNARK's proof process. It's designed to simulate a conversation between the Prover and Verifier, where oracles are sent, queries are made, and responses are verified. Crucially, although this process is originally interactive, we can make it non-interactive by using the *Fiat-Shamir transformation*. This trick replaces the Verifier's random challenges with deterministic values derived from a cryptographic hash function, allowing the Prover to simulate both sides of the interaction and send a standalone proof.

To ensure the Verifier can verify the proof quickly we introduce a *pre-processing setup* phase. This setup creates public parameters that summarize the arithmetic circuit,

---

[93] SNARKS, IOPs and PCS: the building piece for ZK proofs|Medium.

allowing the Verifier to check polynomial evaluations without needing to parse the entire circuit. This setup can be trusted and circuit-specific, transparent and general-purpose, or universal and updatable—each with different trade-offs in terms of security and scalability.

The SNARK construction process proceeds in several well-defined stages. We start by choosing a finite field, then translate our computation into an arithmetic circuit. This circuit is compiled into a SNARK-friendly format, and a setup algorithm generates public parameters for both Prover and Verifier. The Prover uses these parameters to produce commitments to the relevant polynomials. Then, through a series of evaluation queries (guided by the Fiat-Shamir transformation) the Prover provides proof that these commitments represent valid computations corresponding to the original statement.

What emerges from this process is a compact proof composed of a small number of polynomial commitments and evaluation proofs. The Verifier, using the public parameters and the statement, can check this proof efficiently without learning anything about the underlying witness. Verification time remains constant or logarithmic in relation to the circuit size, while the Prover time has been increasingly optimized in recent years.

SPLONK, then, is the conceptual framework for building SNARKs from the ground up, using an IOP paired with a PCS, transformed into a non-interactive proof via Fiat-Shamir, and supported by a setup phase that makes the entire system practical for real-world use. Through this architecture, we gain powerful cryptographic guarantees: succinctness, soundness, and zero-knowledge, enabling secure, private, and efficient verification of complex computations.

2.38.11 HALO 2

Developed by the Electric Coin Company (the creators of Zcash), Halo leverages a mathematical technique known as polynomial commitment schemes, specifically building on what's known as PLONK arithmetization. It uses inner product arguments to commit to and prove properties of polynomials efficiently. The true power of Halo lies in recursion—it can verify one proof inside another. This capability means it can bundle and compress many computations or proofs into one, enabling scalability improvements for systems like blockchains. What makes Halo unique is its ability to generate recursive proofs without requiring a trusted setup, something that earlier zero-knowledge systems often relied on. A trusted setup can be a security risk because if it's compromised, the whole system can be undermined.

Because of this, Halo is ideal for privacy-preserving blockchain applications, rollup scalability solutions, and even for verifying complex computations across different blockchains. Its second generation, **Halo 2**, is already in use within Zcash's Orchard protocol, allowing for shielded transactions that maintain user privacy while improving trust and efficiency. Unlike many zero-knowledge systems, Halo doesn't rely on large, complicated trusted ceremonies to initialize—it's secure and decentralized from the start.

Compared to traditional zk-SNARKs and zk-STARKs, Halo strikes a balance: it avoids trusted setups like STARKs, supports recursion efficiently, and offers moderate proof sizes with fast verification, though it lacks quantum resistance due to its use of elliptic curve cryptography.

Feature	Halo	zk-SNARKs (e.g. Groth16)	zk-STARKs
Trusted setup	✗ No	✓ Yes	✗ No
Recursion	✓ Yes	⚠ Limited	✓ Yes (with caveats)
Proof size	⚠ Moderate	✓ Very small	✗ Large
Verification speed	✓ Fast	✓ Fast	✗ Slower
Quantum Resistance	✗ No (uses elliptic curves)	✗ No	✓ Yes

2.38.12 Account Abstraction

Account Abstraction is a concept in blockchain architecture, especially within the Ethereum ecosystem, that removes (or at least impacts) the distinction between user accounts and smart contracts. Ethereum has two types of accounts: externally owned accounts (EOAs) controlled by private keys, and contract accounts controlled by code. Account Abstraction proposes merging these into a single, programmable account type, opening new possibilities for how users interact with blockchains. In the current system, user accounts are limited by the rules baked into the Ethereum protocol. For example, to send a transaction, an EOA must sign it with a private key, use Ethereum's standard gas payment system, and follow rigid nonce rules. Account Abstraction allows users to replace these default behaviours with custom logic, enabling things like multi-signature wallets, social recovery, biometric logins, or gasless transactions, all natively supported at the protocol level.

This is achieved by treating all accounts like smart contracts, where the validation of a transaction isn't hardcoded into Ethereum, but instead defined by a "validation function" inside the account itself. This gives users and developers the flexibility to define how an account should approve and process transactions. Want to require two signatures instead of one? Add a delay for large withdrawals? Use facial recognition instead of a seed phrase? All of this becomes possible. One of the most anticipated implementations of account abstraction on Ethereum is ERC-4337, which introduces these features without requiring a hard fork. It achieves this through a clever system of "UserOperations", bundlers, and entry points, allowing smart contract wallets to function like native accounts while remaining backward-compatible with the existing network.

The practical benefits of account abstraction are profound. It can dramatically improve security and usability, especially for non-technical users. Wallets become more like apps with programmable rules, onboarding becomes smoother, and key management becomes more flexible and recoverable. Developers can build wallets that are secure by default, eliminating entire categories of user error. However, the transition to full account abstraction also brings new challenges, such as complexity in gas fee handling, potential DoS vectors, and ecosystem readiness. Despite this, it's widely considered a crucial step toward making Web3 more user-friendly, secure, and accessible.

2.38.13 ERC-4337

ERC-4337 is Ethereum's innovative proposal to bring Account Abstraction to life without changing the core Ethereum protocol.[94] It refactors how accounts and transactions work by turning smart contracts into first-class citizens capable of behaving like user accounts. Ethereum users operate through Externally Owned Accounts (EOAs)—these are tied to a private key and must follow strict rules baked into Ethereum's consensus mechanism. This setup limits flexibility. Want multi-signature security? Social recovery? Biometric login? Gasless interactions? You can't do that with EOAs alone. And upgrading Ethereum to allow for such flexibility would normally require a hard fork, which is risky and slow.

Enter ERC-4337, a smart-contract-based workaround that emulates Account Abstraction at the application layer—no changes to the base protocol needed. ERC-4337 introduces a new transaction flow centered around three main components:

- UserOperation: Instead of sending a typical Ethereum transaction, users submit a UserOperation. Think of it as a package containing instructions (like "send tokens" or "sign a message") along with metadata such as gas limits and signature.
- Bundler: A new actor on the network, the Bundler, listens for UserOperations in a special mempool. It bundles multiple UserOperations into one regular Ethereum transaction and sends it to a smart contract called the EntryPoint.
- EntryPoint Contract: This contract acts like a universal gateway. It verifies the UserOperations (using the logic defined in each user's smart contract wallet), handles gas payments (including via tokens), and executes the requested actions.

This implementation comes with a series of benefits. No trusted setup or protocol fork is required for ERC-4337 to take effect. It also allows for custom signature schemes such as biometrics and hardware modules, allowing more flexibility towards new implementations. Additionally, there is also gas fee flexibility, where users can pay gas in ERC-20

---

[94] ERC 4337.

tokens. Other advantages are the possibility of social recovery and multi-signature is built in on an account level. Finally, batch transactions and programmable logic will become seamless.

2.38.14 Layer-2 Rollups

Layer-2 rollups are another solution to one of Ethereum's biggest challenges: scalability. As more people use Ethereum, the network becomes congested, fees skyrocket, and transaction speeds slow down. But simply making Ethereum faster or bigger at the base layer risks compromising its two core strengths: security and decentralization. That's where rollups come in. They offer a clever alternative: handle the bulk of transaction activity off the main chain while still anchoring everything to Ethereum's secure foundation. At their heart, rollups are about efficiency. Instead of having every transaction processed and stored directly on Ethereum, rollups bundle or "roll up" hundreds or thousands of transactions into a single proof or summary. This bundle is then posted to the Ethereum blockchain, where it's recorded and validated. By doing the heavy lifting off-chain and only posting the essential data back to Layer 1, rollups drastically reduce costs and speed up processing—without sacrificing the trustlessness Ethereum is known for.

There are two main types of rollups, and they differ in how they prove that transactions are valid. Optimistic rollups take a "trust first, verify if challenged" approach. They assume transactions are correct by default and only check for fraud if someone disputes a transaction during a short challenge period. This simplicity makes them efficient and easy to implement, though it comes at the cost of longer finality times. ZK-rollups, on the other hand, are more mathematically rigorous. They use cryptographic zero-knowledge proofs to verify the correctness of every batch of transactions before it ever touches Ethereum. These proofs are tiny and fast to verify, even though generating them is computationally intensive. The result is instant finality and high security. Both models aim to achieve the same thing: to make Ethereum more usable by scaling its capacity without altering its core. And they're already in action—projects like Optimism and Arbitrum use optimistic rollups, while zkSync, StarkNet, and Polygon's zkEVM are building the future of ZK-based scaling.

What makes rollups particularly important is that they inherit Ethereum's security. Unlike sidechains, which rely on their own validators and consensus mechanisms, rollups keep Ethereum as the ultimate source of truth. That means users don't have to sacrifice safety for performance.

2.38.15 Modular Architecture

Modular architecture in blockchain refers to a new and increasingly popular design paradigm that breaks up the traditional, monolithic blockchain into distinct, specialized layers, each responsible for a specific function.[95] Rather than having one tightly integrated system handle everything, from consensus and data availability to execution and settlement—modular blockchains decouple these responsibilities, allowing different layers or chains to focus on doing one thing well, and then coordinate with each other. In traditional (monolithic) blockchains like Bitcoin or Ethereum (pre-2.0), all core functions happen on a single chain. This includes the network reaching consensus, executing transactions, storing historical data, and ensuring that all data is available to participants. While simple and secure, this model faces serious scalability and flexibility limits. Every node has to do everything, which slows the network and makes upgrades complex.

A modular blockchain, by contrast, separates these functions across layers:

- Execution layer: Responsible for processing transactions and smart contracts. This can be offloaded to rollups (like Arbitrum or zkSync) that run on top of Ethereum.
- Consensus layer: Determines the ordering and validity of blocks. Ethereum, for example, plays this role for many rollups.
- Data availability (DA) layer: Ensures that the transaction data needed to verify state changes is accessible to all. New blockchains like Celestia are purpose-built to serve as DA layers, offering scalable and efficient data broadcasting.
- Settlement layer: Serves as the final arbiter and source of truth. It anchors proofs and resolves disputes. Ethereum often plays this role for rollups.

Each component can innovate independently and scale on its own terms. For instance, rollups can experiment with different execution models without changing the base chain, and data availability layers can use techniques like erasure coding or data sampling to scale efficiently without bloating full nodes. The benefits of this approach are immense: better scalability, easier upgrades, and greater flexibility for developers to compose systems tailored to specific needs. It enables a "plug-and-play" blockchain ecosystem, where you can mix and match layers, choosing, for example, Ethereum for settlement, Celestia for data, and your own custom rollup for execution.

Modular architecture is at the heart of Ethereum's rollup-centric roadmap and the rise of new projects like Celestia, EigenLayer, Fuel, and Cosmos. These systems are all built around the idea that blockchains don't need to do everything themselves. Instead, they can specialize, collaborate, and scale in a modular fashion, much like how the internet is made up of independently functioning layers and protocols.

---

[95] What is a modular blockchain? Polkadot's architecture explained.

2.38.16 DAS

Data Availability Sampling, or DAS, is a breakthrough solution to one of the trickiest problems in blockchain scalability: how to ensure that the data behind every block is actually available to all participants, especially when the blocks become large and complex.[96] In any blockchain system, particularly modular ones, it's not enough to just know that a block is valid. You also need to know that the data behind the transactions is accessible. Without this assurance, you can't independently verify what happened, which opens the door to manipulation and undermines trust in the network. Solving this problem in the past meant relying on full nodes, powerful computers that download and store every piece of data for every block. While this works for smaller systems, it's not scalable. As blockchains grow and start handling thousands of transactions per second, the amount of data becomes too heavy for most participants to manage. That's where DAS comes in. It offers a much lighter, smarter approach: instead of downloading the entire block, a node can just sample a few small, random pieces of it. If those samples are all present and retrievable, it becomes statistically very likely that the entire block is available somewhere on the network. This is made possible through techniques like erasure coding, which adds redundancy to the data. Think of it like a puzzle where even if a few pieces are missing, you can still reconstruct the entire picture as long as you have most of them. In a blockchain context, this means that if enough nodes can retrieve small, random parts of a block, we can be confident the whole thing is safely distributed and not being withheld by a malicious actor.

DAS plays a foundational role in modern modular blockchain architectures, especially in data availability layers like Celestia. In these systems, rollups and other off-chain execution layers post their transaction data to the base layer, and thanks to DAS, even light clients—nodes with minimal hardware—can verify whether that data is truly available. They don't need to download gigabytes of information; just a few well-chosen samples can give them high confidence in the integrity of the network. By making it possible to verify large blocks with only a fraction of the data, DAS enables blockchains to scale dramatically without compromising security or decentralization. It empowers lightweight nodes, reduces the burden on the network, and ensures that even as blockchains grow, they remain open and verifiable for everyone.

2.38.17 Verkle Trees

Verkle trees are a next-generation data structure poised to play a critical role in the evolution of Ethereum and other scalable blockchains. They're designed to replace the Merkle Patricia Trie currently used in Ethereum for storing the state of the network—essentially, the giant map of who owns what, smart contract data, account balances, and more. While

---

[96] Data availability sampling|Celestia.

Merkle trees have been reliable for years, they come with some significant limitations, especially as blockchains scale and aim to support light clients and more complex applications. Verkle trees aim to overcome these limitations with elegance and efficiency. Verkle trees work much like Merkle trees in that they allow users to prove the validity of a piece of data (i.e. an account balance or contract storage) without revealing the entire dataset. But instead of relying on cryptographic hash functions at every node, Verkle trees use a different technique: vector commitments. These commitments allow a prover to commit to a large set of values and later reveal just a tiny subset, along with a succinct proof that those values are indeed part of the original set.

The magic of Verkle trees lies in how compact and efficient these proofs are. In Merkle structures, if you wanted to prove something about data deep in the tree, the proof size would grow logarithmically with the size of the tree and involve many hash computations. In Verkle trees, even with millions of entries, you can generate very small proofs, making them ideal for light clients and stateless nodes, which don't want or can't afford to download and store the full blockchain state. This has profound implications for Ethereum's roadmap. One of the network's long-term goals is to become stateless, meaning that nodes wouldn't need to store the entire history and state of the blockchain to verify and relay transactions. This would reduce the hardware requirements to participate in the network, opening the door to greater decentralization. Verkle trees make this possible by enabling users to include small, verifiable state proofs directly in their transactions. That way, nodes don't have to look up anything, they just verify the proof and move on. What makes Verkle trees even more attractive is their support for much wider branching factors than Merkle trees. Instead of having just 16 branches per node like in a Merkle Patricia Trie, Verkle trees can support hundreds or even thousands. This flattening of the structure reduces the depth of the tree and further compresses the size of proofs, making them faster to verify and easier to scale. Mathematically, let a node have a branching factor B, which means it can store up to B child pointers or values. In a Merkle tree, generating a proof for a leaf requires transmitting $\log_B(N)$ sibling hashes, where N is the number of leaves. This scales poorly with deep trees and especially when proofs require multiple branches. In contrast, in a Verkle tree using KZG commitments, a node with B children encodes them into a vector $v = (v_1, v_2, \ldots, v_B)$ and commits to this vector via a commitment $C = KZG(v)$. When a verifier requests proof for the i-th value v_i, the prover supplies a succinct opening proof π_i that is constant in size and verifiable against C using pairing-based cryptography on elliptic curves. The practical impact is substantial. Verkle trees with a branching factor of 256 can produce single-key proofs under 150 bytes, compared to over 500 bytes in typical MPT proofs. This compression scales even more favorably when multiple keys are proven simultaneously due to aggregation properties inherent to polynomial commitments.

2.38.18 Avalanche Consensus

Avalanche consensus is an approach to achieving agreement (consensus) in decentralized networks, designed to be highly scalable, low-latency, and robust against attacks, especially when compared to consensus models like Proof of Work (Bitcoin) or classical Byzantine Fault Tolerant protocols.[97] Introduced by the Avalanche network, this consensus protocol blends ideas from network gossip, random sampling, and probabilistic guarantees to enable fast and secure decisions in a large, decentralized environment. Traditional blockchains like Bitcoin require every node to eventually see and agree on the exact same chain, often through resource-heavy mining and rigid block propagation rules. In contrast, Avalanche uses a gossip-based system of repeated sampling and voting that leads the network toward consensus organically, without needing any single chain or leader.

When a node receives a new transaction or block, it doesn't try to convince the entire network at once. Instead, it randomly selects a small subset of nodes and asks them if they agree that the transaction is valid and preferred. Each of those nodes does the same, checking with their own sample of peers. If the result is consistently positive over several rounds of polling, the network develops confidence that the transaction should be accepted. If the responses start to waver or a conflict arises (like a double-spend), the repeated sampling helps the network naturally resolve the issue in favor of the transaction that receives the most consistent backing. This process is both lightweight and fast. Because it doesn't require global coordination or a massive majority vote in every round, consensus can be reached in a few seconds with minimal communication overhead. And since there's no mining involved, it's also environmentally friendly and energy-efficient.

What's particularly innovative is that Avalanche offers probabilistic finality, meaning once a transaction is accepted after a certain number of successful polls, the probability that it will ever be reversed becomes astronomically low. This stands in contrast to Proof of Work systems, where finality is never absolute and users must wait for multiple confirmations to feel secure.

Avalanche consensus also supports a flexible, modular architecture. Unlike monolithic blockchains, the Avalanche ecosystem can support many interoperable chains, each tailored to specific use cases, yet all secured through the same consensus mechanism. This extensibility has made Avalanche attractive for DeFi platforms, gaming applications, and institutions seeking customizable blockchain solutions.

2.38.19 VRF-Based Proof of Stake

VRF-based Proof of Stake (PoS) is a variation of the Proof of Stake consensus mechanism that introduces Verifiable Random Functions (VRFs) to fairly and securely select

---

[97] Avalanche Consensus|Avalanche Builder Hub.

validators in a decentralized blockchain network.[98] It's used in several modern blockchain protocols (including Algorand, Cardano, and Ouroboros Praos) to enhance security, scalability, and unpredictability in block production without sacrificing decentralization. To understand this model, it helps to start with the challenge in Proof of Stake: how to select the next validator (or block proposer) fairly and securely, especially when thousands of nodes might be competing for the role. Traditional PoS systems use deterministic rules weighted by how many tokens each participant is staking. While this is efficient, it can make validator selection predictable and vulnerable to targeted attacks or manipulation.

That's where VRFs come in. A Verifiable Random Function is a cryptographic tool that allows a validator to generate a random number and a proof that the number was generated correctly. The magic of a VRF is that the output is unpredictable to everyone else, but once revealed, anyone can verify that it was produced honestly based on the validator's secret key and public input. In a VRF-based PoS system, every validator runs the VRF locally during each time slot or epoch, using their private key and some shared input— often the epoch number or block height. If their random output meets certain criteria (like being below a threshold based on their stake), they "win" the right to propose a block. But until they announce it, no one knows who the next validator will be. And when they do, they include the VRF proof in the block, which everyone else can verify to ensure they were indeed the legitimate leader for that round.

This approach has multiple advantages. First, it ensures privacy and unpredictability: since no one knows who the next block producer is until they reveal themselves, it's much harder to target them with censorship or denial-of-service attacks. Second, it maintains fairness and stake proportionality, because the threshold for winning the VRF lottery is based on how much stake a validator holds. And finally, it supports high scalability and low energy usage, since the selection process is lightweight and doesn't require network-wide communication or expensive computations. Protocols like Cardano's Ouroboros Praos use VRFs to choose slot leaders in a way that's both random and verifiable, ensuring that even in a network with tens of thousands of nodes, block production remains fair, secure, and efficient. Algorand, similarly, uses VRFs to select both block proposers and committees of validators in a fully decentralized way, enabling fast consensus with minimal communication overhead.

2.38.20 BFT Improvements

BFT (Byzantine Fault Tolerance) improvements refer to the evolution of consensus mechanisms that make distributed systems more resilient, faster, and scalable.[99] Originally designed for solving the Byzantine Generals Problem, where nodes must agree on a decision despite some of them being dishonest, BFT algorithms have seen major

---

[98] 2008.10189.

[99] Improved dynamic Byzantine Fault Tolerant consensus mechanism—ScienceDirect.

enhancements over the past two decades, particularly in the context of blockchain and decentralized finance. Classical BFT protocols, such as PBFT (Practical Byzantine Fault Tolerance), were groundbreaking in enabling systems to reach agreement even if up to one-third of nodes behave maliciously. PBFT relies on a system of rounds and voting, where nodes exchange signed messages to agree on the next action. It offers fast finality (decisions are instantly final), but it suffers from poor scalability. Every node has to communicate with every other node, which results in $O(n^2)$ message complexity. This becomes a serious bottleneck when the number of validators grows beyond a few dozen.

Modern improvements to BFT focus on solving exactly this scalability problem. Protocols like Tendermint, HotStuff, and DiemBFT introduce more efficient communication patterns and pipelining techniques. HotStuff, for example, significantly streamlines the number of communication rounds needed by structuring the protocol in a chain of consensus proposals, which naturally supports leader changes and parallel execution. It's more resilient to failures and provides a cleaner abstraction for developers. Another major improvement comes from the introduction of threshold signatures. Instead of collecting dozens or hundreds of individual validator signatures, which can bloat message size, modern BFT systems aggregate them into a single, compact signature. This drastically reduces bandwidth and speeds up verification, making it feasible to have hundreds or even thousands of validators participate in consensus.

Protocols like Casper (Ethereum) and Narwhal and Tusk (used in Sui) go even further by separating the data dissemination layer from the consensus layer. This modularization means that data can flow freely through the network without being immediately coupled to agreement, allowing validators to agree on the order of operations only after data has been reliably broadcasted. In asynchronous or partially synchronous settings—where message delivery times can vary unpredictably, improved BFT protocols like HoneyBadgerBFT have introduced techniques to ensure liveness and agreement without requiring fixed timeouts. These systems use randomized leader election and erasure coding to tolerate high network delays while still reaching consensus eventually. BFT improvements aim to preserve the strong security guarantees of traditional Byzantine consensus while making them faster, more scalable, and more practical for real-world blockchain deployments. They're a foundational part of modern blockchain platforms like Cosmos, Solana, Algorand, and the upcoming Ethereum scaling solutions—quietly powering the next generation of decentralized infrastructure.

2.38.21 IBC

IBC, or Inter-Blockchain Communication, is a protocol that allows independent blockchains to securely exchange data and assets, without relying on centralized bridges or intermediaries.[100] It's a key part of the Cosmos ecosystem, but its underlying ideas are

---

[100] What is IBC?|Developer Portal.

broadly applicable to any blockchain that wants to interoperate with others while maintaining its sovereignty and security. Blockchains have been isolated systems, each with its own ledger, consensus rules, and user base. Moving assets or information between them usually involves trusted third parties, like exchanges or wrapped tokens managed by centralized custodians. This creates friction and introduces points of failure. IBC changes this by enabling trustless, direct communication between blockchains through cryptographic proofs and light client verification.

The way IBC works is both elegant and secure. When two blockchains want to communicate via IBC, they establish a channel, similar to a private, authenticated connection. Each chain runs a light client of the other, essentially a compact representation that can verify the other chain's state and consensus. When a transaction happens on Chain A, its result is committed in the chain's state and broadcasted as a packet to Chain B. Chain B then uses its light client to verify that this packet is legitimate before processing it. This ensures that no external party is needed to verify or relay the information, and both chains can continue to operate independently. One of IBC's most visible applications is in cross-chain token transfers. For example, when you send ATOM (the native token of Cosmos Hub) to another chain like Osmosis, IBC locks the ATOM on Cosmos and mints a corresponding representation on Osmosis. This logic can also apply to messages, governance votes, staking instructions, and even smart contract interactions across different chains. Chains don't need to use the same virtual machine, consensus algorithm, or governance model. As long as they implement the IBC protocol and support light clients, they can interoperate. This allows a diverse network of specialized blockchains, each optimized for different use cases like DeFi, gaming, or privacy—to cooperate seamlessly while retaining control over their own infrastructure.

2.38.22 LayerZero

LayerZero is an omnichain interoperability protocol designed to connect multiple blockchains in a lightweight, secure, and trust-minimized way.[101] While other cross-chain solutions rely on centralized bridges or heavy consensus mechanisms, LayerZero introduces a novel architecture that allows different blockchains to communicate directly and share data and assets, without compromising security or decentralization. LayerZero acts as a messaging layer between blockchains. It doesn't create a new blockchain itself. This could be anything from cross-chain token transfers and NFT bridging, to general-purpose communication between smart contracts on different networks. Think of it as a universal messaging bus that lets applications on Ethereum talk to apps on Solana, Avalanche, BNB Chain, or any other supported chain.

The architecture of LayerZero is uniquely composed of three main components: the User Application (UA), the Relayer, and the Oracle. When a dApp wants to send a

---

[101] Home|LayerZero.

message from Chain A to Chain B, the UA constructs the message and sends it to the LayerZero endpoint on Chain A. The Oracle and Relayer then work together to transmit and validate the message. The Oracle sends the block header from Chain A to Chain B, while the Relayer sends the transaction proof. Chain B's LayerZero endpoint uses both of these pieces to verify that the message is legitimate and untampered with. This dual-party model is key to LayerZero's security and trust-minimization. Neither the Oracle nor the Relayer can forge a message on their own; both must provide valid and matching information. And because projects can choose their own Oracles and Relayers, the system is highly customizable. For instance, a DeFi protocol might choose Chainlink as an Oracle and run its own Relayer to maintain high trust, while another dApp might choose different providers for different risk models.

The lightweight nature of LayerZero also means it doesn't require smart contracts to be deployed on new consensus layers or sidechains. Instead, developers integrate with LayerZero's endpoint contracts directly on the chains they already support. This reduces complexity, avoids the need for wrapped tokens or synthetic assets, and minimizes points of failure—an important improvement over older bridge designs. LayerZero powers a range of cross-chain applications, such as Stargate Finance, which enables native asset bridging between chains without requiring users to deal with wrapped tokens. It also supports omnichain NFTs, which can move and operate seamlessly across multiple blockchains, as well as cross-chain governance, lending, and even yield farming strategies.

2.38.23 MEV

MEV, or Miner Extractable Value (now often called Maximal Extractable Value), refers to the profit that can be extracted by validators (or miners) through their control over transaction ordering within a block.[102] It's a phenomenon that occurs in blockchains like Ethereum, where the entity responsible for producing a block can choose the order in which transactions are included, or even insert or exclude transactions altogether. This power, while fundamental to block production, can be exploited in ways that give certain actors unfair advantages and sometimes at the expense of regular users. To understand MEV, imagine a public blockchain as a shared transaction queue. Everyone submits their transactions (i.e. swaps, trades, transfers) and miners or validators choose which ones to include in the next block. Most users assume their transactions are included in the order they're submitted or by gas fees, but that's not always the case. Block producers can reorder, insert, or censor transactions for profit.

One of the most well-known examples of MEV is front-running. Let's say you place a large trade on a decentralized exchange. A validator or a bot can see your pending transaction and insert their own transaction just before yours, taking advantage of the price movement your trade will cause. They can then sell at a profit immediately afterward

---

[102] Maximal Extractable Value (MEV)|Chainlink.

(this is called a sandwich attack), where your transaction is "sandwiched" between two attacker-controlled trades. MEV also appears in liquidation opportunities in lending plat-forms, arbitrage between decentralized exchanges, and even NFT minting wars. Wherever there's financial activity and some actors have a time or information advantage, MEV can occur.

The problem with MEV is that it can be harmful to regular users. It increases slip-page, leads to worse execution prices, and makes the network more congested. Worse, it can incentivize validators to compete in aggressive ways to capture profitable MEV opportunities, which can undermine consensus and network stability. To mitigate MEV, Ethereum and other blockchains are introducing new mechanisms like PBS (Proposer-Builder Separation) in Ethereum's roadmap. This splits the role of block proposer and block builder to reduce the concentration of MEV power. Projects like Flashbots have also emerged to bring MEV out of the shadows. Flashbots offers a more transparent and cooperative marketplace where searchers (who look for MEV opportunities) can submit bundles of transactions directly to block builders, reducing the negative impacts like spam and frontrunning in the public mempool.

2.38.24 Restaking

Restaking is a novel mechanism in blockchain infrastructure that allows staked assets to be reused to secure additional services or networks, thereby maximizing the utility and economic efficiency of those staked tokens.[103] It's an interesting idea that expands the role of validators beyond simply securing one blockchain, enabling them to also provide security for multiple applications, protocols, or chains simultaneously, without needing additional capital. Traditionally, when a user stakes tokens (like ETH) to participate in PoS validation, those tokens are locked and committed solely to securing that one protocol. Restaking changes this by allowing the same staked assets to opt-in to provide security for other systems. This means validators can now extend their cryptoeconomic security guarantees to new projects—like rollups, oracles, bridges, or middleware—by restaking their tokens and committing to additional slashing conditions.

The concept has been popularized by EigenLayer, a protocol built on Ethereum that enables ETH stakers to restake their ETH or liquid staking tokens (like stETH or rETH) and offer their services to external networks. These services might include things like data availability layers, decentralized oracles, cross-chain bridges, or even new consensus layers. In return, validators receive additional rewards for their restaked commitments, effectively layering yield on top of their existing stake. Restaking works through smart contracts that introduce additional slashing conditions. If a validator misbehaves in any of the protocols they've opted into securing, a portion of their original stake on Ethereum could be slashed. This creates strong security guarantees for the new system, backed by

---

[103] What is restaking in crypto and how does it enable capital efficiency?

Ethereum's economic weight. Importantly, this doesn't dilute Ethereum's base security; instead, it extends its economic trust to more applications, enabling a modular and more scalable crypto ecosystem.

The benefits of restaking are multifold. For validators, it's a way to earn more yield from the same capital while participating in multiple roles across the ecosystem. For emerging protocols, it provides an out-of-the-box trust layer without having to bootstrap their own validator set or economic base. For Ethereum itself, it helps strengthen its role as a foundational security provider in a multi-chain world. However, restaking also introduces new risks. If validators become overcommitted or are incentivized to act maliciously for higher rewards elsewhere, the security of the base chain could be indirectly affected. It also adds complexity to the staking ecosystem and shifts more responsibility to participants to understand the slashing conditions and service-level agreements they're entering.

2.38.25 Threshold Signatures

Threshold signatures are a cryptographic technique that enables a group of participants to collaboratively produce a valid digital signature, such that only a predefined subset (or threshold) of them is required to do so.[104] This makes them incredibly valuable in decentralized systems where no single party should have full control, but the group still needs to act as one when signing messages, validating transactions, or approving governance actions. Imagine a digital vault that needs 3 out of 5 key holders to agree before it can be opened. No one can open it alone, but if at least three cooperate, the action is authorized. This is the essence of threshold signatures. It distributes trust and power across multiple parties while keeping the process efficient and secure. In technical terms, a threshold signature scheme allows a private key to be split into multiple secret shares among participants. To sign a message, only a minimum number of these participants (the threshold) must combine their partial signatures to produce a single, unified signature. This final signature looks no different from a normal digital signature—it's compact, verifiable using the public key, and doesn't reveal how many participants were involved or who they were. This approach is especially useful in blockchains and distributed systems, where security, decentralization, and resilience are key. For example, in multi-signature wallets, traditional methods require each signature to be posted individually on-chain, increasing gas costs and exposing the signers. Threshold signatures offer a more elegant solution: multiple parties collaborate off-chain to create one signature, which is then verified on-chain as if it came from a single signer. This improves privacy, efficiency, and scalability. Threshold signatures are also crucial in Proof of Stake (PoS) consensus, decentralized key management, cross-chain bridges, and oracles. In all these scenarios, you want to avoid a single point of failure while still needing the system to act decisively. For instance, a bridge

---

[104] https://scryptplatform.medium.com/threshold-signatures-a0eff03dc29c.

that transfers assets between chains can use threshold signatures to ensure that a certain number of trusted validators approve each transfer—preventing fraud while maintaining decentralization. Several advanced protocols use threshold cryptography in their design. BLS threshold signatures (based on pairing-friendly elliptic curves) are particularly popular in blockchain networks because they support signature aggregation, making them compact and efficient even with large validator sets. Projects like Ethereum 2.0, Dfinity, and Threshold Network leverage threshold schemes to coordinate secure operations across distributed participants.

2.38.26 VRFs

A Verifiable Random Function (VRF) is a cryptographic tool that allows someone to generate a random-looking output along with a proof that this output was generated correctly using a specific private key. It combines two essential properties that are usually hard to achieve together: unpredictable randomness and verifiability. Imagine you're flipping a coin in a room full of people, but you want to prove later that the outcome was fair—without letting anyone influence it or redo the flip. A VRF is like a digital version of that fair coin flip. It generates randomness that can't be predicted in advance, can't be faked, and can be verified by anyone once published. A user with a private key inputs some data—like a timestamp, round number, or message—into the VRF. It produces two things:

- A random output (like a hash).
- A cryptographic proof that this output was generated using the private key and the input.

Anyone with the user's public key can then verify that the output was correctly derived from the input, without learning anything about the private key or being able to reproduce the output themselves unless they control the same key. This is incredibly useful in decentralized systems where randomness is essential but must also be trusted. For example, in blockchain consensus mechanisms, such as in Cardano or Algorand, VRFs are used to select block proposers or validators in a random but verifiable way. The randomness ensures fairness and unpredictability, while the proof ensures that others can verify that the winner was selected honestly.

In these protocols, validators run the VRF locally and, if the output meets a certain threshold (based on how much stake they hold, for example), they "win" the right to propose a block. The VRF proof ensures that this selection was legitimate and tamper-proof. VRFs also help prevent manipulation and grinding attacks, where someone might try to test multiple inputs to find a favorable random result. Because the VRF output is tightly bound to the private key and input, such attacks are infeasible without full control over the signer.

A compelling real-world application of VRFs can be found in the Algorand blockchain, which uses them as the foundation for its consensus mechanism. In Algorand, every round of block production begins with a kind of cryptographic lottery. Every validator uses their private key to run a VRF locally, taking the round number and other protocol data as input. The VRF produces a random-looking output along with a proof that the result was generated honestly. If the output is below a certain threshold—determined by the validator's stake—they are selected to propose the next block. Until the selected validator broadcasts their block and proof, no one else knows who won the round, which helps prevent targeted attacks or censorship. Once a validator reveals their winning result, they include the VRF output and its accompanying proof alongside their proposed block. Other nodes on the network can then use the validator's public key to verify that the VRF was computed correctly and fairly. This way, the network doesn't need a central coordinator or repeated communication to decide who gets to produce the next block. The result is a consensus process that is not only fast and decentralized, but also cryptographically fair and unpredictable.

The underlying math behind VRFs involves advanced cryptography, often based on elliptic curve functions or pairing-based constructions like BLS (Boneh–Lynn–Shacham). Essentially, a VRF is a deterministic function that, given a private key and a message, produces a unique output and a proof. The output appears random to everyone else, but the proof can be publicly verified using the corresponding public key and the original message. Because no one can control or predict the output, and yet everyone can verify its validity, VRFs serve as a trustworthy source of randomness in decentralized settings. This makes VRFs indispensable in scenarios like blockchain consensus, lottery systems, fair NFT minting, decentralized voting, and any system where you need to ensure that randomness is not only fair, but provably so. They are a cornerstone of protocols like Algorand and Cardano, enabling a shift from brute-force mining or centralized coordination to efficient, cryptographically sound randomness that secures the system without sacrificing decentralization.

2.38.27 Maximum Extractable Value

Maximal Extractable Value (MEV) refers to the quantifiable value that a participant in a blockchain consensus process, typically a block proposer, can extract by manipulating the inclusion, exclusion, and ordering of transactions within a block. Originally termed "Miner Extractable Value," the concept has evolved in step with changes in Ethereum's validator architecture and broader consensus models, and now reflects a fundamental economic externality at the intersection of protocol rules and market behavior. At its core, MEV arises because block proposers possess a local monopoly over transaction ordering during their assigned slot. This power enables them to behave strategically, not merely by executing transactions as received from the mempool, but by reordering, injecting, or censoring transactions to capture arbitrage opportunities, front-run user trades, or extract liquidation profits from decentralized finance (DeFi) protocols. The phenomenon is not a design flaw per se, but rather an emergent property of permissionless transaction inclusion coupled with economic rationality. Now, let us consider a proposer P at time t who receives a set $T = \{\tau_1, \tau_2, ..., \tau_n\}$ of pending transactions from the mempool. Each transaction τ_i carries a gas fee g_i, a sender utility function u_i, and potentially induces a side-effect on external protocols (e.g., price changes on DEXes, oracle updates, or stateful triggers). The proposer's objective is not merely to maximize the sum $\sum g_i$, but to maximize total extractable utility, which includes both transaction fees and state-induced arbitrage. This optimization problem is inherently combinatorial and adversarial. The proposer may simulate the execution of permutations $\pi(T)$ of the transaction list and select the permutation $\pi*$ that yields the highest extractable payoff. From a game-theoretic perspective, MEV introduces a form of sequential move game between transaction senders and block producers, where the latter have an informational advantage and unilaterally determine the game's payoff structure. Users act as first movers, broadcasting transactions under the assumption of fair inclusion, while proposers, as second movers, may exploit this informational asymmetry. The equilibrium strategies in such games often deviate from social optimality, resulting in extractive behavior that redistributes value from users to proposers without corresponding increases in network utility. MEV is tightly bound to the deterministic consensus ordering logic of blockchain protocols. In protocols like Ethereum (prior to proposer-builder separation), the proposer has complete freedom to specify the sequence of transactions. This ordering determinism is necessary for state machine replication, but its delegation to a single actor per block creates a point of strategic centralization. The problem is exacerbated in high-throughput settings where transaction ordering can materially affect asset prices, leading to congestion externalities and transaction fee escalation through priority gas auctions (PGAs). Further complexity arises under conditions of MEV-driven reorganization, where validators may be incentivized to revert and re-mine prior blocks to capture previously missed MEV opportunities. This behavior undermines consensus finality and threatens time-based liveness guarantees, particularly in protocols without strong finality layers. In formal terms, if the MEV from re-mining block B_{t-k} exceeds the honest reward trajectory, a rational validator may choose to deviate from canonical consensus, instigating a fork choice instability. To mitigate MEV, recent designs such as Proposer-Builder Separation (PBS) aim to partition block construction and block proposal roles, thereby reducing the unilateral control of ordering. Under PBS, specialized builders compete to create bundles of transactions with provable MEV extraction, while proposers simply choose the bundle with the highest bid. Although this introduces market efficiency, it also shifts the MEV game into a new domain—one with centralization risks among builders and new attack surfaces in bundle simulation and censorship.

2.38.28 PQC

Post-Quantum Cryptography (PQC) refers to a new generation of cryptographic algo-rithms that are designed to remain secure even against attacks from quantum computers. While today's widely used cryptography (like RSA, elliptic curve cryptography (ECC), and Diffie–Hellman key exchange) is robust against classical computers, it would be bro-ken easily by a sufficiently powerful quantum computer using algorithms like Shor's algorithm or Grover's algorithm. PQC aims to future-proof digital security by devel-oping cryptographic systems that are resistant to these quantum attacks. The urgency around PQC stems from the rapid advancement of quantum computing technology. While large-scale quantum computers capable of breaking current cryptography don't exist yet, research and development are accelerating, and cryptographic infrastructure takes years or decades to upgrade globally. A malicious actor could even store encrypted data today and decrypt it in the future once quantum capabilities are available—a threat known as "harvest now, decrypt later." This has made PQC a top priority for governments, banks, tech companies, and critical infrastructure providers.

Unlike traditional cryptography, PQC relies on math problems that are believed to be hard even for quantum computers. These include:

- Lattice-based cryptography: Built on hard problems involving high-dimensional lattices (e.g., the Learning With Errors problem); widely considered the most promising and versatile category.
- Code-based cryptography: Uses error-correcting codes; one of the oldest quantum-resistant schemes.
- Multivariate polynomial cryptography: Involves solving systems of multivariate equa-tions, which is hard for both classical and quantum machines.
- Hash-based signatures: Rely on the security of hash functions, which are relatively quantum-resistant under Grover's algorithm.
- Isogeny-based cryptography: A more recent and compact class based on problems in elliptic curve isogenies, though under intense scrutiny after some schemes were recently broken.

Governments and standardization bodies have been actively preparing for the post-quantum era. The U.S. National Institute of Standards and Technology (NIST) launched a global competition in 2016 to select standard PQC algorithms. In July 2022, NIST announced a first batch of finalists, with lattice-based algorithms like CRYSTALS-Kyber (for key encapsulation) and CRYSTALS-Dilithium (for digital signatures) emerging as the front-runners. These are now being integrated into software libraries and tested in real-world systems. In practice, adopting PQC means redesigning cryptographic protocols in everything from web browsers, emails, and mobile apps to blockchain systems, satellites, and IoT devices. In many cases, hybrid approaches are being used—where classical and post-quantum algorithms are run together—to ensure backward compatibility while preparing for future resilience.

Bitcoin

3.1 How Does Bitcoin Work?

From all cryptocurrencies and blockchain networks, Bitcoin was the first and arguably to this day the most famous of them all. It was the first coin that based itself not on a banking system, a centralized government and/or a payment system but is in fact completely decentralized. The network is completely trustless and trust is based on the actions of all the nodes in the network. Consensus is needed to move forward and is the lifeblood of the network. Bitcoin is also the proponent of what is currently called 'blockchain 1.0' or the first type of blockchain and blockchain implementation to see the light of day. Within the network the proof of work algorithm is being used, more specifically it is based on the secure hash algorithm 256, better known as SHA-256 (see earlier for detailed explanation). The transactions in the network are processed by the miners which generate the hashed output from a block header that is used as input together with a nonce.[1] Why mine for these blocks? It costs time, hardware and energy to find the correct solution of a block. The winning miner receives a number of Bitcoin as reward for his work.[2] This is the high-level story but of course you wouldn't be reading this if you were just happy with the high-level story. We are going to dive into the details and see what makes the Bitcoin network so unique. I would advise all of you to read on if you are interested in development and a technical understanding of blockchain. Even if you just 'skim' through the chapter that follows, you will better understand the choices that were made by other platforms and why there are certain evolutions in the world of blockchain. For those of you that just can't get enough of Bitcoin, I gladly refer you to 'Programming Bitcoin: Learn how to program Bitcoin from scratch' by Jimmy Song where you get an even more

---

[1] The hash value should be lower than the target hash value set by the network.

[2] At this time a miner is awarded 12.5 BTC per block but this has been decreasing over time.

© The Author(s), under exclusive license to Springer Nature Switzerland AG 2026   105
S. Van Hijfte, *Blockchain Platforms*, Synthesis Lectures on Computer Science,
https://doi.org/10.1007/978-3-032-00979-1_3

in-depth explanation of how the network works (and how it is programmed) or 'Mastering Bitcoin' by Andreas M. Antonopoulos. I chose a different approach than other books on the subject of blockchain as I will work 'top-down'. I will start with what most people already know: the chain of blocks. I will work my way down from the chain, towards the blocks themselves and eventually the transactions with signing and verification. This means that sometimes you might see words and concepts pop up that might not be immediately clear to you, but you don't need to worry because everything will become clearer as you go on.

3.2   The Bitcoin Blockchain: The Network

The Bitcoin network is an extensive network in which a heap of nodes are constantly communicating with each other. Transactions and blocks are broadcasted throughout the network while the gossip protocol helps to spread the nonce over all the nodes. But first things first: how do we get inside the network? When we have a node there must be a way to discover other nodes in the network and start to make a connection, otherwise it would be futile to start up a node in the first place. To be able to join the extensive Bitcoin network, only one other node needs to be discovered. That's it. When that happens, you are part of the Bitcoin network. The nodes typically connect to each other by making use of a TCP connection over port 8333 (or another in case another is provided).[3] New nodes can be discovered by making use of so-called seed nodes which help to quickly discover other nodes in the network. Once our new node has established a connection with several of these 'regular' nodes in the network, it will lose the connection with the seed node. When you are making use of the Bitcoin core client, this option is turned on by default (-dnsseed is set to 1). Other ways for a node to discover the address of another node is by making use of a user provided text file on startup, hard coded addresses in the software of the node, stored addresses in a database and reading these on startup or by DNS request. The node will keep a timestamp for each of the addresses and this timestamp is updated every 20 min when a message is received from a specific node via the AddressCurrentlyConnected in net.cpp (one of the files making up the Bitcoin Core implementation. When our node finally discovers one of the nodes that is already part of the network, it starts by sending out a version message. This version message contains the following information:

Version message

Name	Description
PROTOCOL_VERSION	Version of the P2P protocol

(continued)

---

[3] For the testnet the default port is 18333 and for Regtest it is 18444.

(continued)

Name	Description
nLocalServices	List of local services
nTime	Current time
addrYou	The IP address of the 'old' node
addrMe	The IP address of our node
Subvert	Type of software on the node
BestHeight	Block height of our blockchain

Based on this version-message the 'old' node that was already part of the Bitcoin network will respond with a so-called verack-message. With this message the 'old' node acknowledges the version message that has been sent by our new node. Now the 'old' node can do the same thing and respond with a version message so that it can be acknowledged by our node. This way the nodes become peers of each other. The next step will be for our node to start sending 'addr' and 'getaddr' messages through the network. With the first message it sends its own address to the newly connected peer so that this peer can send this address further through the network so that more nodes learn about our node and can start to establish connections.

Name	Description	Field size	Data type
Time	The actual timestamp	4	Uint32
Services	Bitfield of features to be enabled	8	Uint64_t
IPv6/4	IPv6 address/IPv4 mapped to v6	16	Char[16]
Port	Port number or network byte order	2	Uint16_t

The same way our node can ask for a list of addresses by making use of the 'getaddr' message. The response on the getaddr is a list of the addresses of which the timestamp isn't older than 3 h old and a maximum of 2500. If there are more than 2500 addresses, there is a random selection amongst the addresses that have a timestamp that is younger than 3 h. The Bitcoin network is a distributed network and nodes can come and go as they please, therefore our node will have to perform network discovery from time to time. This is not very efficient and would lead the network to send out and receive way too much messages. The problem at hand is solved in 2 different ways: first of all, our node will only connect to a handful of peers. Too many connections are simply not interesting. The second is even more ingenious. When we would disconnect our node, it will make use of a technique called 'bootstrapping' to quickly rediscover nodes and reconnect to the network. How does it do this? By keeping a list of the earlier connections the node had in the network. This way it can easily try to reestablish a connection with a node it knows from before. In case no node can be discovered, it is the seed node to the rescue.

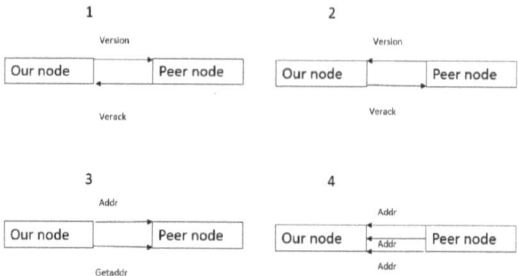

The several steps of node discovery

Of course one can take the more adventurous route and simply turn off the default settings. This is not advisable as the network connections will no longer be automatically maintained. Some final remarks regarding the nodes and addresses in the network need to be made. When a node receives an 'addr'-message, these addresses aren't just simply added. They are checked. It the message is from a node with a really old version, the message is ignored, just as when the version of the other node is not very old (but still older) and you already have 1000 addresses. The addresses also receive a timestamp in the addr-message and if the timestamp is too low or too high, it is simply set to 5 days ago. Otherwise, we always subtract 2 h from the timestamp and add the address. The addAddress function with then check if the address already exists, and if so, update the address record accordingly. Now, our node might want to respond to a 'getAddr'-message itself. This can be done and 'addr'-messages can be sent out but the addresses that are added to the message have to adhere to a certain set of rules:

- After processing, the timestamp of the address < 60 min
- The address must be routable
- The addr-message can contain a maximum of 1000 addresses
- fGetAddr is not set on the node.

The node will also broadcast its own address to all connected nodes every 24 h. The own list of addresses are also being updated and old addresses are removed. This happens every 10 min as long as there are more than 3 connections.[4] A special type of messages that used to be implemented (it has been removed in the more recent versions of Bitcoin core) in most nodes, was the 'alert message'.[5] This was an option which allowed the Bitcoin developers to broadcast an emergency message throughout the network to all nodes. The alert message was used to warn the users if they have to undertake certain actions. Such an action could be an update because of a critical bug in the software in use. So far we have seen discovery messages and alert messages but the bulk of the messages

---

[4] (December 19, 2017) Satoshi Client Node Discovery. *Github—Bitcoin* https://en.bitcoin.it/wiki/Satoshi_Client_Node_Discovery. Accessed November 4, 2019.
[5] Removed with BIP133.

in the Bitcoin network are more 'standard' messages. A network message in the Bitcoin network has the following container structure:

Bitcoin network message

Name	Description	Size
Start string	Start indicator and identifier	4 bytes
Command name	What is the payload	12 bytes
Length of the payload	Length in little-Endian	4 bytes
Checksum field	Identifier	4 bytes
Payload	The actual data	Varies

So what information is hidden in the messages? When we look at the table above, we need to understand that the first items are all in the 'start string'. The network message gives us an indicator of the start of the message that is being transmitted. It also gives us an identifier as each network that makes use of 'start string' has its own unique starting code for each message, like a signature. With the use of network magic the messages send out by other nodes from a different network will never be accepted as they do not have the correct 'fingerprint'. For the Bitcoin main network, this fingerprint is 0xf9beb4d9.[6] The next part is the command field. This gives us a description of what the payload actually is and is meant to be human readable. By examining the command field, we can get therefore a better understanding of what the intent of the message is. The length of the payload is encoded in little-endian and is important for the client to be able to accept a communication or not at all. This can be important as the payload size is variable and can be in some cases too big for a client to accept. The last part of the message header is the checksum field. This checksum field consists out of the first 4 bytes of the SHA256 of the payload. Finally, there is the payload itself. We are nog connected to the network. Interesting. What should we do next? You might have guessed it, information about the blockchain, more specifically the block headers. Why the block headers? Well, it is much smaller in size than the actual blocks themselves and already contain the information necessary for a full node to asynchronously download the full blocks. For a light client the block headers are even enough to get proofs of inclusion. We will go deeper into these different nodes types at the end of the chapter on Bitcoin.

3.3 Bitcoin Blocks

To get these block headers, the node sends out a 'getheaders' message and this message requests a 'headers' message that provides blocks starting from a certain point in the Bitcoin blockchain. It can however, also be done by making use of a 'getBlocks' message.

---

[6] For the testnet the start string is 0x0b110907 and for Regtest it is 0xfabfb5da.

How is determined which headers the node needs to download? Well there are two situations: either you have a completely new client which contains no information yet or you have a client that has been disconnected for a while. In case it has been disconnected, the possibility exists that you have information on stale blocks that are no longer part of the 'main' chain. The reply to both 'getHeaders' and 'getBlocks' is a set of header hashes on several heights within the blockchain. Your node will check which one it recognizes from its own chain and start from that point. If there are stale blocks being replied by the peer node, it is up to our node to make the distinction between what is part of the main chain and what isn't. So what does such a reply usually look like? It has the format that looks like this:

Inventory message that follows getBlocks message

Name	Description	Size
Version	Protocol version	4 bytes
Hash count	Number of header hashes	Varies
Block header hashes	The actual header hashes	Varies
Stop hash	All zeroes	32 bytes

Inventory message that follows getHeaders message

Name	Description	Size
Count	Number of headers	Varies
Headers	Block headers	Varies

The main difference between getHeaders and getBlocks is the number of header hashes. GetBlocks will get you a maximum of 500 header hashes while the getHeaders goes up to a maximum of 2000 header hashes.

The block header itself consists out of 6 parameters:

- **Version**: the version number of the Bitcoin software
- **Parent block hash**: the hash of the last block accepted on the blockchain
- **Merkle tree root hash**: a hash of all the transactions included in the block
- **Time stamp**: the time the block was created
- **Nonce:** a set variable used in proof of work
- **nBits:** the threshold set by the network.

For the genesis block, we could fill out the following information:[7]

---

[7] The encoding of the genesis block can be found on: https://github.com/bitcoin/bitcoin/blob/3955c3 940eff83518c186facfec6f50545b5aab5/src/chainparams.cpp#L123.

Simplified block header

Version	Parent hash	Merkle hash	Time	Nonce	Nbits
1	0	Genesis.buildMerkleTree()	1231006505	2083236893	0x1d00ffff

So how is this data transmitted over the Bitcoin network? It makes use of the following format to provide some kind of inventory:

Data container

Name	Description	Size
Type identifier	Type of the hashed object	4
Hash	Twice SHA256 in internal byte order	32

The data identifier is as you might already know the indicator of what data is being transmitted. An example is MSG_TX which indicates that the hash is a transaction identifier. This is the reply to a getData message (or getBlocks/getHeaders message). Here we took the information that is used in the Bitcoin network, as you will see later, this varies depending on the technology implementation. For now, we will use this as a start to gain a deeper understanding of blockchain. Of course the information that has been provided within the block headers has been evolving over time. The genesis-block is an example of the first version that started out in 2009. In September 2012, the block height was the next parameter that was required and it was in March 2013 that blocks that did not contain this information started to be rejected. Version 3 of the blocks was another soft fork which required DER serialization (you will see later what this is) of all ECDSA signatures. Version 4 (which was also released in 2015, just as version 3), was a soft fork that supported the OP_CHECKLOCKTIMEVERIFY. All these upgrades have been supported by the isSuperMajority() mechanism.

The structure of a block in bitcoin

Field	Description	Size
Block size	Size of the block (bytes)	4 bytes
Block header	See below	80 bytes
Transaction counter	How many transactions	Varies
Transactions	The transactions	Varies

An important rule that is included within the Bitcoin network for the serialization of blocks is that the maximum size is 1 MB. So even though there are several variable parts when we look at the size, the total sum has a hard limit that needs to be respected.

The structure of a block header in bitcoin

Field	Description	Size
Version	Version of the protocol	4 bytes
Previous block hash	Hash of the parent block	32 bytes
Merkle root	Hash of the root of this block	32 bytes
Timestamp	Creation time of the block	4 bytes
Difficulty	Difficulty target	4 bytes
Nonce	Variable number	4 bytes

The genesis block was created by Satoshi Nakamoto and contained within it a hidden message which not only refers to the earliest time of the creation of the block but also at the same time the philosophy behind the creation of Bitcoin: "The Times 03/Jan/2009 Chancellor on brink of second bailout for banks". Every produced block is then being shared with the rest of the network to be checked and approved or discarded based on the participants their results. Your node can receive blocks based on two methods: either your node has send out a request for block data, where you receive a data message with data type MSG_BLOCK or the blocks can be send out as a part of a 'block message' because a peer has just mined a new block. When you are making use of a node, or at least a full client, all the blocks, starting from the genesis block, are being contained within this node. When a node receives a new block, it will start to check if the block follows the criteria[8]:

1. Is the data structure of the block syntactically valid?
2. Is the block header hash < the target difficulty?
3. Timestamp < 2 h in the future (for time errors)
4. Block size within acceptable limits
5. First transaction is a generation transaction
6. All transactions within the block are valid.

The blocks within the blockchain are linked to each other based on the hash of the previous block. A final part that is crucial to understand is the concept of network difficulty. The difficulty of finding a correct hash can be set by increasing or decreasing the target hash value within the network. This way one can change the rate at which correct hashes can be discovered, the pace at which transactions can be approved and the speed at which new blocks can be added to the blockchain. The average speed of the Bitcoin network has been about 10 min per block. Other networks much quicker but as we have seen in earlier sections, faster networks come with risks of their own, just as slower networks might

---

[8] You can find these requirements in the CheckBlock and CheckBlockHeader functions of the Bitcoin Core client.

have their own vulnerabilities. Every 2016 blocks the network difficulty can be adjusted based on the length of time it was necessary to solve and find the previous 2016 blocks. This is done because the network wishes to remain at a pace of 1 block every 10 min but computer power increases over time, so the difficulty needs to be adjusted so that we can maintain the pace of 10 min/block. This recalculation does not happen through a central authority, as this would entirely defeat the purpose of a decentralized and distributed network. Instead, every full node in the network does this completely independently. It does this based on the following equation:

$$\text{Difficulty}_t = \text{Difficulty}_{t-1} * (t \text{ of last 2016 blocks}/20160 \text{ minutes})$$

To make sure that the recalculation is not too volatile, the adjustment must be less than a factor 4.

3.4 Bitcoin Transactions

We already have a good idea of how blocks and block headers are being shared and transmitted throughout the network and how our node can ask for this information from its peers. Problem is that we still don't have an idea how the transactions are being shared among the nodes. Here the 'mempool' message is being used. With this message our node can request transactions that it has already verified as valid while they have not yet been mined in a block. Here the reply also is an inventory (inv) message which contains the transaction IDs (or TXIDs). This list of unconfirmed transactions might not be complete. If you are running a SPV client (see later), you might receive only those transactions linked to your wallet, nothing else. A regular inventory message can contain up to 50,000 of these unconfirmed transactions, so it can take several messages before your node has the complete list and there are also some problems with the 'filterload' message (check out the Bitcoin developer manual for more information as there are a lot more messages that can be transmitted throughout the network). Transactions are being shared among the nodes of the network before they are put inside of a candidate block. Such a transaction has the following structure:

Standard transaction

Field	Description	Size
Transaction hash	Pointer to the transactions spent UTXO	32 bytes
Output index	Index of the spent UTXO	4 bytes
Unlocking-script size	Length in bytes	Varies
Unlocking-script	Script that fulfills UTXO locking-script	Varies
Sequence number	Tx-replacement feature	4 bytes

Every transaction that is received by a node must first be verified by that node to make sure that only valid information is communicated to other nodes in the network while the invalid transactions are immediately discarded. This validation of a transaction occurs in a specific manner as there is a specific set of criteria:

1. The syntax and data structure must be correct
2. $100 \geq$ Transaction size $<$ MAX_BLOCK_SIZE
3. nLockTime $\leq$ INT_MAX
4. Input and output lists are not empty
5. Inputs should not have hash $= 0$ or $N = -1$
6. For each input, if the referenced output exists in any other transaction in the pool, reject
7. For each input, check the main branch/transaction pool to find referenced output transaction. If the output is missing, this is an orphan transaction.
8. For each input, if the referenced output transaction is a coinbase output, it must have at least 100 confirmations
9. Reject if sum of input $<$ sum of output
10. $0 <$ output $< 21,000,000$ and $0 <$ input $< 21,000,000$
11. Number of signature operations $<$ signature operation limit
12. scriptSig can only push number on the stack while scriptPubkey must match isStandard.

These criteria change over time, to prevent certain types of attacks or to allow faster/slower block creation. It helps to prevent double spending, makes sure that there are only new bitcoins created when it is a coinbase transaction and it makes sure that the combined scripts are actually valid. When a transaction is accepted, it will be added to the memory pool[9] until it can be mined with other transactions in a candidate block. Which transactions that will be included in the next block is based on the age of the UTXO[10] that is being spent in their inputs.[11] How can one determine the priority of a transaction? That will be determined based on the sum of the value and age of the inputs divided by the total size of the transaction. There is a specific transaction space for high priority transactions of 50 kb.[12] Here the high priority transactions can be added, even if

---

[9] A transaction is valid for perpetuity but a memory pool is a transient, non-persistent form of storage. So imagine that all the nodes that received a transaction that is not yet in a block is being reset or restarted. The transaction will be wiped of the memory pool. The solution will be that the consequent wallet retransmits the transaction or reconstructs it with higher fees.

[10] The age of the UTXO is the number of blocks that have elapsed since the UTXO was recorded.

[11] It can even be the case that prioritized transactions can be sent without any fees if there is enough space in the candidate block.

[12] A high priority transaction.

they carry no transaction fees.[13] The first transaction that will be added to the block is the generation transaction (or coinbase transaction), which is virtually a payment for the mining effort. This transaction has not UTXO as input but has the so-called 'coinbase' as input which is used by the miner to collect his reward. Good to know is that the miner cannot spend this until there are 100 block confirmations in the blockchain.

Generation transaction

Field	Description	Size
Transaction hash	All bits are 0	32 bytes
Output index	All bits are 1	4 bytes
Height	Block height (required since BIP34)	4 bytes (varies)
Coinbase data size	Length of the coinbase data	Varies
Coinbase data[14]	Arbitrary data	Varies
Sequence number	0xFFFFFFFF	4 bytes

(December 13, 2019) Transaction. *Github—Bitcoin.* https://en.bitcoin.it/wiki/Transaction. Accessed December 26, 2019

If we now return to the chain itself, we can see that there are 3 types of chains being maintained by the network nodes. There are the main chain blocks, the side chain blocks and the orphan blocks. The main chain is the one with the highest associated cumulative difficulty. The side chains are created through forks of the main chain, while orphan blocks are those that are kept in the orphan pool until its parent is discovered so that it can be added to the chain.

Below you can see how the transaction actually looks like when it has been mined in a block. You see that the structure has changed and that different information is given than when the transaction has originally been transmitted throughout the network.

Transaction inside a block

Field	Description	Size
Version	Version number	4 bytes
Flag	Optional (always 0001)	Optional 2 byte
In-counter (tx_int count)	Number of inputs	1–9 bytes
Inputs (tx_in)	The actual inputs	Varies
Out-counter (tx_out count)	Number of outputs	1–9 bytes

(continued)

---

[13] Although some mining nodes choose to ignore these transactions.

[14] It was in here that Satoshi Nakamoto hid his secret message. However, the beginning of this field is no longer arbitrary with BIP00034 which states that version-2 blocks start the coinbase data with the block height index as a script push operation.

(continued)

Field	Description	Size
Outputs (tx_out)	The actual outputs	Varies
Witnesses	List of witnesses (only if there is a flag)	Varies
Lock_time	If $\neq$ 0 and sequence < 0xFFFFFFFF: block height or timestamp when final	4 bytes

Interesting here is the mentioning of inputs and outputs. The inputs of a transaction actually refer to the output of a previous transaction. Each transaction input is linked to a previous output because you can simply not spend what you have never received in the first place. So the network wants to know 2 things: where are these bitcoins coming from and are they actually yours to spend? Similarly the outputs provide this information for the transactions that will follow. Lock time is used to delay a transaction. Based on this value, a transaction can only be added to a block unless a certain block height (or Unix time) has been reached. We have mentioned several times the pubkey script or sciptPubKey. This is a script that is included in the outputs and sets the conditions on when these satoshis can be spent. The data that is needed to fulfill these conditions can be provided by making use of the signature script (or scriptSig). Several opcodes can be used in the scriptPubKey when it comes down to our transactions. Below we give a short overview of the opcodes than can be used in the script:

- OP_TRUE/OP_1: pushes values 1–16 up the stack depending on OP_1–OP_16
- OP_CHECKSIG: consumes a signature and a full public key. It checks if the transaction data specified by the SIGHASH flag was converted into the signature by the same ECDSA private key. If so, TRUE is pushed on the stack, otherwise FALSE
- OP_DUP: pushes a copy of the top item on the stack
- OP_HASH160: computes RIPEMD160(SHA256()) of the topmost item on the stack
- OP_EQUAL: checks if the top 2 items are equal and pushes TRUE or FALSE on the stack
- OP_VERIFY: if the topmost item is 0 (FALSE), it terminates the script in failure
- OP_EQUALVERIFY: runs OP_EQUAL and OP_VERIFY in sequence
- OP_CHECKMULTISIG: consumes the value (n) at the top of the stack, consumes that many of the next stack levels (public keys), consumes the value (m) now at the top of the stack, and consumes that many of the next values (signatures) plus one extra value
- OP_RETURN: terminates the script in failure.

A final point that we should consider with Bitcoin transactions is the concept of 'confirmations'. When you perform a transaction, this transaction has to be confirmed over time. This confirmation can only happen when the transaction that you just performed, is propagated throughout the network and accepted in one of the blocks. In the case of the Bitcoin network, this happens, as you know, every 10 min. However, to be entirely sure, it is better to wait until a couple of blocks have been mined on top of the block containing your transaction. So in actuality, if a vendor wants to be sure that a transactions is really valid, he should wait about an hour (5–6 blocks on top of the block containing your transaction) before he could really accept the transaction as confirmed and valid. For small transactions this process might be a little bit over the top but for payments that have some significance this process can prevent several types of attacks and attempts on double spending. In the world of financial services this is also known as 'clearing'.

3.5   Bitcoin Signing and Verification

So we already went through the chaining of blocks to create the blockchain and we have seen how transactions are structured and shared by the peer nodes. But how do we sign transactions and how are these being verified? Bitcoin makes use of the Elliptic Curve Digital Signature Algorithm, or ECDSA in short. With a signature we sign a scalar for G (we defined this earlier for Bitcoin in the section on elliptical curve cryptography). Signing with ECDSA comes down to the use of the discrete log problem. Signing can only work if you either know the private key or if you are able to break the discrete log problem. We make use of a signature hash to create a fingerprint of the input data (a hash algorithm will always give us a fixed-size output, no matter the size of the input). This to make sure that we sign something that is exactly 256 bits. The equation behind the signing process looks like the following:

$\implies$ The relation between the private key e and the public key P $\implies$ $eG = P$
$\implies$ A target k which has a similar relationship $\implies$ $kG = R$
$\implies$ The discrete log problem implies $\implies$ $uG + vP = kG$ with k a random 256-bit integer and u, v $\neq$ 0 chosen by the signer. We also know P and G.
$\implies$ $u = z/s$ and $v = r/s$
$\implies$ $s = (z + r)/k$ where r is the x-coordinate of R and z the signature hash.

It is this final equation that gives us the final signature algorithm that is being used in ECDSA. Verification is easier (which is also the entire purpose within the blockchain network):

- We know the hash z, the public key P of the signer, the x-coordinate of R and the signature s
- $u = z/s$ and $v = r/s$
- $uG + vP = R$
- We know the signature to be valid if the x-coordinate of R and r are equal.

DER or 'Distinguished Encoding Rules' are used for the encoding of the r and s values that are used to perform the actual signing in a single byte stream. Verification is performed on several levels. Transactions have both inputs and outputs, where the inputs reference the previous transactions and the outputs determine the new owners of the bitcoins. Each of the input needs to have the signature that unlocks the coins from the prior transaction.[15] Most of the time this is a single transaction but there are also other possibilities. It is possible to specify a script in which 2 ECDSA signatures are necessary or 2-out-of-3 schemes are also possible. The script opcode that verifies if the signature of a transaction input is valid is called 'OP_CHECKSIG'. Depending on the script that is being used, OP_CHECKMULTISIG is also possible together with OP_CHECKSIGVERIFY and OP_CHECKMULTISIGVERIFY. Another requirement is that the sum of the inputs must be equal or greater than the output. The amount extra is considered to be transaction fee for the miner of the transaction. Some transactions also make use of locktime and transactions are marked as invalid if the specified time has not yet passed. This is the OP_CHECKLOCKTIMEVERIFY opcode. To complete the story, digital signatures are applied to transactions. There is the SIGHASH flag that indicates which part of the transaction data is included in the hash signed by the private key. This SIGHASH flag is applied to every signature and consists out of a single byte (containing either ALL, NONE, SINGLE or ANYONECANPAY). Depending on the type of transaction you are willing to create, a different flag is needed to indicate this to the other participants that are making use of the transaction type.

Flag	Description	Value
ALL	Signature for all inputs and outputs	0x01
NONE	Signature for all inputs	0x02
SINGLE	Signature for all inputs and 1 output which has the same index as the signed input	0x03
ALL|ANYONECANPAY	Signature for 1 input and all outputs	0x81
NONE|ANYONECANPAY	Signature for 1 input and no outputs	0x82
SINGLE|ANYONECANPAY	Signature for 1 input and all outputs with the same index	0x83

One should keep in mind that a transaction can contain several inputs that each can have a different SIGHASH flag. On top of that, the unlocking scripts can contain a signature that lead to different SIGHASH flags and lead to different parts of the transaction being committed. The SIGHASH will eventually sign the nLocktime field and itself is appended to the transaction as well. This means that it will also be hashed and therefore cannot be changed by any other participant in the network, providing the security necessary to ensure that transactions remain how they were defined when they were send out by the signing party.

---

[15] (December 26, 2018) Protocol Documentation. *Github—Bitcoin.* https://en.bitcoin.it/wiki/Protocol_documentation#Signatures. Accessed November 20, 2019.

3.6   UTXO

UTXO or unspent transaction output is a term we have seen earlier in this chapter. It is the basis of transactions taking place in the network as they are used to balance the ledger.[16] From the second a transaction is confirmed, the coins are removed from the UTXO database and the transaction is recorded on the ledger. To understand the way one can spend bitcoin, we should understand that multiple fractions of bitcoin can be retrieved by an algorithm to fulfill a transaction. The changes made to each of these fractions used, is send to the UTXO database. Of course one needs to take into account the transaction fees that one has to pay to execute a transaction. These fees are removed from the UTXO so that this amount will always be lower than the amount you originally have send out. So while we have the idea in our heads that transactions send bitcoins from one wallet to another, they actually move from transaction to transaction. As explained before, each transaction has an input which is the output from a previous transaction. So as the transaction can in case create several outputs, the outputs themselves can only be used once, otherwise you would be attempting to double spend. That is why we have unique transaction identifiers (TXIDs). So in the world of Bitcoin you have 2 types of outputs: spent and unspent. That is why UTXOs are so important, because the money in your wallet isn't really in your wallet. It is in the UTXO database.

So to explain with a practical example: imagine that there are two participants A and B and participant A wants to send 0.80 BTC to participant B. He will also have to pay a transaction fee of 0.20 BTC. To perform the transaction he will make use of a set of UTXOs as inputs (In the image they are all the same size while in reality this will often not be the case). These unspent UTXOs can be found in a global database that is kept and updated by all full (and up to date) nodes of the Bitcoin network. When UTXOs are used, the set is reduced, while new unspent output is created, enlarging the global UTXO set. This transaction, and all other transactions, reference both the address of the current 'owner' of bitcoins (and a change address which can be the same or different from the input address) and the address of the new owner. Any 'change' from the transaction can be sent to the change address. This is because UTXOs cannot be split before you use them as input.

---

[16] Asolo, B. (December 20, 2018) Bitcoin's UTXO Set Explained. *Mycryptopedia*. https://www.myc ryptopedia.com/bitcoin-utxo-unspent-transaction-output-set-explained/. Accessed on November 28, 2019.

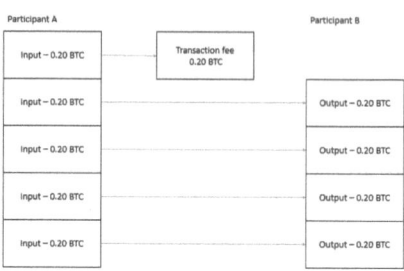

UTXOs

There is also the possibility to create unspendable outputs from transactions, by making use of the Bitcoin scripting language. Specific applications can be developed by making use of this scripting language called 'smart contracts' (explained in detail later on). Sometimes these applications can develop output that cannot be spent and when the RETURN operator is used, these are no longer stored in the UTXO database (otherwise it is stored in there, even though you can no longer spent it, making it ever more expensive to run a full node). Here it is also interesting to note that Satoshi is the smallest indivisible unit of the bitcoin currency. Clearly called after the inventor of the Bitcoin network, a lot of transactions and transaction fees happen in Satoshi instead of in bitcoins.

Satoshi	Bitcoin	Alternative name
1	0.00000001	
10	0.0000001	
100	0.000001	1 Bit/μBTC/you-bit
1000	0.00001	
10,000	0.0001	
100,000	0.001	1 mBTC/em-bit
1,000,000	0.01	1 cBTC/bitcent
10,000,000	0.1	
100,000,000	1.0	

One final aspect is would like to note is the existence of 'bitcoin dust' which is an output that requires a transaction fee that is greater than 1/3 of that outputs value. This is a situation that is very uninteresting for involved parties as the costs are extensive when we look at the actual value. Combining several of these outputs into a more valuable output can create a more interesting transaction for all participants involved.

3.6.1 Timelocks

Another interesting implementation is the one called 'timelocks'. These allow for the restriction of transactions or the use of outputs until a certain point of time. It has been there since the very beginning with the nLocktime-field but new features were later introduced: CHECKLOCKTIMEVERIFY and CHECKSEQUENCEVERIFY. The first field helps define the earliest time that a transaction is valid and can actually be processed and validated. The value given to this field should be below 500,000,000 and is interpreted as a block height. This means that the transaction can only become valid when the blockchain reaches this block height. Above 500 million it is interpreted as a Unix Epoch timestamp and the transaction is only valid when the given time is reached. Problem is that nLocktime can give rise to double spending. As you can send out a transaction with a locktime and another without one. BIP-65 came to the rescue with the CHECK-LOCKTIMEVERIFY implementation or 'CLTV'. The difference with nLocktime is that CLTV really is an output-based timelock while the nLocktime-field is a transaction-level timelock. CLTV isn't meant to replace nLocktime, but rather prevents the spending of the transaction value UTXO until a time where nLocktime is set to a greater or equal value. The previous examples are absolute timelocks while there are also possible relative timelocks that can be used in the Bitcoin network. These timelocks depend on elapsed time based on the confirmation of the output in the blockchain. This can be interesting to keep a set of transactions off-chain and is used in lightening networks and payment channels (see later in this section). A first field that can be used for this is called 'nSequence' and is the transaction-level timelock, while the script-level timelock is called 'CHECK-SEQUENCEVERIFY' or 'CSV'. The 'nSequence'-field is standard set to '0xFFFFFFFF' when the transaction doesn't make use of timelocks. If CLTV or nLocktime is being used, it should be set to a value less than 2^{31}. BIP-68 introduced some uses for this field as a value less than 2^{31} is now being interpreted as a relative timelock transaction. Each of the inputs can have a different relative timelock so the transaction only becomes valid until the last input has become valid. The nSequence ca neither be specified in the number of blocks or seconds. To differentiate, there is a type-flag in the 23rd least-significant bit. If it is set, the value is interpreted as a multiple of 512, otherwise it is interpreted as a number of blocks. The CSV is linked to nSequence, just as CLTV is linked to nLocktime. So what is a possible problem that you can spot here? All of these implementations deal with time. But time in a decentralized peer-to-peer network means something different than in centralized systems where a server can determine the time for all clients. In the world of Bitcoin, each participant has his own interpretation of time. On top of that, there is network latency that puts even more strain on the interpretation of time throughout the network. This can create difficulty for both transaction being interpreted, timestamps and of course timelocks. Miners are incentivized to lie about the timestamp they set on the blocks they mine if they contain timelocked transactions, to earn even more fees (this is

also known as 'fee sniping').[17] This incentive was removed with BIP-113 with the introduction of 'Median-Time-Past'. This timestamp is calculated by taking the last 11 blocks
and calculates the median time. This becomes the consensus time in the network and is
eventually used for the timelocked transactions. The median-time-past will approximately
be 1 h behind the 'wall-clock time'.

3.7   Bitcoin Serialization

Serialization is used to communicate all the information over the Bitcoin network. Several
formats have been used in the past to make use of serialization. Today there is a specific
Bitcoin standard (based on SegWit or non-SegWit). In the past it made use of the uncompressed SEC format, also known as 'Standards for Efficient cryptography' to do so. The
uncompressed SEC format for a point $P = (x, y)$ is generated by following these steps:

- Prefix: 0x04
- Append x-coordinate 32-byts as a big-endian integer
- Append y-coordinate 32-byts as a big-endian[18] integer.

For the compressed SEC format, we use the following procedure for a point $P = (x,y)$:

- Prefix: 0x02 or 0x03 (if y is even the former, otherwise the latter)
- Append x-coordinate 32-byts as a big-endian integer.

From the procedure we can clearly see that the compressed format is 33 bytes opposed to
the 65 bytes of the uncompressed format. For the serialization of signatures we needed to
use a different format. We cannot simply compress the signature because of what we have
seen before (the discrete log problem) we cannot derive s from r. Therefore, we make use
of DER or 'Distinguished Encoding Rules'. We can find this standard in the OpenSSL
library. It has the following format:

- 0x30 (start)
- Encoding of the length of the signature
- 0x02 (marker byte)
- Encode r (big-endian) and prepend the resulting length of r

---

[17] Fee sniping is not lucrative now as the block reward is high enough but in some point in the future
the transaction fees will be high enough to attempt and steal them. This is why nLoctime is set to
'current block + 1' and nSequence to '0xFFFFFFFE' so that locktime is set to the next block and
fee sniping becomes impossible.

[18] Big-endian means that the most important byte is written first, little-endian means the least important byte is written first.

- 0x02 (marker byte)
- Encode s (big-endian) and prepend the resulting length of s.

The current format that is used since SegWit and BIP 141, while before the segregated witness update, Bitcoin was making use of 'raw format'. The raw transaction format, which was in use since October 2014, had the following format:

Raw format

Name	Data type	Description	Bytes
Version	Uint32_t	Transaction version nr	4
Tx_in count	compactSize uint	Nr of inputs in transaction	Varies
Tx_in	TxIn	Transaction inputs	Varies
Tx_out count	compactSize uint	Nr of outputs in transaction	Varies
Tx_out	txOut	Transaction outputs	Varies
Lock_time	Uint32_t	A time or block number	4

We can see in this table a data type called 'compactSize Unsigned Integers'. This data type is used in the raw transaction format to indicate the number of bytes that can be expected in the following data set that is going to pass. When you read up in documentation on the Bitcoin network, you will also find this as 'var_int' or 'varInt' as it is a variable length integer. The table below indicates how the encoding scheme works, with numbers 0–252 looking like regular unsigned integers.

Value	Bytes used	Format
>= 0 && <= 252	1	Uint8_t
>= 253 && <= 0xffff	3	0xfd + number as uint16_t
>= 0x10000 && <= 0xffffffff	5	0xfe + number as uint32_t
>= 0x100000000 && 0xffffffffffffffff	9	0xff + number as uint64_t

Finally there is the 'wallet import format' or WIF which is used for our private keys. It has the following procedure:

- Prefix 0x80 (mainnet)
- Secret encoded (32-byte big-endian)
- If public key is compressed SEC, add 0x01 as a suffix
- Take a copy of the previous 3 combined, SHA256 and take the first 4 bytes
- Combine all and translate to BASE58.

3.8   Bitcoin Script

The Bitcoin network makes use of script to lock and unlock coins. This scripting language is a programming language that processes one command, containing either elements or operations, at a time. As you might have guessed, the elements are data while the operations are functions that are performed on the stack. i.e. OP_HASH160 will perform a SHA256 followed by a ripemd160. These commands are known as 'opcodes' and make up the programming language of the Bitcoin network. It is a living language as opcodes can be added or removed over time. Most of the time opcodes are removed or limited to make sure that the danger to the network is reduced as much as possible. It is a transaction network with a native coin and it was never the intention of the network to be anything else. So with Bitcoin script we have a push and pop style programming language that makes use of a stack and makes use of a last-in first-out data structure. Typically, 'push' can be used to add an element to the top of the stack, while 'pop' removes the top element. During the parsing of the script it is determined whether it is an operation or an element based on the byte (when the value lies between 0x01 and 0x4b, we know the next n bytes are an element). Whenever we would like to perform an evaluation, we combine the ScriptPubKey and ScriptSig fields, which represent the locking and unlocking mechanisms. When we were talking about blockchain addresses in the first section, we already talked about a couple of standard scripts. A couple of these are p2pk (pay to public key), p2pkh (pay to public key hash), p2sh (pay to script hash), p2wpkh (pay to witness pubkey hash) and p2wsh (pay to witness script hash). You are of course not limited to these specific standard scripts and can build your own locking and unlocking scripts. For those of you that aren't following the story so far, you should imagine the world of scripting as a stack of information on top of each other. It is up to the scripts you use to make changes to this stack. An example is the OP_CHECKSIG instruction. This instruction will combine the signature with a full public key and will push TRUE on top of the stack in case the signature and the public key are generated from the same private key, else there will be a FALSE. OP_CHECKMULTISIG does something similar but with multiple signatures and public keys. Several sets of opcodes can be defined: the constants, opcodes used for flow control, opcodes to perform specific stack operations, there is still 1 splice opcode called OP_SIZE, 2 bitwise logic operators (OP_EQUAL and OP_EQUALVERIFY), some arithmetic commands, hashing and signing opcodes, locktime opcodes, reserved and pseudo words. For a more conclusive overview of these instructions and Bitcoin script I would advise you to check out the Bitcoin developer reference and the Bitcoin Wiki pages. As mentioned before you should be aware that changes happen to these OP_CODES and that those that were once in use can perfectly be disabled (in an attempt to increase the security of the Bitcoin network). When you see these instructions, and the way of working (stack), you can understand why this is not immediately that developer friendly. It tells you clearly that the original intent of Bitcoin wasn't the creation of smart contracts (which doesn't mean that this isn't possible).

3.8.1 Ivy for Bitcoin

Ivy[19] is a high-level programming language that was developed by Chain and allows to write smart contracts for the Bitcoin protocol.[20] At the moment it is still a prototype software but it can already be used to test software and look at how you could possibly develop new applications in the future with this (new) programming language. There is a playground available where you can test out contracts you have written. It offers you all the flexibility of the Bitcoin script as you would expect but you have some extras which make it interesting to look into this language: name variables, name clauses, static types and familiar syntax for both functions and operators. It has some similarities to the Solidity or Vyper languages used for Ethereum smart contract development and other platforms (later discussed in more detail). You always have to specify a contract template and pass some arguments to be able to actually make use of the contract. These arguments have several types such as PublicKey, Value and Signature. The contract also needs some contract clauses, the arguments needed to unlock a contract.

The types that are defined in Ivy for Bitcoin script are:

- **Bytes**: a string of bytes
- **PublicKey**: an ECDSA public key
- **Signature**: an ECDSA signature
- **Time**: block height or timestamp
- **Duration**: number of blocks or x times 512 s
- **Boolean**: True/False
- **Number**: an integer
- **Value**: amount of bitcoins
- **HashableType**: any type you can pass to hash functions (Bytes, PublicKey, or result hash functions)
- **Sha256(T: HashableType)**: SHA256 of HashableType T
- **Sha1(T: HashableType)**: SHA1 of HashableType T
- **Ripemd160(T: HashableType)**: RIPEMD160 of HashableType T.

The following functions have been defined in Ivy for Bitcoin script:

- **checkSig(publicKey: PublicKey, sig: Signature)**: Boolean result from the check if the public key is the one that corresponds to the private key used to make the signature
- **checkMultiSig(publicKeys: [], Sigs: [])**: Boolean result from the check that each of the public keys correspond to the private keys used to create the signatures

---

[19] Robinson, D. (2018) ivy-Bitcoin. https://docs.ivy-lang.org/bitcoin/language/IvySyntax.html. Accessed on December 6, 2019.

[20] Chain has been acquired by Lightyear, which is a Stellar-focused company, and together they form now 'Interstellar'.

- **After(time: Time)**: Boolean that checks if the current block height/time is after time. Uses nLockTime and CHECKLOCKTIMEVERIFY
- **Older(duration: Duration)**: Boolean that checks if the contract being spent has been on the blockchain for at least duration. This uses CHECKSEQUENCEVERIFY
- **Sha256(preimage: (T: HashableType))**: SHA256 of preimage
- **Sha1(preimage: (T: HashableType))**: SHA1 of preimage
- **Ripemd160(preimage: (T: HashableType))**: RIPEMD160 of preimage
- **Bytes(item: T)**: turns item into bytestring, cannot be performed on Value or Boolean. Only affects type checking
- **Size(bytestring: bytes)**: returns 'number' type, the length of the bytestring
- **== or !=**: equality or inequality check.

As you can see this feels a lot more familiar for most of you than the actual Bitcoin scripting language. For those of you that are interested, I would certainly advise to visit the website and use the documentation to gain deeper insight. It will help you to get a better understanding of the Bitcoin scripting language, and for those of you that are willing, it might be the start point to actually programming in Bitcoin script (mastering Bitcoin by Andreas Antonopoulos might give deeper insight in the scripting language itself). Below you can find an example in both Bitcoin script and in the Ivy programming language to give you an idea on how the higher-level Ivy programming language actually compiles to opcodes. We are going to take the LockWithPublicKeyHash example as it can tell us how the contract language translates to the Bitcoin scripting language.

```
contract LockWithPublicKeyHash(pubKeyHash: Sha256(PublicKey),
  clause spend(pubKey: PublicKey, sig: Signature) {
    verify sha256(pubKey) == pubKeyHash
    verify checkSig(pubKey, sig)
    unlock val
  }
}
```

LockWithPublicKeyHash

You can see here clearly that you use the hash of the public key to lock the contract, while you need to provide the public key to unlock it. This contract would eventually compile to the following output:

- OP_DUP OP_HASH256 <pubKeyHash> OP_EQUALVERIFY OP_CHECKSIG

The actual script would look like this:

- ScriptSig: <sig> <pubKey>
- ScriptPubKey: OP_DUP OP_HASH256 <pubkeyHash> OP_EQUALVERIFY OP_CHECKSIG

Finally, there is also a JavaScript library that is in its early stages but can be used for testing.

3.9   Bitcoin Miniscript

The latest innovation in Bitcoin scripting is called 'Miniscript' which is a language that should allow developers to write scripts in a more structured way. It also allows statistical analysis for various actions such as spending conditions, correctness, security properties and malleability.[21] It has currently been developed for P2WSH and PS2H-P2WQH scripts (and also adheres to its resource limitations as defined in the Bitcoin scripting language by either standard or consensus[22]).[23] Currently there are Bitcoin core compatible C++ and a Rust implementation. On the dedicated website you can test and analyze Miniscripts and you can see if you have actually achieved what you wanted to. You can also find a thorough reference that you can use in the further development of your scripts. If you look through the list you can clearly see how Miniscript could make the life of many a developer easier. An example is the following Bitcoin script: "SIZE <32> EQUALVER-IFY RIPEMD160 <h> EQUAL" gets reduced to "ripemd160(h)". However, not every Miniscript expression can just be compiled with another. Just as any other Bitcoin script (or even any other programming language) the expressions linked together need to make logical sense. In Miniscript there has been a 'correctness type system' introduced to help developers from making mistakes. There are four types:

- Base expressions (B): these expressions take their input from the top of the stack. This type is used for most of the expressions and is required for the top level expression. If the expression evaluates to true, it pushes a non-zero value to the stop of the stack, otherwise it will be zero.

---

[21] Wuille, P., Poelstra, A. and Kanjalkar.S. (2019) Analyze a Miniscript. *Blockstream.* http://bitcoin.sipa.be/Miniscript/. Accessed December 7, 2019.

[22] The standardness and consensus rules are built-in the Miniscript language so that you can make sure that your scripts adhere to the Bitcoin scripting rules.

[23] The design and implementation has been done by Pieter Wuille, Andrew Poelstra & Sanket Kanjalkar at Blockstream Research.

- Verify expressions (V): these expressions take their input from the top of the stack. If the expression evaluates to true, nothing happens and the script continues. Otherwise, there will be an abort of the script.
- Key expressions (K): taking their input from the top of the stack, they always push a public key onto the stack which requires a signature to satisfy the expression.
- Wrapped expressions (W): these expressions take their input from one below the top of the stack and when it evaluates to true, push a non-zero value to the top of the stack. Otherwise, a zero value is pushed to the top of the stack.

Conversions between these expression types are also possible. You can convert a B expression in a V expression, a K into a B and so on. The Miniscript language also comes with 5 types of modifiers:

- The 'z' or 'zero-arg' that consumes exactly 0 stack elements
- The 'o' or 'one-arg' that consumes exactly 1 stack element
- The 'n' or 'nonzero' that consumes at least 1 stack element
- The 'd' or 'dissatisfiable' which allows an unconditional dissatisfaction to be constructed
- The 'u' or 'unit' that, when satisfied, will add a '1' on the stack.

If we keep the example we looked at previously (ripemd160(h)), we know that this is a base expression (B) and that the properties are 'o', 'n', 'd' and 'u'. The developers of the Miniscript language have also built-in satisfactions and dissatisfactions for each of their scripts. For ripemd160(h), the satisfaction is a preimage while the dissatisfaction is any 32-byte vector except for the preimage. So the correctness of an expression is based on these predefined rules within Miniscript. However, there is 1 important point that we need to take into consideration: malleability. The Miniscript language has been created with the Segwit update in mind. This means (as you hopefully remember) that changing certain parts of the transaction no longer breaks the validity of unconfirmed descendant transactions. Still, there might be certain undesirable effects.[24] Miniscript was designed as such that non-malleable signing is permitted, increasing the security of the transactions that can be created. The non-malleable satisfactions within the language are created by making use of a function that returns the optimal satisfaction/dissatisfaction for a certain expression or a special DONTUSE value and an optional HASSIG marker that shows if the solution contains at least one signature. The function should recursively be used over all the subexpressions in the function you are creating. You should know that certain expressions (such as the ripemd160(h)) are always malleable so that you have to use the DONTUSE value. With each check one should make sure that every possible

---

[24] An example given in the Miniscript documentation is that the witness can be stuffed with additional data, forcing the feerate down and eventually impacting the transactions possibility of being processed and confirmed.

outcome has the HASSIG marker, otherwise the (sub)-expression is malleable in one way or another. There are of course the 'd'-expressions that are unconditionally dissatisfiable, meaning that there must be a non-HASSIG dissatisfaction. Here the rule is that non-HASSIG solutions must be preferred over HASSIG solutions and when there are multiple non-HASSIG solutions, none can be used.

Depending on the expressions you are using, there will be different requirements for one to make sure that their Miniscript is nonmalleable. You should always strife to make a script nonmalleable as this greatly increases security and trust for all the involved participants.

3.10 Bitcoin Addresses

We already offered a short discussion on blockchain addresses. Still, it is of interest to make not of them here and the formats on how we can find them and how they are derived. As we know, we have to make use of a public key and a private key. There are several private key formats that we should take into account.

Type	Description/size	Prefix
Raw	32 bytes	None
Hex	64 hexadecimal digits	None
WIF	Base58check encoding	5
WIF-compressed	Base58check encoding with 0x01 suffix before encoding	K or L

Public keys on the other hand either exist in compressed or uncompressed formats. Depending on the format, the prefix is either 04 (uncompressed) or 02/03 (compressed). As explained before, the compressed version is the standard but some of the older clients that are still part of the network do not yet support these. To resolve the possible problems leading from this difference, when private keys are exported from a Bitcoin wallet to another wallet, the WIF is implemented differently to indicate that these keys have been used to produce compressed public keys, leading to compressed Bitcoin addresses.[25] Commonly the P2PKH (pay to public key hash) and P2SH (pay to script hash) are used. As you can clearly see in the name, these 2 procedures make use of hashing. This increases the inherent security issues that you might find with classic approaches, such as the very first Bitcoin network where you had to pay to the IP-address of a peer. For the P2PKH, you might have guessed, that you have to hash your public key. This hash consists out of SHA256, followed by RIPEMD160. For the P2SH you have to use a similar hashing format but instead of your public key, you hash a so-called 'redeem script'. The

[25] Antonopoulos, A. (2017) *Mastering Bitcoin: programming the open blockchain.* 2nd ed. California: O'Reilly Media.

next step in the creation of your Bitcoin address, consists out of adding a version byte. For the Bitcoin mainnet this is 0x00 for the P2PKH and 0x06 for P2SH.[26] The third step in the process is creating a copy of this hash combined with the version byte and hash this again twice with SHA256. From this result you take the first 4 bytes as a checksum to make sure that your original hash + checksum is transmitted correctly. You append this checksum to the version + hash combination. The final step is encoding the result in a BASE58check string. This is the BASE58 encoding format but with a built-in code that checks for possible errors. In practice, this leads to a checksum with 4 additional bytes being encoded. This checksum is later used by the software to determine the validity of the encoded data. In SegWit the BASE58 is being replaced with Bech32 because it is more user friendly (only lower case letters and numbers). So what are P2SH functions used for currently? Most commonly, it can be used for something such as multi-signature address scripts. These scripts allow the creation of addresses that i.e. have a maximum of 3 participants that can sign, of which 2 need to sign to approve a transaction. We can also introduce the concept of 'vanity' addresses which contain a specific human-readable message. This means that the address contains certain words or numbers that you can choose. This can refer to your company or you as a person. These addresses are just as secure as any other address but the search time to find an address that contains all the letters and numbers you wish for, can take up quite an amount of time. A pattern of up to 6 characters will take about an hour or less, while 8 characters will already take up to 4 months and 9 characters 800 years (considering you use your personal computer at home and not some advanced supercomputer).

3.10.1 Encrypted Private Keys (BIP-38)

There have been several Bitcoin Improvement Proposals to increase the security of the wallets in use. This to provide protection to the users but as it often is, there is also a dark side to some of these implementations. BIP-38 introduces the encryption for private keys. AES is used in this standard to encrypt them so that the information itself can be kept safe. These encrypted keys will always start with '6p'. Current wallets often are able to recognize these encrypted keys and will ask you for your passphrase. This increases the security of the private keys themselves but can lead to other issues. If you lose your passphrase, you no longer have access to your private keys and these cannot be recovered.

---

[26] In the Bitcoin testnet this will be 0x6F and 0xc4 respectively.

3.11 Bitcoin Wallet

We can complete the explanation of the Bitcoin network itself with the wallets that are being used within the network. The usefulness of mining, signing and verifying transactions would be rendered completely useless if there would not be something as a wallet. It is in this wallet that you store your bitcoins (currency is written 'bitcoin', the network as 'Bitcoin'). It is basically a combination of your Bitcoin address and your private key that makes up your wallet. There are nondeterministic wallets which indicates that each key is independently generated by making use of a random generator. We also know these wallets as JBOK wallets or 'just a bunch of keys' wallets. Problem is that each address has to be backed up and used for multiple transactions, reducing privacy and security of the user. The type-0 nondeterministic wallet was introduced by the Bitcoin core implementation but shouldn't be used anymore. Compared to other implementations they take too much work backing up and use, certainly if you take privacy into account. In short we can identify 2 types of wallets that we actually can use, where the first one is the type 1 deterministic wallet, called the single chain wallet. This wallet can only send and receive a specific cryptocurrency, in this case bitcoins. It is the simpler version as it helps to create a single series of keys from a single seed. This immediately implies that if the seed is leaked or stolen, all funds are in jeopardy. The second type of wallet is the Hierarchical Deterministic wallet or HD wallet (based on BIP-32/BIP-44). This is a solution where the wallet software can generate a pattern of public and private keys which do not require a backup and cannot easily be guessed. It is generated from a root seed that consists out of a random number that is either 128, 256 or 512 bits. This seed is inserted in a HMAC-SHA512 algorithm to generate a master private key and a master chain code. From the master private key, the master public key is generated and the chain code is used as entropy for all the child keys that are generated afterwards with the 'child key derivation function' or 'CKD'. The master key and the chain code are concatenated and form the 512-bit '(private or public) extended key'.[27] The CKD makes use of the HMAC-SHA512 hashing algorithm, an index number, the chain code and the parent key are combined to generate a hash. This hash is split in 2 where the right half is used as the chain code for the child while the left half is added to the parent key to generate the child key. The index allows us to create up to 2^{31} children, where the children can become parents again and perform the same process. In practice the CKD is a bit changed to increase security (if the chain code and a child private key are leaked, one could guess the master private key and breach all keys in use). There is a hardened key derivation process which makes use of the parent private key to derive the child chain code instead of the parent public key, breaking the relationship and making it impossible for attackers to derive the master/sibling keys.

---

[27] They are encoded in BASE58Check format and use the prefix 'xprv' or 'xpub'.

It is clear that within HD wallets an infinite number of keys can be generated in a tree-like structure which can be restored by making use of a seed word. This is the set of 12 words you get when you generate such a wallet. When you log in again, the wallet asks typically for a couple of the seed words and this way is capable of regenerating the keys and with it your funds. So it remains crucial that you store the seed key. BIP-44 allows for wallets that introduce both multiple accounts but also multiple currencies! An example of the HD paths and coins you can find below:

HD path	Decription
m/44'/0'	Bitcoin
m/44'/1'	Bitcoin testnet
m/44/2'	Litecoin

These HD wallets are improved by making use of BIP-39 that allows for a standardized way of creating seeds from a specific sequence of English words. This not only enhances the inner working of the wallet but also has a positive impact on the user experience. The number of words that are used, usually are a sequence of 12–14 words. How does the wallet actually create this link? Well, it comes down to this: a random sequence of 128–256 bits are generated, after which a checksum is generated by taking the first (entropy-length/32) bits of its SHA256 hash. The checksum is added to the end of the sequence, and next the entire result is split in 11-bit segments. These segments are mapped to a dictionary of 2048 words. These words from the mnemonic words that you will have to store. These words are hence used to generate a seed by making use of both the words, a salt and the PBKDF2 function. This seed can either be a constant string within the software or a passphrase. This passphrase can provide extra security by making the original mnemonic words useless without the passphrase, and the creation of a duress wallet which can distract attackers from the actual wallet. Another BIP that helps improve the user experience and usability of wallets are the BIP-43 that allows for multipurpose wallets. If you are looking for a specific wallet client, please check out https://bitcoin. org/en/choose-your-wallet where you can find an overview with some amazing wallets to use and create. For each operating system (mobile or desktop), you will find sufficient possibilities.

3.12 Simplified Payment Verification

Simplified payment verification or SPV for short is a technology which allows you to validate transactions without taking into account the transactions of other participants. It makes sure that your transactions are included within a block that can be added to the chain and it provides confirmations of blocks being added to the chain. Why can this be interesting? Do you have an idea what the current size is of the Bitcoin blockchain? As of April 2019 it is a whopping 210 GB! So if you wish to store the entire blockchain database, you need quite some storage space! If you are not interested in supporting the network but only in its feature as a cryptocurrency, this is quite a dilemma. It is not as if you are going to carry around an external hard drive just so that you can keep on making payments. It is here that the Merkle root, one of those pesky elements we explained in the very beginning, comes in handy. It can be used as a proof of inclusion so that the client can verify that a transaction was included in a block without having to know every transaction that at one point has taken place. A clever reader should be able to identify an issue. If you work with a client that has SPV as a way of working, it means it is dependent on a full node to receive information concerning the block so that the light client can verify the transaction with the Merkle root. So if I have a full node and you have the light client, I can try to deceive you. How? You have no assurance that the block I am presenting is actually in the blockchain itself. This way you have no way of knowing for sure that I am speaking the truth. The only way around this, is by connecting with many other full nodes, as they can display the truth. Still, it is advisable to work with full nodes if you are making large payments. If the payment is high enough, nodes might always have the incentive to try and deceive you. A final aspect that I would like to address here before we go on is a change brought by BIP37: the use of bloom filters. I briefly explained what a bloom filter is at the beginning of the section but here we can see its use. Bloom filters are used for network communication within the Bitcoin network. The network makes use of the murmur3 hash function, which is very fast but not cryptographically secure.[28] It is used in light clients so that these can solely focus on transactions of interest for the wallet. It makes use of filterload (set the Bloom filter), filteradd (add data element to the filter) and filterclear (remove the filter) messages.

3.12.1 SPV Wallet Client

There are several SPV wallet client implementations but wallets making use of centralized API servers are far more popular. Currently you can easily make use of BRD wallet, Electrum, Bitpay and several other implementations. There is the native Bitcoin SPV client and the modified SPV wallet client for Bitcoin. There are several Bitcoin native SPV wallets available and in development on Github[29]. To this day it is not advised to use these in a production environment as they are still under development. On the other hand there are the modified SPV wallet clients which make use of other developments, such as OpenBazaar, the lightening network and BTCD.

---

[28] For those among you that have more in-depth knowledge of Bloom filters: it is indeed more efficient to use several hashing algorithms to reduce the space needed by the bit field. Bitcoin just uses the same hashing algorithm but changes the seed, leading to the same efficiency.

[29] For example on https://github.com/keeshux/bitcoinspv.

3.13   Segregated Witness

We have already mentioned it several times in this section so far: witnesses, SegWit and segregated witness but what is it? We mentioned it already a couple of times before that this was a soft fork in the Bitcoin network. An interesting option that was added by the SegWit soft fork is the block size increase. As we have seen before, the maximum size of a block is 1 MB and currently this size, combined with the block time is simply not enough to handle the enormous amount of transactions that is being processed every day.[30] The solution that is being put forward, is that the signature data is moved to an extended block so that space can be freed up in the original block. This is certainly interesting if you know that signature data comprises about 65% of a regular, standard block. By making use of this technique, the block size increases to 4 MB. Next, uncompressed SEC pubkeys are no longer allowed, which will also help to save space.

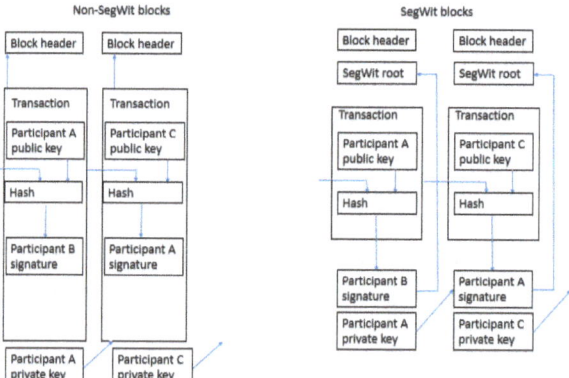

Non-SegWit versus SegWit

Another one of the things it introduced was the pay to witness public key hash or p2wpkh.[31] The only difference with p2pkh is that the location of the data for the Script-Sig is now in the witness field to prevent transaction malleability—here the unique id of a transaction is changed and this is possible because the digital signature in the Script-Sig can be modified and when one modifies this information, the unique ID changes as well.[32] With SegWit and the new location of the data, this is omitted when creating the unique ID and therefore the ID no longer changes when an attacker starts modifying the data. The witness can consist out of the digital signature but it can basically contain any

---

[30] Asolo, B. (November 1, 2018) What is Segregated Witness? *Myencryptopedia.* https://www.myc ryptopedia.com/what-is-segregated-witness/. Accessed December 24, 2019.

[31] BIP0141 and BIP0143.

[32] As long as the transaction isn't mined in a block yet—after this the ID is immutable.

condition that is necessary to unlock the UTXOs and make them available for spending. The introduction of the segregated witness scripts brings also the 'script version' number which tells what type of script we are dealing with (similar to transactions and blocks). The problem with p2wpkh is that it is not backward compatible with older wallet technologies as they cannot send payments to p2wpkh ScriptPubKeys because of the change from BASE58 to Bech32. To address this problem, p2sh-p2wpkh saw the light of day where the new p2wpkh is wrapped inside the p2sh. So it looks like a normal p2sh address but inside you can find the ScriptPubKey of p2wpkh. Even though p2wpkh was able to get rid of the issue of transaction malleability, we needed also a different way of working if multisignature technology was still to be included. For this pay to witness script hash or p2wsh was created, which is the same as p2sh, only with the ScriptSig data in the witness field. Similarly to the example of p2wpkh there were problems when it came to older wallets, so p2sh-p2wsh was invented to circumvent this problem. A final problem addressed by SegWit is the quadratic hashing problem. For the verification of each signature, the amount of data hashing is proportional to the size of the transaction.[33] You can easily see that growing data, will result in longer time necessary to verify the transaction. A second problem that comes out of the 'current' signature process is that the algorithm makes no use of the bitcoin spent by the input. If you have a 'cold' wallet, this becomes a problem because it is impossible to calculate the exact amount spent and the transaction fee applicable. This can only be solved by acquiring the entire transaction, which again might form a problem in itself. If the input value of the transaction would be part of the signature, the cold wallet would no longer have a problem. Why? If the value that is provided is wrong and the transaction is signed, the signature becomes invalid and the transaction will simply not happen. Therefore a new algorithm is used by SegWit to stop both of these problems. A new way of serialization is used with a new transaction digest algorithm (please check out BIP-143 for all the details).

3.14 Bitcoin Improvement Proposals[34]

Bitcoin Improvement Proposals or BIPs are design documents which provide information to the supporting community. When refer to the BIP purpose and guidelines (or BIP0001) we can identify 3 types of BIP:

1. A Standards Track BIP describes a change that will affect most or all Bitcoin implementations. This can be a change in protocol, block criteria, transaction validity rules or any other change that might affect applications using Bitcoin.

---

[33] Stepanov, H. (July 1!, 2019) bip-0143 *Github—Bitcoin.* https://github.com/bitcoin/bips/blob/master/bip-0143.mediawiki. Accessed on December 28, 2019.

[34] BIPS can be found on https://github.com/bitcoin/bips.

2. The Information BIP provides guidance, describes a design issue or offers information to the community. These BIPs are completely voluntarily and members of the community are free to follow the advice of a BIP or completely ignore it.
3. Finally, there is also the process BIP which describes a process surrounding Bitcoin. They are very similar to standards track BIPs but differ in that sense that where the Standards track focuses on the Bitcoin protocol itself, the process BIP focusses on the processes surrounding Bitcoin.

If you are prompted to learn more about the BIPs already in place or how you can make your own suggestions, do not hesitate to visit the Github page!

3.15   Schnorr Signatures

A draft BIP which might improve the Bitcoin network even more in the future is one that focuses on the use of Schnorr signatures.[35] It was invented by Claus-Peter Schnorr while he was working at the University of Frankfurt in the 80s. We have learned that signatures make up a significant part of the data that is being transmitted over the network. SegWit gave already a first push to a more scalable way of working. Schnorr signatures could be the second step in this process as it is security proof and non-malleable. Furthermore one could move away from DER-encoding for signatures and even start with batch verification. Currently, as we have seen before, a transaction is constructed out of a batch of inputs coming from earlier transaction outputs. With Schnorr this would no longer be necessary and 1 signature could be used for all inputs. This could lead to an increase of the capacity of the entire Bitcoin network of almost 25%! Another advantage that is given by making use of this technique is the use of an interactive scheme (i.e. MuSig) where participants can produce 1 signature where they jointly signed for. These are all clear benefits over the current ECDSA signature. Currently, P2SH is being used which is a script smart contract and is therefore not really efficient. Key aggregation with Schnorr signatures would lead to less footprint, lower transaction costs, improved bandwidth and more privacy for the participants. Key aggregation let multisigs become indistinguishable from other regular transactions. If and when the implementation would actually take place, the OP_CHECKSIG and OP_CHECKMULTISIG opcodes would be retired in favor of a new class of opcodes called OP_CHECKDLS. This will lead to the disappearance of Multisigs in favor of musigs. At least for those participants that follow the soft fork with the Schnorr signature implementation. The current work on the implementation of the musig-scheme

---

[35] Asolo, B. (February 16, 2019) Bitcoin Schnorr Signatures Explained. *Mycryptopedia.* https://www.mycryptopedia.com/bitcoin-schnorr-signatures-explained/. Accessed on November 17, 2019.

by Blockstream can be followed on their Github page.[36] A first semi-formal proposal for the activation of Schnorr signatures has been made by the end of 2018 on the Bitcoin mailing list.[37] However, it will probably take some more months and perhaps even years of testing before the next soft fork also actually goes live.

3.16   Taproot, G'root and Graftroot

Taproot follows in the idea of Schnorr signatures to increase the privacy of Bitcoin transactions but on top of that it would allow for smart contract flexibility. Scripts would no longer be distinguishable from other transactions on the blockchain. As we mentioned already several times, the P2SH is currently used, which allows to lock bitcoins and only unlock them based on certain conditions. These conditions can be tailored to the needs of the participants and can create complex schemes. The P2SH allows these conditions to be hidden from the public, or at least at first (the script is included as a hash). When the owner spends the coins, the script and solution are revealed. The initial hash can be used to check if this is the script and can check what the requirements for unlocking were.[38] This is both heavy on data and is not really private. Several solutions have been presented for this in the past. MAST or 'Merkelized Abstract Syntax Tree' was one of these proposals. All conditions are hashed in a Merkle tree and the root is used to lock up the coins. If any of the data is revealed, it can be verified by making use of the Merkle root and path, without revealing the other data. Specifics of the MAST proposal made by Gregory Maxwell can be found online (BIP-114 and BIP-117).[39] This still reveals data and the combination of Schnorr signatures and Taproot will provide even better security. Taproot looks like MAST but always includes a condition where all participants can cooperate to simply send the funds, called the 'cooperative close'. It actually makes use of the special case of a top-level threshold signature or arbitrary conditions, which becomes indistinguishable from a one-party signature, by making use of a special delegating CHECKSIG. If you combine this with Schnorr signatures, you could make the transaction look like any other one. All public keys involved in the transaction could be aggregated together

---

[36] Davies, J. (January, 2019) secp256k1. *Github—ElementsProject.* https://github.com/ElementsProj ect/secp256k1-zkp/tree/secp256k1-zkp/src/modules/musig?source=post_page. Accessed January 4, 2020.

[37] Towns, A. (December 14, 2018) Schnorr and taproot (etc) upgrade. *Linux Foundation* https:// lists.linuxfoundation.org/pipermail/bitcoin-dev/2018-December/016556.html?source=post_page. Accessed January 8, 2020.

[38] Van Wirdum, A. (January 24, 2019) Taproot is Coming: What it is, and ho wit will benefit Bitcoin. *Bitcoin Magazine.* https://bitcoinmagazine.com/articles/taproot-coming-what-it-and-how-it-will-benefit-bitcoin. Accessed October 2, 2019.

[39] Maxwell, G. (January 23, 2018) Taproot: Privacy preserving switchable scripting. *Linux Foundation.* https://lists.linuxfoundation.org/pipermail/bitcoin-dev/2018-January/015614.html. Accessed October 4, 2019.

in a 'threshold public key' and all participants their signatures in a 'threshold signature'. Another addition would be that all other possible ways of spending the bitcoins (so all other non-cooperative outcomes except for the cooperative close) would be combined in a different script. This script is hashed and used to adapt the threshold public key which would also have an influence on the signature. So only if the cooperative close wouldn't be possible, the threshold public key will be revealed for what it really is. There is also an implementation which is called generalized Taproot or G'root.[40] This is recursive taproot by making use of Pedersen commitments. This is a useful implementation when one makes use of additional conditions. If you do this, you could either start spending after the transaction is signed directly, if some extra conditions are satisfied or when the 2 points are revealed (in a Pedersen commitment, explained earlier) which actually satisfy that condition. This improves the privacy, as you can keep initially the lower layers of scripts hidden if you don't need them and you don't reveal the conditions corresponding with other keys, only the ones corresponding to the key you are actually spending with.[41] There is also the idea of Graftroot. This implementation wants to focus on a limitation within the idea of taproot. Namely, that it only provides 1 real alternative. Even if you could create a tree of taproots, they would offer less privacy than a single level.[42] Graftroot tries to solve this by, once again, letting participants establish a threshold key, with optionally a taproot alternative. They can then delegate their ability to sign to a script by signing that script, and only that script, with their taproot key and sharing delegation with whomever they want and choose. When the time comes to spend the coin and all signers aren't available, they can use the script and the redeeming party can satisfy the requirements of the script, combining this with the signer's signature of the script. Using this scheme, an unlimited number of alternatives can be provides which are all executed with equal efficiency to a single alternative and their number is hidden without overhead. The current idea is that Schnorr signatures, taproot and mast should be implemented first, after which graftroot, cross-input aggregation and G'root could be implemented. This would increase both privacy and efficiency while still keeping the transactions open enough for easy auditing. Bitcoin cash has already a first implementation of the Schnorr signatures and is working hard on further improvements, with Bitcoin on its heels. There have been some BIP proposals to make this possible, with a new SegWit version 1 output type to allow spending rules based on Taproot, Schnorr signatures or MAST but also batch validation and signature hash improvements.[43] Therefore the new opcode OP_CHECKSIGADD has been

---

[40] Original proposal was the name 'MAST-ended sc'roots' but as a joke towards the Mimblewimble folks with their Harry Potter references, Anthony Towns went for G'root as a stab at Marvel.

[41] Towns, A. (July 13, 2018) Generalised taproot. *Linux Foundation.* https://lists.linuxfoundation. org/pipermail/bitcoin-dev/2018-July/016249.html. Accessed on October 10, 2019.

[42] Maxwell, G. (February 5, 2018) Graftroo: Private and efficient surrogate scripts under the taproot assumption. *Linux Foundation.* https://lists.linuxfoundation.org/pipermail/bitcoin-dev/2018-February/015700.html. Accessed on October 24, 2019.

[43] Wuille, P. (January 16, 2020) Bip taproot. *Github—Bitcoin bips.* https://github.com/sipa/bips/blob/bip-schnorr/bip-taproot.mediawiki. Accessed on January 20, 2020.

proposed to allow for multisignature policies in a batch-verifiable way. This will probably be combined with some new OP_SUCCESS opcodes to allow the script to run more efficiently. You might be wondering why Bitcoin goes through such lengths to improve its privacy while there are already some other implementations possible and performed by other cryptocurrencies such as zcash (with zk-SNARKs) or Dash and Monero (ring signatures). Well, the main goal of these other cryptocurrencies is to provide privacy, while Bitcoin wants to remain an open network that wants to find a balance between privacy for its users and general adoption by the public. They want to focus on making the network more scalable and allow for transactions still to be audited, which is a requirement for several commerce applications and industries. This is why the developers have searched for and are developing these implementations so that there is a layer of privacy for the external world, while there is still the possibility for general adoption and acceptation by legislation.

Since the publication of the first edition of this book, a lot has changed. Bitcoin's major Taproot soft fork was activated in November 2021.[44] Through the aggregation of different proposals (BIPs 340, 341, 342) which also included Schnorr signatures and MAST (Merkelized Abstract Syntax Trees). As explained earlier, this upgrade comes with improved transaction privacy as well as efficiency by allowing complex items such as multi-signatures and timelocks to appear as simple payments on-chain. With this upgrade, also advanced smart contract capabilities became available and added future upgrade flexibility. At the time of writing, the output of Taproot is growing (also aided through new use cases like Ordinals) but is not yet something we can call 'universal'. The Tapscript linked to Taproot also enables more complex spending logic.[45] To have an idea on how Taproot works (through a Python sample), below you can find a short script where:

- One generates a private key
- Derive the corresponding public key (Schnorr)
- Construct the witness program
- Encode it using Bech32m.

Here is the script:

```
import hashlib
from ecdsa import SigningKey, SECP256k1
from ecdsa.util import sigencode_string
from hashlib import sha256
```

---

[44] https://www.coinbase.com/learn/crypto-glossary/what-is-the-bitcoin-taproot-upgrade-and-why-is-it-important#:~:text=The%20Taproot%20upgrade%20is%20an,is%20backward%20compatible%20with%20older.

[45] https://www.coinbase.com/learn/crypto-glossary/what-is-the-bitcoin-taproot-upgrade-and-why-is-it-important#:~:text=How%20Taproot%20Benefits%20Bitcoin.

```
# Bech32m reference implementation from BIP350
import bech32 # You can find this on the BIP350 GitHub or use a compatible library


# Generate private key
sk = SigningKey.generate(curve=SECP256k1)
private_key_bytes = sk.to_string()
print(f"Private key (hex): {private_key_bytes.hex()}")


# Derive public key
vk = sk.get_verifying_key()
public_key_bytes = vk.to_string("compressed")
print(f"Compressed public key (hex): {public_key_bytes.hex()}")


# Taproot uses x-only public key (32 bytes from compressed pubkey, skipping the
0x02/0x03 prefix)
x_only_pubkey = public_key_bytes[1:]
print(f"X-only public key (Taproot internal key): {x_only_pubkey.hex()}")


# Witness program is SHA256(x-only pubkey)
witness_program = sha256(x_only_pubkey).digest()
print(f"Witness program (SHA256): {witness_program.hex()}")


# Convert to 5-bit format (for Bech32m)
def convertbits(data, frombits, tobits, pad=True):
    acc = 0
    bits = 0
    ret = []
    maxv = (1 << tobits) - 1
    for value in data:
        acc = (acc << frombits) | value
        bits += frombits
    while bits >= tobits:
        bits -= tobits
        ret.append((acc >> bits) & maxv)
    if pad and bits:
        ret.append((acc << (tobits - bits)) & maxv)
```

```
    return ret
```

```
    # Encode using Bech32m
    hrp = 'bc' # Use 'tb' for testnet
    data = [1] + convertbits(witness_program, 8, 5)
    taproot_address = bech32.bech32_encode(hrp, data, bech32.Encoding.BECH32M)
    print(f"Taproot (Bech32m) address: {taproot_address}")
```

3.17 Ongoing Technical Trends

3.17.1 Bitcoin Mining

We have gone in quite some detail when it comes to the Bitcoin network but we skipped 1 significant part: the mining hardware. Nowadays it is no longer profitable to start mining bitcoin from home with your pc or a GPU but this wasn't always the case. This is because of the mining difficulty that was introduced with the network. The goal is to mine a block every 10 min, not slower nor faster. As more miners join the network, there is only 1 way to keep this speed and that is by increasing the difficulty and computer power needed to mine a block. In 2009 all you needed was your pc and the CPU (central processing unit) to mine. You can still find articles from this period discussing the best processors for mining, aiming at 60$ per CPU when you wanted to build a rig.[46] As more people started to join the network (we are 2011), it became too difficult to keep on mining by making use of the CPU and people started to switch to GPUs or Graphical Processing Units. It is used for complex computations and more specifically for those computers which have heavy graphics requirements. These units are much more powerful than CPUs (we are looking to an increase in power × 30). The next phase came with FPGA-mining where the power was increased once more (FPGAs are between 3–100 times faster than the GPUs). It was 2013 when the ASIC-miner (Application Specific Integrated Circuit) joined the mining game and the entire level playing field changed. This is a piece of hardware that was specifically designed for the purpose of mining. Because of the continuous added competition, mining pools and farms came into existence. Mining pools allow you to join with your mining equipment with other miners to work together as one. The profits are shared based on the mining power you bring into the pool. Mining farms are companies that focus on building entire infrastructures, aiming to earn large amounts of bitcoins based on the power they have. Some concerns have been raised in the past because the majority of mining farms can be found in China.

---

[46] Edmonds, R. (March 8, 2018) Best CPUs for Crypto Mining. *Windows Central.* https://www.win dowscentral.com/best-cpus-crypto-mining. Accessed December 18, 2019.

3.18   Bitcoin Relay Networks

Closely linked to the concept of mining, is the existence of Bitcoin relay networks. Again, this relates to the concept of time in the network. It is very important for miners to know when to start mining the next block when the new block is being propagated throughout the network. The relay network is used to minimize the latency in the network. The original network was introduced by Matt Corallo in 2015. It made use of specialized nodes on Amazon Web Services and connected the majority of the miners in the network. This implementation was replaced in 2016 with the introduction of 'FIBRE' or 'Fast Bitcoin Relay Engine' which was also created by Matt Corallo. It is an UDP based network that relays blocks throughout the network and makes use of compact block optimization. Currently, developers are working on Falcon which is based on Cornell University research. It makes use of 'cut-through routing' instead of 'store-and-forward'. With cut-through routing we enter a world of sequential routing where the messages are divided in units called 'flits'. These flits are of a very small size so that their header information must also be minimized, and this is done by forcing all these flits over the same path in sequence.

3.19   Bitcoin: The Cryptocurrency

More famous than the network of course is the cryptocurrency behind the network, also called bitcoin. Bitcoin is being created by making use of the mining process and started at 50 bitcoin per block being created in January 2009. However, the rewards for mining are diminishing over time. Every 4 years[47] the rewards are being halved and now we have arrived at 12.5 bitcoin per block. Currently, over 85% of all bitcoins that will ever be mined, are already mined with a current reward of 12.5 bitcoins per block that will diminish to 6.25 bitcoins on the 17th of MAY 2020.[48] If you follow this formula, we know that there will eventually come an end to the creation of new bitcoins. In the year 2140 there will be approximately 21 million bitcoin and after this no new bitcoins will be created ever again. Does this mean that there will be 21 million bitcoins on the market? No, not exactly, as bitcoins that are lost because of people losing access to their wallets, can never be recovered. It has led to the famous saying that bitcoin is the equivalent of gold in the crypto world (with ether being the oil but more about that later). This mechanism makes sure that we are dealing with a deflationary currency (or at least it should be in theory). This means that the value of the currency will increase over time because we are dealing with a lowering supply while the demand increases over time. This makes sure that we have an increase in value, and the purchasing power increases. There are several ways that you can acquire bitcoin (if you are not a miner taking part in the mining process). First of all, you could make use of one of the several exchanges out

---

[47] Or more exactly, every 210,000 blocks.
[48] https://www.bitcoinblockhalf.com/.

there that offer bitcoin in return for other cryptocurrencies and/or regular currencies such as Euro or US Dollars. A second interesting approach is that of the 'bitcoin ATM'. These accept cash in return for bitcoin and send it to your (smartphone) bitcoin wallet. Finally, there is also the possibility to perform a direct trade with another person their wallet and/ or perform services for bitcoin as you would any other currency.

3.20   Payment Channels on BITCOIN

Over time several proposals have been made to create payment channels on top of the Bitcoin network (and other blockchain platforms). It is a technique that allows users to perform multiple transactions without committing all of the transactions to the Bitcoin blockchain.[49] Over the years several implementations have been proposed to introduce this feature to the network. Below I am going to give a short overview of several of these proposals. These examples clearly show how the network has evolved over time and how developers have tried (and succeeded) to tackle the scalability problem that often comes with blockchain networks. Later in the chapter, you will also find the lightening network explanation and implementation, which is arguably the most famous payment channel protocol to date.

3.20.1 Nakamoto High-Frequency Transactions

This implementation made use of the nLockTime field. It was proposed by Satoshi Nakamoto and could be used in his view to contain payments of multiple parties where each of the participants could sign their own input. To agree on a new version, each participant must sign a higher sequence number, agreeing on the inputs and outputs of the previous state. There were also some other options to only agree to your output (SIGHASH_SINGLE), a pre-agreed default option could also be created with the nSe-quenceNumber and OP_CHECKMULTISIG but the problem was that in the end, the design wasn't secure as a miner and a participant could work together and commit a non-final version of the transactions taking place, stealing from the other participants.

3.20.2 Spillman-Style Payment Channels

Proposed by Jeremy Spillman on the Bitcoin-development mailing list and implemented in BitcoinJ, this technique creates a secure deposit combined with a second transaction by which the 2 parties can release the funds. This way the possible attack that could take

---

[49] Payment channels. *Bitcoin.* https://en.bitcoin.it/wiki/Payment_channels. Accessed October 8, 2019.

place with Nakamoto High-frequency transactions, can't take place. These transactions work unidirectional as there is always a payer and a payee and it is not possible to reverse money back in the opposite direction. The payee needs to close the channel before a certain expiration time.[50] Problem here? The channel was vulnerable to transaction malleability (described in more detail below).

3.20.3 CLTV-Style Payments

Similar to Spillman-style payment channels, the CLTV-style payment channels are unidirectional payment channels that expire after a specific time. They became possible after the BIP-65 specification and the CLTV-soft fork that took place end of 2015. This channel is resistant against the malleability problem but still has limited use, as it only works in a unidirectional fashion. If we want to really scale the network, we need to be able to make payments in both directions, and if it were possible, with multiple parties.

3.20.4 Poon-Dryja Payment Channels

Poon-Dryja payment channels make use of funds that are locked in a 2-of-2 multisig. Commitment transactions of each party must be written and signed, before even the funding transaction is signed. Segregated witness is of key value here as it makes use of unsigned transactions and as such, it requires a transaction format that separates the transaction that is hashed for the txID and the signatures. It are bidirectional channels that have no expiration time and can be closed either unilaterally or bilaterally.

3.20.5 Decker-Wattenhofer Duplex Payment Channels

Christian Decker and Roger Wattenhofer introduced duplex payment channels in their paper.[51] It makes use of nSequence (the nSequence introduced by BIP-68) and consists out of 2 unidirectional payment channels with indefinite lifetime. Between the funding transaction of the channel and the final transactions, there is something called an 'invalidation tree' which contains the off-chain transactions that happen between the parties. The first version of the transaction has the longest relative lock time, while the next has a slightly smaller relative lock time and so on. This channel can be closed by either

---

[50] Spilman, J. (April 20, 2019) Anti DoS for tx replacement. *Linux Foundation.* https://lists.linuxf oundation.org/pipermail/bitcoin-dev/2013-April/002433.html. Accessed October 8, 2019.

[51] Decker C. and Wattenhofer R. A Fast and Scalable Payment Network with Bitcoin Duplex Micropayment Channels. *Ethz.* https://tik-old.ee.ethz.ch/file/716b955c130e6c703fac336ea17b1670/ duplex-micropayment-channels.pdf. Accessed October 13, 2019.

party but it is most efficient if both parties work together to close the channel, as everything comes down to 1 single transaction on the Bitcoin blockchain. This channel can be extended to contain multiple parties.

3.20.6 Decker-Russell-Osuntokun Eltoo Channels

Christina Decker, Rusty Russell and Olauluwa Osuntokun introduced the Eltoo payment channel in their paper on April 30th, 2018.[52] This is one of the many ideas put forward by Blockstream and Lightning labs (as you will discover later in the chapter). The channel makes use of 2 transactions whenever there is an update taking place: the actual update transaction and a CSV-encumbered settlement transaction that spends the update transaction. To make this happen, this channel requires a new type of signing flag called SIGHASH_NOINPUT and OP_CHECKLOCKTIMEVERIFY. The OP_CHECKLOCKTIMEVERIFY is not used to enforce any particular future time but is rather used to enforce an ordering of the update transactions so that each later update can spend an earlier one, but not vice versa. It does not require any punishment features as in Poon-Dryija but the main reason this channel is not being used yet is because of the SIGHASH_NOINPUT that still needs to be implemented. When this happens, this implementation will probably be used by the lightning network.

3.20.7 Hashed Time-Locked Contracts or HTLCs

HTLCs are an integral part of the lightning network nowadays. It uses hashlocks and timelocks which lead to a situation where the receiver of a payment has to either acknowledge that he received a payment by generating a proof of payment or forfeit the payment altogether, after which it is returned to the payer. These hashed time-locked contracts can be combined with Poon-Dryja payment channels which increases the security of the payments and without the necessity of recording these transactions on the Bitcoin blockchain.

3.20.8 Transaction Malleability

Segregated witness was implemented to prevent all forms of transaction malleability. Before Segwit (and to this day for those nodes that didn't follow the soft fork required to implement segregated witness), there was work being done on researching all forms of transaction malleability. BIP-62 was a work in progress to change the Bitcoin transactions

---

[52] Decker, C. and Russell, R. eltoo: A Simple Layer2 Protocol for Bitcoin. *Blockstream.* https://blockstream.com/eltoo.pdf. Accessed October 14, 2019.

so that malleability could be prevented.[53] Even though it is no longer being worked on, it is still an interesting study to see what forms of malleability were identified:

1. **Non-DER encoded ECDSA signatures**: older implementations (before v0.8.0 of the Bitcoin core) non-DER encoded signatures could still be relayed throughout the network.
2. **Non-push operations in scriptSig**: a sequence of operations in scriptSig, resulting in the intended data pushes, including more than only the push, results in a valid transaction
3. **Push operations in scriptSig of non-standard size type**: there are several push opcodes in the Bitcoin scripting language, with each having different possibilities
4. **Zero-padded number pushes**: number inputs in sciptPubKey opcodes can be zero padded
5. **Inherent ECDSA signature malleability**: ECDSA signatures are malleable
6. **Superfluous scriptSig operations**: extra data pushes at the start of the script which are not consumed by the corresponding scriptPubKey
7. **Inputs ignored by scripts**: OP_DROP opcode can be used to ignore the last data push in a scriptSig
8. **Sighash flags based masking**: these flags can be used to ignore certain parts of a script
9. **New signatures by the sender**: the sender can create new signatures that spend the same inputs to the same outputs.

However, at the time of writing the 2nd edition, a lot has changed. BIP350 introduces a modification to the Bech32 address format, known as Bech32m, in order to support newer Segregated Witness (SegWit) versions in Bitcoin, particularly those introduced with Taproot (defined in BIP341). Bech32, as originally introduced in BIP173, was designed to encode SegWit addresses with witness version 0, such as P2WPKH and P2WSH. However, with the implementation of Taproot and the introduction of witness version 1, it became clear that the original Bech32 format was not sufficiently robust for newer versions, especially in terms of error detection. BIP350 addresses this by defining a modified checksum constant for Bech32m. While Bech32 used a constant of 1, Bech32m uses 0x2bc830a3, which results in a significantly different checksum output. This alteration allows software to distinguish between legacy and new SegWit addresses based on the checksum alone. As a result, Bech32m enhances the reliability and security of address interpretation in wallets and other Bitcoin software.

Practically, the usage of Bech32 and Bech32m is now determined by the witness version. Addresses with witness version 0 continue to use the original Bech32 format, while those with version 1 or higher, such as Taproot addresses, must use Bech32m. This clear delineation ensures backward compatibility while enabling forward expansion of Bitcoin's

---

[53] Dashjr, L. (January 19, 2017) Bip-0062. *Github—Bitcoin bips* https://github.com/bitcoin/bips/blob/master/bip-0062.mediawiki. Accessed October 14, 2019.

address encoding system. BIP350 is a minimal but critical upgrade to Bech32, ensuring that the encoding format evolves alongside Bitcoin's technical improvements. It reinforces the system's resilience against errors and supports the continued growth of Bitcoin through upgrades like Taproot.

For a proper comparison between the first proposal and the current version, you can use the table below as a reference:

Feature	Bech32	Bech32m
Used for	SegWit v0	SegWit v1+
Checksum constant	1	0x2bc830a3
Error detection	Good (for v0)	Improved (for v1+)
Introduced in	BIP173	BIP350

For those of you interested in a Python implementation of Bech32m encoding and decoding, you can find a small sample here:

```
import bech32 # You may need to install a bech32 library like 'bitstring' or 'segwit_
addr'
# Example HRP (Human Readable Part) and data
hrp = 'bc' # Mainnet prefix
witver = 1 # Taproot address
witprog = bytes.fromhex('751e76e8199196d454941c45d1b3a323f1433bd6') # 20-
byte witness program


# Convert witness program to 5-bit groups (per BIP173)
def convertbits(data, frombits, tobits, pad=True):
    acc = 0
    bits = 0
    ret = []
    maxv = (1 << tobits) - 1
    for value in data:
        acc = (acc << frombits) | value
        bits += frombits
        while bits >= tobits:
            bits -= tobits
            ret.append((acc >> bits) & maxv)
    if pad and bits:
        ret.append((acc << (tobits - bits)) & maxv)
    return ret
```

```
# Encode using Bech32m
data = [witver] + convertbits(witprog, 8, 5)
bech32m_address = bech32.bech32_encode(hrp, data, bech32.Encoding.BECH32M)
print(f"Bech32m address: {bech32m_address}")
```

```
# Decode and check the encoding type
hrpgot, datagot, encoding = bech32.bech32_decode(bech32m_address)
print(f"Decoded HRP: {hrpgot}, Encoding: {'BECH32M' if encoding ==
bech32.Encoding.BECH32M else 'BECH32'}")
```

3.21   Wasabi Wallet and Zerolink

Privacy is always a concern when developers talk about the Bitcoin network. Zerolink is an implementation that focusses on fungibility of bitcoins and the privacy of the participants that perform transactions. The privacy is extended not to only a single transaction but also to chains of transactions. Zerolinks main goal is to break all links between separate sets of coins.[54] In the end, zerolink is the combination of a wallet privacy network combined with Chaumain CoinJoin. CoinJoin was first introduced by Gregory Maxwell in 2013. It comes down to multiple participants adding inputs and outputs to a common transaction so that the transaction graph becomes obfuscated. The Chaumain CoinJoin uses chaum blind signatures. This means that each participant provides input and a blinded output to the Tumbler which signs the blinded output and gives it back to the participants. The participant then unblinds the output and provides it to the server in a signed form through a different anonymity network identity. The Tumbler eventually constructs CoinJoin transactions and requires the participants to sign. An implementation of this privacy based Bitcoin wallet is called 'Wasabi wallet' and is open for use.

3.22   Meta-Coin Platforms on Top of Bitcoin: Colored Coins

There have been several implementations over time on top of the Bitcoin protocol. The first implementations that occurred focused on various techniques to add metadata to the existing Bitcoin processes. This was done by making use of unused transaction fields to encode extra information in the transactions. It was with the introduction of the OP_RETURN transaction script opcode that more possibilities arose to include more information directly on the blockchain. This also meant that a new type of coin saw the light of

---

[54] Nopara73 (April 28, 2020) ZeroLink: The Bitcoin Fungibility Framework. *Github—ZeroLink*. https://github.com/nopara73/ZeroLink?source=post_page. Accessed October 15, 2019.

day: the so-called colored coins.[55] These colored coins are used to represent other cryptocurrencies but can also refer to digital and even physical assets. The first implementation of colored coins is called 'Enhanced Padded-Order-Based Coloring', or 'EPOBC', which assigns assets to 1 satoshi. Of course, the OP_RETURN opcode allows for more data to be stored, while these can also refer to external data which in turn can be used to reference specific assets. Over time there have been several implementations of which the most famous were OpenAssets (used by coinprism) and Colored coins by Colu. However, nowadays the use of colored coins is mostly gone because of the introduction of the ERC-20 standard and others (explained later) which are easier and cheaper to use.

3.23 OpenAssets Protocol

Even though the protocol isn't used anymore that often (or not at all), it can still be interesting to play with the protocol. It can give you a better understanding of the workings of the Bitcoin network and how the developers wanted to interact with the network. How is the metadata association actually performed for assets? Well it works in three stages:[56]

- **Blockchain association**: the asset definition URL is embedded in the Bitcoin blockchain by the issuer
- **Asset definition file**: the definition file of the asset is made available at the URL stored in the blockchain
- **Proof of authenticity**: SSL has to guarantee the identity of the issuer.

In the blockchain, the association can be performed by making use of an asset definition pointer that can have several formats but of which only 1 can only be used anymore because of limitation imposed in 2015 (marker output limited to 40 bytes) and to provide privacy for the parties exchanging the asset.

---

[55] These coins do not actually have a color, it is rather a reference to changing the attributes in some way, such as color would have done.

[56] Charlon, F. (May 13, 2015) Open Assets Protocol. *Open Assets* https://github.com/OpenAssets/open-assets-protocol/blob/master/asset-definition-protocol.mediawiki. Accessed October 17, 2019.

```
{
  "asset_ids": [
    "<base 58 asset id>"
  ],
  "name_short": "<string>",
  "name": "<string>",
  "contract_url": "<url>",
  "issuer": "<string>",
  "description": "<string>",
  "description_mime": "<mime type>",
  "type": "<string>",
  "divisibility": <integer>,
  "link_to_website": <boolean>,
  "icon_url": "<url>",
  "image_url": "<url>",
  "version": "<string>"
}
```

Asset definition

The assets themselves, when included in transactions, give these transactions 2 new characteristics: an asset ID which is a hash of 160-bits, and the asset quantity being stored. The ID of an asset is the RIPEMD-160 hash of the SHA-256 hash of the output script referenced by the first input of the transaction that initially issued that asset. The transactions that make use of the protocol, must have a 'marker output'. The marker output always starts with OP_RETURN and must have a PUSHDATA opcode containing a parsable marker payload.[57] The payload looks like this:

Field	Description	Size
OAP Marker	Always '0x4f41'	2 bytes
Version	The version number	2 bytes
Asset quantity count	Number of items in asset quantity list	1–9 bytes
Asset quantity list	0 or more LEB128-encoded unsigned integers	Variable
Metadata length	Length of the metadata field	1–9 bytes
Metadata	Empty or arbitrary data associated with transaction	Variable

There are two submodules where the first focuses on the transaction interpretation as colored coins while the second focuses on building the transactions themselves. If you would like to test out for yourself, do not hesitate to consult the Github page and make sure that you are deploying it on a Bitcoin core instance with both RPC enabled and the –txindex = 1 parameter.

---

[57] If there are multiple payloads, only the first one is used and the rest is ignored.

3.24   Bitcoin 2.0

Below you will find a substantial list of sidechains of the Bitcoin network but also new layers or protocol improvement projects. These all bring their own adaptations and innovations to the original Bitcoin network and try to offer a solution for an existing problem. Depending on what you are looking for, you will find some of these projects more interesting than others. Still it will show you that there is a major community supporting the Bitcoin network and looking for ways to improve the network so that there can be an even larger adoption of the network and the underlying technology. The Bitcoin network isn't dead, it is thriving and ever looking for new ways to ensure its future.

3.25   Bitcoin Hivemind

Hivemind is a peer-to-peer oracle protocol that wants to provide Bitcoin users with accurate data from outside the blockchain environment (see a more general description of oracles in the Ethereum chapter) so that participation in the prediction market (event derivatives) becomes a possibility. It is one of the implementations that sprung from Truthcoin (others are Amoveo, Augur and Gnosis). The focus lies on the problem of information aggregation. The problem lies in the fact that we can never know when journalist, politicians and so on actually tell us the truth. Similar to other projects such as Rootstock, they make use of merge-mining to ensure that the Bitcoin miners will also help to secure the Hivemind sidechain. To receive an extra incentive to do so, by receiving dividend revenue of the Bitcoin Hivemind. Within the network there would be the creation of 2 types of coins: CashCoins (CSH) and VoteCoins (VTC).[58] Participants with CashCoins can actually create so-called 'prediction markets' of which the shares can be bought, sold or transferred and there is a value pegging in place where 1 CSH = 1 BTC. The VTC-coins represent equity in the oracle corporations which are also called branches. Each of these branches has their own VoteCoins. It is used to prevent Sybil attacks, provide proof of reputation within the network and can be used to punish participants that do not provide the necessary work within the overall network. The more VTC you have in a branch, the more voting power you have and the larger your share from the branch revenues. From the second you start to vote away from the majority or refuse to vote, you can lose your VTC-coins in the branch. In a similar way you can gain more VTC-coins if you participate in voting and with the majority. The distribution of VTC-coins is based on a reputation based redistribution scheme. This includes measures for deviant behavior, movements against the existence of an oligarchy and too volatile network environments. The system is also created in such a way that the minority vote gets the least reward (lower than 50% agreement on vote) and is maximized at 51% (preventing voting pools).

---

[58] Sztorc, P. (December 14, 2015) Truthcoin. *Truthcoin.* http://bitcoinhivemind.com/papers/truthc oin-whitepaper.pdf. Accessed November 18, 2019.

These prediction markets can be created by any user which then becomes an 'author'. This author should have a certain believe that the market he is creating will be sufficiently liquid for trading and linked to this these authors only have an incentive to write 'decisions' that by a certain day will be a locked fact. VoteCoin owners or 'voters' have an incentive to maintain the long-run trading volume of their branch and have a strong incentive to vote on all decisions and vote the way they believe other voters will vote. The voters can be seen as the 'employees' within the network. There are several concepts that you need to understand: vote, decision and ballot. The decision is what we are voting on. This can be something very simple as 'Person A will be elected president'. Or these can be much more complex statements on which the voters need to vote. Based on the decision, the voter will cast a vote (0 means false, 1 means true, NA means you didn't vote and there are also some possibilities in-between when it comes to pricing calls for example). The ballot consists out of the matured decisions and the votes that have been cast on these decisions. At this moment the votes are revealed and the consensus algorithm determines the outcome of the vote. In case there wasn't a clear outcome of the vote, an 'audit' takes place. Voters also have the right to vote after a waiting period and in case this is more than 50% of the blocks, there must be a re-vote.

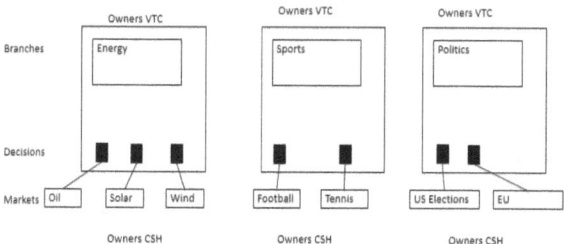

Bitcoin Hivemind

The users of the CashCoins are the 'customers' and don't have to interact at all with VoteCoins if they don't wish to do so. They can trade on any prediction market they wish depending on what they think will increase in value. The trading is being facilitated by an automated market-maker as long as the voting is in progress. Between several rounds of voting there is a time called 'Tau' or the intervote period. From the second the decision has been resolved, the trading ends and one enters the state of 'redeeming'. You can also understand that this is a very scalable project in that sense that you can keep on creating more specialized branches. However, an unlimited amount of branches is undesirable, as it increases computational and economic cost, can create branches where voters no longer receive enough incentives to vote as they really want to vote and markets that are simply empty. That is why there is a system of 'intelligent' splitting where voters have to decide whether or not they agree with a new branch. That is why there is a 'main' branch to start with, from which we can specifically start to split. If we refer to the image above, a market such as 'football' could perfectly become its own branch, leaving a sports branch without football. If there is no activity left in branch for 3 consecutive intervote periods, it will be removed from the chain. The number of participants per branch will be limited to a number around 100,000 because of computational costs. This will mean that when the number increases, those with the lowest values will be removed from the branch. These participants would probably not have shared in any dividends or have participated in the process, leaving room for new active members to join. This limit only extends to the voters on the branch, not the owners! The current transaction speed for the Bitcoin network is too low for a competitive trading environment (even though low transaction speeds certainly help prevent double spending within the ordered list of transactions) and this is why Bitcoin Hivemind is looking at the GHOST protocol (or something similar) to provide a higher throughput speed.

3.26   The Mimblewimble Protocol

For those of you that are Harry Potter fans, the phrase 'mimblewimble' will be well-known.[59] It is also the name of a protocol that was introduced in a paper on the 19th of July 2016 by an author who called himself 'Tom Elvis Jedusor' (oh yes, he did).[60] The author wanted to provide an answer to some of the privacy concerns that are linked with the Bitcoin network. The problem lies in the fact that all transactions must be stored in the blockchain while in fact they only relate to a small set of unspent transaction outputs or 'UTXOs'. You cannot remove the other transactions because the final state and with it the UTXOs are only valid if the entire blockchain is valid. Transactions are also cryptographically atomic, which means the transaction graph can be used to identify users. The paper references several solutions put forward by Dr. Greg Maxwell, Nicolas van Saberhagen and Shen Noether to improve the privacy within the blockchain but the author notes that these approaches lead to more data being used (KBs for confidential transactions), signatures that must be stored forever and the need for interactivity. The need for interactivity refers to the solution of Dr. Maxwell called 'CoinJoin' where users can interactively combine transactions. CoinJoin is a trustless method of combining trans-actions by multiple spenders in 1 single transaction to make it more difficult for outsiders to determine who paid who. The number of transactions that are actually making use of this scheme is increasing over the years.[61] You do not need to change the Bitcoin protocol as such and the Wasabi wallet makes it easy to implement. This data storage requirement and need for interactivity was solved by Dr. Yuan Horas Mouton who made

---

[59] It is the curse that prevents one from speaking in the Harry Potter-world.

[60] Jedusor, T.E. (July 19, 2016) MimbleWimble. *Scaling Bitcoin.* https://scalingbitcoin.org/papers/mimblewimble.txt. Accessed November 26, 2019.

[61] Manning, L. (May 1, 2019) Percentage of CoinJoin Bitcoin Transactions Triples over past year. *Bitcoin Magazine.* https://bitcoinmagazine.com/articles/percentage-coinjoin-bitcoin-transactions-triples-over-past-year. Accessed November 6, 2019.

transactions freely mergeable but at a cost. Because he uses paring-based cryptography, everything becomes much slower. This solution was called OWAS or 'One-way aggregate signatures'. The proposal put forward is to remove Bitcoin script because it doesn't allow for merging of transactions with general scripts. Next, he took the idea of 'confidential transactions' of Dr. Maxwell to allow authorization of spending outputs and the combinations of transactions without interaction (OWAS). This means that the Bitcoin structure and way of working is completely changed. Instead of individually signing each input and output there is a multisignature for all inputs and outputs. This is all thanks to the use of the Pedersen Commitment scheme where you no longer need addresses but instead use something called a 'blinding factor' which is shared among the actors. Both inputs and outputs, together with the public and private addresses are encrypted so that only the involved parties know that they are involved in the transaction. So how does this Pedersen Commitment scheme actually work? First of all the full nodes check whether the inputs and outputs totals are a balanced equation, making sure that no new coins are being produced out of thin air. The inputs and outputs totals are multiplied by a 'blinding factor' that is made up out of both the private and public keys. This way the equation still has to hold but no one has an idea of the amounts that are involved while at the same time the involved parties can prove that they are the owners. The involved parties are eventually asked to sign a multisignature header to approve the transaction. But it also offers a solution for the storage of the data. While in fact there is a 'cut through' feature which allows for much less information to be stored in the blockchain. In the Bitcoin world, each stage of an UTXO needs to be stored, as a proof of the transation of ownership throughout the transactions that took place. In the Mimblewimble-world only the first input UTXO and the final output UTXO need to be stored, this way removing all the in-between steps and freeing up a lot of space. In January 2019 this Mimblewimble protocol was put into use with the launch of the Grin mainnet after years of development on the Github project started by 'Ignotus Peverell' (Harry potter fans rejoice).[62] There is also another active implementation called 'Beam'. Both implementations have their own specific features even though they make use of the same protocol. Grin has no cap on the number of coins that can be mined (60 per block) while Beam is limited to 263 million. Also the proof of work consensus protocol differs: Grin uses the Cuckoo cycle (CuckARoo for 90% and CuckAToo for 10% while slowly shifting towards CuckAToo over time), Beam equihash. However, the block time remains the same: for both it has landed on 1 minute per block. What is the main difference with other coins that focus on privacy? Probably you have heard of coins such as Monero, Dash and Zcash which all bring their own ideas to the table when it comes to protecting the user from prying eyes. We will go in more detail when we discuss these coins separately but you should know that Zcash is much slower than either Grin or Beam, up to 64% of Monero inputs

---

[62] https://github.com/mimblewimble/grin/blob/master/doc/intro.md.

do not have the required 'mixins' leading to traceable transactions and Dash is a centralized solution. Although we should note that these coins could try to incorporate the Mimblewimble protocol in their solutions, increasing the privacy even further.

3.27 The Elements Project

The elements project is another sidechain project created by Blockstream (it can also be run as a standalone project) that wishes to solve several problems that are encountered by participants in blockchain networks such as the lack of privacy, transaction latency and the risk to fungibility.[63] All these problems are being addresses by the developers behind the elements project by making use of federated block signing and confidential transactions. Block creation is no longer done by miners solving a proof of work algorithm but rather by 'block signers' which are a federation of notaries who can create new blocks. In case Elements is being run as a sidechain, some notaries will take the role of 'watchmen', making sure that there is a controlled and secure transfer between the 2 chains. Similarly to mimblewimble, here the Elements project makes use of confidential transactions and a blinding factor. When using Elements as a sidechain, this is more often than not the Bitcoin blockchain and there will always be a 2-way peg in place, allowing for the transfer of goods between the 2 chains. This ensures that Elements is interoperable with other blockchain platforms. It is the role of the watchmen to make sure that the token of the 'main' chain are effectively frozen and it is only when the transaction is verified that the equivalent amount of tokens on the Elements blockchain are released. The reverse transaction (from Elements to the main blockchain) is a little bit more complicated. First the 'peg out' transaction is checked by watchmen who then sign the transaction that leaves a multi-signature wallet on the main chain. Only if enough members of the federation sign, the transaction becomes valid. In that case the tokens on the Elements chain are destroyed. Because of this way of working the speed of transactions and the creation of blocks is increased while the need for a 3th party isn't necessary. When you make use of the Elements blockchain, you can create new assets all you like which is open to all network nodes (as long as you possess reissuance tokens which invoke the right of creation). Similarly you can destroy tokens (if you possess these in your personal wallet). Furthermore, Elements is implementing new opcodes to the ones that already exist within the Bitcoin network (such as DETERMINISTICRANDOM and CHECKSIGFROMSTACK) allowing for more scripting possibilities and is similarly researching the possibilities of Schnorr signatures to further improve the efficiency of the network.

---

[63] How Elements works and the roles of network participants. *Blockstream.* https://elementsproject. org/how-it-works. Accessed July 13, 2019.

3.28   Siacoin

Siacoin is another ambitious and interesting project, focusing on decentralized cloud storage. It is a decentralized way of storing files without a single point of failure. Because of the distributed way of working, there is no way to assure that enough nodes stay live and connected to the network for a participant to download his file. Well, they have a solution: Reed-Solomon erasure coding. What? This is how it works: when you upload a file to the Sia platform, your file gets divided in 30 segments which are distributed all over the world. This allows for maximum distribution and makes sure that at least a few of these nodes will stay online. Okay, now step two. Reed-Solomon codes were developed in 1960 by Irving S. Reed and Gustave Solomon. They proposed an encoding scheme which used a variable polynomial based on the target message where only a fixed set of evaluation points are known to both encoder and decoder. The decoder then has to generate potential polynomials based on subsets of unencoded message length of the encoded message length. This way the code can be used to detect mistakes that might have happened during transmission. Similarly this technique is used by Sia. If 10 of the 30 divided segments of a file can be found, the entire file is available for download by the user. On top of this, each file segment is encrypted before it is distributed over the nodes by making use of the twofish algorithm. This way the users receive maximum protection from possible malicious participants. Finally, the up- and downloading facilities are facilitated by smart contracts so that no node can try to extort you for your file, it is locked in a secure way which does not require third party interventions. On top of that, the nodes have to pay collateral for each file contract, ensuring their participation and they receive 'rent' from the participants that upload files. This rent is paid via micropayment channels. The host has to proof it is providing the storage in order to get paid, otherwise he is penalized. To increase adoption of the Sia network, there are several integrations with technology partners such as NextCloud (to host your own data storage similar to Dropbox), Duplicati (to allow for full computer backups) and Minio (distributed object storage server). To pay for all of this you can make use of Siacoin which is integrated with the blockchain solution of the platform.

3.29   The Counterparty Protocol

The counterparty protocol is another implementation on the Bitcoin network which wants to extend its use as much as possible. It is used to write specific digital agreements or even smart contracts with built-in scripts.[64] It allows for the creation of tokens for any type of asset digitalization or the creation of a cryptocurrency. To further enhance the speed, counterparty makes use of the lightening network (explained below) to speed up

---

[64] https://counterparty.io/platform/.

swaps between XCP and BTC. An even more interesting use case of the Counterparty protocol is the 'asset exchange' where the roles of both escrow agent and clearing house are fulfilled by the protocol itself. The contracts exist on the network itself and funds from participating parties are immediately debited from their respective addresses. Only when the conditions of the contract is met, the distribution of funds can begin. Finally, they are also working on an alternative way of voting secured by their implementation of the Counterparty protocol and XCP-transactions. Securing both the identity of the participants and the result of the vote.

3.30 Drop Zone

The original paper on Drop Zone was released in 2015 by 'Miracle Max' but still receives attention on its ideas for creating a decentralized peer-to-peer market place.[65] It is another project that aims to work on top of the Bitcoin protocol.[66] The main idea (related to other P2P market places) is to prevent censorship and the freedom to sell and buy products. The difference here is that a blockchain is used as a solution. The project is not yet finished but it should work following these principles: a seller uploads the brief description of the good, an expiration and a hashtag. Buyers on the other hand search for goods close to their given location. In case the buyer finds a good it wants, the 2 parties can open a communication channel on the Bitcoin testnet so they can negotiate a price. Upon agreement, the buyer pays the seller on the mainnet and the location of the seller is revealed (GPS coordinates). However, the whitepaper also reveals a lot of weaknesses that need to be addressed. There is the vulnerability to Sybil attacks and reputation selling, but also non-fungible transactions, abuse of API sources, unresolved sales, unscrupulous selling and the fact that URL-identifiers are centralized. It is still a project that has a lot of work to do but if established, might have a serious impact on P2P markets in an age where instances such as the SilkRoad have disappeared.

3.31 Omni Protocol

Mastercoin was the first implementation which tried to leverage the power of the Bitcoin network while at the same time building a new platform on top of it. The term 'Master' was derived from 'Metadata Archival by Standard Transaction Embedding Records'. The main goal is to become a user-friendly platform where you can easily implement new development. It immediately also introduced the new cryptocurrency called, how could

---

[65] (March 26, 2015) Drop Zone: P2P E-commerce paper. https://www.metzdowd.com/pipermail/cryptography/2015-March/025212.html. Accessed August 4, 2019.

[66] ScroogeMcDuckButWithBitcoin (2016) Drop Zone. https://github.com/17Q4MX2hmktmpuUKHFuoRmS5MfB5XPbhod/dropzone_ruby. Accessed on August 3, 2019.

you even guess it, 'Mastercoin' or 'MSC'. The idea put forward by the developers of Mastercoin is that their layer can be seen as the HTTP layer on top of the TCP/IP stack where the Bitcoin network becomes their protocol and Mastercoin the top layer.[67] This way they hope to open up development on the Bitcoin network to a much wider group of participants as you no longer have to be an 'expert' to be able to participate and solve some common issues such as instability and insecurity. This was an attempt to stop the division of the developer community over all the rivalling alt coins. By pushing developers on top of the Bitcoin network and let them create their new cryptocurrencies on this protocol layer, the entire community would benefit as all developers would be pushing to a greater adoption of the network which would in turn lead to reward for every participant. The first release of their own coin, was mainly intended to support their own growth so that developers could get paid to work on the new protocol layer. They even state they have an "exodus address", similar to the "genesis block" on the Bitcoin blockchain, which is the first Bitcoin address from where Mastercoins were generated.[68] It was later renamed to the 'Omni protocol'[69] (and with it the OMNI token) and now aims at a broader target of developers including blockchain based crowdfunding where participants can send bitcoins or other tokens directly to the issuer and the sender receives the alternative token in return. The goal still remains to create a user-friendly developer environment where one can easily develop and release a cryptocurrency. First it made use of fake Bitcoin addresses and afterwards it made use of a multisignature scheme to embed data onto the Bitcoin blockchain. Currently, it makes in a large extent use of the OP_RETURN opcode of the Bitcoin network to lock data in the blockchain. Tether is probably the most (in)famous example of a cryptocurrency that makes use of the Omni protocol to leverage the power of the Bitcoin network. In the chapter on stablecoins you can find more information on this specific cryptocurrency.

3.32   Lightning Network[70]

We very, very much need such a system, but the way I understand your proposal, it does not seem to scale to the required size.—James A. Donald, November 2, 2008[71]

---

[67] https://en.bitcoinwiki.org/wiki/mastercoin.

[68] The Exodus address is: 1EXoDusjGwvnjZUyKkxZ4UHEf77z6A5S4P.

[69] https://www.omnilayer.org/.

[70] Poon, J. and Dryja, T. (January 14, 2016) The Bitcoin lightening network: scalable off) chain instant payments. http://lightning.network/lightning-network-paper.pdf. Accessed October 21, 2019.

[71] Donald, J. A. (November 2, 2008) Bitcoin P2P e-cash paper. https://www.metzdowd.com/piperm ail/cryptography/2008-November/014814.html. Accessed August 9, 2019.

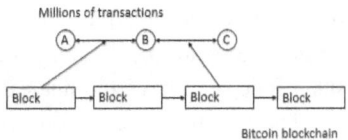

The above sentence may mean nothing to you but it was the first public comment made on the Bitcoin whitepaper that was put forward by Satoshi Nakamoto. Now, many years later, indeed scaling is one of the main issues that Bitcoin is dealing with. The system can only deal with about 7 transactions per second, which is immediately the reason why they are so slow nowadays and why the transaction fees are so high.[72] Over the years the Bitcoin community has struggles with the limitations of the network and came up with several proposals. One of these is the lightning network. The general idea is that not every transaction needs to be recorded on the blockchain itself. It has added an extra layer on top of the Bitcoin blockchain so that any participant can create a channel with another participant to send and receive transactions nearly instantly with low or even no transaction fees. Several problems can be seen when we think about such payment channels. The paper written by joseph Poon and Taddeus Dryvja largely focus on these. The first is the hostage taking problem. If you open a payment channel and you actually send the money, the other participant could simply say 'I will never sign, unless you give me most of the transaction'. To prevent this from happening, as you will learn from the description below, the money isn't actually send when the payment channel is opened. This is because the transaction isn't signed until the very end. So both participants know what is going to happen, but it only happens when they both sign, so equally crossing the lines. Secondly, there is the problem of old commitment transactions.[73] The first transaction is the so-called 'funding transaction' (to fund the payment channel) while all the other transactions happening between the participants are called 'commitment transactions'. If the payment channel is open for a long time, and we eventually want to close it, what prevents me from choosing an earlier transaction to close it on that is more in my favor? If this sounds confusing, think about this. Let's say you and me are funding the channel with both 1 BTC. A month ago you paid me 0.8 BTC, leaving the balances to 1.8 and 0.2 BTC. After 2 weeks I had to pay you 1.2 BTC, leaving the balances to 0.6 and 1.4 BTC. Why wouldn't I try to close on the balance leaving me with 1.8 BTC? Well there are 2 securities built in. First there is the opcode OP_CHECKSEQUENCEVERIFY that uses the sequence field to freeze the output until enough miners have confirmed that the output can actually be spent. This still doesn't prevent me from lying and taking the older transaction best of all it gives you time. Time to do what? Well, if I lie and close my part

---

[72] Visa has an average of 24,000 transactions per second with a peak capacity of over 50,000 transactions per second!

[73] Bergmann, C. (April 29, 2017) The lightning network explained, part I: how to build a payment channel. *Btcmanager.* https://btcmanager.com/lightning-network-primer-pt-i-building-payment-cha nnels/?q=/lightning-network-primer-pt-i-building-payment-channels/. Accessed July 25, 2019.

of the channel, you still have the option to take the whole fund of 2 BTC. What? Yes, as long as there are 2 participants watching the channel and waiting for the transaction to be accepted, all is fine. But if I lie, you have the nuclear option: you can just take it all. Now a bit more technical. The Lightning network works by making use of a multisignature wallet so that each participant can access this wallet by making use of their respective private keys, deposit some cryptocurrency and perform transactions between each of them. It is only when this wallet is closed and with it the channel, that the final results of all the transactions will be broadcast to the network, where it will be recorded as a single transaction. So how does this wallet actually look like? It makes use of something called a hashed timelock contract. It consists basically of a smart contract aimed at eliminating counterparty risk and implements time-bound transactions. It consists out of two participants where the first hashes his private key and sends it to the second participant. The first participant also generates a preimage which is used at the end to validate the transaction (a preimage is a datastring that is passed into a hash function and is sometimes called a 'secret'). The second participant hashes his private key and sends it back to the first. Again the second participant also generates a preimage by making use of a nominal transaction with the first participant. The first can now sign the transaction with the original key that is available in the preimage. The second participant can now do the same. There are still limitations though. The Lightning network does not solve the problem of the high transaction fees on the network. On top of that, the safest way of storing bitcoins is by making use of 'cold storage'. This is not possible as nodes making use of the Lightning network need to remain online at all times. Finally, it is still largely dependent on adoption of the network by the participants. As long it is not wide-used, it does not live up to its full potential. Several parties developed an actual implementation on the lightning network. One of these is Lightning Charge by blockstream but an extensive list can be found on the following repository: https://github.com/bcongdon/awesome-lightning-network.

Since this book first came out, the lightning network (LN) has matured significantly. Since 2020, the capacity of the network has grown with ~ 384% in BTC terms.[74] It even exceeded 5000 BTC in public channels by early 2023! As of the year 2024, larger channels and more nodes have become more common but also major exchanges and wallets integrate with the network for withdrawals and payments. Taproot-enabled channels and MPP (multi-path payments) have also entered the story to improve reliability and to ensure the future of LN through channel splicing and enhanced privacy. In traditional Lightning channels, the funding transactions and certain on-chain actions are relatively easy to identify, making them stand out to blockchain observers. But with Taproot, these channels can be disguised as ordinary Bitcoin transactions, significantly improving privacy. This is critical for users and developers who want to shield their financial activity from surveillance or simply value discretion. Taproot unlocks technical possibilities like channel splicing, a

---

[74] https://bitcoinmagazine.com/takes/my-top-3-takeaways-from-fidelity-and-voltages-recent-lightning-report#:~:text=,1%20seconds.

feature that allows users to add or remove funds from an existing channel without closing it. Previously, managing channel liquidity often meant closing and reopening channels which is a cumbersome, expensive, and privacy-leaking process. Taproot makes splicing seamless and discreet, helping users keep their channels active while adjusting their balances in the background. This is a game changer for wallet usability, as it removes much of the friction from managing funds on LN.

Alongside Taproot-enabled upgrades, the Lightning Network also benefits from another powerful feature called MPP, or Multi-Path Payments. Normally, if Alice wants to pay Bob via Lightning, she needs to have a single channel with enough capacity to cover the whole amount. But what if she doesn't? Before MPP, the payment would fail. With MPP, however, Alice can split her payment into smaller parts, sending them through multiple routes and channels to reach Bob—who receives them as a unified payment. This significantly improves payment reliability, liquidity utilization, and network resilience. It also helps reduce the need for large, capital-heavy channels, allowing more users to participate effectively in the network with modest balances. Combined with Taproot, MPP even benefits from better privacy, because each fragment of a payment takes a potentially different path, making it harder to link or trace. Together, Taproot-enabled channels and MPP represent a leap forward in making the Lightning Network more robust, private, and user-friendly. Taproot lays the cryptographic groundwork for flexible, indistinguishable smart contracts, while MPP makes payments more fluid and accessible. These upgrades are key to LN's future—enabling features like non-interactive channels, channel factories, and cross-wallet payment coordination—and bringing us closer to a vision of Bitcoin as a fast, private, everyday currency for the entire world.

3.33   Ark[75]

In the evolving landscape of Bitcoin Layer 2 protocols, most attention has long centered on the Lightning Network (LN), which is a fast and scalable micropayment solution built around payment channels. While powerful, LN requires users to actively manage these channels, fund them in advance, and maintain network connectivity—tasks that can be complex, especially for less technical users. This is where Ark, a new Layer 2 proposal introduced by developer Burak, presents a compelling alternative.

Ark's goal is to offer a simpler, more accessible way to make off-chain Bitcoin payments, without the need for users to open or manage their own payment channels. It introduces the concept of "virtual UTXOs", a mechanism that allows users to share liquidity and transaction space while still maintaining individual control over their funds. These virtual UTXOs behave like typical Bitcoin outputs, but instead of existing on the base layer, they are co-managed off-chain through a shared transaction pool, coordinated

[75] https://bitcoinmagazine.com/takes/my-top-3-takeaways-from-fidelity-and-voltages-recent-lightn ing-report#:~:text=,still%20slowing%20Lightning%20adoption%3B%20in.

by a central participant known as the Ark Service Provider (ASP). This design offers several key benefits. First, it abstracts away the complexity of channel management. Unlike the Lightning Network, where users must carefully maintain liquidity in both directions (and may face failed payments due to unbalanced channels), Ark users can simply make payments through the shared pool without worrying about channel capacity or routing. The ASP acts as a liquidity hub, facilitating batched transactions that are eventually settled on-chain in a compact and privacy-preserving way. Secondly, Ark is designed to maximize user privacy and on-chain efficiency. By batching many virtual UTXOs together into a single periodic on-chain transaction, Ark reduces the number of entries that appear on the Bitcoin blockchain, saving space and minimizing fees. Because each user's payment is mixed with others in the batch, it also becomes much harder for outside observers to trace who paid whom, improving transactional anonymity.

Ark can be thought of as a shared ledger for off-chain payments, where each participant holds a claim to a slice of value represented in the ASP's UTXO pool. Users are free to withdraw their funds to the base layer at any time, and they can do so independently, without needing permission from anyone else. This non-custodial design is essential for maintaining Bitcoin's trustless and decentralized ethos. Ark is not meant to replace the Lightning Network but to complement it. While LN excels in high-frequency, peer-to-peer payments among power users and merchants, Ark aims to lower the entry barrier for casual users, mobile wallets, and microtransactions—offering a "plug-and-play" experience with minimal overhead. It also provides an alternative design path in the broader effort to scale Bitcoin beyond its base layer constraints. Ark represents a fresh and pragmatic step forward in the Bitcoin scaling story, leveraging virtual UTXOs and a hub-based model to bring faster, more private, and easier-to-use payments to the average user. As the Bitcoin ecosystem continues to grow, this kind of protocol diversity ensures that scalability doesn't come at the cost of usability, and that Bitcoin remains a robust foundation for global, decentralized finance.

3.34 Liquid Network[76]

The liquid network is an implementation created by Blockstream, which in turn was founded in 2014 by a group of open-source coders behind Bitcoin. The network went officially live on September 27, 2018. It had an impressive range of launch participants: Altonomy, Atlantic Financial, Bitbank, Bitfinex, Bitmax, BitMEX, Bitso, BTCBOX, BTSE, Buull Exchange, DGroup, Coinone, Crypto Garage, GOPAX, Korbit, L2B Global, OKCoin, The Rock Trading, SIX Digital Exchange, Unocoin, Xapo, XBTO and Zaif. The idea behind the liquid network was already started in 2015 with the white paper titled 'Enabling blockchain innovations with pegged sidechains'. Liquid is a federated

---

[76] https://blockstream.com/liquid/.

sidechain which has been built on the Bitcoin network to facilitate faster bitcoin transactions between businesses and individuals, with a main focus on exchanges, financial institutions, and large traders. Small players can also use the network by making use of wallets or member exchanges. In the liquid network, you will not find the classic miners you would otherwise find but a group of so-called 'block signers'. These collect transactions into blocks, sign them and broadcast them over the network.[77] Within the network, block time has been reduced to a minute opposite to the 10 min in Bitcoin. However, all the functionalities of the Bitcoin network are still present in liquid, so you can still create wallets, use block explorers and keys. As explained before, the liquid network is a sidechain, which means it has its own native cryptocurrency, called 'liquid bitcoin' or LBTC which is backed with a 2-way peg to bitcoin. The 2 currencies are interchangeable at any time. However, the network also leaves the possibility to issue other assets over the network that are linked to the real world. All of this information is safely encrypted so that it cannot be read by the public, while the hash of the asset can still be tracked through the transactions over the network. This way the transactions can still be audited and information can be shared with accountants and other interested parties.

3.35   Rootstock

So what is Rootstock? Rootstock is the (first) implementation that aims to build a smart contract platform (later explained in more detail) on top of the Bitcoin network. It aims to be the most secure decentralized network in the world (the Bitcoin network has the most hashing power to date in the network). Immediately, they also want to make their chain and smart contracts compatible with the Ethereum network, understanding and accepting their power and position in the market when it comes to these implementations and preventing a further divide in the community of developers supporting the different networks.They also have their own coin, called 'smart bitcoin' or 'SBTC' which is linked 1:1 with BTC '(regular bitcoin). There is a 2-way peg between RBTC and BTC so the coins are always interchangeable. Though the miners in the Bitcoin network are also rewarded because of a feature which RSK calls 'merge-mining'. This means that the miners in the network will be effectively mining the RSK-chain and the Bitcoin chain, improving the security of both chains. The reward for the miners is 80% of the transaction fees while 17.5% goes to RSK labs, 1% to the RSK federation, 1% to RSK full nodes and 0.5% to Bitcoin full nodes. The federation consists out of the set of semi-trusted notaries that need to sign the transactions described below. However, they can also provide oracle services (explained in Ethereum chapter) and other modules (check the docs for more information). sTo get a good-working relationship between their RSK-chain and the main Bitcoin network, they make use of a special hybrid relationship model. To lock the coins at the Bitcoin side of the network, they are using the classic drivechain implementation where

---

[77] These block signers are often exchanges, market makers and other big players.

the miners of the Bitcoin network need to vote and mine the block, effectively locking Bitcoin and unlocking SBTC. To reverse the transaction, the relationship is a bit more complex. To unlock the Bitcoin (and lock the SBTC), there is a combination of the multisignature approach combined with the drivechain approach. This means that both chains have to give their approval before this transaction actually can take place.

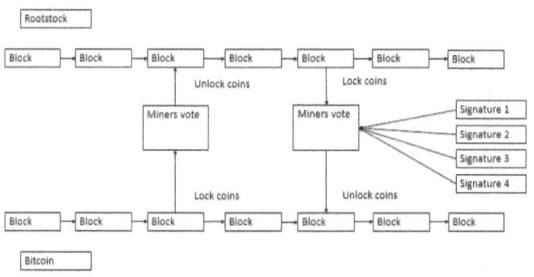

Rootstock pegging system

The ultimate goal is, when there are enough participants that engage in the relation between the two chains, this way of working will end. In the beginning, only the notaries can vote, then the combined relation will take place while the goal is to completely get rid of the signatures from the notaries and remove these completely so that only the drivechain relation remains. It is only the question if there will be enough participants so that this can actually be achieved. The implementation of smart contracts on Bitcoin has some consequences for other competitors in the market space such as Ethereum. This is another platform that brings the feature of smart contracts, and Ethereum is without a doubt the oldest and best known brand when it comes to smart contracting and DApp development. They wish to increase even more the adoption of the Bitcoin network but also allow industry to start developing applications on top of the Bitcoin network while still adhering to regulation. Their aim is to create (just like Ethereum) a Turing-complete chain with unlimited code size and memory with a persistent state and execution time. The consensus protocol in place is a combination of GHOST and DECOR with PBFT as a fallback mechanism which leads to a block time of 10 s. While we will go into much more detail in the chapter on Ethereum, you just need to know for now that there is the possibility for smart contracts (and therefore DApps) on the RSK-network. We also move away from UTXO-scheme that is being used in Bitcoin to the use of accounts. The ECDSA-algorithm is used to produce the public and private keys that are in use in the network. The smart contract in the Rootstock world consists out of several elements. The smart contract can both receive and send out messages combined with deposits or payments. Furthermore, the contracts have their own persistent memory and vaults to store a certain amount of SBTC. The next thing that Rootstock would like to achieve is to become a more scalable solution for Bitcoin than the lightening network. While the lightening network helps to increase the speed of the transactions, you still need a connection to the Bitcoin network and propagate the transactions through the network itself. Therefore, Rootstock is aiming at the 'Lumino Transaction Compression Protocol' or LTCP that is built on top of the RSK-network. This would lead to a transformation where Bitcoin can only do 3–5 transactions per second, to 100 transactions per second via RSK, to 2000 on-chain transactions via the LTCP layer. On top of this layer, there should come the 'Lumino' network that would be able to carry up to 20,000 of off-chain transactions. With this network, it would greatly overcome the limitations of the lightening network and the Lumino network would be able to reach billions of people (if you consider that each person settles their account once a month.

3.36   Zcash

Zcash is one of the cryptocurrencies that in fact was built on top of the Bitcoin code base. The main goal of Zcash is once again to improve the privacy that is not offered by the Bitcoin protocol and to improve the transaction speed and scalability of the network.[78] On the other hand, the developers promise that the transactions can be auditable, but only with user permission. Within the world of Zcash, several transaction types exist as there are also 2 types of addresses: private or 'z-addresses' and transparent or 't-addresses'. As you might have guessed, a z-address starts with a 'z' while a t-address starts with a 't'. When a transaction takes place between 2 private addresses, the transaction is recorded but the addresses, transaction amount and the memo field are all encrypted to make sure that all this information remains private. A transaction between 2 public addresses remains completely visible when it becomes part of the blockchain. Tricky are the transactions between a public and a private address. When a transaction takes place from a private to a public address we call this a 'deshielding' transaction. The address and input remains encrypted but the receiving address and the amount are shown to the world. The reverse gets called 'shielding' and also has the reverse implications. The developers also explain the implications of this increased level of security. If you send a balance, you normally need 2 addresses for the receiver: the receiving address and an address of your own to receive the remaining balance (unless you want to send to entire amount). This because sending a balance in the blockchain world actually means sending the entire balance that you have. If you just use your sending address, this is fine but not really private as you can create an identity profile based on this. One possible action might be to change the receiving address you use for the remaining amount to obfuscate anyone trying to uncover your identity. Not really helpful, as all transactions are linked and all these new addresses will just be linked one after another. Well hello, private (or shielded) addresses! I can just reuse my original sending address, as this is encrypted on the blockchain anyway.[79] But

---

[78] https://z.cash/technology/.

[79] Peterson, P. (November 23, 2016) Anatomy of A Zcash Transaction. *Electric coin.* https://electr iccoin.co/blog/anatomy-of-zcash/. Accessed October 4, 2019.

how does it provide this security? By making use of zero-knowledge proofs. These zero-knowledge proofs can be best explained by making use of the Ali Baba's Cave Parable put forward by Jean-Jacques QuisQuater (and others). In essence the story goes that two people, A and B stand in a ring-shaped cave with a door locking the end of the cave. B claims to know the secret to opening the door but does not wish to share this secret with A. Together they decide that A can choose which path B should take, and only if B comes out on the other side, it is proven that B actually knows the secret.

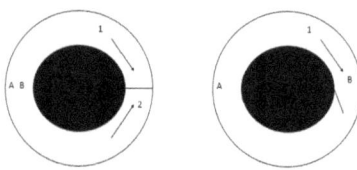

Ali Baba's cave

3.36.1 Zk-SNARKs

Zcash makes use of something called 'zk-SNARKs' or 'Zero-Knowledge Succint Non-Interactive Argument of Knowledge' (so let's just keep saying zk-SNARKs). This is a form of cryptography where the prover can provide a proof of knowledge without actually revealing that knowledge AND without interaction between prover and verifier. This means that there is only a single message sent from prover to verifier. Currently the most efficient way to achieve this is by making use of an initial setup where a common reference string, created with secret randomness, is shared between prover and verifier. If one could get access to the secret randomness to generate these parameters, one could attack the entire network and start creating counterfeit coins. Zcash went to extreme lengths to prevent this from happening. There was a multi-party ceremony with participants taking part so that the knowledge was well-spread and at afterwards some of the computers were even blowtorched! To start there is the creation of a public key—private key set with several participants in the multi-party ceremony. The reason behind this is that the private key linked to the public key needs to be destroyed. Otherwise this would allow the participants to create counterfeit coins.[80] Because Zcash makes use of a multi-party process, all the participants their secret randomness is concatenated so that the private key will be destroyed unless all participants act maliciously. The final aspect we need to complete the process is the function that can actually determine whether a transaction is actually valid without revealing the secret information. Therefore, some of the Zcash network rules are encoded in the zk-SNARKs. 'Succint' means that this proof is smaller

---

[80] Gabizon, A. (September 25, 2016) Zcash Parameters and how they will be generated. *Electric coin.* https://electriccoin.co/blog/generating-zcash-parameters. Accessed November 11, 2019.

and can be faster verified. Next there is the 'arguments' part of SNARKs which means that a malicious actor only has a very low probability of cheating the system because he has a limited amount of computing power. This might become a problem in the future of course with the rise of quantum computing. Finally there is the 'knowledge' which means that without the knowledge of the secret, the prover cannot create the proof. Now how does the algorithm actually work? The transaction validity function must be broken down to the lowest level, the arithmetic circuit where you can find single steps such as AND, OR and NOT.

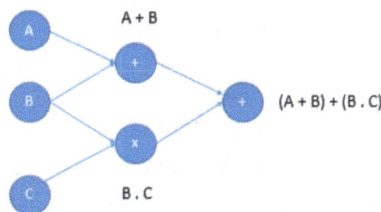

Arithmetic circuit

Based on the outcome of these steps within the circuit, you come to what is called a 'Rank 1 Constraint System' or 'R1CS'. This representation makes sure that all parameters have followed the correct path to the outcome. The verifier has a heavy computational task of checking the outcome of each of these paths. With Quadratic Arithmetic Program or QAP[81] this has been reduced to 1 computation of a polynomial. This in itself is again a great computational task but the verifying itself isn't that difficult. If an attacker were to generate a fake polynomial but doesn't know the right identity, the polynomial will fail almost every point, so that only 1 point needs to be checked to verify the proof with a high probability. Below we will give a short description of how the process actually functions and what we can find under the hood when we talk about zk-SNARKs. In essence, it comes down to 'homomorphic hiding' functions.[82] They are similar to computational hiding commitments with that difference that hiding functions are deterministic functions of the input while commitments use additional randomness. For these HH's we have the following properties:

- When $E(x)$, it is hard to find x
- For $x \neq y \implies E(x) \neq E(y)$
- If we know $E(x)$ and $E(y)$, we can perform operations such as $E(x + y)$

[81] Gennaro, R., Gentry, C., Parno, B. and Raykova, M. (2012) Quadratic Span Programs and Succinct NIZKs withpout PCPs. *IBM T.J. Watson Research Center.* https://eprint.iacr.org/2012/215.pdf. Accessed November 11, 2019.

[82] Gabizon, A. (February 28, 2017) Explaining SNARKs. *Electric coin* https://electriccoin.co/blog/snark-explain. Accessed on December 3, 2019.

These expressions are used on a finite group $\mathbb{Z}^*_p$ instead of integers with the following properties:

- There is a generator g so that all elements of $\mathbb{Z}^*_p$ can be written as g^a for some a in $\{0, ..., p - 2\}$ (cyclic group)
- With a large p, it is hard to find the integer a so that $g^a = h \pmod p$ (discrete logarithm problem)
- For a, b in $\{0, ..., p - 2\}$ $g^a \cdot g^b = g^{a + b \pmod{p - 1}}$.

From these properties one can know that $E(x + y) = g^{x + y \bmod (p - 1)} = g^x \cdot g^y = E(x) \cdot E(y)$ or similarly that $E(ax + by) = (g^x)^a \cdot (g^y)^b = E(x)^a \cdot E(y)^b$.

Next, we have the polynomial P of degree d over a finite field F_p which is of the form $P(x) = a_0 + a_1 \cdot x + a_2 \cdot x^2 + \cdots + a_d \cdot x^d$ for $a_0, ..., a_d \in F_p$.

This polynomial can be evaluated for a point $s \in F_p$ where x is replaced by s.

Now we combine the principles of homomorphic hiding and the polynomial so that we can perform blind evaluation.[83] For 2 participants A and B, one knows the polynomial P while the other wants to learn E(P(s)) for a certain point s. However, the participants do not wish to share either P or s. This is solved by participant A sending $E(1), ..., E(s^d)$ to participant B who replies with E(P(s)). This way no one learns the true value from the other participant. The next logical step in the process is forcing participant B to actually reply with the truthful answer from his polynomial calculation. In this process we make us of the knowledge of coefficient test or 'KC' test. The generator g we defined before becomes the generator of a group G with order $|G| = p$.[84] We also define $\alpha \in F^*_p$ where α is a pair (a, b) in G and a, b $\neq$ 0 and b = $\alpha \cdot$ a

The KC test:

- A computes b = $\alpha \cdot$ a and chooses at random a $\in$ G
- A sends B (a, b)
- B responds with (a', b') which is also an α-pair
- A checks and accepts in case this is true.

The response by B can only be calculated by choosing a $\gamma \in F^*_p$ so that (a', b') = ($\gamma \cdot$ a, $\gamma \cdot$ b) so that b' = $\gamma \cdot$ b = $\gamma\alpha \cdot$ a = $\alpha(\gamma \cdot$ a) = $\alpha \cdot$ a' and therefore is an α-pair. The KCA or Knowledge of Coefficient Assumption states that this final statement is always the case. This sounds fine for 1 α-pair while there are multiple of these pairs being send out. It is up to the receiver to use these α-pairs together to create a new one following these properties:

[83] Gabizon, A. (February 28, 2017) Explaining SNARKs. *Electric coin* https://electriccoin.co/blog/snark-explain2. Accessed on December 3, 2019.

[84] Gabizon, A. (February 28, 2017) Explaining SNARKs. *Electric coin* https://electriccoin.co/blog/snark-explain3. Accessed on December 3, 2019.

$$c_1, \ldots, c_d \in F_p \text{ and} (a', b') = \left(\sum_{i=1}^{d} c_i a_i, \sum_{i=1}^{d} c_i b_i \right) \Rightarrow a' = \sum_{i=1}^{d} c_i . a_i$$

From which we can create the d-power KCA[85] in G where participant A chooses a set of α-pairs with a polynomial structure $\alpha \in F^*_p$, $s \in F_p$ and sends participant B the α-pairs $(g, \alpha . g), (s . g, \alpha s . g), \ldots, (s^d . g, \alpha s^d . g)$. Participant B knows $c_0, \ldots, c_d \in F_p$ (with a certain high probability) and then responds with $a' = \sum_{i=0}^{d} c_i s^i . g$.

To reduce the calculations we have to do over the arithmetic circuit, we make use of QAPs (as we mentioned before). For a strongly reduced explanation below (find an excellent explanation by Ariel Gabizon on electriccoin.co), you can look at the image below.

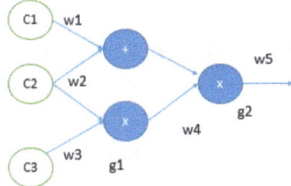

Participant B wants to proof he knows the inputs C_1, C_2 and $C_3 \in F_p$ and that these lead to a certain outcome when combined. We make use of the arithmetic circuit to proof the outcome. In the image, the first set of wires are 'the input wires' and the final wire 'the output wire'. Furthermore, if we would like to translate to a QAP the following properties hold:

- If an outgoing wire goes to more than 1 gate, we still see it as 1 wire (w_2)
- Multiplication gates have exactly 2 input wires (left and right)
- The addition gate and wires going from addition to multiplication gate aren't named.

The multiplication gates are associated with a field element g_x associated with a target point $\in F_p$ and we will also define a set of left wire polynomials ($L_1, \ldots, L_d$), right wire polynomials ($R_1, \ldots, R_d$) and outgoing wire polynomials ($O_1, \ldots, O_d$). These polynomials will usually be 0 on the target points, except for those involved in the target's point corresponding multiplication gate.[86]

When we start from fixed values $c_1, \ldots, c_a \Rightarrow L := \sum_{i=1}^{a} c_i . L_i, R := \sum_{i=1}^{a} c_i . R_i$ and $O := \sum_{i=1}^{a} c_i . O_i$.

From this we can define the polynomial $P := L . R - O$

[85] Groth, J. (October 26, 2010) Short Pairing-based Non-interactive Zero-knowledge Arguments. *University College London.* http://www0.cs.ucl.ac.uk/staff/J.Groth/ShortNIZK.pdf. Accessed October 1, 2019.

[86] Gabizon, A. (February 28, 2017) Explaining SNARKs. *Electric coin* https://electriccoin.co/blog/snark-explain5. Accessed on December 3, 2019.

We can state that c_1, ..., c_a is legal assignment if and only if P vanishes over all the target points. For this to work out there must be a target polynomial T that divides P. This is where QAP comes in as a QAP of degree d and size m consists of polynomials L_1, ..., L_d, R_1, ..., R_d, O_1, ..., O_d and a target polynomial T of degree d. The QAP can only hold if $L = \sum_{i=1}^{a} c_i.L_i, R = \sum_{i=1}^{a} c_i.R_i, O = \sum_{i=1}^{a} c_i.O_i, P = L.R - O$ and T divides P. This all comes together in the Pinocchio protocol. The steps before only gets us to B providing the proof over the right degree of polynomial but doesn't force B yet to use the correct assignment c_1, ..., c_a. For each $i \in \{1, ..., a\}$ we create the polynomial $F_i = L_i + X^{d+1} . R_i + X^{2(d+1)} . O_i$ where we need to use X^{d+1} and $X^{2(d+1)}$ because we cannot mix the coefficient L, R or O in F. Therefore coefficient 1, X, ..., X^d are the coefficients of L, the next $d + 1$ coefficients X^{d+1}, ..., X^{2d+1} are the coefficients of R and the last $d + 1$ coefficients are those of O. With QAP we learn that $F = \sum_{i=1}^{a} c_i.F_i, L = \sum_{i=1}^{a} c_i.L_i, R = \sum_{i=1}^{a} c_i.R_i$ and $O = \sum_{i=1}^{a} c_i.O_i$ for the same coefficients c_1, ..., c_a and if F is a linear combination of the produced F_i's, we know that these were produced from the same coefficients. Again, we have to apply the homomorphic hiding functions when we want to know how zk-SNARKs function. Participant A sends a set of hidings $E(\beta . F_1(s))$, ..., $E(\beta . F_d(s))$ to participant B and asks B to produce the hiding outcome of the assignment $E(\beta . F(s))$. Problem is that participant A could try to deduce information of the hidden L, R, O and T by applying a set of coefficients $(c_1, ..., c_d)$, discovering whether the hidden L, R, T and O he produces match or not and when this is not the case, he knows this is not participants B coefficients set. To prevent this, there is a random T-shift to each polynomial applied by participant B.[87] Now we need two more steps to complete the entire protocol: we need a homomorphic hiding function that supports both addition and multiplication and we need to shift from an interactive system to a non-interactive system. For this to happen, we need to apply elliptic curves. You can find the explanation on elliptic curve cryptography in the chapter on 'technologies to understand'. This is combined with something called 'Optimal Ate Pairing'. By combining these 2 techniques, we arrive at a situation where we actually can compute the multiplication hidings based on the correct hidings of two other elements (an in-depth explanation would lead us too far from the description here). To allow for the non-interactive part, we make use of the common reference string or CRS. So first, before any communication takes place between the parties, the CRS $(E_1(1), E_1(s), ..., E_1(s^d), (E_1(1), E_1(s), ..., E_1(s^d), E_2(\alpha), E_2(\alpha s), ..., E_2(\alpha s^d)) E_2(\alpha), E_2(\alpha s), ..., E_2(\alpha s^d))$ is published which is based on random data. These elements are hence used to help compute the a set (a, b) based on a random chosen $s \in F_p$ and $\alpha \in F^{*}_p$.[88] Verification follows by the other participant who verifies that $E(\alpha x) = Tate(E_1(x), E_1(\alpha)) E(\alpha x) = Tate(E_1(x), E_2(\alpha))$ and $E(y) = Tate(E_1(1), E_1(y))$ from x, y $\in F_r$ so that $a = E_1(x)$ and $b = E_2(y)$.

[87] Gabizon, A. (February 28, 2017) Explaining SNARKs. *Electric coin* https://electriccoin.co/blog/snark-explain6. Accessed on December 3, 2019.

[88] Gabizon, A. (February 28, 2017) Explaining SNARKs. *Electric coin* https://electriccoin.co/blog/snark-explain7. Accessed on December 3, 2019.

3.36.2 Zk-STARKs

Future implementations of cryptocurrencies wishing to preserve privacy might make use of a new implementation called 'zk-STARKs' which refers to 'Zero-Knowledge Scalable Transparent Arguments of Knowledge' and can act as a faster and cheaper alternative to zk-SNARKs. Zk-STARKs remove the need for the initial trusted setup and also remove the computation difficulty (and the linked theoretical quantum computer attacks). Finally, the time needed to compute the outcomes of zk-SNARKs should be improved to further improve scalability of the network.[89] StarkWare industries is the first one to try and develop an industry ready implementation of this new way of working. In broad terms, STARK makes use of arithmetization. It is the reduction of the problem of verifying a computation to the problem of checking that a certain polynomial, which can be evaluated efficiently on the verifier's side, which is the succinctly part, is of low degree. The arithmetization used in zk-STARKs is composed of 2 steps: generating an execution trace and polynomial constraints, after which these are transformed in a single low-degree polynomial. The prover and verifier agree in advance on what the polynomial constraints are in advance so that, when the prover generates the execution trace, the prover can convince the verifier that the constraints have been satisfied without actually showing the execution trace. It makes use of Collatz conjecture to create a Collatz sequence execution tree which leads to the polynomial constraints. Starkware, together with 0x, has come up with StarkDEX which allows the creation of decentralized exchanges on top of the Ethereum blockchain with a higher throughput of trades compared to other current solutions and an improvement in the use of gas.

3.37 Ordinals and On-Chain Inscriptions

A striking new development in Bitcoin's evolution emerged in early 2023 with the rise of Ordinals and on-chain inscriptions, a phenomenon that has redefined how data can be stored and interacted with directly on Bitcoin's base layer. Traditionally viewed solely as a peer-to-peer currency or store of value, Bitcoin has now, somewhat unexpectedly, become a home for digital artifacts, including Bitcoin-native NFTs. This shift began with the launch of the Ordinals protocol by developer Casey Rodarmor in January 2023.[90] Built atop the technical groundwork laid by the Taproot upgrade, Ordinals introduced a novel way to embed arbitrary data (images, text, videos, and more) into individual satoshis, the smallest unit of Bitcoin. Unlike previous Bitcoin NFT attempts, which relied on Layer-2

---

[89] Ben-Sasson, E., Bentov, I., Hresh, Y. and Riabzev, M. (March 6, 2018) Scalable, transparent, and post-quantum secure computational integrity. *Israel Institute of Technology*. https://eprint.iacr.org/2018/046.pdf. Accessed November 23, 2019.

[90] https://chain.link/education-hub/ordinals-bitcoin-nfts#:~:text=videos%2C%20and%20more%20to%20an,on%20the%20base%20Bitcoin%20blockchain.

protocols or sidechains, Ordinals operate natively on Bitcoin's base layer, using a clever method to insert data directly into the witness fields of Taproot transactions. These witness fields, enabled by SegWit and expanded by Taproot, allow for large data payloads without bloating the core transaction logic or breaking consensus rules. Taproot's key contribution to this functionality was the removal of hard limits on witness data size per transaction, effectively opening the door for larger and more flexible data insertions. This architectural shift meant that a single satoshi could now carry a uniquely inscribed payload (an image, poem, or code snippet) thereby transforming it into a digital artifact with collectible or artistic value. In practice, this meant that Bitcoin users could now "mint" NFTs directly on-chain, without leaving the main Bitcoin network or relying on external smart contract platforms like Ethereum. The response to Ordinals was explosive. Within the first few months, over 200,000 inscriptions were created. By the end of 2023, that number had surged into the tens of millions, sparking a wave of creative experimentation and financial speculation. This surge in inscriptions had a measurable impact on the network itself: average Bitcoin block sizes climbed well above 1 MB, reaching some of the largest sizes ever recorded. Taproot usage hit all-time highs, driven by the massive influx of Ordinals transactions that leveraged its advanced scripting capabilities. However, this new use case has not been without controversy. The influx of Ordinals transactions has led to significantly fuller blocks and rising transaction fees, which some see as a healthy development, increasing miner revenue and giving Bitcoin a more sustainable long-term fee market. Others, however, have raised concerns about blockspace congestion, the storage burden on full nodes, and the philosophical implications of turning Bitcoin into a medium for NFTs and digital art. Critics argue that this activity constitutes "spam" that dilutes Bitcoin's original purpose as sound money and clutters the blockchain with non-financial data. This has sparked intense debate within the Bitcoin community. Some developers and maximalists see Ordinals as a misuse of blockspace, advocating for limits or filtering mechanisms. Others embrace the open nature of Bitcoin's protocol, arguing that as long as users pay fees, they should be free to inscribe whatever data they wish. This tension underscores deeper questions about Bitcoin's identity and future: is it strictly a monetary protocol, or is it a neutral, programmable ledger with space for broader digital expression?

3.38 Ongoing Technical Trends and Changes

Bitcoin's scalability constraints remain a defining aspect of its technical architecture. With a base-layer throughput of approximately seven transactions per second, constrained by the 1 MB block size (or 4 million weight units under SegWit), Bitcoin's on-chain capacity is deliberately limited to preserve decentralization and validate transactions efficiently on modest hardware.[91] The protocol's scaling roadmap has largely shifted toward

---

[91] https://bitcoinmagazine.com/takes/my-top-3-takeaways-from-fidelity-and-voltages-recent-lightning-report#:~:text=,1%20seconds.

off-chain and second-layer solutions rather than increasing base-layer throughput. The Lightning Network (LN) represents the most mature expression of this approach, offering a mechanism for executing high-speed, low-cost transactions off-chain. Since its early deployment, LN has seen substantial growth, particularly in enabling microtransactions and instant payments. By routing transactions through payment channels and settling only the net outcomes on-chain, Lightning significantly alleviates pressure on base-layer bandwidth. More recent advances in the LN ecosystem, such as multi-path payments and experimental channel constructions like channel factories, aim to improve liquidity management and allow multi-party coordination with fewer on-chain commitments. Parallel to Lightning, newer architectures are emerging such as Ark. It proposes a novel Layer 2 model based on virtual UTXOs and coordinated batch transactions via service providers. Though still in early development, Ark performs a push toward abstracting channel management and simplifying user experience while retaining the trustless properties central to Bitcoin's ethos. Another noteworthy development is Fedimints, which fuse federated custody with Lightning payments through Chaumian e-cash protocols. These arrangements enable community-level custody models with enhanced privacy, allowing users to benefit from both custodial efficiency and off-chain scalability. Bitcoin's core protocol development maintains a conservative posture toward increasing block sizes or making invasive changes to base-layer throughput. Instead, incremental improvements—such as package relay in the mempool and optimized transaction propagation—are designed to maximize utilization of existing block space. This conservatism reflects a foundational design goal: to ensure that full nodes remain accessible, reinforcing decentralization and verifiability even as demand on the network grows.

Bitcoin's scripting capabilities, though deliberately limited compared to platforms like Ethereum, continue to evolve through incremental improvements and Layer 2 innovation.[92] The activation of Taproot in 2021 marked a significant enhancement by introducing MAST (Merkelized Abstract Syntax Trees) and enabling Schnorr signatures, both of which expand Bitcoin's expressive potential without increasing complexity at the base layer. These features have already facilitated more efficient multi-signature schemes and enabled the practical deployment of Discrete Log Contracts (DLCs). DLCs, a form of financial smart contract that relies on external oracles, have gained adoption in use cases such as prediction markets and binary bets, leveraging Taproot's privacy and efficiency gains to execute contracts with minimal on-chain footprint. Beyond Taproot, several proposals are under active discussion. Simplicity, a formal verification-friendly scripting language proposed by Blockstream, aims to provide a powerful but safe alternative to Bitcoin Script. Simplicity could enable more expressive contracts without increasing the attack surface of the core protocol. Meanwhile, Taro, developed by Lightning Labs, offers a mechanism to issue assets on Bitcoin through Taproot-based commitments. This design allows stablecoins or other tokens to be transacted over Lightning,

---

[92] https://www.deltecbank.com/news-and-insights/bitcoins-taproot-upgrade/#:~:text=Bitcoin%27s%20Taproot%20Upgrade%20,functionality%2C%20and%20other%20privacy%20increases.

extending Bitcoin's utility in the domain of digital assets. Drivechains (proposed via BIPs 300/301) also continue to stimulate debate. These would allow Bitcoin to interoperate with sidechains—independent blockchains that peg-in to Bitcoin's security model— thus expanding programmability without altering the main chain. While not yet active, such mechanisms remain part of the broader conversation on whether and how Bitcoin can safely accommodate more complex application layers. Bitcoin does not prioritize general-purpose programmability on its base layer, the ecosystem is gradually expanding through carefully vetted enhancements, second layers, and opt-in protocols. This ensures the platform remains secure and robust while supporting a limited but growing set of programmable applications.

Privacy in Bitcoin remains an important and actively researched area. While the protocol is pseudonymous by design, base-layer transactions are fully transparent, and the rise of chain surveillance has amplified awareness of this limitation.[93] The introduction of Taproot offered modest privacy gains by making complex spending conditions indistinguishable from standard payments until spent. Combined with Schnorr signatures, this enables signature aggregation techniques such as MuSig2, reducing the footprint of multiparty transactions and enhancing privacy by minimizing distinguishable patterns on-chain. At the application layer, privacy-enhancing techniques such as CoinJoin, PayJoin, and Whirlpool have gained traction in user wallets since 2020. These approaches allow users to obfuscate transaction origins and ownership, although they require active participation and do not provide default privacy. Ongoing protocol-level research includes proposals like cross-input signature aggregation, which would significantly reduce the cost and visibility of CoinJoin-style transactions, and adapter signatures, which facilitate trustless atomic swaps with privacy-preserving properties. Other ideas under exploration include CoinSwap, which allows transaction participants to swap UTXOs in a non-linkable way, and new privacy-focused opcodes. None of these have been deployed as of 2025, but they represent active areas of research and prototyping. It is worth mentioning that privacy on Bitcoin today remains opt-in rather than built-in. While second layers like Lightning offer improved privacy by keeping transactions off-chain, base-layer anonymity continues to face both technical and cultural challenges. Any future privacy improvements will need to be compatible with Bitcoin's backward-compatible soft-fork upgrade path and subject to extensive community review.

Decentralization remains a cornerstone of Bitcoin's design and community ethos. On the mining side, the geographic distribution of hash rate has improved since regulatory changes in China pushed miners to relocate across North America, Europe, and Central Asia. Mining pools such as Foundry USA and Antpool continue to command a significant share of total hash rate, prompting ongoing discussions about the role of Stratum

---

[93] https://www.coinbase.com/learn/crypto-glossary/what-is-the-bitcoin-taproot-upgrade-and-why-is-it-important#:~:text=How%20Taproot%20Benefits%20Bitcoin.

V2.[94] This protocol upgrade allows individual miners within a pool to construct their own block templates, potentially reducing the centralizing influence of pool operators. From a network perspective, running a full node remains feasible on consumer-grade hardware. Despite growth in blockchain size and increased average block weights—driven in part by Ordinals and inscription activity—tools like pruned nodes and efficiency improvements in software clients help mitigate storage burdens. The decision to limit block size remains integral to Bitcoin's decentralization model, ensuring that participation in consensus does not require enterprise infrastructure. Bitcoin governance continues to follow a decentralized, open-source model based on rough consensus and wide review. The departure of long-time maintainer Wladimir van der Laan in 2022 marked a symbolic transition, but the development process remains resilient, with core contributors supported through grants from multiple independent organizations. The activations of SegWit (2017) and Taproot (2021), both of which relied on miner and node signaling, demonstrate how the community uses coordination mechanisms like BIP signaling and user-activated soft forks (UASF) to implement protocol changes when broad support emerges. Proposals such as BIP-119 (OP_CHECKTEMPLATEVERIFY) in 2022 sparked renewed interest in how consensus is reached and how features are introduced in a system where centralized decision-making is intentionally absent. While slow and conservative by design, Bitcoin's development process reflects a strong commitment to stability, decentralization, and backward compatibility—values that are essential for its long-term resilience and trustworthiness.

3.39   Bitcoin Core and BIP Developments

The most consequential protocol upgrade in recent years was the activation of Taproot, integrated into Bitcoin Core v22.0 and formally adopted via a series of BIPs: BIP-340 (Schnorr signatures), BIP-341 (Taproot), and BIP-342 (Tapscript). Together, these BIPs form a unified enhancement to Bitcoin's scripting and signature system.[95] BIP-340 introduces Schnorr signatures, replacing the ECDSA signature scheme for Taproot-spending outputs. Schnorr's mathematical properties enable linear aggregation, which is critical for threshold signature schemes (e.g., MuSig2), improving both privacy and efficiency in multi-party transactions. BIP-341, which defines the Taproot construction itself, enables the encapsulation of complex scripts behind a single public key. These scripts remain hidden unless executed, allowing for private and flexible spending conditions without

---

[94] https://insights.glassnode.com/ordinal-theory-and-the-rise-of-inscriptions/#:~:text=The%20c hart%20below%20shows%20how,following%20the%20SegWit%20soft%20fork.

[95] https://www.coinbase.com/learn/crypto-glossary/what-is-the-bitcoin-taproot-upgrade-and-why-is-it-important#:~:text=The%20Taproot%20upgrade%20encompasses%20three,capabilities%20of%20the%20Bitcoin%20network.

compromising verification integrity. This upgrade significantly reduces the on-chain foot-print of sophisticated contract logic. BIP-342 (Tapscript) complements these changes by updating Bitcoin's script evaluation semantics. It introduces new opcodes and modifies signature checking logic to support the expanded capabilities of Taproot and Schnorr, paving the way for future extensibility without requiring further consensus upgrades.

These enhancements collectively mark a meaningful evolution in Bitcoin's scripting model: enabling more expressive contracts with minimal impact on node performance or security. BIP-350 introduced the Bech32m address encoding standard to support Taproot addresses. This change corrects a subtle checksum mismatch issue in the original Bech32 format when applied to newer witness versions. Wallets, exchanges, and hardware signing devices have adopted Bech32m as the standard for SegWit v1 (Taproot) outputs, ensuring compatibility and usability across the Bitcoin ecosystem. From versions 0.21 through 25, Bitcoin Core has steadily introduced a suite of low-level networking and performance enhancements. These include:

- Compact Block Relay v2, improving block propagation efficiency through better transaction prefill mechanisms.
- Support for Tor v3 addresses (via BIP-155), modernizing peer connectivity in line with privacy-respecting network architectures.
- Preliminary support for P2P encryption (BIP-324, still under discussion), which proposes transport-level encryption of peer-to-peer messages to mitigate metadata leakage and traffic analysis.

These changes, though less visible to the end user, are vital to preserving Bitcoin's robustness under adversarial conditions and ensuring that its full node architecture remains secure and performant. Infrastructure-oriented improvements like Output Descriptors and the AssumeUTXO framework are now integrated or in late-stage testing. Output Descriptors offer a standard method for describing script types in wallets, enhancing interoperability and code clarity. AssumeUTXO allows new nodes to bootstrap by importing pre-validated UTXO snapshots, substantially reducing the time to sync with the active chain without compromising trust assumptions. While many enhancements have been implemented, the Bitcoin community continues to explore further changes through a deliberative and peer-reviewed BIP process. Several proposals are of particular relevance in 2025:

- BIP-118 (SIGHASH_ANYPREVOUT) proposes a new sighash flag enabling more flexible transaction replacement—critical for enabling Eltoo, a streamlined Lightning channel update mechanism that minimizes the penalty model and simplifies channel state management.
- BIP-119 (OP_CHECKTEMPLATEVERIFY or CTV) introduces a covenant-based opcode that enables restrictions on how outputs can be spent. Though it saw extensive

community debate in 2022, CTV remains under discussion as a potential primitive for vault constructions, congestion control, and batched payments. Its inclusion in this text contextualizes an important shift in how Bitcoin might support more structured transaction flows without general-purpose programmability.

- BIP-324, as mentioned, continues to be refined for deployment as a privacy enhancement in the P2P layer.
- BIP-156 (Dandelion Relay), although not yet implemented, deserves brief mention as a promising mechanism to obscure transaction origination by routing broadcasts through an anonymizing stem-and-fluff relay system.
- Other minor but cumulative changes (e.g., BIP-147, a malleability fix related to scriptSig modifications) highlight the ongoing maintenance of Bitcoin's protocol-level invariants and compatibility guarantees.

3.40   Zcash and HAWK

HAWK continues on the ideas of privacy and protection of personal information with a blockchain-based smart contract system that stores encrypted transaction on the blockchain itself. It is being promoted by students and faculty staff at Cornell University and the University of Maryland. The goal of HAWK is to allow non-technical people to create privacy preserving systems without having to know the details of cryptography.[96] The program is split in 2 parts: private and public. The private portion of HAWK is actually responsible for the encryption of the data while the public portion doesn't come into contact with the actual data.

3.41   Hard Forks

This is only a limited overview of the hard forks that have happened or are planned. There were also so many in the past that failed to reach their target or simply never gained any support. Over the years there have been over 105 fork projects.[97] There was during the heights of the crypto-craze a whole set of attempts to fork Bitcoin which included: Super Bitcoin, Bitcoin Platinum, Bitcoin Uranium, Bitcoin Cash Plus, Bitcoin Silver, Bitcoin Diamond and so on. Some crypto coins are already forks based on forks (such as Bitcoin stash which is a working fork of Bitcoin cash). I chose to list here some of the more significant changes that happened in the past while a hard/soft fork was still something considerable. Others in the future might still be considerable and might have significant

---

[96] Kosba, A., Miller, A., Shi, E., Wen, Z. and Papamanthou, C. (2015) Hawk: the blockchain model of cryptography and privacy-preserving smart contracts. *University of Maryland.* https://eprint.iacr. org/2015/675.pdf. Accessed November 23, 2019.

[97] https://forkdrop.io/how-many-bitcoin-forks-are-there.

impact on the network and the community. If you would like to go into detail in all the Bitcoin forks, be my guest. I am certain it will be an interesting journey although I am not sure where your journey will end. Each of the forks over time wanted to achieve something specific, to change something inherent to the Bitcoin protocol as it existed. Some of the forks focused on privacy, others on the transaction speed and still others on the block size and/or transaction costs. Another famous one developers like to focus on is the limited supply of Bitcoin. Either way, some of these were successful, or even more successful (up to your personal opinion) than the original Bitcoin release, others were doomed almost from the start.

3.42   Bitcoin XT

One of the first (software) hard forks of the Bitcoin network was Bitcoin XT.[98] Its software was created by Mike Hearn in 2014 so that several new features could be included. It increased the number of transactions from 7 to 24 a second and increased the block size significantly to 8 Mb. The first proposal was released as BIP 64, so at first it was considered as a change proposal for the original Bitcoin network. BIP 64 called for a small P2P protocol extension that performs UTXO lookups given a set of outpoints. The first release of Bitcoin XT (version 0.10) included this change. Following the first release, some other changes were added to the protocol. Gavin Andresen published BIP 101 to call upon the increase in size of the Bitcoin blocks. This was implemented in Bitcoin XT on the 6th of August 2015 but eventually reverted, and made place for the 2 MB-blocks that are also supported under the Bitcoin Classic protocol. While it had some initial success, Bitcoin XT was mostly abandoned by the end of 2015. Since August 2017, Bitcoin XT is a Bitcoin Cash client by default since release G.[99] For each of the Bitcoin Cash upgrades, there have been subsequent Bitcoin XT upgrades to keep on supporting the network (respectively called releases H and I).

3.43   Bitcoin Classic

After the failure of Bitcoin XT, some of the community still supported some of the ideas behind this hard fork. Bitcoin classic proposed to increase the block size to only 2 MB instead of any bigger block size.[100] Very similar to Bitcoin XT, this was a software hard fork and was building on top of the Bitcoin Core reference client. The fork was less aggressive as Bitcoin XT and therefore was able to gain a level of support that remained

---

[98] Reiff, N. (June 25, 2019) A history of Bitcoin hard forks. *Investopedia.* https://www.investopedia.com/tech/history-bitcoin-hard-forks/.

[99] https://github.com/bitcoinxt/bitcoinxt/releases.

[100] https://bitcoinclassic.com/devel/blocksize.html.

for a certain time. After a while the control over the block size was put in the hands of the miners and the nodes.[101] Ultimately, on the 10th of November 2017 Bitcoin Classic ceased operations after the New York agreement failed which also had as aim to increase the block size of the 'Legacy Bitcoin chain' as it was called by Bitcoin Classic.[102] In the ending notes, you can clearly read that the developers call Bitcoin Cash 'the last hope' for Bitcoin scalability and direct all their supporters in this direction.

3.44   Bitcoin Unlimited

The difference within this hard fork was that it would allow nodes and miners to decide for themselves what the size of their blocks would be and this without restarting the node or compiling new executables.[103] It was also the first implementation that allowed for Xthin (Xtreme thin blocks) where the inefficiency of receiving the same transaction twice or more is fixed. On top of that the client allowed for parallel validation so that nodes can validate more than one block. It presents itself as not being a 'hard fork' but rather a new form of consensus mechanism to allow change throughout the Bitcoin network based on a democratic voting system. Emergent consensus is introduced so that underlying incentive mechanisms might help consolidate a consensus on block size between minders, users, companies, wallets and holders. Nodes also have the possibility to set an excessive block size (EB) and acceptance depth (AD) to enable them to delay the acceptance of extra-large blocks from miners by orphaning their blocks until they have reached a certain depth in the blockchain. There was some interest in the implementation but eventually also this hard fork lost interest of the community. However, since version 1.1.0.0 the Bitcoin Unlimited client is compatible with the Bitcoin Cash client. There is still support for this hard fork and it has a steady community but time will tell if this currency will stand the test of time.

3.45   Bitcoin Cash

Bitcoin Cash or Bcash was the most successful hard fork of the Bitcoin network to date.[104] It was a response to the SegWit update because a part of the community refused to work with the updates of SegWit. They felt that certain changes, also introduced by BIP91 would favor those that saw Bitcoin as an investment mechanism rather than a means of payment. To this day, these differences can be seen in the setup of the Bitcoin network

---

[101] Zander, T. (November 30, 2016) Classic is back. https://web.archive.org/web/20170202055402/https://zander.github.io/posts/Classic%20is%20Back/.

[102] https://bitcoinclassic.com/news/closing.html.

[103] https://www.bitcoinunlimited.info/.

[104] https://www.bitcoincash.org/.

(which favor smaller blocks and see it mainly as a store of value) and the community supporting Bitcoin cash, which support it as a means of payment. The Bitcoin network was around this period (mid 2017) also dealing with rising transaction costs which further pressured the Bitcoin community. Eventually a group proposed a hard fork that would try to deal with all of these pain points.This protocol allows blocks of 8 megabytes, it comes with low fees and fast transaction times. They also promise reliable confirmations, which make the use of the coin much more scalable. More functionalities are on its way as there is a focus on faster block propagation, UTXO commitments, Schnorr signatures and more. The opcode OP_CHECKDATASIG is already available allowing for oracles and advanced scripts within the network. There is still a certain competition with the original Bitcoin network to implement some of these features faster, to proof that one of them is the 'true' future of Bitcoin in the long run. The hard fork was created in August 2017 and has achieved a huge market cap.

3.46   Bitcoin SV

Within the camp of Bitcoin Cash there was a further division between 2 main camps. The first camp, which was supported by Roger Ver and Johan WU promoted a software entitled Bitcoin Adjustable Blocksize Cap (bitcoin ABC) which aimed at keeping the block size at 32 MB. A second camp was led by Craig Steven Wright and Calvin Ayre wanted a software called Bitcoin Satoshi's Vision (Bitcoin SV) that would increase the block size to 128 MB.[105] They have a clear view on what they believe the vision of Satoshi Nakamoto was and aim to bring back certain aspects such as the opcode OP_ RETURN. All of this to create a scalable solution that has a big block size. As always, only time will tell of their success.

3.47   Bitcoin Gold

A second hard fork after the SegWit update (and following Bitcoin Cash) followed in October 2017. The main goal of the creators was to return to mining with GPU's against the current development of too specialized hardware. An interesting feature created by the developers was a so-called 'post-mine' of 100,000 coins which were placed in an endowment to finance further development of this fork. Another difference with Bitcoin is its proof of work algorithm.[106] Several attacks have taken place on the coin with a major DDOS attack at the launch of the currency on the website, but later on (in May 2018) there was also a 51% hashing attack where 338,000 BTG were stolen with a value

---

[105] https://bitcoinsv.io/.

[106] https://bitcoingold.org/.

at the time of about 18 million US dollars.[107] It still knows market success despite the setbacks it has had in the past.

3.48   Bitcoin Diamond

Bitcoin diamond launched in November 2017 and they promise faster transaction times at about 2–7 transactions per second being processed. On top of that, they offer lower transaction fees and want to encourage new users by lower prices of their cryptocoin.[108] There is, opposed to most other forks from Bitcoin, a higher cap on the total amount of cryptocurrency that can be mined. Instead of 21 million, the possible total amount has increased to 210 million. It also has a block size of 8 MB and offers connectivity to the lightening network. At the time of writing, the valuation is quite low but this could change over time depending on the changes that will be introduced in the future, and as always, the popularity of the currency itself.

3.49   Bitcoin Interest

In January 2018, a new interesting fork took place that rewarded participants based on mining and holding their tokens for a certain amount of time. When mining a block, the reward is split in 1 part for the miner (13.5 BCI) and 1 part for the interest pool (3.24 BCI). You can choose to participate in a weekly or monthly interest round and receive an even share (based on your input) of the generated interest. It is one of the few projects that managed to keep a 'steady' price for the time being.[109] It has a very low valuation at the time of writing and it doesn't seem to change soon in the near future. It certainly shows how the clash between the different ideals behind Bitcoin (store of value versus a means of payment), can come to new and innovative ways of interpreting cryptocurrencies. It was also meant as a way of stabilizing the network so that market volatility could be contained as much as possible, creating a stable and trustworthy environment for everyone.

---

[107] Cimpanu, C. (September 4, 2018) Bitcoin gold delisted from major cryptocurrency exchange after refusing to pay hack damages. *Zdnet.* https://www.zdnet.com/article/bitcoin-gold-delisted-from-major-cryptocurrency-exchange-after-refusing-to-pay-hack-damages/. Accessed December 19, 2019.

[108] https://www.bitcoindiamond.org/.

[109] https://www.bitcoininterest.io/.

3.50   Bitcoin Private

In March 2018 another interesting implementation launched which was called 'Bitcoin Private' and is based on both Bitcoin and Zclassic (which in turn is a fork of Zcash). It introduces both an alternative private way of transactions (with zero knowledge proofs) and at the same time uses a proof of work algorithm that is GPU resistant.[110] By combining these techniques, its aim is to be open for the community that wishes to participate in the mining, while at the same time helping to secure the privacy of all participants. Some interesting and user friendly tools are offered to quickly test out the network and the possibilities of mining but currently there is not a very high market cap or valuation for this fork.

3.51   How to Fork Bitcoin

We have now been talking a lot about the forks that have happened in the past on the Bitcoin network, so it seems only natural that we should discuss at least high level how one would be able to fork the network. Take into account that this is only a tutorial describing the process, while in reality you should think about possible attacks on your new network, glitches, scrutiny and more. Hash power is of key importance, just as trust in what you are doing. As there are several ways of approaching this question, we will focus on the client software from Bitcoin Core. Reasons to try out the Bitcoin Core software, is because it is released under the MIT license (free of charge), there have been hundreds of developers working on it and it has because of this built-in features and security measures that could only help your own project a whole way along.[111] For the explanation below, we based ourselves on the explanation provided by Jordan Baczuk. First of all, make sure that you have an environment ready to go and install all the dependencies. To be able to start a fork, you need to start from the original code of course which you can clone from https://github.com/bitcoin/bitcoin. Baczuk suggests to put an upstream remote to pull updates later, which is not the focus of this text but for a functioning coin in a live environment, this could be interesting to think about. Based on the latest version, we will branch of the latest release (here as dummy 1.0). Finally, we make sure that we can build the project and all dependencies are installed.

- Sudo apt-get update
- Sudo apt-get install software-properties-common libssl-dev libevent-dev libboost-system-dev libboost-filesystem-dev libboost-chrono-dev libboost-test-dev libboost-thread-dev –y

---

[110] https://btcprivate.org/.
[111] Baczuk, J. (May 24, 2019) How to fork Bitcoin—Part1. *Medium*. https://medium.com/@jordan.baczuk/how-to-fork-bitcoin-part-1-397598ef7e66. Accessed on September 19, 2019.

- Sudo add-apt-repository ppa:bitcoin/bitcoin –y
- Sudo apt-get update
- Sudo apt-get install libdb4.8-dev libdb4.8++-dev -y
- Git clone https://github.com/bitcoin/bitcoin && cd bitcoin
- Git remote add upstream https://github.com/bitcoin/bitcoin
- Git checkout v0.18.1
- Git checkout –b 1.0
- ./autogen.sh
- ./configure
- Sudo make.

Now you are ready to go and start to make changes on the actual code such as renaming the project, change the address prefixes, work on message prefix bytes, RPC and P2P ports, seeds, max supply, distribution, block size and more. Do not think this is a light exercise or that this will not require much effort from your part. An example is the renaming the project to a name of your choice, because in the code there are thousands of references to bitcoin, Bitcoin or BITCOIN, which have to be replaced by the equivalents of your 'new coin'. Below you can find the proposed scripts with $NAME$ for the new name you would like to use. Be aware that the code below also changes all bitcoin urls, breaking the link to Bitcoin Core, so you will have to change these again if you want to make the documentation accurate.

- Sudo apt-get install rename-y
- Git clean –xdf
- sudo find -type f -not -path "./.git/*" -exec sed -i 's/bitcoin/$name$/g' {} +
- sudo find -type f -not -path "./.git/*" -exec sed -i 's/Bitcoin/$Name$/g' {} +
- sudo find -type f -not -path "./.git/*" -exec sed -i 's/BITCOIN/$NAME$/g' {} +
- sudo find . -iname "bitcoin*" -exec rename 's/bitcoin/$name$/' '{}' \;
- sudo find . -iname "*bitcoin*" -exec rename 's/bitcoin/$name$/' '{}' \;
- ./autogen.sh
- ./configure
- Sudo make
- sudo find -type f -not -path "./.git/*" -exec sed -i 's/$Name$* Core developers/Bitcoin Core developers/g' {} +[112]

Congratulations! You just have completed the first step in creating your own coin based on the Bitcoin Core source code. Next, we can change the address prefixes to something

---

[112] With this command you can fix licensing and copyrights but more links would have to be restored.

more suitable for our new coin. An entire list of prefixes can be found online.[113] These values can be adapted in the source file src/chainparams.cpp.

```
319        base58Prefixes[PUBKEY_ADDRESS] = std::vector<unsigned char>(1,111);
320        base58Prefixes[SCRIPT_ADDRESS] = std::vector<unsigned char>(1,196);
321        base58Prefixes[SECRET_KEY] =     std::vector<unsigned char>(1,239);
322        base58Prefixes[EXT_PUBLIC_KEY] = {0x04, 0x35, 0x87, 0xCF};
323        base58Prefixes[EXT_SECRET_KEY] = {0x04, 0x35, 0x83, 0x94};
324
325        bech32_hrp = "bcrt";
```

These values you can adapt to reflect the values you would like from the prefix table. In the same file you can adapt the network parameters so that your new network will not conflict with the Bitcoin network when your coin is going live.

```
pchMessageStart[0] = 0xf9;
pchMessageStart[1] = 0xbe;
pchMessageStart[2] = 0xb4;
pchMessageStart[3] = 0xd9;
nDefaultPort = 8333;
nPruneAfterHeight = 100000;
m_assumed_blockchain_size = 280;
m_assumed_chain_state_size = 4;
```

You should always look out for values that are already in use by other networks or that are unlikely to occur in normal data. You can make use of several sources to make sure that your choices are valid and won't generate any conflicts.[114,115] After you implemented these changes, we should always make sure we run again:

• sudo make

To adapt the RPC and P2P ports, we should look in the src/chainparamsbase.cpp and src/chainparams.cpp files. With the first example below:

---

[113] https://en.bitcoin.it/wiki/list_of_address_prefixes.

[114] https://www.utf8-chartable.de/unicode-utf8-table.pl.

[115] http://www.asciitable.com/.

```
std::unique_ptr<CBaseChainParams> CreateBaseChainParams(const std::string& chain)
{
    if (chain == CBaseChainParams::MAIN)
        return MakeUnique<CBaseChainParams>("", 8332);
    else if (chain == CBaseChainParams::TESTNET)
        return MakeUnique<CBaseChainParams>("testnet3", 18332);
    else if (chain == CBaseChainParams::REGTEST)
        return MakeUnique<CBaseChainParams>("regtest", 18443);
    else
        throw std::runtime_error(strprintf("%s: Unknown chain %s.", __func__, chain));
}
```

And the second example:

```
99          pchMessageStart[2] = 0xb4;
100         pchMessageStart[3] = 0xd9;
101         nDefaultPort = 8333;
102         nPruneAfterHeight = 100000;
```

Also these can be adapted to the values you want, depending on how you want the network to run (not interfering with frequently used ports, …). The seeds in the chain-params file are the nodes that new nodes will connect to first when they are synchronizing with the network. As you are starting a new network, it is better to comment these out (assuming you have no seed nodes).

```
116     vSeeds.emplace_back("seed.bitcoin.sipa.be"); // Pieter Wuille, only supports x1, x5, x9, and xd
117     vSeeds.emplace_back("dnsseed.bluematt.me"); // Matt Corallo, only supports x9
118     vSeeds.emplace_back("dnsseed.bitcoin.dashjr.org"); // Luke Dashjr
119     vSeeds.emplace_back("seed.bitcoinstats.com"); // Christian Decker, supports x1 - xf
120     vSeeds.emplace_back("seed.bitcoin.jonasschnelli.ch"); // Jonas Schnelli, only supports x1, x5, x9, and xd
121     vSeeds.emplace_back("seed.btc.petertodd.org"); // Peter Todd, only supports x1, x5, x9, and xd
122     vSeeds.emplace_back("seed.bitcoin.sprovoost.nl"); // Sjors Provoost
123     vSeeds.emplace_back("dnsseed.emzy.de"); // Stephan Oeste
```

For the coin distribution we have to look into the initial block subsidy (50 BTC for Bitcoin) and the block halving interval (210,000 blocks for Bitcoin), as there is no simple 'max supply' parameter that we can adjust. In validation.cpp you can find the information you need to adjust. For the initial supply:

```
1231    CAmount GetBlockSubsidy(int nHeight, const Consensus::Params& consensusParams)
1232    {
1233        int halvings = nHeight / consensusParams.nSubsidyHalvingInterval;
1234        // Force block reward to zero when right shift is undefined.
1235        if (halvings >= 64)
1236            return 0;
1237
1238        CAmount nSubsidy = 50 * COIN;
1239        // Subsidy is cut in half every 210,000 blocks which will occur approximately every 4 years.
1240        nSubsidy >>= halvings;
1241        return nSubsidy;
1242    }
```

While the halving interval can be adjusted in the now well-known chainparams.cpp:

```
class CMainParams : public CChainParams {
public:
    CMainParams() {
        strNetworkID = "main";
        consensus.nSubsidyHalvingInterval = 210000;
        consensus.BIP16Exception = uint256S("0x00000000000002dc756eebf4f49723ed8d30cc28a5f108eb94b1ba88ac4f9c22");
        consensus.BIP34Height = 227931;
        consensus.BIP34Hash = uint256S("0x000000000000024b89b42a942fe0d9fea3bb44ab7bd1b19115dd6a759c0808b8");
        consensus.BIP65Height = 388381; // 000000000000000004c2b624ed5d7756c508d90fd0da2c7c679febfa6c4735f0
        consensus.BIP66Height = 363725; // 00000000000000000379eaa19dce8c9b722d46ae6a57c2f1a988119488b50931
        consensus.CSVHeight = 419328; // 000000000000000004a1b34462cb6aeebd5799177f7a29cf28f2d1961716b5b5
        consensus.SegwitHeight = 481824; // 0000000000000000001c801d9cb3b742ef25114f27563e3fc4a1902167f9893
        consensus.MinBIP9WarningHeight = consensus.SegwitHeight + consensus.nMinerConfirmationWindow;
        consensus.powLimit = uint256S("00000000ffffffffffffffffffffffffffffffffffffffffffffffffffffffff");
        consensus.nPowTargetTimespan = 14 * 24 * 60 * 60; // two weeks
        consensus.nPowTargetSpacing = 10 * 60;
        consensus.fPowAllowMinDifficultyBlocks = false;
        consensus.fPowNoRetargeting = false;
        consensus.nRuleChangeActivationThreshold = 1916; // 95% of 2016
        consensus.nMinerConfirmationWindow = 2016; // nPowTargetTimespan / nPowTargetSpacing
        consensus.vDeployments[Consensus::DEPLOYMENT_TESTDUMMY].bit = 28;
        consensus.vDeployments[Consensus::DEPLOYMENT_TESTDUMMY].nStartTime = 1199145601; // January 1, 2008
        consensus.vDeployments[Consensus::DEPLOYMENT_TESTDUMMY].nTimeout = 1230767999; // December 31, 2008
```

In the same block above you can adjust the block time (PowTargetSpacing), the target difficulty (nPowTargetTimespan). Take into account that these are the parameters for the main net, while there are similar blocks for the test nets. The block size is even trickier. By now you have a little bit of an idea of the previous forks that took place and the 'factions' that came into being because of these divisions. With the introduction of Segregated Witness within the Bitcoin network, we have to take into account the scriptSig data. The formula for the transaction weight so far is:

- Transaction weight = base transaction * 3 + total transaction size
- Base transaction size = the size of the transaction serialized and witness data stripped
- Total transaction size = transaction size in bytes serialized according to the description in BIP144 (including the base and witness data).

When you check the consensus.h file, you can see that the current weight is set at 4,000,000, so that the maximum block size is 1MB without witness data.

```
/** The maximum allowed size for a serialized block, in bytes (only for buffer size limits) */
static const unsigned int MAX_BLOCK_SERIALIZED_SIZE = 4000000;
/** The maximum allowed weight for a block, see BIP 141 (network rule) */
static const unsigned int MAX_BLOCK_WEIGHT = 4000000;
/** The maximum allowed number of signature check operations in a block (network rule) */
static const int64_t MAX_BLOCK_SIGOPS_COST = 80000;
/** Coinbase transaction outputs can only be spent after this number of new blocks (network rule) */
static const int COINBASE_MATURITY = 100;
```

Based on what you would like to include in your 'new' cryptocurrency, you can activate certain BIPs. Some of these needed the approval of miners in the network to be activated. As you cannot perform these activations anymore, you can do it directly in the chainparams.cpp file. You can find a short example below, where you should adjust the values accordingly (remove or turn to 0).

```
consensus.BIP16Exception = uint256S("0x00000000000000002dc756eebf4f49723ed8d30cc28a5f108eb94b1ba88ac4f9c22");
consensus.BIP34Height = 227931;
consensus.BIP34Hash = uint256S("0x000000000000024b89b42a942fe0d9fea3bb44ab7bd1b19115dd6a759c0808b8");
consensus.BIP65Height = 388381; // 000000000000000004c2b624ed5d7756c508d90fd0da2c7c679febfa6c4735f0
consensus.BIP66Height = 363725; // 0000000000000000379eaa19dce8c9b722d46ae6a57c2f1a988119488b50931
```

An important one to remember is to remove the checkpoint data that is hard coded in the application. We talk about the minimum work that should be in the chain (nMinimumChainWork), assume by default that the signatures in ancestors of this block are valid.[116] With all the previous work, we arrive at the piece where most of you probably wanted to start: the genesis block. You can personalize the message you want to embed inside of your new currency, to what you believe in or would like to support with your new implementation. Remember that if you are serious, it is meant to last and that your message may just stand the test of time.

```
52   static CBlock CreateGenesisBlock(uint32_t nTime, uint32_t nNonce, uint32_t nBits, int32_t nVersion, const CAmount& genesisReward)
53   {
54       const char* pszTimestamp = "The Times 03/Jan/2009 Chancellor on brink of second bailout for banks";
55       const CScript genesisOutputScript = CScript() << ParseHex("04678afdb0fe5548271967f1a67130b7105cd6a828e03909a67962e0ea1f61deb649f6bc3f4c
56       return CreateGenesisBlock(pszTimestamp, genesisOutputScript, nTime, nNonce, nBits, nVersion, genesisReward);
57   }
```

On top of that, you should also generate the coinbase transaction, public key that should receive the transaction, timestamp and the nBits. To mine the block, you can use the cpp_miner program to start the process. To ease the mining of the genesis block, you can add an exception in the validation.cpp and pow.cpp files so that you can lower the difficulty of this first block. If you would like to be able to spend the first transaction, you will have to adapt the code a bit as this was not possible with the original Bitcoin Core setup. This change you would have to do in the validation.cpp file. With all these changes, you can adapt it further so that it reflects your vision of what a cryptocurrency should be. Of course this example with Bitcoin, accounts also for all other cryptocurrencies that were originally based on Bitcoin. You might have to focus on other aspects as well, but as you should understand by now, you can adapt in the code what you want. Important is to keep in mind what you want to achieve and the security of the participants.

---

[116] chainTxData is used to estimate the sync progress.

3.52   Altcoins Based on Bitcoin

It might shock you, or you might already know this, but a lot of the cryptocurrencies to this date make use in one form or another of the code base that was once provided by the Bitcoin network. The code is open source, so that it can be reviewed and adapted by developer communities that have their own idea of what a coin should be or what features are important to them. Have all of these 'altcoins' been successful? Of course not. A lot of coins barely saw the light of day without any support. A community that underlies a coin is of upmost importance if it wishes to stay 'alive'. I am not going to list all cryptocurrencies that are based on Bitcoin but I will give you a couple of examples below of the most successful ones (to date of course). Previously, we had the hard forks on Bitcoin, which still heavily refer to Bitcoin and why they believe they are better or necessary. The following examples you will see here, have lost most of their references to Bitcoin and really want to stand on their own, with their own vision and specific issues they are trying to solve or focus on. Important is that, just as with the list of hard forks, this list is only a sample and a picture set in time. This means that when you are reading this book, there are probably already new and popular cryptocurrencies that aren't included here (just as there are already some popular cryptocurrencies that I haven't included). The reason is that I only make a specific description of what is out there, while trying to cover everything, would be an endless and even hopeless task. I hope those that I disappoint, can forgive me for this.

3.53   Litecoin

The next cryptocurrency based on Bitcoin is called Litecoin, also sometimes called the silver if Bitcoin is gold. It promises transactions that are nearly instant and near-zero transaction costs.[117] The number of coins that can be mined in the Litecoin network is also limited, just as in the Bitcoin network but the total number has increased to 84 million coins. An importance difference between the 2 networks is the block time: it has been reduced to 2.5 min. The mining algorithm in place is called 'Scrypt' (which requires fewer resources than the mining algorithms in place for Bitcoin or Monero) and is just as in the case of Monero, designed to be more ASIC resistant so that CPUs and GPUs are the preferable method for mining Litecoin. Over time, Scrypt ASIC miners have come to the market but the majority of the miners in the network still seem to be participants that make use of CPU/GPU miners. The Scrypt algorithm is a proof of work algorithm that hashes the input value with a salt. So very similar to Bitcoin, Litecoin tries to provide a cryptocurrency but the focus is already much stronger on the practical use, as it offers a higher transaction rate.

---

[117] https://litecoin.org/.

3.54 Dash

Next in the list of cryptocurrencies that I would like to shortly introduce is called Dash, which was created on the 18th of January 2014 and originally named Darkcoin. Similar to Monero and Zcash, this currency aims to protect the privacy and anonymity of the participants in the network.[118] It forked the Bitcoin code and introduced except for privacy also quick transactions and the use of masternodes.

The total supply that will be generated by the network will amount to a maximum of 18 million coins of which the final coin will be mined around 2300. Still quite a way to go, don't you think? The mining algorithm in use is the X11-algorithm which was developed by Even Duffield.[119] It is another algorithm that wants to build in a resistance against ASICs. The name 'X11' literally refers to the fact that 11 different hash functions have been incorporated into the algorithm: BLAKE, BLUE MIDNIGHT WISH, Grøstl, JH, Keccak, Skein, Luffa, CubeHash, SHAvite-3, SIMD and ECHO. Very simply explained, a value is provided to the first hash function and the output of that function is provided to the next, and the next until the very end. You can clearly understand that the combination of all these hash functions made Dash more secure than Bitcoin was before but the goal, namely being ASIC-resistant, is no longer achieved. We already mentioned shortly before the masternodes. These were installed to simplify the system in use within the Bitcoin and other networks. Masternodes are full nodes that have a bond of collateral (basically a stake in the network of 1000 DASH), which "allows the users to pay for the services and earn a return on their investment". Another differentiator between Dash and other popular networks, is the split in block rewards. Every mining reward is split in 3 ways: 45% for the miner, 45% for the masternodes and 10% goes to the treasury. The treasury is used to fund the further development of the network and future Dash projects. It are the votes from the masternodes that determine the future development and projects of Dash. One of the main goals of Dash, is to really become a day to day currency, both in the US but also for abroad, in countries that are in financial distress. So that people maintain a means of payment. It is investing in these countries but also research to further the future of blockchain as a whole.[120]

---

[118] https://www.dash.org.

[119] Asolo, B. (October 30, 2018) X11 Algorithm Explained. *Mycryptopedia*. https://www.mycryp topedia.com/x11-algorithm-explained/. Accessed November 27, 2019.

[120] Sharma, R. (June 25, 2019) What is Dash Cryptocurrency? *Investopedia*. https://www.investope dia.com/tech/what-dash-cryptocurrency/. Accessed November 27, 2019.

3.55   Namecoin

When you visit the website, you will learn that Namecoin is "an experimental open-source technology which improves decentralization, security, censorship resistance, privacy, and speed of certain components of the Internet infrastructure such as DNS and identities."[121] It came into being on the 18th of April, 2011 thanks to a developer named 'Vinced' following a discussion on Bitcoin and its possibilities. To make sure that miners wouldn't just simple economic incentives and jump on the token that would provide them with the most profit, merge mining was introduced. With merge mining it was possible to mine both Bitcoin and Namecoin and the same time. According to the website it has several possible uses, as it can enhance the protection of free speech (censorship resistance), attach identity information (GPG, OTR keys, …) to an identity of your choice, human-meaningful .onion domains, decentralized TLS certificate validation, websites with .bit top-level domain and promote other technologies such as file signatures, voting, web of trust, notary services and more. There are some clear similarities with Bitcoin, such as the proof of work algorithm in use and the maximum cap of 21 million coins. It also has a mining rate of about 10 min on average but the block size is a bit lower than that of Bitcoin. It is stated that about one-third of all Bitcoin miners merge-mine Namecoin. This gives the network a hashrate security that is far more than most other altcoins. Where we find the clear difference, is in its ability to store data within the blockchain transaction database.[122] The market cap isn't that great, certainly not for a coin that was one of the earliest ventures to increase and enhance the possibilities offered by Bitcoin. Nevertheless, it is a coin and network worth mentioning and looking into as its ideas are to this day still innovative and worth considering towards the future. It has a loyal base of supporters that understand and push for the decentralized DNS system which could be the fundaments of internet privacy and censorship resistance. The coin makes also a clear reference to Aaron Swartz, who was a prominent internet activist.[123] He published a text with a proposal for so-called 'Nakanames' which was one of the concepts that was later on implemented in Namecoin.[124]

---

[121] https://www.namecoin.org/.

[122] Frankenfield, J. (March 5, 2018) Namecoin. *Investopedia.* https://www.investopedia.com/terms/n/namecoin.asp. Accessed November 28, 2019.

[123] The smallest unit of Namecoin is called Swartz.

[124] Schwartz, A. (January 6, 2011) Squaring the triangle: secure, decentralized, human-readable names.   https://web.archive.org/web/20170424134548/http://www.aaronsw.com/weblog/squarezooko. Accessed November 28, 2019.

3.56   Dogecoin

Next on the list is a cryptocurrency that listens to the name 'Dogecoin', referring to the well-known meme from the internet.[125] It first started out as a joke by Billy Markus in 2013, but quickly found a user base and now has a market cap of about 500 million dollar. Jackson Palmer was encouraged to help make the idea a reality and together they were able to eventually make Dogecoin a success.[126] It is actually based on Luckycoin, which in turn is based on Litecoin. Similarly to these coins, it makes use of Scrypt for its proof of work algorithm, making it ASIC resistant. However, the block time is only 1 minute for Dogecoin and there is no limit on the number of coins that can be produced. A remarkable occurrence in the history of Dogecoin, is the hack on the 25th of December 2013 of the Dogewallet platform, which lead to the theft of millions of coins.[127] To aid those that lost funds due to the hack, an initiative called 'SaveDogemas' was set up to donate coins to those people that had coins stolen.[128] On January 2014, enough tokens were donated to refund all participants that were victim of the attack.[129] Later on the fundraising didn't stop, as the community behind Dogecoin funded the Jamaican Bobsled team to go to the Sochi Winter Olympics, to help build a well in the Tana river basin in Kenya and Nascar driver Josh Wise.

3.57   Peercoin

Peercoin calls itself 'the pioneer of proof of stake' and is based on a paper that was released on August 2012 by Scot Nadal and Sunny King (who is also the creator of Primecoin). As you might have guessed, it is a proof of stake based network that generates new coins based on the holdings of individuals. The network does still contain a proof of work component, making it more a hybrid system than a pure 'proof of stake' network. The idea is that the proof of work algorithm becomes increasingly difficult, so that participants are more and more rewarded via a proof of stake system, eventually phasing out the proof of work aspect of the network. Peercoin also clearly sees cryptocurrency more as a store of value, as your chances of reward increase over the time you are actually holding the coins in your wallet. The main goal when this network was created, was to

---

[125] https://knowyourmeme.com/memes/doge.

[126] https://dogecoin.com/.

[127] The platform's filesystem was hacked and the send / receive page was modified in such a way that all transactions were sent to a specific static address.

[128] Couts, A. (December 27, 2013) Such Generosity! After Dogewallet heist, Dogecoin community aims to reimburse victims. *Digital trends.* https://www.digitaltrends.com/cool-tech/dogecoin-dogewallet-hack-save-dogemas/. Accessed November 29, 2019.

[129] Feinberg, A. (December 26, 2013) Millions of Meme-based Dogecoins stolen on Christmas day. *Gizmodo.* https://gizmodo.com/millions-of-meme-based-dogecoins-stolen-on-christmas-da-148981 9762. Accessed Novemebr 30, 2019.

reduce the high-energy consuming proof of work algorithm that is in use by the Bitcoin network, but also wanted to provide increased security and energy efficiency.[130] There is also no limit on the number of peercoins that can be generated, as the proof of stake algorithm ensures a 1% yearly inflation of the minted coins. Next to that, the block time was around the starting time about 7 min (opposed to the 10 min in the Bitcoin network) and the transaction fees within the Peercoin network are driven by the protocol itself.

3.58 Gridcoin

Gridcoin has a unique approach to blockchain technology as it focuses on crowdsourcing of calculations for the scientific community.[131] It was published on the 16th of October, 2013 by Rob Halförd and it was constructed in such a way that proof of research is applied. Participants in the network are rewarded based on their computational contribution to science on BOINC (Berkely Open Infrastructure for Network Computing). Similar to Peercoin, also Gridcoin makes use of a proof of stake validation scheme so that it may become more ecofriendly than the Bitcoin network. Participants receive a reward of 1.5% on the staked coins while they can receive a payment on top based on the participation of the user on BOINC projects that are whitelisted. A lot of guides and examples are provided on the website, to show how you might contribute and be rewarded as you are going solo, as part of a pool or rather just invest in the token.[132]

3.59 Primecoin

The last token I would like to describe here, is called 'Primecoin'.[133] It was launched on the 7th of July 2013 by Sunny King. Blocks are generated every minute and block difficulty is changed every block and the block reward is adjusted based on the difficulty of the block. What makes this network unique is the proof of work algorithm in place. It is based on the computation of prime numbers based on Cunningham chains and bi-twin chains. The results of the computation are stored on the blockchain, and shared with the scientific community for further research. The symbol of the network is the Greek letter psi, referring to Riemann and his zeta function. You can actually check in each block the primes by making use of the 'getblock' output and combine it with the 'primeorigin' field.

---

[130] Frankenfield, J. (July 5, 2018) Peercoin. *Investopedia.* https://www.investopedia.com/terms/p/peercoin.asp. Accessed on November 30, 2019.

[131] https://en.bitcoinwiki.org/wiki/GridCoin.

[132] https://gridcoin.us/.

[133] http://primecoin.io/.

Ethereum

4

> *If crypto succeeds, it's not because it empowers better people. It's because it empowers better institutions.*
>
> —*Vitalik Buterin*

Ethereum, or 'the world computer' as it is often called by the supporting community, is a deterministic but practically unbounded state machine, consisting of a global singleton state and a virtual machine that applies changes to that state.[1] This seems to be a very complex sentence but it really well shows what the Ethereum network actually is. In the following sections we will start to dissect every part of the sentence stated above and try to explain what makes it so very different from Bitcoin, and why it is also the first proponent of a new type of blockchain, introducing concepts of its own, and more importantly: blockchain 2.0. The reason why this is important, is that Ethereum was developed to fix an existing problem, the problem that the Bitcoin network wasn't immediately able to solve. Vitalik Buterin, the inventor of Ethereum, was a Bitcoin enthusiast and believed in the possibilities of blockchain but encountered a rather difficult problem when it came to development on the platform. As we have described before, the possibilities for development on the Bitcoin platform is rather difficult and limited. Combined with the fact that possibilities are more and more limited due to the fact that certain scripting modules are being removed to increase the stability and security of the Bitcoin network, creating applications on top of this network is quite difficult. There was of course the possibility to

---

[1] Antonopoulos, A. and Wood, G. (2018) *Mastering Ethereum.* 1st ed. California: O'reilly Media.

S. Van Hijfte, *Blockchain Platforms*, Synthesis Lectures on Computer Science, https://doi.org/10.1007/978-3-032-00979-1_4

create a layer on top of the network but this removed in part the possibilities and opportunities that were brought by the blockchain technology itself. Knowing that this could be done differently, Vitalik Buterin published his white paper on Ethereum[2] in 2013 where he defended his idea of what could unlock the full potential of blockchain technology by creating a universal state machine. His efforts were soon supported by a lot of other people, willing to work on this new solution. The network also came with some clear goals towards the future participants and developers that would join the network. First of all, it makes use of something that is called 'the sandwich complexity model' where the goal is that the bottom level architecture of the network should be as simple as possible. This means that the Ethereum platform wants to be as user-friendly as possible and that all things concerning network protocol, machine-level language, serialization and so on shouldn't be that developers' main concern. This is whenever possible, pushed to the other layers so that the developer can focus completely on the development part of smart contracts and dApps in high-level languages. Secondly, the network focuses on freedom and generalization. This means that the developers behind the Ethereum platform believe in the values of 'net neutrality' and do not wish to judge over which applications and smart contracts are developed on top of the network. They also aim to make the possibilities as broad as possible for those people that wish to develop on top of the platform. This means that there are opcodes defined for which currently there doesn't seem a clear use but this can always change in the future. This generalization goes quite far because the developers of the network refuse to build in even very common features. The reason is that they want to keep the protocols and the network open for everyone and if you want a specific feature to be used, you can perfectly define it yourself in a smart contract. The responsibility is up to you and you alone. Finally, there is no risk aversion, which means that the choices of the network include faster block times, generalized state transitions and so on. This again in part with the user and developer in mind so that they can have the best experience while maintaining some general principles.

In the next couple of pages, you will find an explanation on how the network and Ethereum functioned in 2019. Many of these concepts remain very relevant to understand Ethereum but some of these might look outdated. Not to worry! Later on in the text, you will find the relevant updates and changes that took place between 2019 and 2025. It might not seem long but you might be surprised what can happen in a short timespan like 6 years!

---

[2] http://blockchainlab.com/pdf/Ethereum_white_paper-a_next_generation_smart_contract_and_dec entralized_application_platform-vitalik-buterin.pdf.

4.1   The Ethereum Virtual Machine

An important concept to understand in Ethereum is the 'Ethereum Virtual Machine' or EVM in short. It was first defined by Gavin Wood in his yellow paper on improvements for the Ethereum network.[3] In short, The EVM is a 256-bit register stack which is designed to run the code presented by a smart contract. It creates a level of abstraction between the executing code and the executing machine. This allows for a separation both between applications as well as their hosts. This is one of the key features that we want to see in smart contracts, as you will later see in the section called 'smart contracts'. These smart contracts are written in a programming language that is called Solidity (even though Vyper or Bamboo are also viable options).[4] These separate languages came into being because in the EVM a separate language must be used to code the applications. The EVM should be seen as a generalized, secure, ownerless, virtual machine.[5] This virtual machine will accept the programs running on top which we know as smart contracts. These will always produce the same result given a specific input (which means they are 'deterministic'), which implies that the underlying state[6] changes will also be the same. Every possible task that can be executed by a computer, can in some way also be executed by the Ethereum Virtual Machine, making it Turing complete. However, there is one limitation: the EVM is bound by the use of gas that must pay for the computations that are taking place. These smart contracts cannot be executed directly by the Ethereum Virtual Machine but need to be compiled in a set of low-level machine instructions. These instructions, or 'opcodes' allow the EVM to be Turing-complete. This stack-based way of working can remind one of how Bitcoin scripting works and in part this is certainly true, only the possibilities with Ethereum are much, much broader. Each of these opcodes is 1 byte so there can only be 256 opcodes (for now we already have 140 unique opcodes) which can be divided in a specific set of categories[7]:

- Stack-manipulating codes
- Memory-manipulating opcodes
- Storage-manipulating opcodes
- Environmental opcodes
- Program counter related opcodes
- Halting opcodes
- Arithmetic/comparison/bitwise opcodes.

---

[3] You can always check the yellow paper called 'Ethereum: a secure decentralized generalized transaction ledger" by Gavin Wood (2018).

[4] Deprecated programming languages are Serpent and Mutan.

[5] Dannen, C. (2017) *Introducing Ethereum and Solidity.* 1st ed. New York, NY: Apress.

[6] To know more about state changes and a state machine, please consult the glossary.

[7] Do not hesitate to consult the reference with all the opcodes on: https://ethervm.io/.

A sample set of these opcodes can be found in the table below.

Opcode	Name	Description	Gas
0x00	STOP	Halts execution	0
0x01	ADD	Addition operation	3
0x02	MUL	Multiplication operation	5
0x03	SUB	Subtraction operation	3
0x04	DIV	Integer division operation	5
0x05	SDIV	Signed integer division operation (truncated)	5
0x06	MOD	Modulo remainder operation	5

Because the goal of the Ethereum network is to work efficiently, these opcodes are stored in so-called bytecodes. During the execution of the code, the bytecode is being split in bytes, each representing an opcode. However, there are also limitations to the use of the EVM as it uses a 256-bit register stack from which only the 16 most recent items can be manipulated at once. Furthermore, the stack can only hold 1024 items. This is why the opcodes use contract memory to retrieve data. To store this data indefinitely, one has to make use of storage. However, writing to storage is very expensive! The EVM, is just as any other computer, always looking for changes to its state. Every time it encounters instructions of any kind, it will start to translate and run its own code. Each change the machine makes in its state, will be based on the previous state. This makes sure that these changes are linked to each other and that changes in memory are made for a reason. The EVM is in a non-stop loop checking for new instructions to be executed. What is specific to Ethereum and differs it from other computers is that the network here will constantly check for transactions taking place and the state of the EVM is the representation of the balances that at that moment of time exist. Of course this brings with it a whole set of problems of its own.

> There exist far more invalid state changes than valid state changes. Invalid state changes might, e.g., be things such as reducing an account balance without an equal and opposite increase elsewhere. A valid transition is one which comes about through a transaction.— Gavin Wood, Yellow paper

The ultimate goal of the EVM is to create a representative and trustworthy history that reflects each legitimate change in its state.

4.2   Network Communication in Ethereum

The Ethereum network makes use of the RLPx transport protocol, which is a TCP-based transport protocol and is named after the serialization format used by the network, to allow communication between the nodes that make up the network.[8] The protocol makes use of 'Elliptic Curve Integrated Encryption Scheme' or 'ECIES' and is an asymmetric encryption method. ECIES in RLPx consists of the following parts:

- Secp256k1 elliptic curve with generator G
- The NIST SP 800-56 Concatenation Key Derivation function
- HMAC using the SHA256 function
- The AES128 encryption function—CTR mode.

All the cryptographic operations are based on secp256k1 and the nodes are required to keep a static secp256k1 static key. However, before there can be any communication there is another step that needs to happen. The initial connection is created by making use of a handshake between the nodes. There is first an 'auth'-message send by the initiator that wishes to make a connection. The receiver decrypts the message and verifies if the message has been correctly signed (signature = keccak256(ephemeral-pubk)). The receiver will also derive the secrets from the message. Only if this is the case, it responds with the 'auth-ack'-message to the initiator together with the first encrypted frame containing the 'Hello'-message. The initiator derives in turn the secrets from the auth-ack and replies in kind with the first frame containing the 'hello'-message. Both will authenticate this first frame and the handshake is complete if the MAC of the first encrypted frame is valid on both sides.

The Hello-message looks a bit like this:

(example taken from https://github.com/ethereum/devp2p/blob/master/rlpx.md):

```
[protocolVersion: P, clientId: B, capabilities, listenPort: P, nodeKey:
B_64,…]
```

Once the authentication is complete, the communication between the nodes can begin. Important is that all messages after the authentication are framed. This allows multiplexing multiple capabilities over a single connection and because of the demarcation points that are created for message authentication codes, encrypted communication is easier. The multiplexing allows messages with different capabilities to be transferred over the same connection. Furthermore the message authentication in RLPx makes use of 2 keccak256 states: egress-mac (sent) and ingress mac (received).

---

[8] https://github.com/ethereum/devp2p/blob/master/rlpx.md.

4.3   Blocks and Chains

We already went through a lot of information regarding the Ethereum network and how it is developing over time. As before we will start from the top and move down to how the Ethereum blockchain (currently) looks like. We will go through the several parameters that make up blocks in the blockchain and it is always interesting to start at the very beginning: the genesis block.

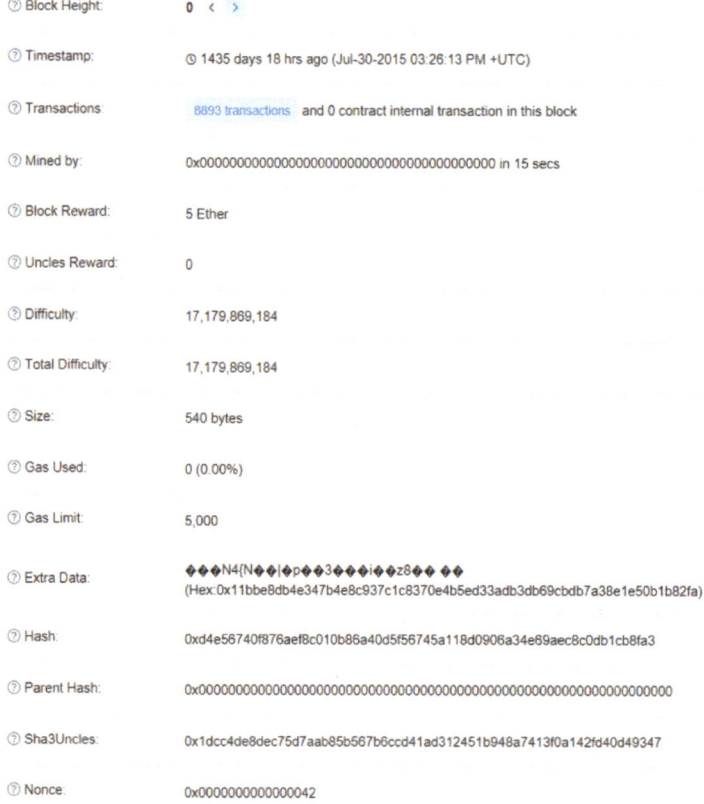

The block height is obviously 0 as it is the first block and the timestamp gives us the 30th of July 2015. There are a lot of transactions included which refer to the first addresses receiving the first reward from the genesis block. Below you can see a short example from what these transactions look like.

Txn Hash	Block	Age	From		To	Value
GENESIS_756f45e3...	0	1435 days 18 hrs ago	GENESIS	→	0x756f45e3fa69347...	200 Ethe
GENESIS_f42f9052...	0	1435 days 18 hrs ago	GENESIS	→	0xf42f905231c770f0...	197 Ethe
GENESIS_2489ac1...	0	1435 days 18 hrs ago	GENESIS	→	0x2489ac126934d4...	1,000 Et
GENESIS_ddf5810a...	0	1435 days 18 hrs ago	GENESIS	→	0xddf5810a0eb2fb2...	17,900 E
GENESIS_c951900...	0	1435 days 18 hrs ago	GENESIS	→	0xc951900c341abb...	327.6 Et
GENESIS_6806408...	0	1435 days 18 hrs ago	GENESIS	→	0x680640838bd07a...	1,730 Et
GENESIS_9d0f347e...	0	1435 days 18 hrs ago	GENESIS	→	0x9d0f347e826b7dc...	4,000 Et
GENESIS_9328d55...	0	1435 days 18 hrs ago	GENESIS	→	0x9328d55ccb3fce5...	4,000 Et
GENESIS_7e7f18a0...	0	1435 days 18 hrs ago	GENESIS	→	0x7e7f18a02eccaa5...	66.85 Et

We also receive information on who was the miner, the reward for mining this block and the uncle rewards. Finally, there is the difficulty of the mining (as Ethereum started out with a proof of work consensus protocol), size of the block, the gas used in the block and the limit, extra data that can be added by the miner, the hash from the block header from the previous block, the parent hash, the SHA3uncles and the Nonce. Clearly, there is a lot more information included in the Ethereum blocks when we compare these with the Bitcoin blocks. The image below gives us an initial idea of how the block headers look like (based on the Ethereum Yellow paper).[9]

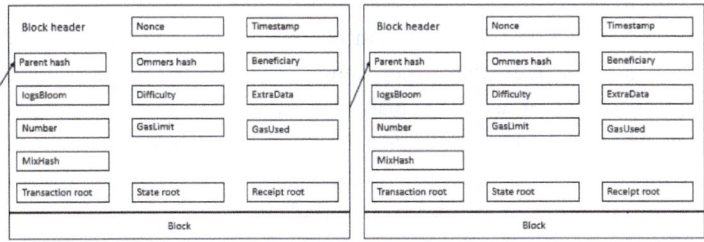

Several of these parameters we have discussed before when we were looking at the genesis block of the Ethereum blockchain. This information is based on the information given by Gavin Wood in his Yellow paper. There are three Merkle Patricia Tree roots in the block headers: transactions root, state root and receipts root. The transactions root is, as you might have expected, the root of the Merkle Patricia Tree, linking together the transactions in the block. The state tree represents the entire state after the block has been processed. The receipts tree is a little bit more difficult to understand. It represents the 'receipts' from the transactions. It is itself made up out of 4 separate items: medstate, gas_used, logbloom and logs. In short[10]:

[9] Wood, G. (2019) Ehtereum: a secure decentralized generalized transaction ledger Byzantium version. https://ethereum.github.io/yellowpaper/paper.pdf.

[10] https://github.com/ethereum/wiki/wiki/Design-Rationale.

- The medstate is the state root after the transaction has been processed
- The gas_used is the gas used after processing the transaction
- The logs is a list which again consists out of some other elements: logger's account address, a certain amount of topics and data that are produced by the LOG0. LOG4 opcodes during execution of the transaction
- The logbloom is a bloom filter made up of the addresses and topics of all logs in the transaction.

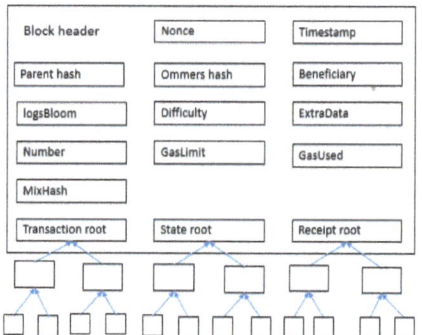

Other information that is stored in the block header is:

- The parent hash is the hash of the parent block's header (using keccak256).
- The nonce is a 64-bit hash that, when combined with the mixHash proves that there was enough computation used to actually mine the block.
- The beneficiary is the successful miner of the block that will receive the fees from mining the block
- The timestamp which is the Unix timestamp of the block
- The logsBloom which is the Bloom filter on the logs
- The difficulty which shows at which difficulty level the block was mined
- The extraData which has in it... you guessed it: extra data
- The number is the block number of the block, starting from 0 for genesis
- The gasLimit which represents the gas (explained later) limit per block
- The gasUsed which is the sum of total gas used by the transactions in the block.

And then we still have one value to explain: the ommershash. This is the hash of the ommers in the block. So what the hell are ommers? In short, these are the stale blocks that arise in the network because of the high block time. They are called ommers or uncles and have the same grandparent as the current block that is being mined. Because of the GHOST protocol, the miners of these blocks also receive a reward, which is smaller than the reward for the miner that was able to mine the full block but still provides enough incentive to follow the main chain. What else can be found in the blocks of the Ethereum blockchain except for the block header? Well there is the set of transactions of course but also the other block headers of the current block's uncles.

4.4 GHOST Protocol

The Ethereum network also makes use of the GHOST protocol because of the high block time of the network. This fast processing time leads to a lot of stale blocks or 'uncles' which are now used within the calculations of the network to prevent too many forks. It is a limited version of the GHOST protocol that is being used by Ethereum though, to prevent high calculation costs. Uncles can only be included up until the '7th generation'. On top of that, unlimited GHOST would allow miners to mine any block and still claim reward, pushing them away from the main chain. So what is the design rationale behind all this? The goal of the network is to have a block time of 12 s. We have learned before however, that this is in reality a bit longer due to network latency. On top of the 7th generation limitation, there is also a 1 block descendant limit. This both for security and simplicity reasons.

Interesting to know is that when it comes to the validation of the uncles, only the headers are checked. This is done to make the process lighter and easier but incorporates of course limited risks.

4.5 UTXOs?

In the section on Bitcoin I talked quite extensively about UTXOs and why they are of such a major importance in the network (and in many other networks that use the same mechanism). Ethereum chose to leave this approach and wanted to make use of accounts. These accounts consist out of a balance, and in some cases out of a code and internal storage. If you wish to make a transaction, it is simple: your account is checked and if the account has enough balance on it, the account is debited for the payment you wish to make while the receiver has his account credited. If there is a code, this code can be executed based on the result of the transaction, and even the internal storage can be adapted as a result of the transaction. Discussions on what is the best strategy for dealing with transactions are manifold but the main points are these: UTXOs provide better privacy when it comes down to the transactions you are making and it can give you a certain advantage when we are talking about certain scalability paradigms (but both are arguable when you wish to make use of smart contracts and dApps, and even so, in the past it has been proven that frequent users of the Bitcoin network could be identified, whether they liked it or not). The advantages of accounts are given by simplicity as it is easier to understand, greater fungibility as the source of the coins is no longer a blockchain-level concept, it is easier for light clients to access all data related to an account when they simply need to look for the account in the state tree. Finally, the main advantage is the space saving compared to UTXOs both in storing information (account has one truth versus UTXOs which need to be combined to make a transaction work) and the transactions can be smaller as you again, only need 1 input, 1 output and 1 signature. In the world of Ethereum, there are two types of accounts: externally owned and contract accounts. The first are owned by owners with a private key, just like you and me (in case you have an Ether account). These can be freely used to send transactions to other externally owned accounts or to contract accounts when the correct private key is used to sign the transactions. The contract account has code associated with it and is controlled by contract code. This means that it can only be activated when it actually receives a transaction. So what comprises the 'account state'? There are four components that are essential: the nonce, the balance, the storageRoot and the codehash. The nonce is the number of transactions actually send from the eternally owned account or the number of contracts created by the account in case it is a contract account. The balance is the number of Wei owned by the address (details later). Next, there is the storageRoot which is the Merkle Patricia tree root of the storage contents. Finally, there is the codeHash which is the hash of the Ethereum Virtual Machine code for the account.

4.6   Transactions

Just as with the Bitcoin blockchain, also here we are dealing with transactions and messages that are being send throughout the network. We can basically define 2 types: message calls and contract creations but both have the same basic structure:

- The nonce is the number of transactions send by the sender
- The gasPrice is the price the sender is willing to pay for the execution of the transaction
- The gasLimit is the maximum amount of gas the sender is willing to pay
- The "to" is the recipient-address
- The value is the amount of Ether/wei that is to be transferred
- The "v", "r" and "s" are used to generate the signature of the sender
- The init-field is only included when we have a contract-creating transaction which gives us an Ethereum Virtual Machine fragment that is used to initiate the new contract account
- The data-field is only used for message calls and contains the input data for the transaction.

We know from before that contract accounts can only be initiated when they receive a transaction from an externally owned account. This is not entirely true as in some cases contract code, once initiated, can call other contracts by making use of internal transactions.[11] Important for developers to know is that these subsequent transaction don't have a gas limit which means that the initial transaction should contain enough gas to power the first transaction and all subsequent transactions that follow. There are some other rules to consider when we talk about transaction execution in the Ethereum network environment. Within the transaction there must be a valid signature and a valid nonce (the counter if you remember). There are also validity checks on the intrinsic and upfront gas costs (defined later in this chapter) before we can move on to the actual execution. During execution there will always be a so-called 'substate' that tracks the changes in the state while the transaction is executing. This substate tracks the following items:

- The 'refund balance' which contains the amount to be refunded to the sender
- The 'log series' which are a number of logs referring to the Ethereum Virtual Machine execution
- The 'self-destruct set' which is a set of accounts that will be deleted once the operations are finished. Refers to the self-destruct opcode that can be used to delete a contract and send the remaining gas to the senders account.

4.7 Serialization

We learned before that the transaction has to follow a specific format called 'Recursive Length Prefix' or 'RLP' which is the serialization format used in Ethereum. The RLP function takes in an item or a set of items and follows a specific encoding procedure[12]:

- If the input is a single byte in the range 0x00–0x7F, we know that byte is its own RLP encoding
- If the input is a special byte, the encoding starts with 0x81
- If the input is a string between 2 and 55 bytes long, the encoding scheme consists of 0x80 + the length of the string in bytes followed by the hex value of the string
- If the input is a string longer than 55 bytes, the encoding scheme consists out of 3 different parts. We end with the hex value of the string upmost to the right, in the middle we have the length of the string in hex, and to the left we have 0xb7 + the length of the middle value
- If the input is a non-value, the RLP encoding is 0x80
- If the input is an empty array, the encoding is 0xc0

---

[11] Kasireddy, P. (September 27, 2017) How does Ethereum work, anyway? *Medium*. https://medium.com/@preethikasireddy/how-does-ethereum-work-anyway-22d1df506369. Accessed on December 13, 2019.

[12] Chinchilla, c. (August 2, 2019) RLP. *Ethereum wiki*. https://github.com/ethereum/wiki/wiki/RLP. Accessed on December 13, 2019.

- If the input is in the range 0x80–0xFF, the RLP encoding concatenates 0x81 to the input
- If the input is a list with a total payload between 0 and 55 bytes, the RLP encoding starts with 0xc0 + length of the payload + the hex value of the items
- If the input is a list with a payload longer than 55 bytes, the encoding scheme consists out of 3 different parts. We end with the hex value of the items upmost to the right, in the middle we have the length of the payload in hex, and to the left we have 0xb7 + the length of the middle value

The decoding of the RLP encoded transactions will always start with the first byte as this will make immediately clear which data types are being handled. The decoding reverses the rules which were set before and make clear what needs to happen and what information is being transferred.

4.8   Signing

To sign a transaction, one can call the 'eth_sign' method from an Ethereum client which makes use of the keccak256 hashing algorithm. It looks like this: eth_sign(keccak256("\x19Ethereum Signed Message: \n" + len(message) + message)). As mentioned before, there is a nonce included in the transaction once it is being sent, to prevent replay attacks from attackers that are able to capture our messages. The elliptical curve digital signature algorithm being used makes use of the parameters in the transaction called 'r', 's' and 'v' to create the actual signature. 'r' and 's' are both 32 bytes and concatenated together to form the first part of the signature. The 'v' is the 65th byte of the signature itself. To be able to verify the signature, these have to be split out and this way the sender's address can be recovered. In case the transaction was tampered with, the sender's address will no longer be correctly identified. On top of that also the message needs to be verified, it can perfectly be that the signature is correct but that the message has been altered. The message is recreated by making use of the same parameters that should have been used and verify if the outcome is similar to what has actually been sent.

4.9   Ether, Fees, Gas and Fuel

The cryptocurrency linked with Ethereum is the coin called 'Ether'. Opposite to the Bitcoin network, the main goal of the network wasn't the creation of the cryptocurrency but rather Ether is an enabler for the development for smart contracts and DApps on the network. It is used to power the applications and prevent certain forms of abuse while at the same time making sure that the miners and participants get paid. Another major difference is that there is no hard cap on the creation of Ether which makes it a coin that is much more susceptible to inflation. We have seen clear evolutions over time where there have been inflation rates around 14% in the years 2015 and 2016, which decreased to a steady 7.4% in 2018.[13] To give you an idea, Bitcoin has a yearly inflation rate of about 4.25%. However, when the Casper protocol will be implemented, it is suspected that the inflation rate will decrease to as low as 0.1%. If you have ever worked with the Ethereum platform and network before or have at least read about it, you will have certainly seen the word 'gas' of 'fuel'. But what is it? As we already shortly described above, gas was invented to deal with several problems that Turing complete machines might run into. One of these is the halting problem which can lead to the infinite loop but also DoS-attacks and others are mitigated by the use of this new concept. If we are talking about 'simple' transactions, gas can be seen as the transfer fee that must be paid for your transaction to take place. It is also the reward that miners get for mining your transaction into a block. But as you know now, a lot more can take place on the Ethereum platform, so what does gas measure when it comes to executing smart contracts? Gas is the computational effort that it will take to execute all the operations that are enclosed within a smart contract.[14] Making use of the Ethereum Virtual Machine takes up a lot of effort and should therefore only be used for simple tasks and the fees help encourage all participants to keep their computations to a minimum. The denomination for gas can be found in the table below.

Unit	Wei value (Wei)	Weis
Wei	1	1
Babbage	1e3	1000
Lovelace	1e6	1,000,000
Shannon	1e9	1,000,000,000
Szabo	1e12	1,000,000,000,000
Finney	1e15	1,000,000,000,000,000
Ether	1e18	1,000,000,000,000,000,000

The actual transaction fee is calculated based on a simple formula: gas limit X gas price = max transaction fee. The limit is set by the sender and represents the maximum amount he is willing to pay for the transaction to be executed. If there is enough Wei to be found on the account of the sender, the transaction will be executed otherwise the transaction is invalid. This fee will eventually end up as a reward for the miner that mines the block which includes the transaction that was executed by the sender. There is also a check on this gas limit when the transaction is created. The gas limit should be equal

---

[13] Conner, E. (July 27, 2018) A case for Ethereum block reward reduction to 2 ETH in Constantinople (EIP-1234). *Medium.* https://medium.com/@eric.conner/a-case-for-ethereum-block-reward-reduction-in-constantinople-eip-1234-25732431fc77. Accessed December 11, 2019.

[14] Rosic, A. (2018) What is Ethereum gas? *Bockgeeks.* https://blockgeeks.com/guides/ethereum-gas/. Accessed December 11, 2019.

or greater than the intrinsic gas used by the transaction. This intrinsic gas consists out of 21,000 gas + 4 gas for every byte of data equal to 0 or 68 gas for every byte of data $\neq 0$. On top of this an additional cost of 32,000 gas is possible when we are dealing with a contract creation transaction. A final check is performed on the account of the sender by adding the maximum transaction fee and the value of the transaction together. This is called the upfront gas price and the account of the sender should contain a high enough balance to cover these costs. If this is the case, the transaction can move to the next steps of execution. Similarly, you can store data on the Ethereum blockchain but also for these services you have to pay. Here the fee is calculated based on the smallest multiple of 32 bytes used. If you execute an operation that has as aim to free up space, you don't have to pay a fee for this transaction and even a refund is given for the freed up space.

4.10 The Milestones of Ethereum

The development of the Ethereum platform has followed several prototypes which had each their own code names. Below you can find an overview of the several versions of the platform that have already been created so far. The first really stable version of the network came with the Homestead update which brought several improvements to the network.[15] Serenity is supposed to be the final version of the network with the implementation of Casper 2.0.

Ethereum platform versions

Version	Code name	Release date
0	Olympic	May, 2015
1	Frontier	30 July 2015
2	Homestead	14 March 2016
3	Metropolis (vByzantium)[16]	16 October 2017
3.5	Metropolis (vConstantinople)[17]	28 February 2019
4	Serenity	TBA

Just as with the Bitcoin network, also Ethereum has seen its protocol updates over time and its subsequent hard forks (later more). The Ethereum network differs in several ways from the Bitcoin network. One of these differences, is the use of accounts and balances (called state transitions). So unlike Bitcoin, it does not have to rely on UTXO's. Another major difference is that the block time is only 15 s (compared to 10 min for Bitcoin).

---

[15] Improvements to transaction processing, gas pricing and security among others.

[16] This was a soft fork which reduced the complexity of the Ethereum Virtual Machine and added support for zk-SNARKS.

[17] This update was a hard fork.

The return of ether for mining a block is consistent, and this is why one sometimes refers to Ether as the oil of the cryptocurrencies. There is also a major change ongoing in the way the protocol works as it is moving from the proof of work protocol to the proof of stake protocol. It does this in several implementations, to make sure that the change in the network is not too significant. The Ethereum also makes use of a concept called 'gas', which is measured in Gwei. This is the transaction fee one has to pay based on the computational complexity, bandwidth being used and the storage needs.

4.11 The Stages of Ethereum Explained

As with the development of Bitcoin and other blockchain platforms, there have been several stages in the development of Ethereum. The difference with the Bitcoin platform was that the development of Ethereum has been clearly staged from the very beginning. Some of these steps were not planned beforehand but the main timeline was always clear. I would like to point out that not everything described below will be immediately clear but will be explained on the next pages. So no panic, everything will become clearer when you move along and don't hesitate to refer back to this section on the timeline. It will make clear what is already there and what will be added in the near future.

4.12 Frontier

This was the first stage of the Ethereum platform and started on the 30th of July 2015 and lasted to March 2016. To be completely honest, before the release of Frontier there was another version that was released called 'Olympic'. It was the final pre-release version that was opened up to the world so that the limitations of the network could be tested by willing participants.[18] There was the focus on transaction activity, virtual machine usage, mining prowess and general punishment. It lasted for about 14 days before the launch of the Frontier 1.0 version of Ethereum. The Olympic testnet was replaced with the release of Frontier with 'Morden' which was a Frontier-equivalent testnet. The mining on this first version of Ethereum could start once the hardware was installed and the genesis block could be generated. As it was the first version of the network software, the network was plagued with initial bugs and updates propagated through the network to adjust for these issues. There was also the implementation of so-called 'canary contracts' which were only used in this version of the platform. It was a centralized check that was created to follow up on the frontier clients and possible consensus issues. There were 4 'switches' that could be either 1 or 0 and these were controlled by the Ethereum developers. From the second that 2 of these were turned on, the mining would stop and the participant was

---

[18] Buterin, V. (May 9, 2015) Olympic: Frontier pre-release. *Ethereum blog.* https://blog.ethereum. org/2015/05/09/olympic-frontier-pre-release. Accessed on December 17, 2019.

forced to update their client so that these wouldn't prevent a chain upgrade. The used consensus algorithm was the proof of work algorithm called ETHhash even though the developers already knew they wanted to move to a proof of stake protocol in the future.

4.13   Ice Age

This stage started at block 200,000 (7th of September 2015) and introduced a time bomb that would increase the difficulty in the proof of work protocol used by the network. The name 'ice age' refers to the 'freezing' of the blockchain because of the increased difficulty, the fact the miners wouldn't be able to keep up and as a direct effect that the block time would increase. The main reason was to stimulate the participants in the network to move to the proof of stake protocol when it was ready to be implemented. So this means that at the moment the network is ready to implement the new proof of stake 'Casper' protocol (the Serenity update), there will be a hard fork with the remaining proof of work network which would force every miner to switch to the new network. Why? Remaining on the old network would leave the participants on a PoW network where the difficulty would eventually become so high, that the participants could no longer mine. Stephen Tau stated that the bomb would go off at block 200,000 but that the results would only be noticeable after about a year.[19] After this time, the difficulty would increase significantly, leading to higher block times. The goal was that the Serenity update would be ready by this time. It seems clear now that this timeline wasn't met and the difficulty bomb has been delayed several times already to prepare for the Serenity update. The algorithm behind the time bomb looks like this:

Block_diff = parent_diff + parent_diff//2048 * max(1 − (block_timestamp − parent_timestamp)//10, − 99) + int(2 ** ((block.number//100,000) − 2) with//the division operator resulting in 8//4 = 4 and 9//4 = 4.[20]

4.14   Homestead

The next stage started at block 1,150,000 (14th of March 2016 or Pi-day) and was the second implementation of the Ethereum network. It was a hard fork because it brought protocol changes that were not backward compatible. Similarly to the Bitcoin network, also in the Ethereum world there are 'Ethereum Improvement Proposals' or 'EIPs'. Several of these were implemented with Homestead such as EIP 2 which increased the cost

[19] Tual, S. (August 4, 2015) Ethereum Protocol Update 1. *Ethereum blog.* https://blog.ethereum.org/2015/08/04/ethereum-protocol-update-1/. Accessed December 17, 2019.

[20] Rosic, A. (2017) What is Ethereum Metropolis: the ultimate guide. *Blockgeeks.* https://blockgeeks.com/guides/ethereum-metropolis/. Accessed December 18, 2019.

of contract creation from 21,000 to 53,000.[21] In case there is no gas enough to create the contract, it simply fails (instead of leaving an empty contract). Also transaction signatures are now checked. There are also EIP 7 and EIP8. The first introduced a new opcode called DELEGATECALL which can be used for contracts that create contracts but don't repeat additional information. The second changed the RLPx discovery protocol and RLPx TCP transfer protocol so that clients could deal with future network upgrades (before the client would simply stop communication).

4.15   DAO

Later in this chapter explained in more detail, around block 1,192,000 a hard fork took place when there was a hack in the DAO. Discussions followed, after which a part of the community decided to refund the victims of the hack. A part of the community would remain in the old chain, creating 'Ethereum classic'.

4.16   The DAO Attack

It was in 2016 that a major event occurred which would influence not only the perception of the Ethereum platform but also the concept of the 'decentralized autonomous organization'. There was a fund raising project that made use of a decentralized autonomous organization, called 'the DAO' (real original, I know). The DAO was created by Christoph Jentsch together with his brother Simon. Their goal was to fund projects using ether via the DAO. It was a very popular organization and at the time (May 2016) it had attracted almost 14% of all ether that had been issued to that date. The idea was that the members could vote on which projects could win the investments and several security features were built in the decentralized autonomous organization to prevent abuse of these voting rights.

However, darkness loomed and soon an important security vulnerability was discovered in the code supporting the organization. This flaw was pointed out by several people and in June several solutions had been proposed to fix the recursive call issue but it would be too late. It was the 17th of June 2016 when an attacker exploited several vulnerabilities and transferred 3.6 million Ether from the DAO to an account that had a 28-day holding period. Following this event, the community got torn over the question whether a hard fork should occur so that the lost funds could be returned. With no consensus in the community, a hard fork occurred with Ethereum continuing on this fork, while the original chain remains to be used by what is now known as Ethereum Classic. Ethereum Classic also had to deal with the time bomb that was part of their code and hence the Ethereum Classic chain had to perform a hard fork themselves to get rid of this feature. Eventually the tokens related to the DAO would be de-listed by the end of 2016.

---

[21] https://ethereum-homestead.readthedocs.io/en/latest/introduction/the-homestead-release.html.

4.17   Tangerine Whistle

This hard fork was implemented to address the gas calculation in I/O-heavy operations and to address the results of DoS attacks so that it addresses the immediate network health issues which were the result from previous attacks. The idea was that the opcodes that read the state tree were in fact underpriced. These opcodes were easy to add to smart contracts but difficult to process for the clients, which lead to delays in the network. We were at that moment at block 2,463,000 and the change was based on EIP 150.[22]

4.18   Spurious Dragon

Starting at block 2,675,000 other defense mechanisms were implemented to address other DoS-attacks and replay attacks and hence the next hard fork took place on the 22nd of November 2016. EIP 155 (replay attack protection), 160 (EXP opcode cost increase), 162 (state trie clearing to further help prevent DoS-attacks) and 170 (the contract code size limit was brought to 24,576 bytes) were all implemented with this update.[23]

4.19   Metropolis Byzantium

The next stage in Ethereum development was called Ethereum Metropolis Byzantium and occurred at block 4,370,000. It brought to Ethereum the introduction of zk-SNARKs to improve privacy on the blockchain. Next, also the time bomb was delayed another 18 months to allow the developers more time to work on the next implementations and versions of the Ethereum network. Finally, the implementation of smart contracts has been made even more flexible and robust. Specifically, if a contract cannot move on to the next 'state' during execution because of a shortage of gas, the contract is reversed to the previous state without spending all the gas. On top of that, the RETURNDATA opcode is added so that variable length values can be returned. Finally, the upgrade of the network wants to achieve account abstraction, making the network more user friendly so that users will no longer need technical knowledge to make use of the platform.

---

[22] http://eips.ethereum.org/EIPS/eip-608.

[23] Jameson, H. (November 18, 2016) Hard Fork No. 4: Spurious Dragon. *Ethereum blog.* https://blog.ethereum.org/2016/11/18/hard-fork-no-4-spurious-dragon. Accessed December 18, 2019.

4.20   Metropolis Constantinople

The next phase in the Ethereum timeline is Metropolis Constantinople. It was normally planned for the beginning of 2019 but has been pushed forward. Several reasons can be thought of for this push towards the future but one of them was the fact that an auditing team discovered that the upgrade contained a vulnerability that was linked with EIP 1283 that would introduce cheaper cost of storage which in turn introduced the reentrancy attack. What does this mean? Easily explained, an external contract might communicate with a smart contract. If the external contract is in any form malicious, it might try to take control of the smart contract's code and make unexpected changes. Particularly, it can try to re-entering in a particular spot in the code, withdrawing Ether from the smart contract (withdrawBalance() function is abused here). It would have affected only a small number of smart contracts, but still, the developers are now working on the problem to make sure that no vulnerabilities are introduced. It was also this type of attack that was used in 2016 on the DAO (see earlier). The following EIPs would be implemented during this hard fork: EIP 145, 1052, 1283, 1014 and 1234. The first introduces bitwise shifting which allows code (and the underlying operations) to become better optimized so that the code can be processed faster and at lower cost. Next EIP 1052 introduces a new opcode EXTCODEHASH which returns the keccak256 hash of contract code. This can be interesting for contracts which have to check the bytecode of other contracts without actually using it. Again, this will lead to efficiency and lower cost. EIP 1283 refers to the SSTORE opcode which can be used for gas metering. Again, the aim is to reduce costs for developers.[24] The next EIP introduces state channels (explained in more detail below) which are similar to the Lightning network that we find in the Bitcoin world. Finally, there was the plan for the transition to the proof of stake consensus protocol with the introduction of Casper FFG (explained in detail below). However, this plan was cancelled late 2018 where the developers eventually decided to move away from Casper FFG and immediately go for the full implementation.

4.21   Serenity

When you have arrived here, you have already read a lot about the past developments of the Ethereum network. However, what follows is in part outdated and no longer reflects with the reality of how the network developed. "Ethereum 2.0" has become something completely different and the terminology being used here is seen as deprecated. Nevertheless, I kept this part in the book as it reflects the original plans for the network. Beyond these items, you will find the actual developments which took place and an explanation on why these adaptations on the original plan took place.

---

[24] Mitra, R. (2019) Understanding Ethereum Constantinople: A hard fork. *Blockgeeks*. https://blockgeeks.com/guides/ethereum-constantinople-hard-fork/. Accessed December 20, 2019.

Serenity is the final stage of the Ethereum network development, and is also known as Ethereum 2.0. One of the main goals of this final upgrade is to create a more scalable and efficient platform that is capable of handling thousands of transactions per second. Several implementations are expected divided over phases, such as the beacon chain without shards (phase 0), shard chains without EVM (phase 1), the implementation of a new execution engine (phase 2), Phase 3 with the light client state protocol, phase 4 will bring cross-shard transactions, phase 5 tight coupling with main chain security and finally phase 6 with upper-quadratic sharding.[25] This all will eventually lead to 'Ethereum 3.0' which will contain several new implementations.

4.21.1 Phase 0

So in a little more detail, phase 0 brings the implementation of the beacon chain without sharding and validators create an RNG via RANDAO in block proposals, organize into proposers and attestation committees based on the RNG output and create crosslinks for stubbed shards. The beacon chain will be the proof of stake based blockchain version of Ethereum. So far the Ethereum network has always made use of proof of work but with the beacon chain this is supposed to change with the introduction of Casper protocol. The beacon chain will also be used for sharding in the later phases of Serenity. Validators will have to put up a stake of 32 ETH to be able to join the process. These validators will be organized into committees so that they can vote on the proposed blocks. These committees and their validators will make use of 'attestations' to vote on these proposed blocks (beacon blocks and shard blocks). All of this will be done by the beacon chain. On the beacon chain there will also be a new ether called 'ETH2' which is a new asset to be used by the validators. In this phase there will be no way yet for the participants to withdraw this new currency. Finally, RANDAO will introduce sufficient randomness into the system when it comes to organizing validators in proposers and committees.[26]

In this phase the proof of work blockchain that has always been used by the Ethereum blockchain environment will coexist with the beacon chain and all transactions and smart contract computations will still take place on this 'old' chain.

4.21.2 Phase 1

Phase 1 starts with shards (without chain state execution or account balances) and binary large objects (or BLOBs) are collated in shards without transactions. Also notaries will see the light of day in this phase. Sharding is the solution that has been put forward by

---

[25] Ray, J. (March 4, 2019) Sharding roadmap. *Ethereum Wiki.* https://github.com/ethereum/wiki/wiki/Sharding-roadmap. Accessed December 20, 2019.

[26] https://docs.ethhub.io/ethereum-roadmap/ethereum-2.0/eth-2.0-phases/.

Ethereum to deal with the scaling problems that are currently plaguing public blockchain implementations. The problem relies on the fact that a public blockchain cannot be at the same time decentralized, secure and scalable: a choice needs to be made between 2 of the 3.The Bitcoin network tries to solve this with implementations like the Lightening network or sidechains that sparsely interact with the main chain. Sharding leads us to a completely new approach. Before the implementation of sharding, each node has to process each and every single transaction from the network. This again leads to the network only being as fast as the individual nodes.[27] Therefore sharding allows the entire state of the network to be divided in so-called 'shards' which represent each their own piece of state. Each of these shards would be linked to the beacon chain by making use of the Merkle trees (combined data roots) creating a connection between the two which are also called 'crosslinks'. Once such a block with a 'combined data root' has been accepted on the beacon chain, the other shards know they can rely on it for cross-shard transactions. Each of the shards will store receipts of each transaction so that they can still communicate with the other shards and perform transactions with each other. One of the issues is that sharding is way easier to implement when the network makes use of proof of stake instead of proof of work. Active validators can just be assigned to different shards.[28] This is why the Ethereum developers are working on sharding as a part of the Casper protocol implementation (explained below). So in short, basically it means that the main chain is chopped into smaller chains where the node is acting as a full node for a certain shard and as a light client for the other shards. Similar to phase 0, the proof of work chain and the beacon chain with the shards will friendly coexist with one another in this phase as well. This means in practice that validators and miners both will receive rewards for the time being, leading to the necessary inflation but it is during this time that the proof of work chain should lose its appeal while participants are crossing to the beacon chain.

4.21.3 Phase 2

Phase 2 will introduce structured chain states to the shards combined with the use of smart contracts. This will bring with it also accounts, contracts, states and all other basic concepts that we are already using on the Ethereum network today. Perhaps most important to understand is the introduction of eWASM or Ethereum flavored WebAssembly. WebAssembly (or Wasm as a contraction) is a new, portable, size- and load-time-efficient format. WebAssembly aims to execute at native speed by taking advantage of common

---

[27] Jordan, R. (January 10, 2018) How to scale Ethereum: sharding explained. *Medium.* https://medium.com/prysmatic-labs/how-to-scale-ethereum-sharding-explained-ba2e283b7fce. Accessed December 21, 2019.

[28] https://education.district0x.io/general-topics/understanding-ethereum/ethereum-sharding-explained/.

hardware capabilities available on a wide range of platforms and WebAssembly is currently being designed as an open standard by a W3C Community Group.[29] All of this means that it is a virtual machine within the computer that can optimize the execution of commands and operations. It does this by converting or immediately executing of commands because it has a knowledge of the hardware it is running on. The introduction of eWASM is another answer to the question of scalability and is aimed at EVM. Currently, when EVM has to compile code, every node has to compile the node. This is not only very costly but also limits the speed of Ethereum to the speed of the Ethereum Virtual Machine. In this specific implementation WebAssembly is being designed exclusively to work with the smart contracts that exist in Ethereum. It is the goal that eWASM will be able to replace the EVM, optimizing how code is run in the Ethereum network and dramatically improving the transaction throughput in the network. On top of that it can be more secure as it is standardized and it delivers support for more programming languages, leading to a broader developer base. Finally, there would also be the implementation of state rent so that developers would have to pay for eWASM storage over time to make sure that unused data is removed in a timely fashion.

4.21.4   Phase 3

Phase 3 (and the other phases) are still very speculative. I have added the information here but as the previous steps and phases already have shifted and changed a lot, these steps are even more speculative). This phase follows with the introduction of state minimized executions. This with the focus on light clients because the previous phases were all focused on full nodes. How this would be implemented is still under discussion.

4.21.5   Phase 4, 5 and 6

Phase 4 comes with cross-shard transactions. The main introduction that comes with phase 5 is the introduction of fork-free sharding. Finally, there will be phase 6 which, as we mentioned before, comes with super-quadratic sharding. All of these implementations are aimed at increasing the scalability of the network while adhering to the security that we would like to see in the network.

4.21.6   Ethereum 3.0

So what is Ethereum 3.0? The first lines put forward talk about the integration of zk-STARKs in the network and heterogeneous sharding.

---

[29] https://github.com/ewasm/design.

4.22   An Update in 2025

While the book was first published in 2020, a lot has happened. The transition from proof of work to proof of stake has taken place on the 15th of September 2022.[30] This switch from the Mainnet to proof of stake is also known as 'The Merge'. During this event, the legacy Ethereum chain was merged with the Beacon Chain (which was launched in 2020) and officially deprecated proof of work mining.[31] The results were amazing: a reduction of 99.95% in energy consumption and a fundamentally different security model through validators staking ETH rather than miners expending energy. In total there are about 500.000 active validators now in the network instead of the miners in the past.

But I already skipped a couple of steps here. A key transformation in Ethereum's protocol architecture was the introduction of the Beacon Chain, launched on December 1, 2020, as the foundational component of Ethereum's transition from Proof of Work (PoW) to Proof of Stake (PoS). Initially operating in parallel with the existing Ethereum mainnet, the Beacon Chain was designed to serve as the coordination and consensus engine of Ethereum's future PoS-based architecture. It introduced validators, epochs, attestations, and finality, a new framework for how blocks would be agreed upon and finalized, independent of block execution.

Prior to The Merge, Ethereum's state transitions and consensus were intertwined within the PoW paradigm: miners produced blocks, executed transactions, and secured consensus through energy-intensive computation. The Beacon Chain, by contrast, did not originally process user transactions or execute smart contracts; instead, it maintained a registry of validators, assigned block proposal and attestation duties, and implemented a fork-choice rule based on Casper FFG (Friendly Finality Gadget) and LMD GHOST. The critical shift occurred with The Merge, finalized on September 15, 2022, when Ethereum's execution layer (formerly the PoW mainnet) was formally joined with the Beacon Chain's consensus layer. Post-Merge, Ethereum's architecture is defined by this two-layer separation:

- The Execution Layer is responsible for transaction processing, state updates, account balances, and smart contract execution. This corresponds to the original Ethereum mainnet, now stripped of its mining-based consensus logic.
- The Consensus Layer—the Beacon Chain—handles validator orchestration, finality, proposer selection, and the underlying security of the chain via PoS. It determines which blocks are canonical and finalized, irrespective of their execution content.

In this dual-layer model, when a new block is produced, it is first proposed by a validator selected by the Beacon Chain. This validator packages a block containing execution

---

[30] https://ethereum.org/en/roadmap/merge/#:~:text=Shipped%21.

[31] https://ethereum.org/en/roadmap/merge/#:~:text=The%20Merge%20was%20executed%20o n,99.95.

payloads (transactions, state transitions) and propagates it through the network. Other validators then attest to the block's validity, both in terms of its position in the chain (via the fork-choice rule) and the correctness of its execution layer content (via inclusion of the payload and block hash). Once enough attestations are collected and checkpoints finalized, the block becomes part of Ethereum's immutable history. This architectural decoupling offers several long-term benefits. First, it allows consensus and execution logic to evolve independently, enabling modular upgrades. For instance, future enhancements like sharding will focus on scaling the consensus layer, while the execution layer may evolve through EVM extensions or rollup-centric designs. Second, the PoS model introduced by the Beacon Chain is significantly more energy-efficient and provides a clear economic structure around validator rewards and penalties (including slashing for misbehavior).

4.23   Data Sharding

Data sharding is something that will keep coming up when we are discussing Ethereum. Hence, it is a key term for us to understand if we want to know where the network is evolving towards. Ethereum's journey toward scalability has undergone a transformation, moving from traditional sharding concepts to a more refined approach known as Danksharding. This evolution reflects the network's commitment to enhancing throughput and reducing costs without compromising security or decentralization.[32] Initially, Ethereum's scalability roadmap included the implementation of shard chains, which would divide the network into multiple parts, each processing its own transactions and smart contracts. However, this approach presented complexities in terms of cross-shard communication and state management. Recognizing these challenges, Ethereum's developers pivoted toward a model that emphasizes data availability over execution sharding. This shift led to the development of Proto-Danksharding, introduced through Ethereum Improvement Proposal (EIP) 4844.[33] EIP-4844, also known as Proto-Danksharding, represents a foundational step toward full Danksharding. It introduces a new transaction type that carries "blobs" of data, which are large binary objects stored in the consensus layer but not directly accessible by the Ethereum Virtual Machine (EVM). These blobs provide a more efficient and cost-effective method for rollups to post transaction data, significantly reducing gas fees and alleviating network congestion. By decoupling data availability from execution, Proto-Danksharding lays the groundwork for future scalability enhancements.[34]

The implementation of Proto-Danksharding has had a profound impact on Layer 2 (L2) solutions, which rely on Ethereum for data availability. By providing a dedicated space for rollups to store data, Proto-Danksharding has enabled these solutions to operate more

---

[32] https://www.techopedia.com/definition/danksharding.

[33] https://www.gsr.io/insights/updated-ethereums-roadmap-A-guide-to-the-merge-and-beyond.

[34] https://arxiv.org/abs/2409.11043?utm_source=chatgpt.com.

efficiently and at lower costs. This development aligns with Ethereum's rollup-centric roadmap, which envisions L2 solutions handling the majority of transaction execution while the mainnet ensures data availability and security.

Building upon the foundation laid by Proto-Danksharding, Ethereum's roadmap includes the transition to full Danksharding. This advancement aims to further enhance data availability by increasing the number of blobs per block and implementing data availability sampling (DAS). DAS allows validators to verify the availability of data without downloading entire blobs, thereby maintaining network efficiency and scalability. By expanding the capacity for data storage and verification, full Danksharding is expected to support a significant increase in transaction throughput, potentially reaching hundreds of thousands of transactions per second. The progression from Proto-Danksharding to full Danksharding shows Ethereum's commitment to a modular architecture that separates concerns of execution, data availability, and consensus. This design philosophy facilitates scalability while preserving the network's core principles of security and decentralization. As Ethereum continues to evolve, these innovations position the network to meet the growing demands of decentralized applications and users worldwide. Ethereum's shift toward Danksharding represents a strategic and technical advancement in its scalability roadmap. By focusing on data availability and leveraging innovations like blob transactions and data availability sampling, Ethereum is poised to achieve significant improvements in throughput and cost efficiency. These developments not only enhance the performance of the network but also reinforce its role as a foundational platform for decentralized applications in the years to come.

4.24   A Rollup-Centric Roadmap

In the following pages (as well as already in some of the text before) we talked about rollups. It is important to understand what exactly this means, to truly understand the new roadmap for the network. Ethereum's evolution from a monolithic blockchain to a modular, rollup-centric architecture marks a shift in addressing scalability challenges. This transformation has been driven by the development and adoption of Layer 2 (L2) scaling solutions, particularly Optimistic and Zero-Knowledge (ZK) rollups. These technologies have enabled Ethereum to handle increased transaction volumes while maintaining security and decentralization. The rollup-centric roadmap, introduced by Ethereum co-founder Vitalik Buterin, emphasizes the use of rollups to scale Ethereum. Rollups process transactions off-chain and post compressed data back to the Ethereum mainnet, reducing congestion and gas fees. This approach allows Ethereum to maintain its security model while significantly increasing throughput. Optimistic rollups, such as Arbitrum and Optimism, assume that transactions are valid by default and only run computations in case of disputes. They batch multiple transactions off-chain and submit a summary to L1, reducing gas costs. A challenge period (usually seven days) allows for fraud proofs to be submitted if discrepancies are found. This design choice simplifies implementation and has led to faster deployment and adoption. ZK rollups, including zkSync and StarkNet, use validity proofs to ensure transaction correctness. They generate cryptographic proofs for each batch of transactions, which are then verified on L1, providing immediate finality and enhanced security. This approach offers strong security guarantees and faster finality but requires more complex proof computation.[35] The adoption of rollups has significantly increased Ethereum's scalability. By mid-2023, L2 networks processed approximately 61% of all Ethereum transactions, indicating significant adoption. Arbitrum, for instance, handled around 1 million transactions per day, rivaling L1 Ethereum's throughput. This shift has led to reduced transaction fees, with L2 fees often below $0.05 compared to L1's ~$0.30.[36]

4.25   Berlin and London (2021): Paving the Way for Monetary Reform in Ethereum

The year 2021 marked a turning point for Ethereum's economic policy and transaction processing mechanism. While both Berlin and London were incremental upgrades in terms of their codebase and EVM refinements, London (specifically EIP-1559) introduced a paradigm shift in Ethereum's fee market and monetary dynamics, reshaping incentives, predictability, and long-term tokenomics. The Berlin hard fork was primarily a technical upgrade that optimized gas costs and enabled several low-level EVM improvements. Key changes included:

- EIP-2565: Reduced gas cost for the ModExp (modular exponentiation) precompile.
- EIP-2929: Increased gas costs for state access operations to better defend against DoS attacks.
- EIP-2718: Introduced a *transaction type abstraction*, allowing the protocol to support multiple transaction formats in the future.
- EIP-2930: Added access lists, improving efficiency for transactions that interact with multiple contracts or state entries.

While Berlin laid essential groundwork for more flexible and secure transaction types, its reforms were evolutionary. The London hard fork, on the other hand, was transformative. It introduced EIP-1559, which fundamentally restructured Ethereum's transaction fee market, departing from the traditional auction model and moving toward a more deterministic and user-friendly pricing mechanism. Before EIP-1559, Ethereum employed a first-price auction model: users would submit bids (gas prices) to have their transactions

---

[35] https://www.tastycrypto.com/blog/layer-2-networks/.

[36] https://www.coingecko.com/learn/starknet-zk-rollups-zk-stark.

included in a block. This system suffered from volatility, inefficiency, and unpredictability—particularly during network congestion. Users frequently overpaid to get prioritized, and fee estimation was imprecise. Some key features were:

- Base Fee Introduction: Each block has a dynamically adjusted "base fee", which represents the minimum price per gas unit required for inclusion. The base fee is algorithmically adjusted based on network demand: it increases when blocks are full, and decreases when demand subsides. This creates a more predictable and transparent pricing environment.
- Fee Burn Mechanism: Crucially, the base fee is *burned*, not paid to miners (now validators), effectively removing ETH from circulation. Only an optional "tip" (priority fee) is sent to validators as an incentive for timely inclusion. This introduces deflationary pressure on the ETH supply, especially during periods of high network activity.
- Block Gas Limit Elasticity: Blocks can be up to twice the target gas limit (e.g., 30 million vs. a target of 15 million), allowing for smoother adaptation to short-term demand spikes.

EIP-1559 represents Ethereum's move toward a more disciplined and algorithmically governed economic model, akin to central bank monetary policy but executed through deterministic code. It aligns Ethereum with the principle of programmatic scarcity—an emergent counterweight to inflationary dynamics common in traditional fiat systems and even earlier blockchain protocols. Combined with Ethereum's shift to Proof-of-Stake, EIP-1559 has reinforced the idea of ETH not just as a utility token, but as a store of value, potentially comparable to Bitcoin in terms of monetary policy integrity, yet more flexible and expressive.

4.26 Post-merge Scalability: From "Ethereum 2.0" to Danksharding and Beyond

In earlier accounts of Ethereum's development, the term "Ethereum 2.0" was often used to describe a sweeping redesign that would transition the network from Proof of Work to Proof of Stake, introduce sharding, and significantly increase throughput. By 2025, however, this terminology has been formally deprecated in favor of a modular, phased upgrade strategy anchored around Ethereum's existing architecture. This transition in narrative, from monolithic rebrand to incremental execution-layer and consensus-layer improvements, reflects a maturing design philosophy that prioritizes backward compatibility, modularity, and layer separation. With the successful completion of The Merge in 2022, Ethereum replaced its energy-intensive PoW consensus with the Beacon Chain's PoS mechanism. This was a foundational upgrade that preserved the execution layer—Ethereum's state, accounts, contracts, and applications—while migrating consensus duties to a parallel infrastructure. The result is a clean architectural separation between execution (the former mainnet) and consensus (the Beacon Chain). In pre-Merge projections, sharding was envisioned as Ethereum's primary method for scaling throughput. Drawing inspiration from distributed database systems, sharding was to involve splitting Ethereum's state and execution into multiple parallel chains, or shards, each capable of processing transactions independently. However, this design posed formidable challenges both in terms of cross-shard communication complexity and the burden placed on validators to synchronize fragmented global state. These constraints, coupled with the rapid ascendance of Layer-2 (L2) scaling solutions such as rollups, led Ethereum's core developers to reassess and reprioritize the roadmap. This recalibration gave rise to what is now called "The Surge", the next major milestone in Ethereum's development after The Merge. The Surge is centered around scalability, not by distributing computation or state directly across shards, but by augmenting the network's data availability capacity to better support rollup-centric scaling. This approach acknowledges that Ethereum's long-term scalability is most effectively achieved through rollups for execution, paired with base-layer support for abundant, verifiable data availability. The result of this architectural pivot is Danksharding, a fundamentally reimagined form of sharding tailored to the rollup-centric roadmap. Rather than enabling each shard to process transactions and maintain independent state, Danksharding focuses on creating multiple data shards—essentially modular containers for posting large quantities of calldata used by rollups. These data shards do not execute transactions or store state; instead, they provide a scalable medium for compressed rollup data, which is subsequently verified and interpreted by the L2 protocols. The first step toward full Danksharding is represented by EIP-4844, also known as proto-danksharding. This upgrade introduces a new transaction type (blob-carrying transactions) which allows rollups to submit large bundles of data ("blobs") to Ethereum in a cost-efficient and bandwidth-conscious manner. These blobs are made available through the consensus layer but are not retained permanently by the execution layer. This mechanism creates a temporary data availability substrate, sufficient for rollups to perform fraud proofs or zero-knowledge validity proofs, and then discard the raw data after a predetermined window. From a systems design perspective, this model offers substantial scalability benefits. By offloading data-heavy payloads from the execution layer and minimizing the permanent state burden, Ethereum can increase effective throughput by several orders of magnitude while preserving the decentralization and verifiability of the base chain. Furthermore, the use of data availability sampling and KZG commitments ensures that light clients and validators can efficiently verify that data has been made available without downloading it in full. A critical feature for preserving lightweight node participation in a high-throughput environment. In this evolved framework, the Beacon Chain continues to play a central role not only in managing validator duties and finality, but also in coordinating shard data availability. Validators are assigned to sample, attest to, and ensure the availability of data blobs posted to these shards. However, the execution layer remains unified, ensuring that Ethereum's global state, smart contracts, and composability are not fragmented across shards, as originally envisioned in earlier sharding designs. This architecture avoids the pitfalls of complex cross-shard contract calls and preserves atomic composability, a property considered crucial for many DeFi and multi-contract applications. The design thus reflects a strategic trade-off: shard data is distributed, but execution remains centralized to maintain usability and developer experience.

Ethereum's post-Merge roadmap has transitioned from a monolithic "Eth2" vision to a modular, rollup-centric paradigm. The term "Ethereum 2.0" has been retired in favor of a more accurate description of continuous protocol evolution: each milestone—The Merge, The Surge, The Scourge, The Verge, and others—targets specific bottlenecks in scalability, decentralization, or sustainability. Danksharding, as part of The Surge, represents Ethereum's solution to scaling without compromising on decentralization or composability. It redefines sharding from a state-splitting mechanism to a data-layer scalability strategy, optimizing Ethereum for a multi-layer environment where rollups handle execution and the base layer provides data availability, consensus, and settlement.

4.27 The Surge: Scaling via Rollups and Data Sharding

The Surge addresses Ethereum's long-standing scalability bottlenecks. Rather than scaling execution directly on Layer 1, Ethereum has adopted a rollup-centric roadmap, which envisions Layer 2 (L2) rollups as the primary locus for transaction execution, while the base layer focuses on data availability and consensus. To support rollup throughput, The Surge introduces data sharding, with a specific implementation called Danksharding. This architecture avoids sharding execution or state, focusing instead on scaling data availability through shard blobs, large containers for rollup calldata. The initial step toward this vision is proto-danksharding (EIP-4844), which introduces blob-carrying transactions. These transactions store data off-chain in a temporary but verifiable manner, dramatically lowering costs for rollups while preserving data accessibility for fraud or validity proofs.

Key components of The Surge:

- Danksharding: Redesign of sharding to provide scalable data storage, coordinated by the Beacon Chain.
- EIP-4844 (proto-danksharding): Intermediate upgrade enabling scalable blob storage before full shard implementation.
- Data availability sampling: Efficient verification of large data sets by light clients.

Goal: Support 100,000 + transactions per second via rollup execution and optimized Layer 1 data throughput.

The original timeline for The Surge looked like the following (but in May 2025 EIP-4844 was still not implemented!)[37]:

- **Q1 2024—Dencun Upgrade (Proto-Danksharding Launch)**
  - Introduced Proto-Danksharding (EIP-4844) to improve data availability through data "blobs."
  - Lays the foundation for further rollup scaling.
  - Ethereum's Layer 2 solutions begin leveraging improved data availability for faster and cheaper transactions.
- **2024–2025—Rollup Expansion and Maturing Proof Systems**
  - Rollups like Arbitrum, Optimism, and zkSync will implement updates to enhance scalability.
  - New cryptographic proofs (e.g., SNARKs) will improve the trustlessness of rollups.
  - Data Availability Sampling (DAS) systems such as PeerDAS and 2D DAS will expand to support higher transaction throughput.
- **Late 2025—Gas Pricing Optimization and Layer 1 Enhancements**
  - Introduction of EOF (Ethereum Object Format) for more efficient smart contract execution.
  - Potential adoption of multidimensional gas pricing to separate fees for computation, data, and storage.
  - Possible native rollup solutions directly integrated into Ethereum's protocol.
- **2026 and Beyond—Full Danksharding Rollout**
  - Transition from Proto-Danksharding to full Danksharding, dividing Ethereum into multiple shards to boost scalability further.
  - Ethereum aims to fully reach over 100,000 transactions per second across Layer 1 and Layer 2 ecosystems.
- **Post-2026—Ongoing Monitoring and Upgrades**
  - Introduction of advanced consensus mechanisms, including post-quantum cryptography, to secure the network.
  - Ethereum continues to optimize and integrate cross-L2 interoperability for a seamless user experience.

4.28   The Scourge: Censorship Resistance and MEV Neutrality

The Scourge is Ethereum's forthcoming initiative to address the risks of censorship, centralized block production, and Maximum Extractable Value (MEV). While Ethereum's shift to PoS improved environmental sustainability and security, it also heightened concerns around MEV—the practice of reordering or inserting transactions in blocks for profit. These risks are intensified by the rise of builder-centralized ecosystems, where a

---

[37] What Is The Surge Phase in Ethereum 2.0 Upgrade?|KuCoin Learn.

small number of block builders, often external to validators, dominate block construction. This dynamic introduces economic centralization and poses threats to transaction neutrality and censorship resistance.

The Scourge proposes several countermeasures:

- Implementation of Proposer-Builder Separation (PBS): A design that splits block proposal and block building to reduce centralization and enable competitive block markets.
- Encrypted mempools or delayed transaction revelation to mitigate frontrunning and MEV extraction.
- Mechanisms to ensure transaction inclusion fairness, possibly through protocol-enforced orderings or privacy-preserving submission methods.

The Scourge is thus about safeguarding Ethereum's credibility as a neutral public infrastructure, ensuring that transaction inclusion is not captured by economic or political actors.

4.29   The Verge: Statelessness and Verkle Trees

The Verge addresses Ethereum's long-term goal of becoming a stateless blockchain, thereby reducing the burden on full nodes and improving scalability and decentralization. The current model requires nodes to maintain and access the entire Ethereum state (balances, contract storage, etc.) to validate new blocks, a model that becomes increasingly costly as state grows. The Verge introduces Verkle trees, a more efficient data structure than Merkle Patricia Tries (used today). Verkle trees enable compact state proofs that can be verified without requiring the entire state database. This advancement supports:

- Stateless clients, which only need proofs rather than full state to verify blocks.
- Faster synchronization and lower hardware requirements for nodes.
- Long-term viability for light clients and mobile verification.

Key features:

- Vector commitments: Cryptographic commitments to sets of data allowing for succinct and verifiable proofs.
- Verkle witnesses: Compact proofs of state that can be bundled in blocks.

Together with other changes (like EIP-4444 for historical data pruning), The Verge moves Ethereum toward a more scalable and inclusive network, where running a validating node is feasible for a broader population.

4.30   The Purge and the Splurge: Finalizing Ethereum's Evolutionary Trajectory

Following the execution of transformative protocol shifts such as *The Merge* and *The Surge*, aimed at achieving massive scalability via rollups and data availability enhancements, Ethereum's development roadmap culminates in two conceptually elegant yet technically formidable phases: The Purge and The Splurge. These stages are not simply afterthoughts or clean-up operations; rather, they represent a philosophical and architectural maturation of the Ethereum protocol, aligning it with its long-term vision of decentralization, modularity, and usability at planetary scale.

I. **The Purge: Toward Minimalist Protocol Architecture**

The Purge is envisioned as a large-scale simplification initiative whose objective is to excise vestigial technical debt and legacy burdens that have accumulated in the protocol's codebase since its inception. At its core, the Purge seeks to reduce the systemic load on node operators by minimizing historical state data requirements and streamlining protocol complexity. This goal is both functional and ideological: a more lightweight Ethereum is one that lowers barriers to entry, promotes wider node decentralization, and upholds the network's resistance to centralization pressures. Among the most significant features in this phase is EIP-4444, which introduces *history expiration*. This is a mechanism whereby Ethereum nodes are no longer required to retain execution layer history older than a predefined window (e.g., one year). This aligns with a broader push toward statelessness, where nodes can validate blocks without maintaining full state, facilitated by cryptographic constructs like Verkle Trees. The Purge includes state expiry mechanisms, ensuring that dormant or obsolete contract states are pruned from the network, further mitigating state bloat. This not only reduces storage overheads, but also enhances synchronization speed for new or recovering nodes, ensuring faster participation in consensus and reducing the asymmetries between lightweight and full nodes.

II. **The Splurge: Protocol Refinement and Ideological Realization**

Following the systematic simplification of the Purge, Ethereum enters The Splurge, a phase that represents the culmination of its architectural evolution, a space for creative expression, protocol polish, and user-experience enhancement. In Vitalik Buterin's own formulation, the Splurge is reserved for "all the other fun stuff". Key advancements targeted in the Splurge include the implementation of Verkle Trees, which not only support the stateless vision initiated in the Purge but also significantly optimize proof sizes and verification times. Another landmark development is EIP-4337, which paves the way for account abstraction, allowing users to create programmable and flexible wallets with built-in logic such as social recovery, automated gas fee payments, and multisignature configurations—previously unfeasible within the canonical externally owned account (EOA) structure. The Splurge seeks to refine Ethereum's gas accounting mechanisms, upgrade smart contract tooling, and integrate improved support for zero-knowledge (ZK) cryptographic primitives, thereby enhancing both privacy and scalability. Whereas the earlier phases were largely infrastructural, the Splurge reflects a maturation into a user-centric protocol, replete with developer affordances, UX upgrades, and architectural coherence.

Together, the Purge and the Splurge represent Ethereum's final steps in transitioning from an experimental blockchain infrastructure into a robust, accessible, and future-proof global computation layer. While the Purge champions minimalism and modularity, the Splurge embraces expressivity and elegance, reflecting a dialectical progression in Ethereum's design philosophy, from necessity to possibility, from burden to liberation. This roadmap not only improves Ethereum's technical robustness and performance, but also embodies a deeper principle: that sustainable decentralization requires both architectural restraint and creative flexibility. In its final form, Ethereum aims to be a platform not only for smart contracts but for sustainable, sovereign computation at scale.

4.31   Execution Layer Hard Forks

With the landmark completion of *The Merge* in September 2022, Ethereum's execution layer entered a new epoch, no longer tasked with orchestrating its own consensus, but instead co-evolving alongside the now-independent consensus layer, underpinned by Proof-of-Stake. This architectural decoupling cleared the way for Ethereum to fully embrace its modular roadmap, specifically the transition to a rollup-centric scalability paradigm. In this context, the execution layer's subsequent hard forks—Shanghai, Cancún, Prague, Osaka, and Amsterdam—represent not isolated software updates but rather milestones in a coordinated trajectory toward statelessness, data availability optimization, and EVM evolution.

4.31.1   Shanghai (April 12, 2023): Completing the Proof-Of-Stake Transition

The Shanghai hard fork was the first major post-Merge update to the execution layer. While the Merge unified Ethereum's execution under Proof-of-Stake, it left one critical feature incomplete: validator withdrawals. Shanghai closed this loop by introducing EIP-4895, which enabled stakers to withdraw both principal and reward balances from the Beacon Chain to the execution layer. Though primarily an infrastructural update, Shanghai symbolized the *operational finality* of Ethereum's PoS transformation, allowing for a more dynamic and accessible staking ecosystem. It also marked the first tangible integration between the two previously decoupled layers post-Merge, establishing a template for future interlayer coordination.

4.31.2 Cancún (March 13, 2024): Proto-Danksharding and the Rollup Scalability Thesis

The Cancún hard fork, together with its consensus-layer counterpart Deneb, delivered one of Ethereum's most anticipated scalability upgrades: EIP-4844, also known as proto-danksharding. This proposal introduced a novel transaction format containing *blobs*: ephemeral, non-execution data fields specifically designed to accommodate rollup data at lower cost. Blobs are not directly accessible to the EVM and are retained for a limited period (e.g., ~30 days), drastically reducing the cost and permanence of storing large volumes of Layer 2 data on Ethereum. This was a paradigm shift in data availability architecture, acknowledging that Ethereum's base layer need not directly execute every transaction, but rather function as a high-integrity data availability layer for rollups. EIP-4844 can be seen as a prototype of full danksharding, where future implementations will integrate multiple data shards, ultimately allowing Ethereum to scale to 100,000 + transactions per second while preserving decentralization and verifiability. Cancún thus instantiated the rollup-centric vision not just as theory, but as economic and infrastructural reality.

4.31.3 Prague (Late 2024, Tentative): A Fork in Deliberation

The next anticipated fork, Prague, remains under active community discussion. Initially envisioned as part of a composite upgrade (Prague-Electra or Pectra), its final scope is as yet undetermined. However, proposed features include enhancements to account abstraction, further progress toward EVM Object Format (EOF) standardization, and potential auxiliary upgrades aimed at enhancing both developer ergonomics and L2 synergy. The indeterminacy of Prague reflects Ethereum's increasingly pluralistic governance ecosystem, where proposals undergo rigorous community vetting and inter-client coordination before being ratified. In a sense, Prague embodies Ethereum's constitutional commitment to decentralized evolution—a protocol whose direction is shaped not by singular vision but by multi-stakeholder consensus.

4.31.4 Osaka (2025): Consolidating Execution Efficiency and Data Sharing

Slated for deployment in 2025, Osaka is expected to consolidate several significant features into a coherent upgrade. Foremost among them is the implementation of EVM Object Format (EOF), a comprehensive redesign of the EVM's binary structure that introduces code validation rules, versioning, and modularity. EOF not only improves execution-layer efficiency and security, but also lays the groundwork for *future-proofing the EVM*, enabling the safe inclusion of advanced features like zero-knowledge opcodes and formal verification mechanisms. Complementing this is PeerDAS (Peer-to-Peer Data Availability Sampling), a mechanism that allows nodes to validate data availability without needing to download full datasets—essential for future sharded or rollup-heavy Ethereum. These upgrades aim to optimize execution performance while preparing Ethereum for a decentralized, bandwidth-efficient data-sharing future.

4.31.5 Amsterdam (2026): Realizing Stateless Ethereum with Verkle Trees

Finally, the Amsterdam fork, projected for 2026, is expected to introduce Verkle Trees. A cryptographic commitment scheme designed to replace Ethereum's current Merkle-Patricia Trie structure. Unlike traditional Merkle trees, Verkle Trees allow for dramatically smaller proof sizes, enabling clients to verify specific parts of the state with minimal data overhead. This is the critical technological enabler for stateless Ethereum, wherein nodes can validate blocks without maintaining full access to the global state. Statelessness democratizes node participation, drastically reducing storage requirements and enhancing Ethereum's decentralization at the infrastructure level. Verkle Trees also facilitate a host of auxiliary benefits, including faster state syncing, reduced block propagation latency, and enhanced compatibility with zero-knowledge proof systems, making them a cornerstone in Ethereum's pursuit of modular, verifiable, and scalable computation.

4.31.6 The Consensus Layer Hard Forks

Ethereum's consensus layer has been the silent yet foundational counterpart in the protocol's metamorphosis. Formally initiated with the Beacon Chain genesis on December 1, 2020, the consensus layer represents Ethereum's deliberate and methodical departure from energy-intensive Proof-of-Work (PoW) toward a scalable, energy-efficient Proof-of-Stake (PoS) paradigm. Each subsequent upgrade to this layer—Altair, Bellatrix, Capella, Deneb, and the upcoming Electra, Fulu, and G-Star—reflects a phased evolution toward not only finality and validator efficiency, but also Ethereum's broader aspirations of modular scalability and cryptographic provability.

4.31.7 Beacon Chain Genesis (December 1, 2020): the Inauguration of PoS Consensus

The launch of the Beacon Chain inaugurated Ethereum's consensus layer as a parallel construct to the existing execution environment. Though initially disconnected from transaction execution, it marked a critical milestone: the instantiation of a validator-based consensus engine built entirely on PoS principles, governed by cryptoeconomic incentives, and structured around epoch-based finality checkpoints. This separation of consensus from execution was not just architectural—it was ideological, laying the groundwork for Ethereum's modular future.

4.31.8 Altair (October 27, 2021): Operationalizing the Beacon Chain

The first upgrade to the Beacon Chain, Altair, introduced tangible enhancements to the protocol's internal mechanics. Most notably, it implemented:

- Sync committees, enabling the development of *light clients*—resource-efficient clients capable of tracking consensus with minimal data, essential for decentralization.
- Validator inactivity penalties and *slashing refinements*, improving protocol liveness and security.

Altair served as a *testbed* for upgrading the consensus layer under live conditions, demonstrating that Ethereum's PoS system could evolve without disruption.

4.31.9 Bellatrix (September 6, 2022): the Merge Catalyst

Bellatrix was a crucial preparatory hard fork, integrating the necessary logic within the Beacon Chain to enable the Merge. Specifically, it introduced support for a new block structure—*execution payloads*—to be sourced from the PoW chain until the Terminal Total Difficulty (TTD) was reached. Once this threshold was crossed, the Beacon Chain assumed full responsibility for block finalization, thus triggering the Merge. While Bellatrix did not change consensus rules per se, it was essential for the orchestration of the Merge, functioning as a synchronization and compatibility layer between consensus and execution.

4.31.10 The Merge (September 15, 2022): Ethereum's Constitutional Moment

The Merge itself is *not a traditional hard fork* but rather a deterministic, *difficulty-triggered consensus transition*. Upon reaching the Terminal Total Difficulty, Ethereum permanently disabled PoW and began proposing and finalizing blocks exclusively through PoS validators on the Beacon Chain.

This event was arguably the most complex and politically significant upgrade in Ethereum's history. It slashed the network's energy consumption by over 99.9%, removed miner incentives, and introduced finality—a cryptoeconomic guarantee that finalized blocks cannot be reverted without incurring enormous slashing penalties.

4.31.11 Capella (April 12, 2023): Enabling Validator Withdrawals

With Capella, the consensus layer underwent its first major functional enhancement post-Merge. It introduced EIP-4895, enabling validators to withdraw staked ETH and accrued rewards—a capability previously locked since the Beacon Chain's inception. Capella, synchronized with its execution-layer counterpart Shanghai, marked the completion of Ethereum's staking lifecycle by closing the loop between deposit and withdrawal. This unlocked staker liquidity, improved validator incentives, and provided a critical stress test of Ethereum's withdrawal queue mechanism and consensus stability.

4.31.12 Deneb (March 13, 2024): Scaling the Data Layer with EIP-4844

The Deneb fork paralleled the execution-layer Cancún upgrade and together they delivered EIP-4844, or proto-danksharding. While Cancún enabled blob-carrying transactions on the execution layer, Deneb introduced the consensus logic to validate, propagate, and store these blobs temporarily. This bifurcation, execution handles transaction logic, consensus governs blob data, illustrates Ethereum's move toward modular scalability, where the base layer coordinates data availability rather than direct computation. Deneb's design ensures that rollup data remains verifiable and retrievable, supporting trust-minimized Layer 2 solutions at dramatically lower costs.

4.31.13 Electra (Late 2024, Tentative): A Fork in Flux

Electra, expected by the end of 2024, is currently in the specification and deliberation phase. Although its final scope remains under community review, proposed features are expected to align with those of Prague on the execution side—possibly including further EOF extensions, validator UX improvements, and enhancements to staking dynamics. Like Prague, Electra reflects Ethereum's iterative governance model, where protocol evolution is the outcome of community-driven decision-making rather than top-down imposition.

4.31.14 Fulu (End of 2025): Deeper Modular Enhancements

The Fulu upgrade is anticipated to consolidate consensus-layer support for features such as:

- EOF extensions, allowing for more predictable execution environments.
- PeerDAS, enabling decentralized data availability sampling, essential for scaling Layer 2 rollups and eventually sharded architectures.

Fulu will further Ethereum's commitment to decentralized validation and data integrity across a bandwidth-constrained and heterogeneous validator set, emphasizing computational efficiency without compromising verifiability.

4.31.15 G-Star (End of 2026): Toward Stateless Finality

Projected for the end of 2026, G-Star is expected to be the consensus-layer counterpart to Amsterdam. It is tentatively reserved for the implementation of Verkle Trees, a next-generation cryptographic commitment scheme designed to replace Merkle-Patricia tries. Within the consensus context, Verkle Trees will:

- Enable stateless block validation, allowing validators to confirm blocks without holding the full state.
- Drastically reduce sync and storage requirements, democratizing validator participation.
- Improve light client compatibility, further promoting accessibility and decentralization.

G-Star, thus, represents a culmination of Ethereum's state minimization thesis, pairing the guarantees of finality with the elegance of stateless design.

4.31.16 Account Abstraction and New Protocol Features

Ethereum's evolution includes advancements in usability and security at the protocol level. A key development is the introduction of Account Abstraction (EIP-4337), which redefines user interactions with the Ethereum network. Ethereum distinguishes between Externally Owned Accounts (EOAs), controlled by private keys, and Contract Accounts, governed by smart contract code. This bifurcation imposes limitations on user experience and flexibility. EIP-4337 addresses these constraints by enabling account abstraction without necessitating changes to the consensus layer. This proposal introduces a higher-layer mechanism that allows users to operate smart contract wallets with customizable verification logic, effectively transforming the way accounts function on Ethereum. The core innovation of EIP-4337 lies in its utilization of a new transaction type called "UserOperation," which is processed by a decentralized network of "bundlers." These bundlers collect UserOperations from an alternative mempool and submit them to a central EntryPoint contract deployed on the Ethereum mainnet. This architecture facilitates a range of enhanced functionalities, including multi-signature security, social recovery mechanisms, gas fee payments in various tokens, and batched transactions, all executed at the account level. Such capabilities significantly improve the user experience, aligning it more closely with that of custodial wallets while preserving the principles of self-custody. The deployment of the EntryPoint contract on March 1, 2023, marked the operationalization of EIP-4337 on the Ethereum mainnet. This implementation has led to the creation of over 26 million smart wallets and the processing of approximately 170 million UserOperations, indicating substantial adoption and utility. By circumventing the need for a hard fork, EIP-4337 exemplifies a pragmatic approach to protocol enhancement, leveraging existing infrastructure to deliver meaningful improvements in account management and security.

Beyond account abstraction, Ethereum has introduced several other protocol-level enhancements aimed at improving network efficiency and security. EIP-1559, implemented in August 2021 as part of the London hard fork, overhauled the transaction fee mechanism by introducing a base fee that is burned, thereby reducing fee volatility and contributing to the deflationary pressure on Ether's supply. This change not only improved user predictability in transaction costs but also aligned economic incentives within the network. The Shanghai/Capella upgrade, activated on April 12, 2023, enabled staking withdrawals, allowing validators to retrieve their staked Ether and rewards. This development completed Ethereum's transition to a Proof-of-Stake consensus mechanism, enhancing the network's sustainability and providing validators with greater flexibility and liquidity. In addressing concerns related to Maximal Extractable Value (MEV), Ethereum is exploring the implementation of Proposer-Builder Separation (PBS). This approach delineates the roles of block proposers and builders, aiming to mitigate the centralization of power and reduce the potential for transaction manipulation. By distributing responsibilities, PBS seeks to enhance fairness and security within the block production process. Ethereum plans to integrate Verkle trees into its state management architecture. Verkle trees offer a more efficient data structure compared to the current Merkle Patricia trees, enabling smaller proof sizes and facilitating stateless client designs. This advancement is expected to significantly reduce the storage requirements for nodes, promoting greater decentralization and scalability across the network. Collectively, these developments underscore Ethereum's commitment to continuous improvement in usability, security, and scalability. By implementing innovative solutions like account abstraction, fee mechanism reforms, staking flexibility, MEV mitigation strategies, and advanced data structures, Ethereum is positioning itself to meet the evolving demands of its user base and maintain its prominence in the decentralized ecosystem.

4.32   Gnosis Safe

Among the tools that have risen to prominence in addressing these concerns is Safe (formerly known as Gnosis Safe), a multi-signature wallet solution that has become the de facto standard for treasury management among decentralized autonomous organizations (DAOs), DeFi projects, and various blockchain-based entities. Safe's architecture allows for the creation of smart contract wallets that require multiple approvals before executing transactions. This multi-signature approach ensures that no single individual has unilateral control over significant funds, thereby mitigating risks associated with key compromises or malicious actors. For instance, the Uniswap DAO, one of the largest DAOs by treasury size, manages over \$2.2 billion in assets using a Safe multisig wallet configuration. This setup necessitates multiple delegate approvals for large transactions, enhancing security and promoting collective decision-making.[38]

The adoption of Safe extends beyond Uniswap. Numerous DAOs and blockchain projects have integrated Safe into their operational frameworks. Its compatibility with various Ethereum-based wallets, including MetaMask, Ledger, and Trezor, as well as its support for multiple networks like Ethereum Mainnet, Arbitrum, and Polygon, make it a versatile choice for organizations seeking robust asset management solutions.[39] Beyond its core multi-signature functionality, Safe offers modularity through the integration of various modules and plugins. These extensions allow for enhanced features such as transaction guards, spending limits, and role-based access controls. For example, the implementation of Safe Guard modules can restrict transaction types, adding an additional layer of security against unauthorized activities.[40] The significance of Safe in the Ethereum ecosystem is further underscored by its integration with institutional tools. MetaMask Institutional,

---

[38] https://blockchainreporter.net/top-15-daos-ranked-by-treasury-size-mantle-uniswap-optimism-lead-the-pack/.

[39] https://pexx.com/chaindebrief/not-just-institutions-how-gnosis-multi-sig-wallets-keep-your-coins-safe/

[40] https://markaicode.com/dao-treasury-security-gnosis-safe-multisig/.

for instance, has incorporated Safe into its suite of offerings, providing organizations with streamlined access to multi-signature functionalities alongside other custody solutions.

4.33 Scalability and the Casper Protocol

So far we have been focusing on how the network works and how it will be changed in the future but we still have some concepts to explain. State channels and plasma are 2 projects that also focus on the scalability of the network and aim to improve it for the participants. Finally, I also added an explanation on the Casper protocol.

State channels in 2025 remain relevant for specific use cases but are no longer one of the key solutions for scalability (here rollup technology has taken up a much more prevalent role). State channels proof their worth still for use cases where instant finality and privacy are a key concern. When we look at the Casper protocol, this has proven its worth during the transition from proof of work to proof of stake. However, now we have evolved beyond the initial Casper implementations to a system where Casper FFG with LMD-GHOST fork choice rule are the current system.

4.33.1 State Channels

State channels are one of the several solution put forward to deal with the scalability issues that Ethereum is facing. State channels are very similar to the Lightening network that is being used by the Bitcoin platform, allowing for off-chain transactions to take place, which can be propagated later when the channel is being closed. The state channels in the Ethereum world also allow for something else: they support state updates (hence the name). Comparable to the Lightening network, a certain amount of Ether is locked by sending the amount to a multisignature smart contract which can both accept and pay out the coins. Once the Ether is in the contract, the participants can sign transactions (of which each party contains a copy) that each have nonce to keep track of the chronological order. The channel can eventually be closed by emitting a transaction to the Ethereum main chain.[41]

4.33.2 Plasma[42]

Plasma is yet another solution put forward to deal with the scalability issues of the Ethereum network. With this implementation it allows the creation of child chains that

---

[41] https://education.district0x.io/general-topics/understanding-ethereum/basics-state-channels/.

[42] http://plasma.io/

use the main chain (or a shard of the main chain) as a trust and arbitration layer.[43] Plasma allows for the creation of chains that can be used for specific implementations that currently aren't feasible with the existing main chain. These chains can be adapted when looking at block size, consensus algorithm, block times and so on. Of course there are some limitations as there is still a need for a consensus algorithm that enforces the Nakamoto consensus incentive and a bitmap-UTXO commitment structure to enforce the state transitions. This way DApps can be created that fit any purpose depending on the needs of the participants, and increasing the scalability of the Ethereum network tremendously. How is all of this linked together? By making use of 'plasma contracts' that connect to the root chain. These allow the transfer of assets between the main chain and the child chains. The general rule is that these assets have to be first created on the main chain before they can be moved to a child chain, this to prevent malicious activity from the child chain to propagate to the main chain. Another possible problem is the centralization on the child chains, which could lead to mined blocks that do not represent true transactions. Plasma has a solution for this: the possibility for each participant to show fraud proofs (by making use of a MapReduce computing framework). The main concern with plasma is that it takes quite a long time to withdraw assets (between 7 and 14 days).

4.34 The Casper Protocol[44]

The Casper consensus protocol is a hybrid of the proof of work and proof of stake protocols. While the first is deemed undemocratic and is very costly in terms of hardware and energy. On the other hand the proof of stake protocol is efficient and more secure but has the 'nothing at stake' problem to deal with. Enter: the Casper consensus protocol. Casper differs from other proof of stake protocols as it punishes malicious actors in the network. We again work with validators that have to stake a portion of their Ether to enter the position. The validators are starting to validate blocks and when they have discovered a block that they deem to be a valid candidate to enter the chain, they have to place a bet on the block. If the block is accepted, the validators get rewarded for the bet they placed on the block, if the block is denied, they lose everything. Actually there were two research projects undertaken by the Ethereum development team. At the one hand there is the Casper the Friendly Finality Gadget (or FFG) and the Casper the friendly ghost: correct-by-construction (or CBC). The FFG version[45] was first proposed to aid the transition from proof of work to proof of stake. The proof of work protocol was still active but instead, every 50th block had a proof of stake checkpoint where the

---

[43] https://education.district0x.io/general-topics/understanding-ethereum/understanding-plasma/.

[44] Rosic, A. (2017) What is Ethereum Casper Protocol? Crash Course. *Blockgeeks.* https://blockgeeks.com/guides/ethereum-casper/. Accessed December 22, 2019.

[45] Also known as 'Vitalik's Casper'.

Table 4.1 CBC protocol design

Normal protocol design	CBC protocol design
Formally specify the protocol	Formally but partially specify the protocol
Define protocol properties that must be satisfied	Define properties that the protocol must specify
Prove that it satisfies the properties	Derive the protocol so that it satisfies all the properties that it was stated to specify

finality was assessed.[46] It provides extra finality over the standard proof of work protocol because there is total economic finality. About 2/3rd of the miners in the network put up there entire stake when validating a block, so they stand to lose a lot when they would try to act maliciously. There is also the possibility of a double finality, where in the case of Casper, the participants would have to choose a chain and the majority vote would select the main chain (resulting in a hard fork). This protocol was proposed several times but eventually was moved entirely from the implementation timeline (Table 4.1).

The CBC[47] version will bring even more changes to the use of the protocol.[48]

If we want to derive the full protocol, we would have to implement an 'ideal adversary' which would raise exceptions and list out any future failures that might happen.

4.34.1 Safety Oracles

In this Casper V2 implementation, there has been a lot of confusion on how this might look like. Also because the developer team behind the Ethereum network has several times changed the roadmap and the approach to this new protocol. In the latest update (at the time of writing) there has been the following proposal. The Ethereum network would be split into several separate chains of which there would be 1 Ethereum proof of work chain, 1 beacon chain and a number of sharding chains. The first is the current chain which still uses the proof of work protocol. If miners want to continue mining, they will have to deposit 32 Ether to the beacon chain, after which they will receive the roll of 'validator'. This beacon chain will become the main proof of stake chain within the Ethereum network and will also be the base layer of the sharding chains. It will link to these separate chains and make clear which blocks from these shards can be added to the main chain. This main chain will be the beacon chain. So what are these sharding chains? To prevent that every node will be working on every transaction, there will be

---

[46] Finality means that when a transaction (or any operation really), once done, is locked in the blockchain without the possibility to revert this. In realiy this can never be achieved for 100%.

[47] Also known as Vlad's Casper.

[48] Check out the presentation of Vlad Zamfir on https://www.youtube.com/channel/UCNOfzGXD_C9YMYmnefmPH0g/videos.

a division in separate sharding chains, where nodes will be working on a specific subset of the transactions in the overall network. Simply put, validation and finality will be provided by the beacon chain while transactions and account data will be stored on the shard chains.

4.35   Smart Contracts

We now had a very thorough discussion on how the Ethereum network works and what the blockchain looks like and often there was a specific term that kept on coming back: smart contracts. Smart contracts that can be executed on the network is one of the central concepts and most important addition brought by Ethereum. It allows for the execution of automated contracts when certain conditions are met. It is one of the main reasons why Ethereum is so popular and why there is an entire ecosystem of developers and independent projects that all refer to this main concept. An important concept to understand in the world of Ethereum and smart contracts is the so-called 'halting problem' that keeps on coming back when you talk about Turing complete machines. It was a concept that was first stated by Alan Turing, and in short it means that it is impossible to create an algorithm that is capable of knowing if a program will actually terminate its execution for all possible inputs. In Ethereum this means that we cannot known if a smart contract will ever end. To solve this problem (but also other security related vulnerabilities), the concept of 'gas' was invented to deal with this directly. This way the execution of a smart contract will always be halted and why we say that smart contracts in Ethereum must be 'terminable'. This problem does also arise to other blockchain/distributed ledger technologies that aim to be Turing complete. The Bitcoin blockchain isn't Turing complete, so this issue doesn't arise as such in this environment. Every command is bound to finish in the Bitcoin environment. Furthermore we state that smart contracts must also be deterministic, meaning that for a given input, the output must be the same every time. A final characteristic is that the smart contract must be 'isolated'. The smart contract and more importantly, the results of a smart contract are isolated from the rest of the network. This to prevent certain malware or issues of influencing the entire network and compromising the entire ecosystem. This is where the Ethereum virtual machine comes in, as we explained before. Smart contracts are one of the novel innovations brought by the Ethereum network. The main purpose and meaning behind the term is that we are talking about a contract that can be executed without the intervention of a third party, but completely based on computerized transaction protocols. The idea here is that contractual obligations between several parties can be based upon computer code, which does not leave any room for interpretation but is executed from the second the necessary conditions are met for execution. This in combination with a blockchain network makes sure that the contract is replicated and stored while at the same time providing the necessary security and immutability. This concept was first brought to life with the advent of the Ethereum network but it is certainly no longer limited to Ethereum. A short distinction that we are going to make here is the difference between smart contracts and Ricardian contracts. If we follow the definition, a Ricardian contract is "a digital contract that defines the terms and conditions of an interaction, between two or more peers, that is cryptographically signed and verified. Importantly it is both human and machine readable and digitally signed." The main goal of a Ricardian contract is that it is a legally valid document that is stored in such a way that it can be executed by software. You can clearly see that there are certain points where both smart contracts and Ricardian contracts match but there are also points where they differ. A smart contract can be a Ricardian contract but certainly doesn't has to be and vice versa. If we can achieve both than that is nice, but in reality this will often not be the case. Now how are contracts actually created on the Ethereum platform? Well, in fact we need a completely new account for the contract so this needs to be created. This is done by following a specific set of steps:

- The nonce = 0
- Account balance = value that sender is sending with the contract creation transaction
- Storage = empty
- codeHash = hash of empty string.

The creation is finalized by the 'init code' in the transaction which can in itself create more accounts, call other contracts or send out some transactions.

4.36   Blockchain Oracles

Blockchain oracles are agents that reside on the blockchain to gather and verify real-world information and use this for the execution of smart contracts. This might seem a bit abstract but it comes down to this. A blockchain is a data structure and this is not capable of accessing data outside of its own network. Here the oracle enters the story as this is a third-party service that comes into play to provide the data necessary for a smart contract to be resolved. You might instantly spot a security issue. How do we trust the oracle? It is no part of the blockchain so there is no way of knowing if it is actually feeding us truthful data. Several techniques have now already been implemented to help build a security on top of these oracle. Notable examples are Oracalize with TLS notary-based proofs and Town Crier that makes use of Intel Software Guard Extensions. Furthermore, there are several types of oracles that we can identify. There is the difference between software and hardware oracles. The first provides us information from the online world, while the second feeds information from the physical world. We can also make a distinction between inbound and outbound oracles where the first feeds information to smart contracts, while the second sends information out of the blockchain environment. We will see later on several examples of blockchain oracles and how they interact with smart contracts and decentralized application on the Ethereum platform (and other platforms). They provide even more possibilities for the development of applications and new ways of working in a decentralized world.

4.37 DApps

The DApp or the decentralized application is the next step when we enter the world of blockchain and smart contracts. It adds another layer on top of smart contracts. This layer makes it a full-fledged application that can be used in a user friendly way. For the user not that much changes. They can still work with a user interface with which they are familiar while at the same time they are dealing with a completely different underlying structure. Does this matter? In reality, this will only aid the adoption of blockchain based technology and applications, as users do not want to be confronted with the technological part of things, they just want to use applications for what they were intended. Nowadays, users do not want to go through lengthy processes of learning how something works, an (d)app has to be quick and easy to understand.

4.38 Decentralized and Autonomous

With the introduction of smart contracts and decentralized applications, comes the introduction of something different: the decentralized autonomous organization. This is an organization that is ruled by the code that has been imposed in the smart contracts that make up the organization. These rules are recorded and maintained on the blockchain together with all financial records. We already mentioned shortly in the timeline of Ethereum that there have been some issues in the past with the most famous one the hack of the DAO. Still, it is an interesting concept that is worth exploring as there are numerous future possibilities based on this a bit foreign concept. Several advantages can be thought of when this is implemented correctly. The need for third parties to approve and verify transactions taking place is removed and the code in place clearly defines the rules one has to live by when one wants to be part of the organization. You can solidify democratic voting systems and prevent fraud in a basic way, allowing all participants to aid in the future determination of the organization. Problem of course is the participation of all users in these votes. You could implement a system that forces participants to cast a vote but how far does the system remain democratic in that sense? Another challenge for the future is the legal status of such an organization. In the current legal frameworks, a decentralized organization would probably be considered a general partnership or a joint venture where all participants bare full legal responsibility. This means that all personal belongings of each party involved in a decentralized organization could be seized for the debtors of the organization.[49] Something to think about before you jump into unknown waters. Even more important is that the SEC in the US has determined that this can be seen as unregistered securities offerings, which are illegal and can lead to prosecution.[50] It proves to be scalable, resilient and decentralized governance, enabling broader adoption of DAOs by the public. DAOs have to deal with several problems, which are immediately also the reason why we haven't seen many of them out there as of yet. Daostack tried to solve these with their own interpretation of the problems and the possible solution. Scalability is an obvious problem as the participation of all members of a DAO for each decision is inherently unlikely, leading to a situation where the entire DAO is in an endless state of indecisiveness. While the opposite leads to misrepresentation of the real consensus within the DAO, or even worse: collusion and malicious decisions. A possible solution that is now in use is called holographic consensus, which is based on decisions made on a local level with limited attention and voting power.[51] It makes use of relative majority which means that the only majority needed is the majority provided by those participants that actually voted in the given timeframe, very much like modern democracies nowadays tend to work during elections. Of course there is also a minimum amount of participants that actually need to participate before the vote can be seen as valid. As a lot of proposals are propagated throughout the DAO, proposers can actually give their proposals a value, so that it goes up in the collective attention. To motivate voters to actually vote, they need to become motivated and their efforts compensated. They get rewarded with the native DAO token. There is, however, also the need of another token. Proposals need to be filtered to protect the decision process and create a better executed open, economic and permissionless network for the predictors. When proposals are accepted, the predictors are rewarded, if not, they lose part of their stake in the network.

4.39 Web 3.0

With the coming of blockchain, the digital world has entered a new phase which is often called 'Web 3.0' a term once coined by Gavin Wood and aimed at a completely new way of working and application building. This term has been popularized with the rise of decentralized applications and the support of the Ethereum community but it refers to a broader change and evolution of the internet. Critics state that it is nothing more than a marketing term to help people push to this new type of applications. In short, web 1.0 was the 'read-only web' meaning that you could look up information and read it but the fun stopped there. There are still a lot of websites that still follow this basic concept, though

---

[49] Hinkes, A. (May 29, 2016) The Law of the DAO. *Coindesk.* https://www.coindesk.com/the-law-of-the-dao. Accessed December 28, 2019.

[50] https://www.sec.gov/news/press-release/2014-111.

[51] Field, M. (November 12, 2018) Holographic consensus—part 1. *Medium.* https://medium.com/daostack/holographic-consensus-part-1-116a73ba1e1c. Accessed January 12, 2020.

a new type of websites joined the world around 2002–2004 where users could also start adding their own content and upload information to websites. Social media applications are a prime example of how users are now influencing the world around them. Web 3.0 is only just the next natural step with the use of 3D, AI algorithms that will filter out the best data for the user combined with semantic web that will be able to interpret the data and match even better the records that are registered on a website, therefore giving more information and even meaning to what can be found on the world wide web. But it goes even further. In web 2.0 you basically need to contract your financial institution to make a payment while web 3.0 aims to create a world of payable machines and internet. For the user this will mean a completely new understanding of the internet as it is. Even though web pages might just appear as they do now, the possibilities that are being offered will increase vastly over time and the 'power houses' that we know today will be confronted by an entirely decentralized opposition of web applications and developers that have adapted to a new way of working and creation. Ethereum has offered a new web stack for developers on how they can adapt to this new world and how they see the future of development but again, this is a much broader evolution that you should aim to understand. Below you can find the web stack as envisioned by Ethereum and others (largely based on an abstraction made by Stephan Tual in 2017).

Several of these components we are going to discuss below so that you can have a better understanding of how decentralized applications are created and what we can find in the several layers of the architecture. Some of these components have already been discussed in previous chapters so I will not repeat these here.

4.39.1 Ethereum Whisper

Ethereum Whisper is a communication protocol which allows DApps to communicate with each other over the blockchain platform. It was called an 'identity-based pseudonymous low-level messaging system' by Gavin Wood. This protocol can be necessary for the execution for certain transactions but can also be the focus for the internal workings of application. Over the years there has been a struggle in mainstream adoption of decentralized applications and one of the reasons is that applications often need to be able to exchange transient messages but it doesn't make sense to make use of a blockchain for this. That is where Whisper comes in as a decentralized messaging protocol. However, in the past the protocol hasn't received the necessary attention and at the moment it isn't really as scalable as it should be for the applications that are currently being developed. Developers are now working on the Whisper 2.0 version that should allow for this scalability and incorporate the necessary privacy precautions so that centralized infrastructure providers aren't able to monitor the information that is being exchanged between these decentralized applications. Currently a setup is ongoing to gain support for further development between researchers, protocol implementers and application builders.[52] But how does this protocol look like? It consists of 3 elements called 'envelopes', 'messages' and 'topics'. The envelopes are packets that contain several pieces of information:

- Time-to-live (in seconds)
- Expiry (in Unix time)
- Topics (hash tags, hashed public key of recipient with session nonce, ...)
- Nonce (provides proof of work requirements)
- Message data field (the encrypted payload combined with flags and signature).

Based on the nonce and the work performed on the message, there could be a prioritization of the messages that are received. On top of that nodes can choose which privacy or performance features they prioritize and accept or reject. An example of an application running on top of Whisper is Status.im. Currently in beta, it is an app for both desktop as smartphone which integrates a messaging service and other existing DApps on one location.[53] The main goal of the newfound browser is to lower the threshold to make use of Ethereum and the decentralized applications that run on top of the network.

4.39.2   Ethereum Swarm

Similar to Whisper, Swarm is the solution that has been put forward by Ethereum to offer a decentralized and distributed storage platform. It is another layer in the native web3 stack that is proposed and supported by the community. The main goal of swarm is to provide a decentralized and redundant store of Ethereum's public record, in particular to store and distribute DApp code and data as well as blockchain data.[54] Some of the services that are offered or are under development are messaging, data streaming, p2p accounting, mutable resource updates, storage insurance, proof of custody, scan and repair, payment channels and of course database services. On top of that it is DdoS-resistant, censorship-resistant and promises high availability. This offers a lot of possibilities for the developers of decentralized applications while for the users there changes nothing compared to the normal use of the World Wide Web. Several APIs are offered to developers such as CLI, JSON-RPC, HTTP interface and JavaScript. Just as with Whisper, the Swarm implementation is still under development and one should use the protocol with care. Proof of concept version 0.4 has been released in May 2019 which has provided a stable deployment infrastructure and stable testnet combined with file sharing, access control and notifications. Future

---

[52] https://github.com/w3f/messaging/.

[53] Jankov, T. (June 1, 2018) Ethereum messaging: explaining whisper and status.im. *Sitepoint.* https://www.sitepoint.com/ethereum-messaging-whisper-status/. Accessed January 13, 2020.

[54] https://swarm-guide.readthedocs.io/en/latest/introduction.html.

updates will bring push syncing, upload progress bars, redundancy with erasure coding, pinned content, proof of custody challenge protocol and more. Still it can be interesting for developers to test the implementations of Ethereum Swarm in the development of DApps.

4.39.3 IPFS

IPFS or 'Interplanetary File System' is a distributed system for the storing and accessing of files, setup of websites, applications and data in general. It is similar to Ethereum Swarm as it also wants to offer a decentralized storage layer and a content delivery protocol for decentralized applications. Just as Swarm, IPFS wants to offer an incentivization layer for the participating nodes to encourage participation and insurance to users. Similarly, the storage model used is a block model that chops up large documents into pieces that can be fetched in parallel.[55] Both IPFS and Swarm also make use of content addressing. What is content addressing? Well, standard computer users are used to location addressing where a user will type in an URL and expects a webpage based on that URL. In content-based addressing you can find webpages based on the content instead of the location. The URL of IPFS for example contains a hash of the content of the webpage you are accessing. This way you can verify if what you are accessing is truly what you have asked for. Finally, there is transparent and efficient mapping of file system directories. So why create two different implementations that have the same goals? Well, there are some differences between the projects that will probably keep them both alive. First of all, the development (and the adoption) of IPFS is much further along than that of Ethereum Swarm. Swarm on the other hand has a stronger relation with Ethereum bringing advantages such as the live network of users, funding from the non-profit behind Ethereum and the strong ecosystem it could be implemented in. Secondly, there is a 'philosophical' difference between the 2 projects. Swarm is part of the Ethereum and Whisper development stack for web 3.0 and focuses on privacy, censorship resistance and is developed specifically for the needs of the Ethereum ecosystem. IPFS on the other hand is developed to be open for any protocol that wishes to develop towards web 3.0 and therefore it also offers options such as blacklisting and source filtering. Finally, there are also some technical differences between the 2 projects such as different network communication and peer management protocols. Swarm makes use of the same protocols that are used by the Ethereum network. IPFS on the other hand makes use of libp2p network layer. Another difference is that you can upload to Swarm and use it as a cloud hosting provider while IPFS requires you to have the file on your hard drive. Closely linked to the implementation of IPFS is IPNS or 'Interplanetary Name System' and is a system for creating and updating mutable links to IPFS

---

[55] https://github.com/ethersphere/swarm/wiki/IPFS-&-SWARM.

content.[56] The name specifically is a hash of a public key and takes the form of: /ipns/ QmSrPmbaUKA3ZodhzPWZnpFgcPMFWF4QsxXbkWfEptTBJd. A similar implementation that currently still works faster (and is more human readable) is DNSlink. It uses the domain name instead of the hashed public key and comes closes to what users are used to today.

4.39.4 Filecoin

Filecoin is a project that is linked to IPFS and is the incentivization layer that enables the participants in the protocol. This implementation will make sure that there is an ongoing compensation for those participants that provide storage for the standard users of IPFS. Proof of retrievability mining is the consensus protocol in use here and is a positive reinforcement protocol while Swarm on the other hand has also some punitive measures in place to makes sure that the participants remain truthful to the purpose of the protocol.

The cryptocurrency behind Filecoin is also freely interchangeable. This is used as an extra incentive to convince people to open up storage that is currently not being used. Some part of it is aimed at creating a decentralized market for storage. If the reader remembers correctly (and has read the section on Bitcoin) some of the goals behind File-coin are similar to Siacoin. The difference between the 2 is that Filecoin is really focused on IPFS as well, while Siacoin is a separate implementation in the world of Bitcoin. The Filecoin network makes use of 2 proof of storage protocols: proof of replication which allows participants to prove they have replicated the data on their own storage device and proof of space–time which is a proof of work consensus protocol that allows participants to proof that they have stored some data over a certain amount of time.[57] Their implementation also makes use of zk-SNARKs to improve the security over the network. The idea is to create a market where participants can offer space or request it and when there is a match on pricing, the order can be carried out. Similarly, when the user wants to request a file it has put on decentralized storage, there is an order matching and settlement phase. This is why there are retrieval miners and storage miners with each their own responsibilities towards the participants that make use of the storage facilities. The Filecoin network also wants to provide the capabilities for a smart contracting platform, even though it is rather limited in its setup. The platform supports basic 'put' and 'get' requests but file contracts could be developed in the future that would allow participants to code under which circumstances they are willing to provide storage. There is also the idea to implement smart contracts that are more generic and allow for asset tracking, naming systems and more. However, still a lot of work must be done to make Filecoin completely ready for wide use such as: specification of the Filecoin state tree in every block,

---

[56] https://docs.ipfs.io/guides/concepts/ipns/.

[57] https://filecoin.io/filecoin.pdf.

full implementable Filecoin protocol specification, SNARK/STARK implementation and more.

4.39.5 Libp2p

Libp2p is a networking stack and library that has been modularized out of the IPFS project and is now open to use for other tools and implementations. The networking protocols used by Ethereum are largely based on the research and work done on libp2p and it is an implementation that means to facilitate the use of peer to peer networks. It has implementations that are being supported in Go, JavaScript, Rust and Python and covers a wide arrange of services such as discovery and identification of peers, plaintext protocols that are insecure but can be interesting for certain networks, but also implementations for communication based on pre-shared keys, circuit switching protocol, TLS handshake and transport security protocol.[58]

4.39.6 IPLD

IPLD or 'Interplanetary Linked Data' is closely linked to IPFS and also under development by protocol labs. It aims to bring a data model that can support the content-addressable web as it is created in the world of web 3.0 and IPFS. The idea is that hash-linked data structures can be treated as subsets of a unified information space, unifying all data models that link data with hashes as instances of IPLD.[59] The implementation of IPLD would allow for content-addressing across blockchain networks and protocols (as long as it has some basis in hashing for content-addressing). When this would be in use, it would allow commits to a git branch to be referenced by i.e. a Bitcoin transaction as a timestamp or allow Ethereum contracts to reference media on IPFS. In Go you can already find packages to support Git, Bitcoin, Ethereum and IPFS but also in JavaScript a lot of implementations can be found.

4.39.7 Multiformats

The final addition to the next generation of web applications that is being offered by Protocol labs is multiformat protocols. What are multiformat protocols you ask? Good question. The main goal of this implementation is that there is a set of protocols that aim to future-proof systems by enhancing format values with self-description. The self-description of the protocols has to adhere to a specific set of rules: they must be in-band

---

[58] https://github.com/libp2p/specs.

[59] https://ipld.io/.

with the values, must help to avoid lock-in and promote extensibility, must have a binary-packed representation and must have human-readable representation.[60] Currently there are already the following implementations:

- Multihash—self-describing hashes
- Multiaddr—self-describing network addresses
- Multibase—self-describing base encodings
- Multicodec—self-describing serialization
- Multistream—self-describing stream network protocols
- Multigram—self-describing packet network protocols
- Multikey—self-describing cryptographic keys and artifacts.

Currently IPLD, IPFS and libp2p is making use of multiformats.

4.39.8 0x protocol

The 0x protocol was developed to facilitate the exchange of Ethereum-based tokens (ERC-20 and ERC-721). The goal is to increase the liquidity in these tokens and assets so that businesses can integrate these new ways of payment into their current portals and way of working. By making a modular and user friendly design, it can be integrated without extensive extra development. An extensive set of APIs eases developers into the use of this layer. The use cases advertised on the webpage[61] of the 0x protocol go into games and collectibles as the implementation can also be used for non-fungible tokens (remember the crypto kitties!). It facilitates the trade of these tokens in the marketplace. There are also the prediction markets. Several examples can be found in this book when it comes to decentralized prediction markets where financial stakes are represented by tokens which in turn can be traded. The 0x protocol can help making these markets more liquid as these tokens can more easily be traded with this implementation. A third example are order books that can be facilitated, just as decentralized loan markets that can gain increased liquidity with the buying and re-selling of loans in the form of tokens. Finally, there are the stable tokens which require efficient and liquid markets to succeed in their efforts. 0x can also play here a crucial role for these tokens to succeed in their efforts.

---

[60] http://multiformats.io/.

[61] https://0x.org/why#benefits.

4.39.9 Dat Protocol

The dat:// protocol is a peer to peer protocol that was developed especially for decentralized networks by a strong developer community.[62] It is a protocol that must help the sharing of data directly between computers. The protocol even works in networks with poor connectivity and even offline. It is able to handle large datasets and you can add or modify data while keeping a full history on your machine. It is very user friendly so that it is also accessible to people who don't necessarily have a deep technical knowledge. The protocol is in use for websites but also for art, music releases, chat programs and more.

How does a dat URl look like? Well, there are 3 main parts:

Dat://668f8d955175f92e4ced5e4f5563f55bvch0c86cc6f670352c451233777ab879/
welikedat.gif.

The protocol is identified by **dat://**. Even if you are not an IT professional, you will recognize the format from http://, it is just replaced with another protocol, one suitable for the decentralized world. The second part consists out of a long list of letters and numbers, representing the ed25519 public key in a hexadecimal format. This public key allows participants to find and discover others that have the data and verify that the data wasn't changed while passing through the network. Finally, there is the suffix, which is an optional path to data within the Dat. It will most often look a bit like a file path which you can recognize from directory structures. A browser that makes use of this structure and protocol is called Beaker. Ok, so you know now how an URL looks like in the decentralized world of Dat. But how does your client discover peers from which they can download data? There is no longer a central server that we can connect to, as we are used to in the world of http. The solution comes in the form of discovery keys. Based on the public key of the Dat you are looking for, you can easily calculate the discovery key, however, the reverse isn't possible making it impossible for malicious participants to discover the URL you are looking for.[63] The discovery key is produced by making use of the BLAKE2b hashing function, to hash the word 'hypercore'. Peers trying to reach a certain dataset or website will broadcast Dats in their local network. In the future hyperswarm will be used to improve the process of finding and connecting with peers in the network so that data can be found even faster and shared among the participants.[64] Currently, there is a multicast DNS which are similar to regular DNS queries, except that they are broadcasted throughout the network. The packet itself is an UDP-packet that is sent to the special broadcast MAC 01:00:5e:00:00:fb and IP address 224.0.0.251 with

---

[62] https://dat.foundation/.

[63] Based on traffic, attackers might still figurre out how many Dats are popular, their size, IP addresses, traffic times and volumes.

[64] https://github.com/hyperswarm.

source and destination port 5353. The DNS header looks like this for a client asking for peers:

Transaction ID	Flags	Questions	Answers	Authority records	Additional records
0 0	0 0	0 1	0 0	0 0	0 0

While the response from a peer that he is interested in the same Dat looks like this:

Transaction ID	Flags	Questions	Answers	Authority records	Additional records
0 0	132 0	0 1	0 1	0 0	0 0

Responses can eventually contain 2 TXT records: the token record and the peers record. The first is a random value that makes sure that clients don't connect to themselves. The second is a base64-encoded list of IP addresses and ports of peers interested in the same Dat. However, there is also still a centralized approach to DNS discovery which introduces once again a single point of failure but helps for a fast and global reach. To date, this is the server discovery1.datprotocol.com with a fallback discovery2.datprotocol.com. Peers have to re-announce themselves every 60 s to remain connected and the server also cycles its tokens so that peers have to remember their last received token and update it when necessary. The destination IP address will change to 45.55.78.106 (the first discovery server) and the destination port will be 53. The peer announce request to the server has the following header:

Transaction ID	Flags	Questions	Answers	Authority records	Additional records
189 150	1 0	0 1	0 1	0 0	0 1

While the response from the discovery server looks like this:

Transaction ID	Flags	Questions	Answers	Authority records	Additional records
189 150	128 0	0 1	0 1	0 0	0 0

Finally, the SRV push notifications look like this:

Transaction ID	Flags	Questions	Answers	Authority records	Additional records
135 100	1 0	0 0	0 0	0 0	0 1

When our client has discovered a peer and the port number, it will open a TCP-connection. The first message that is send after opening the connection is a feed message. This message consists out of a discovery key and a nonce that is randomly generated for the TCP-connection. The 2nd message that is generated will always be a handshake message that is sent on each side of the connection. It looks like this:

Number	Name	Description	Type
1	ID	Random ID so that peer doesn't connect to itself	Length-prefixed
2	Live	0 (end connection) or 1 (keep open)	Varint
3	User data	Arbitrary bytes for higher level applications	Length-prefixed
4	Extensions	Name of the extensions the peer wants to use	Length-prefixed
5	Acknowledge	0 or 1 (no need to acknowledge/acknowledge)	Varint

To prevent eaves dropping, the connection is encrypted after the 2nd message with the XSalsa20 encryption cypher. The messages that are being relayed between the peers have the following structure until the end of the connection: length, channel and type, followed by the actual body of the message (this is the structure of the so-called wire protocol). This is repeated over and over as long as the connection lasts. The length is the number of bytes until the next length field (and thus the next message). The channel and type consists out of 11 bits that encodes the channel number (up to a maximum of 127) and the message type (up to a maximum of 15). With the same TCP-connection you can communicate with several Dats, starting the number of channels at 0 for the first Dat and so on. For the types, you can refer to the following table:

Type	Name	Description
0	Feed	I want this Dat
1	Handshake	Negotiate on TCP connection
2	Info	Start/stop downloading/uploading
3	Have	I have the data you want
4	Unhave	I no longer have the data/I didn't save the received data
5	Want	I want this data
6	Unwant	I no longer want this data
7	Request	Please send me this data
8	Cancel	Don't send me
9	Data	Here is the data
10–14	N/A	Unused
15	Extension	Message is not part of core protocol

Finally, there is the body of the message which is the actual content of the message. The first 2 fields in the message are varints or variable length integers. They are easy in use as they can encode with few bytes small numbers and can be expanded based on the need. Encoding and decoding on the other hand takes a bit more time compared to normal integers. The body consists out of field tags that are each time followed by values. The field tag consists out of 2 important parts: the field number (determined by the most significant bit) and the field type. Because the field number can have a variable length, also the field flag is a varint. In the network, the peers also send keepalive messages. These are completely empty and are discarded upon arrival but are purely used to keep the network alive in case there are TCP-connections being cut when they haven't send data for a while. But what if you want a certain dataset from another peer? Say welcome to the 'request'-message!

Number	Name	Description	Type
1	Index	Number of the chunk to send	Varint
2	Bytes	Ignore index if this is present, looks for specific byte	Varint
3	Hash	0/1 (send data and hashes/send only hashes)	Varint
4	Nodes	0/1 (send all hashes to verify the chunk/send only the data)	Varint

And cancelling the request has the following format:

Number	Name	Description	Type
1	Index	Number of the chunk to cancel	Varint
2	Bytes	Ignore index field and cancel specific byte	Varint
3	Hash	Cancel the hash you are forwarding	Varint

The data that is being exchanged between the peers consists out of variable-length data chunks. When there is an existing dat, new chunks can be added at the end but existing chunks can't be deleted or modified. To make sure there haven't been any modifications, there are also hashes that help verify the data hasn't been tampered with. There is also a tree like structure (Merkle tree) so that the sets of data chunks can also be verified. The tree consists out of the root hash, the parent hashes (2 or more linked) and eventually the chunk hashes that verify a single chunk of the dataset. The dataset is being sent to other peers based on the 'want/unwant' and 'have/unhave' messages. The data message looks a bit like this:

Number	Name	Description	Type
1	Index	Chunk number	Varint
2	Value	Contents of the chunk	Length-prefixed
3	Nodes	This is repeated for each hash that verifies the chunks integrity	Length-prefixed
4	Signature	Ed25519 signature of the root hash for this chunk	Length-prefixed

Dats make use of two coupled fields to represent both files and folders: metadata feed and the content feed. The metadata feed contains names, sizes and other metadata for each of the files while the content feed contains the actual file content.

Several future updates and implementations are currently being worked on to improve the Dat protocol. The hyperdrive (the folder and file system) will completely change as they want to start working with a prefix tree to make it faster. There is also hyperswarm (as mentioned before) which will introduce new discovery mechanisms in the network. Next, there is multi-writer which will allow dats to be updated by several authors and devices at the same time. Finally, there is the NOISE protocol which has to fix the current situation where connections can be eavesdropped.

4.39.10 Cryptocurrency Implementations on Ethereum

So we have learned so far that Ethereum opened the door to a completely new world of smart contracts and decentralized applications. However, Ehtereum also opened the door to something else that we all know as cryptocurrencies that run on top of the network. Some tokens have their own blockchain but a lot of them run on top of Ethereum. For this, several standards were developed over the years and even tokens that are independent from the network tend to follow these standards as they are now generally accepted by the broader community.

4.39.11 EIP 20: ERC-20 Token Standard

ERC-20 is the first of the standards that I am presenting to you as it was the first standard that was released to define the design of a token in a smart contract on the Ethereum network and was originally proposed by Fabian Vogelsteller on the 19th of November 2015. At the time of writing there are almost 200,000 tokens on the Ethereum main network that comply with the ERC-20 standard. Paradoxically enough, Ether itself does not conform to the ERC-20 format so that it has the 'wrapped' and converted to WETH which can then be held in a smart contract and a 1:1 peg to ether. Steps are being undertaken to change this so that ether can directly be used for the ERC-20 tokens. Until that time, Radar relay[65] and 0x protocol[66] offer interfaces that allow you to trade directly between WETH and ERC-20 tokens. The following methods are defined in the standard and can be found on the Ethereum EIP website[67]: An important first notice is that callers also must be able to handle 'false' responses from Boolean outcomes.

- Function name() public view returns (string)
- Function symbol() public view returns (string)
- Function decimals() public view returns (uint8).

---

[65] https://radarrelay.com/.
[66] https://0x.org/portal/account.
[67] https://eips.ethereum.org/EIPS/eip-20.

These first 3 functions are optional and meant to improve the usability of the token. The standards website states that interfaces should not expect these values to be present but nowadays it is almost a given that for a token, one can call the name and the symbol. It also doesn't seem a lot of a stretch that you would like to see how many decimals a token is using. This determines how far this token can be split and used in real-life transactions.

- Function totalSupply() public view returns (uint256)
- Function balanceOf(address _owner) public view returns (uint256 balance).

These two functions are mandatory and call for the total supply of the token and the balance of a specific address.

- Function transfer (address _to, uint256 _value) public returns (bool success)
- Event Transfer(address indexed _from, address indexed _to, uint256 _value)
- Function transferFrom(address _from, address _to, uint256 _value) public returns (bool success).

The transfer function transfers a certain amount '_value' to the address '_to' and calls the Transfer event. Similarly the transferFrom function transfers an amount '_value' from '_from' to a certain address '_to'. The transferFrom function is a function used in case of a withdraw workflow i.e. with a contract to transfer tokens, and should throuw unless the '_from' is specified and has authorized the sender of the message. Important note is that transfers with a value of 0 should also trigger the transfer event.

- Function approve(address _spender, uint256 _value) public returns (bool success)
- Event Approval(address indexed _owner, address indexed _spender, uint256 _value).

The approve function allows the '_spender' to withdraw from the account up to '_value'.

- Function allowance(address _owner, address _spender) public view returns (uint256 remaining).

Finally, the allowance function defines the '_spender' that is allowed to withdraw from '_owner'. Critical flaw in all of this: the difference between transfers to someone's address and to a smart contract. If you want to deposit in a smart contract, you must make use of the 'approve' and 'transferFrom' functions while the 'transfer' function is used for a deposit in a standard wallet. If you use the 'transfer' function to transfer to a smart contract, the transaction will succeed but the recipient will not be able to receive the tokens, and therefore they will be lost in limbo. Several implementations have already been created such as the OpenZeppelin implementation and the ConsenSys implementation.

4.39.12 ERC-223

The ERC-20 standard is easy to understand and therefore often used by participants to create tokens but it also has a set of flaws. One of these flaws is that once tokens are lost, because they are send to a smart contract by the process that should send them to a wallet (ordinary address account). This has already resulted in millions of dollars in losses. ERC-223 was proposed by u/Dexaran and is specifically aimed at improving the ERC-20 standard and has taken care of this nasty problem by throwing an error in case of invalid transfers and canceling the transaction so that no tokens are lost. There is also the addition of an extra data parameter to the transfer function to allow for more than only token transfers. On top of that it introduces process efficiency and reduces the gas needed to make transfers.[68] And even with these advantages, it remains backward compatible with ERC-20 not secluding the tokens based on the ERC-20 standard. The main assumption in this standard is that there is a 'tokenFallback' function in the smart contract on which his 'transfer' function is based. This means that the 'transfer' function checks whether the receiving address is a smart contract and if this is the case, assumes that the 'tokenFallback' function is there. However, if this is not the case, the tokens can still be lost!

4.39.13 ERC-721[69]

ERC-721 is a free open standard that describes how one can create non-fungible tokens on the Ethereum blockchain. It is the format of a smart contract that allows you to securily manage, own and trade these tokens while at the same time leaving space for extra metadata or supplemental functions.

The most famous example of ERC-721 are the cryptokitties from Axiom Zen which was released end 2017 and some of these kitties were sold for over \$ 100.000! Today it is used by many platforms to create unique tokens representing real assets. The template can simply be copied and adjusted from the GitHub page so that it can be used in the correct fashion.[70] Below we will show a short example on ERC-721.

---

[68] Wiigo Coin (January 2, 2019) ERC223 Token Standard Pros and Cons. *Medium*. https://medium.com/@wiiggocoin/erc223-token-standard-pros-cons-93a01f0239f. Accessed January 14, 2020.

[69] erc721.org/.

[70] https://github.com/OpenZeppelin/openzeppelin-solidity/blob/master/contracts/token/ERC721/ERC721.sol.

4.39.14 ERC-777

Another standard that is aiming to improve the ERC-20 token standard is the ERC-777 standard. This standard makes use of an alternative way to recognize the contract interface: the central registry of contracts on the Ethereum network that was introduced and defined in ERC-820 (contract pseudo-introspection registry). Every participant can make use of this interface to see if a contract makes use of certain functions or not. You could in theory create a token based on ERC-20 integrated with the functions provided by the ERC-777 standard. This would lead to positive network effects and of course to faster adoption by the participants and the community as well. Exchanges i.e. can easier support this standard than ERC-223 because of these integration possibilities.

4.39.15 ERC-827

The ERC-827 token standard is an extension of the standard interface of ERC20 tokens so that the execution of calls inside transfer and approvals are possible.[71] This means that the token proxy can execute a function in the receiver contract after the transfer is approved. To accomplish this, a proxy contract is used to forward the calls from the token contract. It adds 3 methods to the standard ERC20 methods that are already in use:

- approveAndCall: it only allows the receiver contract to use approved balances.
- transferAndCall: there is no check if the transferred balance is in fact the correct one
- transferFromAndCall: same as transferAndCall, allowing contracts to transfer tokens on your behalf before execution of a function.

4.39.16 ERC-664

The ERC-664 token standard wants to adapt the ERC-20 tokens so that the user balances are abstracted away from the business logic. An entire set of functions and methods are defined on the ERC page, which is still open at the time.[72]

4.39.17 ERC-677

With ERC-677, there is the introduction of functionality to allow the transfer of tokens to contracts and have the contract trigger logic on how to respond to receiving tokens

---

[71] https://github.com/ethereum/eips/issues/827.

[72] https://github.com/ethereum/EIPs/issues/644.

within a single transaction.[73] It enters a new transaction type called 'onTokenTransfer' and wants to solve the vulnerability that still persists with the ERC-223 standard. It is meant as a transitional measure towards the wider adoption of the ERC-223 tokens.

4.39.18 And an Update in 2025

By 2025, Ethereum's ecosystem has matured significantly, with a suite of standards enhancing usability, interoperability, and user experience. Among these, the Ethereum Name Service (ENS), EIP-681, and EIP-7093 stand out for their contributions to simplifying interactions and bolstering security within the network. The Ethereum Name Service (ENS) has become a cornerstone of Web3 identity and domain management. Functioning as a decentralized, open-source naming system, ENS translates complex Ethereum addresses into human-readable names ending with ".eth". This simplification not only reduces the risk of errors in transactions but also enhances the user experience by making blockchain interactions more intuitive. As of May 2025, the ENS token has seen significant growth, reflecting its increasing adoption and the expanding needs of the Web3 space.[74] EIP-681 introduces a standardized URL format for transaction requests, enabling the creation of payment links and QR codes that can be easily interpreted by wallets. This standard facilitates seamless interactions between users and decentralized applications, streamlining processes such as payments and contract interactions. By embedding transaction details within URLs, EIP-681 allows for robust cross-application signaling, enhancing the interoperability of Ethereum-based applications.[75] Security and account recovery have also seen advancements through proposals like EIP-7093, which outlines a social recovery interface for Ethereum accounts. This standard allows users to designate trusted entities, or "guardians," who can assist in account recovery processes. By providing a standardized approach to social recovery, EIP-7093 enhances the resilience of Ethereum accounts against loss of access due to compromised or lost keys.

4.40   Ethereum Classic

We already shortly discussed Ethereum Classic (ETC) in the section on the DAO but it seemed important to me to have a separate section discussing this particular hard fork of the Ethereum blockchain. While in many forms it is the same as Ethereum, there are some key differences to take into account when we look at this blockchain platform. To shortly recap, the Ethereum Classic hard fork came into being because of the aftermath of the

---

[73] https://github.com/ethereum/EIPs/issues/677.

[74] https://www.gate.io/blog/7935/ENS-Price-in-2025--Buying-Staking-and-Web3-Wallet-Integr ation?utm_source=chatgpt.com.

[75] https://eips.ethereum.org/EIPS/eip-681?utm_source=chatgpt.com.

DAO attack. Specifically, there was a part of the community that refused to participate in the hard fork that refunded the victims of the attack and stayed on the original chain. The first block of the Ethereum Classic chain was block number 1,920,000 on the 20th of July 2016. On the 23th of July 2016, Poloniex lists the ETC-token and the price goes up to 1/3th of the ETH token. The first days and even months the community of Ethereum was in disarray and a lot of discussions were held to such an extent that some even speak of a community 'war'.[76] It didn't take long for the supporters of Ethereum Classic to form their own community and when block 2,050,000 was mined, there was the official 'declaration of independence' on the website which stated that ETC was no longer associated with the Ethereum Foundation. In the meantime, a group called the 'Robin Hood Group' which was responsible for securing about 70% of the funds of the DAO after the hack, dumped large amounts of stolen ETC on the market in an attempt to destabilize the young market of Ethereum Classic. Poloniex took preventive action and froze the funds. In the months that followed, the community started to rebuild the Classic network. An important step was on the 31st of August 2016 when the frozen funds of the DAO attack were released to the DAO token holders and the hacker. However, the predictions seemed gloomy, the price of ETC remained quite stable. The ETC monetary policy regarding emission of tokens to align the interests of platform users, miners, investors and developers took place by the end of 2016. At block 3,000,000 there was the ETC Diehard upgrade that resolved several issues such as the possibility of replay attacks and took away the difficulty time bomb that was part of Ethereum. In 2017 the monetary policy is adapted so that there is a fixed-cap with an emission schedule similar to Bitcoin. Other innovations were the embedded SVM which allows the EVM and SputnikVM for embedded applications and support the Byzantine + Constantinople hard forks. Also the JSON RPC schema has been automated so that the operational costs related to libraries are reduced and make DApp development more efficient. Similarly, there has been research towards better tools for DApp deployment and UX research. The ETC JIT compiler has also been translated in EVM byte-code so that the execution time of programs has been reduced by 3 times. There has also been the Atlantis hard fork so that the Spurious Dragon and Byzantium network protocol upgrades are also available on the Ethereum Classic network. The beginning of 2020 saw the Agharta hard fork to allow the Constantinople and Petersburg network protocol upgrades on the ETC network and the next hard fork will be the Aztlan hard fork which should allow the Istanbul network upgrade on the Classic network.

4.41 Some Comparisons

In 2025, there are some notable platforms which have also matured and show their worth. As such, Ethereum is facing some competition and hence it seems interesting to have a quick view on how these measure up against one another. We mention here Solana,

---

[76] https://ethereumclassic.org/roadmap/.

Polkadot and Avalanche, which have each their own design choices. This in turn means that each of them have their own trade-offs and depending on your own use case, one might be more interesting than the other.

4.41.1 Ethereum Versus Solana

Solana is known for its high-performance, monolithic design. It forgoes maximum decentralization to achieve very high throughput on a single chain. Solana can theoretically process up to ~65,000 transactions per second, far above Ethereum's ~15–30 TPS on L1.[77] It does this through a combination of a unique consensus mechanism (Proof of History + PoS), aggressive parallelization, and requiring powerful hardware for validators (e.g., high-core-count CPUs, 128 + GB RAM, etc., far beyond Ethereum's node requirements). Solana's block times are ~400 ms (sub-second) and it aims for near-instant finality, which makes it attractive for use cases like trading or gaming that demand low latency. However, the trade-off is centralization risk: running a Solana validator is expensive, leading to a smaller, more heavyweight set of validators. Solana's approach has also led to stability issues—the network has experienced multiple outages and downtimes in recent years.[78] For example, Solana suffered a 17-h outage in Sept 2021 and several shorter outages (even as recent as Feb 2024, a 5-h outage due to a bug).[79] These incidents highlight the fragility that can accompany pushing performance limits. By contrast, Ethereum (especially post-merge) prioritizes stability and decentralization; it deliberately processes fewer TPS on L1 and relies on L2 scaling, but has *rarely if ever gone down*. This comparison underscores Ethereum's design philosophy: favoring a robust, decentralized base layer even at the cost of immediate throughput, whereas Solana makes opposite trade-offs (maximizing speed, accepting more complexity/centralization). An academic discussion might also note differences in programming: Ethereum uses the EVM and Solidity, while Solana uses Rust or C for smart contracts, which can be more efficient but less standardized compared to EVM (where Ethereum has broader tooling and developer base).

---

[77] https://www.onesafe.io/blog/solana-gaming-revolution-metalcore-migration#:~:text=Why%20S peed%20Matters.

[78] https://www.onesafe.io/blog/solana-gaming-revolution-metalcore-migration#:~:text=The%20D ouble.

[79] https://www.onesafe.io/blog/solana-gaming-revolution-metalcore-migration#:~:text=The%20D ouble.

4.41.2 Ethereum Versus Polkadot

Polkadot offers a different approach: a heterogeneous multi-chain network. Conceived by
Ethereum co-founder Gavin Wood, Polkadot aims to improve scalability *and* flexibility
by allowing multiple specialized blockchains (called parachains) to run in parallel, all
tied to a central Relay Chain for security and interoperability. The chapter should explain
that Polkadot's parachains can each be optimized for specific use cases (one might be
tuned for DeFi, another for identity, etc.), and they communicate via Polkadot's cross-
chain messaging (XCMP). This is analogous in some ways to Ethereum's future sharded
design, but Polkadot launched with this from the start. A key point is Polkadot provides
shared security, parachains inherit security from the Relay Chain, which has its own set
of validators staking DOT (Polkadot's token).[80] This means a smaller project can launch
as a parachain and be protected by Polkadot's overall security, which is an appealing feature. However, Polkadot's model also has trade-offs. There is a fixed number of parachain
slots (currently about 100),[81] which creates competition, projects must win slot auctions
(locking up large amounts of DOT) to secure a parachain. This economic gatekeeping con-
trasts with Ethereum, where anyone can deploy a contract or even launch an L2 without
permission (though L2s need their own security or bridging). Polkadot's design emphasizes on-chain governance and upgradability (forkless upgrades), which Ethereum has
been slower to pursue on L1. Technically, Polkadot uses a nominated PoS and a consensus scheme (BABE + GRANDPA) that provides rapid block production and finality
within seconds. But because each parachain's throughput is limited and there's overhead
in cross-chain operability, the scalability gains are in aggregation rather than single-chain
performance. To highlight design trade-offs: general-purpose settlement layer with opt-
in external rollups versus built-in multi-chain framework. Polkadot's approach achieves
scalability by "uniting different blockchains into a single network" of parachains, which
can *execute transactions in parallel* and share data/assets with each other. This is a more
complex architecture, which has taken time to fully materialize (Polkadot's parachains
became operational in late 2021). Meanwhile, Ethereum has pursued a more incremental
path: improving L1 modestly (PoS, data sharding in the future) and relying on external
L2 networks for parallelism. In Ethereum's eventual sharding (if fully realized beyond
data availability shards), each shard will be roughly identical (general-purpose, like a
mini-Ethereum), whereas Polkadot's parachains can each have their own state transition
function (one might even be an Ethereum-like EVM chain, another a smart contract platform using WebAssembly, etc.). This heterogeneity allows innovation but complicates
cross-chain compatibility to some extent. Ethereum's rollup-centric model, by contrast,

---

[80] https://pixelplex.io/blog/what-are-polkadot-parachains/#:~:text=Polkadot%20parachains%
20are%20controlled%20by,added%20to%20the%20finalized%20chain.

[81] https://pixelplex.io/blog/what-are-polkadot-parachains/#:~:text=Polkadot%20parachains%
20are%20controlled%20by,added%20to%20the%20finalized%20chain.

uses the EVM as a common denominator (most rollups are EVM-compatible) to leverage network effects. Another key difference is interoperability: Polkadot was built with
cross-chain communication natively, while Ethereum is gaining that via standards and
bridges.

4.41.3 Ethereum Versus Avalanche

Avalanche is another prominent smart contract platform that positions itself as a faster,
scalable alternative to Ethereum. Avalanche introduced a novel consensus protocol (Snow-
ball/Avalanche consensus) that uses repeated random subsampling of validators to quickly
achieve agreement. Thanks to this design, Avalanche finalizes transactions in under 1–2
s, much quicker than Ethereum's ~ 12-s block times (and ~ 6–12 min to full finality on
PoS).[82] Avalanche's approach to scaling is to have multiple built-in blockchains and allow
custom "subnets". The primary Avalanche deployment has three chains: X-Chain (asset
exchange), P-Chain (platform chain for metadata and staking), and C-Chain, which is
EVM-compatible and where most smart contracts live. The C-Chain can process around
4500 TPS in ideal conditions, significantly more than Ethereum L1. Avalanche's typical time-to-finality being < 2 s means it can support near real-time applications. This
is a selling point for Avalanche when comparing to Ethereum. Avalanche's subnet feature allows anyone to create a new blockchain (a subnet) with its own set of validators
(which must also validate on the main Avalanche network). Subnets can have custom
rules, for example, a subnet could be permissioned (for KYC/regulated use cases) or use
a different VM entirely. This architecture gives Avalanche flexibility to meet enterprise or
specific dApp needs, it's somewhat analogous to Polkadot's parachains or Cosmos zones,
but with the ability for subnets to optionally share validation with the main network.
By 2025, Avalanche has seen subnets used for things like gaming (e.g., DeFi Kingdoms
moved to an Avalanche subnet) and institutional chains. The chapter should mention that
Avalanche's design sacrifices almost no decentralization at the base layer—it still has
thousands of validators—but it is more complex (multiple chain structure) and relatively
younger (thus less battle-tested than Ethereum). Avalanche's consensus is indeed impressive in scaling properties, but the ecosystem is smaller: Avalanche's DeFi TVL is on the
order of only ~ \$1.5B versus Ethereum's \$90B+, and developer count is roughly 1/15th
of Ethereum's. This suggests that while Avalanche is technically strong, Ethereum's network effects (developers, assets, users) remain dominant. Avalanche achieves fast finality
(~ 1 s) and high throughput (~ 4500 TPS) on its C-Chain, outperforming Ethereum's
base layer. It also provides app-specific chains via subnets which encourage innovation

---

[82] https://tradesanta.com/blog/ethereum-vs-solana-vs-avalanche-which-blockchain-will-win-in-
2025#:~:text=Avalanche%20also%20achieves%20impressively%20fast,April%20launch%20of%
20the%20Octane.

in niches (for instance, regulated enterprise chains on Avalanche for institutions). However, Avalanche's approach means liquidity and activity can be fragmented across subnets, whereas Ethereum (with L2s) often still settles back to one main security layer (Ethereum L1). Also, Avalanche requires validators to stake AVAX (minimum 2000 AVAX) and its reward mechanism differs from Ethereum's (which has fee burn and minimal net issuance post-1559). These details might be too granular, but academically it's interesting that Avalanche chose a fixed-cap supply for AVAX versus Ethereum's now quasi-deflationary model.

Different Private and Public Platforms 5

In this chapter you will find different platforms, both for private and public purposes. While the original chapter was written in 2019, now we are seeing in 2025 new competitors popping up and other platforms which have become less relevant. In the original work, we were still talking about Ethereum which made us of proof of work, Bitcoin with low throughput, first generation DAGs such as the older version of IOTA and others. Nowadays, we are seeing the new version of Ethereum, the new implementations on Bitcoin, but also the rise of Polkadot, Cosmos, Avalanche, Celestia, Aptos, Sui and others.

5.1 Monero

For the privacy lovers among you, Monero will be a well-known name. It is a cryptocurrency that has as a main focus the privacy of the participants and censorship resistance. To achieve this, the developers behind Monero implemented their code in such a way that sending and receiving addresses, just as amounts are clouded for prying eyes.[1] The code base is open source and open for review, and is well maintained by 500 developers and 30 core developers (this was the case in 2019 but seems hard to verify in 2025). They offer quite welcoming webpages explaining the functionalities of Monero and how you can participate in the network. To achieve their goals of privacy, there was no premine or instamine, no tokens were sold nor did they have any presale. The proof of work algorithm they used in the past was called CryptoNight which was developed in 2013 as part of the CryptoNote suite. The algorithm is based on AES encryption combined with 5 (!) hashing functions: Keccak, BLAKE, Groestl, JH and Skein. However, this is no longer

---

[1] https://web.getmonero.org/get-started/what-is-monero/.

in use (it was removed in 2020) due to ASIC resistance failure. As several of the other cryptocurrencies you will see in this book, the developers also wanted to create an ASIC resistant algorithm, meaning that it would be difficult for specialized hardware to mine the coin, leaving some power to the CPU miners. The goal of the algorithm is to find a small-enough hash, meaning that they have to find a hash that fits under a specified threshold (sounds familiar?). The input for the hash function is the block header, Merkle tree root and the number of transactions in the block. With a block time of 2 min, it well surpasses the Bitcoin network. How does the CryptoNight hash function actually work? It is a memory-hard hash function where the function makes use of a scratchpad with pseudo-random data It takes the input and hashes it with the Keccak hash function where the parameters are $b = 1600$ and $c = 512$.[2] From the resulting hash, the bytes 0..31 are used as an AES-256 key and expanded to 10 round keys. The bytes 64..191 from the Keccak hash are split in 8 blocks where each block is AES encrypted with the round keys (there are some differences with standard AES encryption). The resulting blocks are written in the first 128 bytes of a scratchpad, the blocks are encrypted following the same procedure again and written in the second 128 bytes. This process is repeated until 2MiB is filled. Next to this loop, there is the memory-hard loop where bytes 0..31 and 32..63 of the Keccak hash are XORed and the resulting 32 bytes are eventually used to initialize variables a and b. these variables are then used in the main loop for 524,288 times. In case the 16 byte value needs to be converted to an address in the scratchpad, it is interpreted as a little-indian integer and the 21 low order bits are used as a byte index. However, the 4 low-order bits are used as the byte index. The read/write actions to the scratchpad happen in 16-byte blocks where each iteration is expressed by a pseudo-code. Finally, after the memory-hard loop, the bytes 32..63 from the original Keccak hash are expanded in 10 AES round keys. The bytes 64..191 from the Keccak hash are XORed within the first 128 bytes of the scratchpad. The result is encrypted just as in the first part, but with new keys, and the result is XORed with the second 128 bytes from the scratchpad, and so on. After XORing with the last 128 bytes of the scratchpad, the result is encrypted one final time, and then the bytes 64..191 in the Keccak state are replaced with this final result. The final encoded result is then passed through the Keccak-f (the Keccak permutation) with $b = 1600$. Based on the 2 low-order bits of the first byte of the hash are used to select a hash function: 0 = BLAKE-256 [BLAKE], 1 = Groestl-256 [GROESTL], 2 = JH-256 [JH], and 3 = Skein-256 [SKEIN]. The chosen hash function is then applied to the hash, and the resulting final hash is the output of CryptoNight. Over time the CryptoNight hash function has been modified to the current version which is also called 'CryptoNightR' which is the 4th version of the hashing function. Also this CrytoNightR has been superseded in 2025! There was some criticism on the use of this hash function, as it is an expensive hash to verify, which leads to a specific vulnerability: mining nodes can be the victim of DOS-ing attacks where incorrect proofs are used on

---

[2] Seigen, Jameson, M., Nieminen, T., Neocortex and Juarez A.M. (March 2013) Cryptonight Hash Function https://cryptonote.org/cns/cns008.txt. Accessed on November 12, 2019.

the nodes for verification. Another important point of criticism is the fact that the hash function was ultimately not able to prevent ASIC-mining. This is why the proof of work algorithm might be changed in the future but to this day, this is the hashing algorithm in place. The difficulty target changes every block, where the target is based on the last 720 blocks where the 20% of timestamp outliers are excluded. The reward for the mining decreases (just as in the Bitcoin network) but there is also a penalty in place. If you mine a block greater than the median size of the last 100 blocks, you are penalized with a lower reward. This immediately means that the block size is dynamic. The eventual supply is also uncapped, opposed to Bitcoin which is limited. How is the privacy of the users ensured? Well, the network makes use of something called ring signatures. This is used to protect the input side of a transaction, where a group of possible signers are merged together so that they can eventually create a signature to authorize a transaction.[3] This group of signers consist of the actual signer of the transaction, and a couple of non-signers which create a ring. All the participants are considered equal and valid. The non-signers are past transaction outputs that are taken from the Monero blockchain, while the actual signer uses a one-time key that corresponds with an output sent from the spender's wallet. All the inputs appear equally likely to be the output being spent to an outsider. The actual verification of transactions, to prevent double spending, is done by making use of key images. Such a key image is a secure key that is derived from the actual output being spent and is part of every ring signature transaction. It is not possible to determine which output of a ring signature actually created the key image and a list of all the used key images are being stored on the blockchain of the network. Another feature that helps to ensure privacy in the Monero world is the use of stealth addresses.[4] This are one-time used stealth addresses which further obfuscate the destination of a transaction. Finally, there is the implementation of the Kovri invisible internet project. The Kovri project is an open source network layer which allows for censorship-resistant internet use by routing traffic through nodes. The network traffic is encrypted so that your IP address cannot be linked to specific transactions. However, in 2025 the Kovri project is discontinued or inactive. As such it cannot be mentioned here as a 'core' Monero privacy feature.

Also the dream of ASIC resistance was never achieved despite the design attempts. The emphasis over time has shifted toward adaptive algorithm switching (RandomX). The concern of block verification DoS has become less prominent through RandomX as it is designed to be more verifiable and fairer to CPUs. RandomX as such has become the replacement for CryptoNightR and makes use of random code execution and memory-hard techniques such as scratchpads. It is CPU-optimized and ASIC/GPU unfriendly. Other changes in 2025 are that RingCT (ring confidential transactions) are still used but improved with a ring size which has increased to 16 mandatory participants (2021)

[3] Asolo, B. (November 1, 2018) Monero Ring Signature Explained. *Mycryptopedia.* https://www.mycryptopedia.com/monero-ring-signature-explained/. Accessed November 26, 2019.

[4] (April 15, 2019) *Liquid.* https://blog.liquid.com/examples-of-privacy-coins-monero-zcash-dash. Accessed November 26, 2019.

improving plausible deniability. Dandelion++ was adopted as well for network-level privacy to hide IP address leaks during transaction broadcasts. Current research is looking into triptych/Lelantus-MW as an alternative to Ring CT for scaling privacy and improving efficiency. The developers are also exploring zk-SNARK integration for more efficient, private transactions.

5.2   Cosmos

Cosmos used to define itself as blockchain 3.0 and as the natural successor of Bitcoin (blockchain 1.0) and Ethereum (blockchain 2.0). Or at least, it used to do so in the past (nowadays the blockchain 3.0 is no longer commonly used). The developers behind Cosmos envision it being easier for developers to actually build blockchains themselves and interconnect these chains with each other.[5] The solution that they have created is built on Tendermint, Cosmos SDK and IBC. So that developers can quickly build interoperable blockchain implementations. One of the implementations that were built with the Cosmos SDK is Ethermint (which has been rebranded to Evmos) which is a combination of the Ethereum Virtual Machine and the Cosmos SDK module. This means that it works exactly as Ethereum with the added benefits of Terderminft Byzantine Fault Tolerance.

While below I still talk about Tendermint, in 2023 it was rebranded to CometBFT due to organizational restructuring. This CometBFT is now used as the consensus engine for the Cosmos network. Cosmos acts more as a cross-ecosystem bridge nowadays integrating with other networks such as Polkadot and Ethereum via IBC-compatibility layers such as Hyperlane and Axelar.

5.2.1   Cosmos SDK

Cosmos SDK is a framework that has been specifically built for multi-asset public proof of stake blockchains. The SDK can be used on top of the Tendermint solution to create secure state machines/applications. As you can see in the documentation, it is an implementation of the ABCI of Tendermint in Golang together with a multistore to persist data and a router to handle transactions.[6] This means that the 'baseApp' is the implementation of ABCI as we know it. On top of this there is the multistore so that a number of KVStores can be declared which accept [] byte-type as value. Finally, the real power of the Cosmos SDK is in the extra modules that can be added. Each of these modules defines a subset of the state and they have their own message/transaction processor while the SDK is responsible for routing each message to the correct module. The SDK modules are further defined by the 'x/' folder of the SDK. Some of these modules include x/auth, which is

---

[5] https://cosmos.network/intro.

[6] https://cosmos.network/docs/intro/sdk-design.html#baseapp.

focused on managing accounts and signatures, x/bank, which enables tokens and token transfers and x/staking/x/slashing, which is used to create proof of stake blockchains. The implementation of the Cosmos SDK for the Cosmos hub is called 'gaia' and it comes with 2 main entrypoints: a gaia daemon (gaiad) and a command-line interface (gaiacli). It comes with a defined set of modules that have defined the actual implementation of the hub. In 2025, the Gaia implementation is now functionally limited and often used for reference.

Since its early days, the Cosmos SDK has evolved into a mature, modular development framework for building sovereign, application-specific blockchains. One of its most powerful extensions is CosmWasm, which enables developers to write custom WebAssembly-based smart contracts, significantly broadening the SDK's utility beyond its original scope. The SDK now also supports Interchain Accounts (ICA) and Interchain Queries (ICQ), features that allow one blockchain to control or retrieve data from another securely, paving the way for deeply integrated, multi-chain applications. Additionally, the SDK includes Governance V2 modules that incorporate advanced, DAO-like governance capabilities, supporting decentralized on-chain decision-making with granular control. At the heart of Cosmos' interoperability vision lies the Inter-Blockchain Communication (IBC) protocol, which has seen widespread adoption across dozens of production networks. Originally designed for basic token transfers, IBC has now expanded to support ICA and ICQ, enabling cross-chain account management and query execution. The Cosmos ecosystem also introduced Interchain Security (ICS)—often referred to as Mesh Security—which allows "consumer chains" to leverage the validator set of a "provider chain" such as the Cosmos Hub. This model strengthens economic security across the network while preserving the autonomy of individual chains. Furthermore, innovations like ICS-721 extend IBC's functionality to support cross-chain NFTs, promoting composability across creative and financial sectors. The consensus engine formerly known as Tendermint Core has been rebranded to CometBFT. It remains a Byzantine Fault Tolerant protocol but has undergone substantial abstraction to support modular consensus mechanisms. CometBFT now integrates smoothly with light clients and finality gadgets, enhancing both scalability and client-side verification. The power of the Cosmos stack is best illustrated through its vibrant and diverse set of real-world deployments. Celestia utilizes IBC as part of its modular data availability (DA) layer, facilitating scalable, rollup-based applications. Osmosis stands out as an automated market maker (AMM) and decentralized exchange that natively leverages IBC to provide interchain liquidity. Neutron is a smart contract platform secured by the Cosmos Hub via ICS, and Evmos offers full EVM compatibility while maintaining seamless IBC interoperability—bridging the Ethereum and Cosmos ecosystems.

5.3   CometBFT: Evolution of Tendermint in the Modular Blockchain Era

What was once known as Tendermint has, by 2025, evolved into CometBFT, marking both a technical and institutional reorientation within the Cosmos ecosystem. At its core, CometBFT remains a Byzantine Fault Tolerant (BFT) consensus engine designed to support state-machine replication in adversarial environments—tolerating up to one-third of faulty or malicious nodes while maintaining network consistency and liveness. CometBFT serves as the foundational consensus layer across a wide array of application-specific blockchains. Its architecture is based on a clean separation of concerns, distinguishing between the consensus process and application logic. This is achieved through the Application Blockchain Interface (ABCI), a socket-based protocol that connects the consensus engine with the state machine. ABCI enables developers to implement their own blockchain logic in virtually any programming language, while leveraging CometBFT to ensure transaction ordering, block production, and fault-tolerant execution.

The ABCI operates through three main connection types:

- Consensus Connection: Used for block lifecycle management, encompassing methods such as InitChain, BeginBlock, DeliverTx, EndBlock, and Commit.
- Mempool Connection: Primarily for transaction validation via CheckTx, ensuring only well-formed transactions are propagated through the network.
- Info Connection: For application metadata, configuration, and state queries, utilizing methods like Info, SetOption, and Query.

Additional methods such as Flush and Echo serve auxiliary roles for message ordering and debugging, respectively. This modular communication pattern enables precise synchronization between the application and consensus layer, whether the blockchain manages a UTXO set, account-based model, NFT ledger, or a more exotic state representation. What distinguishes CometBFT in today's landscape is its interoperability and adaptability. It is not tied to any specific blockchain design, allowing developers to plug in their own logic—from token economies and smart contract platforms to rollups and enterprise solutions—while relying on a robust consensus core. This plug-and-play flexibility has led to widespread adoption in the Cosmos ecosystem and beyond, including in projects like Celestia (as a consensus option for modular chains), Evmos, and Neutron, as well as external use cases in Hyperledger Burrow and legacy integrations like BigchainDB. In recent years, CometBFT has expanded its utility by integrating light client support and finality gadgets, making it suitable for resource-constrained environments and interoperable blockchain networks. These features are increasingly relevant in a modular architecture where chains may outsource execution or data availability to external providers. CometBFT stands as a powerful enabler of sovereign blockchain development—one that abstracts the complexity of consensus while embracing the heterogeneity of decentralized applications in a multi-chain world. Its evolution from Tendermint Core is not merely a name change but a reaffirmation of its role as a critical infrastructure layer in Web3's modular future.

5.4 Hyperledger

By 2025, the Hyperledger Project, still hosted by the Linux Foundation, has matured into a modular and diverse suite of enterprise-grade blockchain frameworks and tooling, each serving distinct use cases in finance, supply chain, identity, and interoperability. Rather than a single blockchain platform, Hyperledger is best understood as an umbrella project encompassing a family of frameworks and libraries, united by open governance and industrial applicability. At the core of the ecosystem are the blockchain frameworks, several of which continue to evolve, while others have become reference implementations or seen diminished adoption. The most actively maintained and widely used frameworks as of 2025 include:

- Hyperledger Fabric: The flagship permissioned blockchain platform, Fabric supports modular consensus, private channels, and rich access control policies. It remains a top choice for regulated industries like banking and healthcare due to its fine-grained privacy model and endorsement-based transaction validation.
- Hyperledger Besu: A full Ethereum client written in Java, Besu operates across public networks (e.g. Ethereum mainnet) and private, permissioned deployments, making it a bridge between enterprise and decentralized ecosystems.
- Hyperledger Indy: Specializing in decentralized identity (DID), Indy underpins Self-Sovereign Identity (SSI) architectures. It integrates with Hyperledger Aries, providing interoperable protocols and credential exchange logic for verifiable identity systems.
- Hyperledger Iroha v2: Aimed at mobile-first and embedded systems, Iroha now includes support for WASM-based smart contracts and efficient Byzantine fault tolerance—ideal for lightweight deployments in IoT and supply chains.

While frameworks like Hyperledger Burrow and Sawtooth were instrumental in early experimentation with smart contracts and modular consensus, they are now either archived or maintained primarily for legacy or research purposes. Supporting these frameworks is a robust ecosystem of developer tools and infrastructure components, collectively advancing the utility and interoperability of Hyperledger deployments:

- Hyperledger Aries: A foundational stack for peer-to-peer identity communications, Aries supports DIDComm protocols and secure credential exchange between agents.
- Hyperledger Avalon: A framework for off-chain computation and confidential workloads, Avalon helps bridge trusted hardware with blockchain networks.

- Hyperledger Cactus: Now central to Hyperledger's interoperability stack, Cactus facilitates secure and pluggable integration across heterogeneous blockchains, supporting use cases like cross-ledger asset transfer and composite workflows.
- Hyperledger Caliper: A benchmark tool for evaluating blockchain performance, Caliper remains essential for comparing throughput, latency, and fault tolerance across various configurations and consensus protocols.
- Hyperledger Cello: Providing blockchain-as-a-service (BaaS) capabilities, Cello enables managed deployment of Hyperledger networks in cloud-native environments.
- Hyperledger Transact: A transaction execution engine designed to decouple state management from consensus logic, Transact underpins flexible, modular blockchain architectures.
- Hyperledger Ursa: Serving as a shared cryptographic library, Ursa consolidates reusable primitives for zero-knowledge proofs, encryption, and signature schemes, reducing redundancy and audit complexity across the ecosystem.

Tools like Hyperledger Explorer and the now-archived Composer provided early user and developer experiences, but have largely been supplanted by more robust DevOps workflows, containerized deployment, and external observability solutions.

5.4.1 Hyperledger Besu

Hyperledger Besu, originally developed under the name *Pantheon* by PegaSys (the protocol engineering arm of ConsenSys), has emerged as one of the most mature and versatile Ethereum clients in production today. As the first Hyperledger project capable of running on the Ethereum mainnet, Besu represents a unique convergence of enterprise-grade architecture with full public chain compatibility.

Written in Java, Besu has become a go-to solution for organizations seeking Ethereum compliance alongside customizable, permissioned deployments. Its design is inherently modular, offering pluggable consensus mechanisms and a flexible runtime architecture that caters to both regulated enterprise environments and open, decentralized networks.

Besu supports multiple consensus algorithms, including:

- Ethash, Ethereum's original Proof-of-Work engine (now historical, post-Merge)
- Clique, a lightweight Proof-of-Authority (PoA) protocol ideal for testnets and rapid deployment
- Istanbul Byzantine Fault Tolerance (IBFT 2.0), offering fault-tolerant consensus with finalized block guarantees, often used in consortium chain deployments
- Emerging compatibility with Proof-of-Stake (PoS) networks and Ethereum's post-Merge architecture via the Engine API, enabling use in validator and execution client roles within Ethereum 2.0-style stacks.

For state persistence and data storage, Besu utilizes RocksDB, a high-performance key-value store. It supports efficient separation between blockchain data (blocks, receipts) and world state (account balances, contract storage), facilitating state pruning, archival modes, and optimized replay.

Besu also offers a rich set of networking and API interfaces:

- Peer discovery is handled via UDP (using Ethereum Node Discovery protocols v4/v5), while communication is layered over TCP, following Ethereum's standard eth/66+ subprotocols.
- On the client-facing side, developers can interact with Besu via:
  - JSON-RPC (both HTTP and WebSocket)
  - GraphQL API, offering a flexible and query-optimized alternative for decentralized applications and analytics tools
  - Native metrics endpoints for Prometheus and integration with OpenTelemetry for observability.

While Besu was initially incubated within the Hyperledger project, it has now graduated to full project status and is actively maintained by ConsenSys and the broader Ethereum client community. It plays a critical role in Ethereum's client diversity strategy, alongside Geth, Nethermind, and Erigon, especially post-Merge where execution clients like Besu interface with consensus clients over the Engine API. Besu's ability to bridge public Ethereum ecosystems and private, permissioned networks makes it a compelling choice for hybrid deployments. It is widely used in enterprise consortia, DeFi sandboxes, compliance-aware rollups, and regulatory pilots, particularly where modularity, auditability, and enterprise-grade support are required. In 2025, Hyperledger Besu stands not just as an Ethereum-compatible client, but as a robust execution environment platform for public, private, and cross-domain blockchain applications. It exemplifies the fusion of open source transparency with enterprise-grade architecture, positioning itself as a key player in the evolving modular blockchain infrastructure landscape.

5.4.2 Hyperledger Burrow

Hyperledger Burrow represents one of the earliest efforts to fuse Ethereum-style smart contract functionality with a permissioned, enterprise-friendly architecture. Originally designed to explore deterministic and auditable smart contract execution in regulated environments, Burrow continues to be recognized as a pioneering effort in combining the Ethereum Virtual Machine (EVM) with Byzantine Fault Tolerant consensus. At its core, Burrow functions as a compact, modular blockchain node built around several key components:

- The consensus engine, originally built atop Tendermint (now CometBFT), delivers transaction finality through a Byzantine Fault Tolerant protocol, ordering blocks deterministically across a permissioned validator set. This consensus layer ensures safety and liveness even in adversarial enterprise environments.
- The smart contract execution environment leverages a permissioned variant of the Ethereum Virtual Machine, where execution is gated by access control rules enforced at the virtual machine level. Unlike public EVM implementations, Burrow checks permissioning constraints before contract execution, enabling fine-grained governance over who can deploy or invoke contracts.
- The Application Blockchain Interface (ABCI) acts as the bridge between the consensus layer and the execution layer. Using socket-based communication, ABCI passes transaction batches from CometBFT to the smart contract engine for validation and state transition.
- Transactions are processed using the Application Binary Interface (ABI), adhering to Ethereum's standard encoding for function calls and contract interaction. This preserves compatibility with Ethereum tooling, while offering deterministic execution in a permissioned context.
- For integration and interaction, Burrow exposes both JSON-RPC and REST APIs, providing standard entry points for wallet software, enterprise services, and administrative tooling.

While Burrow was initially at the forefront of permissioned smart contract platforms, its role has shifted over time. In recent years, its primary use has been as a reference implementation and experimentation environment—particularly for testing hybrid permissioned-EVM architectures or serving as a lightweight smart contract layer for domain-specific applications. Other frameworks like Hyperledger Fabric, Besu, and newer WASM-enabled chains have since surpassed Burrow in terms of enterprise adoption and scalability. Nonetheless, Burrow remains an important case study in deterministic smart contract design, modular blockchain architecture, and fine-grained permissioning models within EVM-compatible systems. For organizations and researchers investigating compliant or sector-specific blockchain use cases—such as central bank digital currency prototypes, regulated DeFi, or private tokenization environments—Burrow still offers a lean and auditable platform to explore controlled smart contract execution in a trusted setting.

5.4.3 Hyperledger Fabric

Among enterprise blockchain platforms, Hyperledger Fabric remains the flagship solution for building permissioned, high-throughput distributed ledger systems. Initially contributed by IBM and Digital Asset, Fabric has matured into a robust framework designed specifically for scenarios where participant identity, data confidentiality, modularity, and governance are critical. Fabric's architecture is built from the ground up to support pluggable components, allowing developers and architects to tailor the platform to specific use cases. Core services such as the consensus mechanism, membership service providers (MSPs), and certificate authorities can be substituted or extended without modifying the rest of the stack. This modularity enables deployment in a wide variety of regulatory and organizational settings, from banking consortia to logistics networks. Unlike public blockchain platforms, Fabric does not rely on a native cryptocurrency for transaction execution or network security. Instead, it employs a membership-based trust model where all participants are known and authenticated using public-key infrastructure (PKI). This structure is particularly suited for compliance-focused environments, where accountability and legal contracts matter as much as cryptographic guarantees. A defining feature of Hyperledger Fabric is its unique "execute-order-validate" transaction lifecycle, which inverts the traditional "order-execute" approach common in other platforms:

- Execution Phase: Endorsing peers simulate proposed transactions by executing the chaincode (smart contract) without committing them to the ledger. This simulation checks for correctness and generates cryptographic read/write sets.
- Ordering Phase: Valid simulated transactions are submitted to an ordering service (e.g., Kafka, Raft, or BFT-SMaRt) which establishes a total order across the network.
- Validation Phase: Transactions are finally validated against endorsement policies and checked for read–write conflicts before being appended to the ledger.

This architecture enables parallel transaction execution, improves scalability, and supports fine-grained access control and data confidentiality, with features like private data collections that restrict visibility to authorized participants within the same channel. Smart contracts, referred to as chaincode in Fabric, run in isolated Docker containers for security and modular deployment. They can be written in widely used languages such as Go, JavaScript (Node.js), and Java, making them accessible to a broader developer base. Support for newer languages and WebAssembly (WASM) is under active development, expanding Fabric's reach to more modern runtime environments. In 2025, Fabric has become a foundational element in consortium networks, financial infrastructure pilots, supply chain automation, and government-backed blockchain solutions. It supports real-world applications that require transaction confidentiality, regulated identity management, and high throughput, while maintaining traceability and verifiability. The official Hyperledger Fabric documentation continues to be the best starting point for developers. It provides comprehensive guidance on configuring networks, deploying chaincode, managing identities, and leveraging Fabric's powerful features such as multi-channel architectures, ledger snapshots, and system chaincodes. As enterprise demand for data privacy, regulated interoperability, and fine-grained governance increases, Hyperledger Fabric remains at the forefront, offering a production-ready, modular blockchain framework engineered for the complex trust models of the real world.

5.4.4   Hyperledger Grid

Hyperledger Grid is a domain-specific initiative within the broader Hyperledger ecosystem, designed to streamline the development of blockchain-based supply chain applications. While initially proposed in late 2018 and slower to mature than frameworks like Fabric or Besu, Grid has steadily evolved into a modular set of tools, libraries, and reusable components that enable the creation of cross-industry, interoperable distributed ledger solutions tailored for global supply networks. The vision behind Hyperledger Grid is not to create a monolithic supply chain platform, but rather to offer building blocks, including smart contracts, data models, and software development kits (SDKs), that support customizable and interoperable implementations across diverse use cases. This approach is critical in the supply chain context, where participants range from small producers and logistics providers to multinational corporations, each with different infrastructure needs and regulatory constraints. One of Grid's key contributions is its support for modular domain-specific data models, often based on established industry standards such as GS1. These models promote semantic interoperability, enabling consistent interpretation of assets, shipments, and transactions across different organizations and networks. By adhering to shared schemas, Grid facilitates data harmonization and cross-chain integration—capabilities crucial in fragmented, multi-tiered supply chains. In terms of architecture, Grid builds atop foundational Hyperledger components like Transact (a transaction execution engine), and it supports smart contract logic encapsulated in WebAssembly (WASM). This allows for secure, portable business logic that can be deployed in a wide range of execution environments. Chain logic is modular and extensible, allowing users to compose supply chain-specific workflows such as asset tracking, certification, provenance verification, or demand signaling. Grid also provides client-side libraries and user interface components, enabling rapid development of supply chain applications with intuitive front-ends and direct connectivity to distributed ledgers. These tools abstract away low-level blockchain infrastructure and make it easier for developers to focus on integrating business logic, compliance, and partner collaboration mechanisms. By 2025, Hyperledger Grid is positioned not as a singular solution, but as a flexible framework toolkit embraced by industry initiatives seeking to:

- Enhance traceability and auditability of goods and services
- Improve data integrity across multiple stakeholders
- Enable tokenization of physical and digital supply chain assets

- Support regulatory and sustainability tracking (e.g., carbon footprint, ESG compliance).

Though still more niche than Fabric or Besu in terms of deployment volume, Grid plays a pivotal role in projects where interoperability, modularity, and adherence to global data standards are non-negotiable. It is especially relevant in sectors like food safety, pharmaceuticals, luxury goods, and agriculture, where provenance, certification, and multi-party coordination are mission-critical. For developers and architects exploring blockchain-enabled supply chain transformation, Hyperledger Grid offers a pragmatic, standards-aligned, and developer-friendly approach—one that bridges the technical complexities of distributed ledgers with the operational realities of global logistics.

5.4.5 Hyperledger Indy

Hyperledger Indy remains the cornerstone framework within the Hyperledger ecosystem for implementing decentralized identity (DID) solutions. Unlike general-purpose blockchain platforms, Indy was purpose-built to handle the unique requirements of self-sovereign identity (SSI), offering tools, protocols, and libraries optimized for privacy-preserving, cryptographically verifiable, and user-controlled identities. As digital identity continues to underpin a growing range of applications—from government eIDs and financial KYC to health credentials and cross-border identity verification, Indy's architectural decisions prove prescient. It avoids the common pitfalls of traditional identity systems by aligning with privacy-by-design principles, offering decentralized governance and non-correlatable identifiers by default.

At its core, Indy is not a monolithic platform, but a collection of interoperable components tailored for identity:

- A purpose-specific permissioned ledger, optimized to store DID documents, public keys, and schemas required for verifiable credential issuance and verification.
- A supporting set of cryptographic protocols and zero-knowledge proof systems that allow users to selectively disclose information to verifiers without compromising broader privacy or requiring centralized intermediaries.
- Modular libraries and SDKs that allow developers to build agents and wallets capable of issuing, holding, and verifying credentials across a variety of domains and trust frameworks.

A key distinction in the design of Indy is its support for off-ledger data management. Sensitive personal data is never stored directly on the blockchain; instead, Indy serves as a trust anchor, a place to publish decentralized identifiers and schemas that enable verifiable claims to be shared securely and privately between parties. This architectural separation ensures compliance with emerging data protection regulations such as the EU's GDPR or India's DPDP Act, which prohibit the immutability of personal data on-chain. Hyperledger Indy is often used in conjunction with Hyperledger Aries, a complementary project that provides the agent-to-agent communication protocols (DIDComm) and SDKs needed to build interoperable digital identity agents and wallets. Aries handles the transport layer and interaction logic, while Indy serves as the ledger-based root of trust. Notably, the Sovrin Network remains a high-profile, public utility that leverages the Hyperledger Indy codebase to provide a globally distributed identity ledger governed by a decentralized steward community. However, Indy's design is network-agnostic, and its components are increasingly embedded in private deployments, sector-specific identity networks, and national digital ID programs.

5.4.6   Hyperledger Iroha

Hyperledger Iroha is a modular, permissioned blockchain framework built in C++, designed for digital asset management, identity systems, and regulated financial infrastructure. Unlike general-purpose smart contract platforms, Iroha provides a streamlined API with pre-defined commands and queries, making it particularly suitable for enterprise and government use cases where performance, simplicity, and predictability are prioritized over Turing-complete programmability. Initially contributed to the Hyperledger Foundation by Soramitsu, alongside stakeholders such as Hitachi, NTT Data, and Colu, Iroha has steadily matured into a production-ready platform used in high-stakes environments like central bank digital currencies (CBDCs), interbank settlements, and national identity infrastructure. One of the distinguishing features of Iroha is its Yet Another Consensus (YAC) algorithm—an asynchronous Byzantine Fault Tolerant (BFT) consensus mechanism that enables finality without sacrificing throughput. This is paired with a dedicated ordering service, ensuring that transactions are securely and deterministically ordered across nodes with minimal overhead. These design choices make Iroha highly responsive, with low-latency transaction finalization suited for real-time payment and identity verification systems. Iroha employs PostgreSQL as its underlying state storage engine, allowing the system to leverage rich querying and analytics capabilities natively, while maintaining cryptographic immutability guarantees through the consensus layer. This hybrid approach balances ledger immutability with the flexibility and familiarity of a mature relational database system—ideal for enterprise reporting, audits, and compliance workflows. Rather than requiring developers to write smart contracts, Iroha provides a robust set of built-in commands to perform common blockchain operations, such as:

- Issuing and transferring digital assets
- Registering users and assigning roles

- Managing permissions and peer nodes
- Creating and validating identifiers.

This command-driven model reduces the risk of smart contract vulnerabilities and enables rapid prototyping and deployment in regulated sectors where formal verification and deterministic behavior are critical. It also means that developers without specialized blockchain programming expertise can integrate with Iroha using high-level client libraries. Iroha supports language bindings in Python, JavaScript, Java, and Swift, enabling seamless integration with a wide variety of client-side applications, mobile apps, and enterprise backends. This multi-language support reflects Iroha's strategic emphasis on accessibility and interoperability, particularly in cross-border financial systems and government-backed identity schemes.

Current real-world deployments of Iroha include:

- The Bakong payment system (Cambodia's central bank)
- CBDC pilots across several Asia–Pacific and Eastern European countries
- National identity frameworks leveraging blockchain-secured identity registries
- Supply chain traceability solutions where simplicity and trust are key.

In contrast to Ethereum-based systems, where asset creation and transfer require writing and deploying custom smart contracts, Iroha's native functionality for asset management simplifies development and reduces the surface area for bugs and exploits. This makes it particularly appealing in regulated domains where security, compliance, and auditability are paramount. For developers and architects seeking a low-complexity, high-reliability blockchain framework with real-world government and financial sector validation, Hyperledger Iroha offers a compelling alternative—especially when trust, speed, and built-in functionality matter more than general-purpose programmability.

5.4.7 Hyperledger Sawtooth

Hyperledger Sawtooth represents one of the earliest modular blockchain platforms developed within the Hyperledger ecosystem, emphasizing separation of concerns between application logic and core system infrastructure. This architectural decision allows developers to build decentralized applications or smart contract VMs in any programming language, independent of the underlying consensus or permissioning system. Sawtooth's hallmark is its support for parallel transaction execution, made possible by an intelligent parallel transaction scheduler. This stands in contrast to the strictly serial processing found in most blockchain platforms. By identifying transactions that do not conflict with each other (i.e. that do not read/write overlapping parts of state), the scheduler enables concurrent processing. This model significantly improves throughput and latency while preserving the immutability and double-spend protections expected of any robust DLT system. Sawtooth also supports pluggable consensus, including RAFT, PBFT, and PoET (Proof of Elapsed Time)—a hardware-assisted consensus protocol originally designed for Intel's SGX trusted execution environments. Smart contracts can be deployed either natively or within Wasm- or EVM-based VMs, enabling hybrid environments where business logic and virtual machine contracts coexist on the same chain. Although not as widely adopted in production as Hyperledger Fabric or Besu, Sawtooth remains a highly flexible experimentation platform, particularly for academia and innovation labs testing novel consensus or scheduling paradigms.

5.4.8 Hyperledger Aries

Hyperledger Aries provides protocols and SDKs for peer-to-peer credential exchange and verifiable identity communication, forming the middleware between identity agents and the underlying ledgers (e.g., Hyperledger Indy or others). Aries implements DIDComm, a decentralized messaging protocol for identity agents, and relies on Hyperledger Ursa for cryptographic operations. Aries is now integral to many self-sovereign identity (SSI) and public infrastructure for digital identity (PIDI) initiatives globally.

5.4.9 Hyperledger Avalon

Hyperledger Avalon (previously Trusted Compute Framework) addresses the blockchain scalability trilemma by enabling trusted off-chain processing. It introduces mechanisms for executing transactions securely in Trusted Execution Environments (TEEs) or using zero-knowledge proofs and multi-party computation (MPC). Avalon preserves integrity and auditability while offloading expensive computations, making it ideal for confidential AI inference, private DeFi, and data marketplaces.

5.4.10 Hyperledger Cactus

Hyperledger Cactus, developed by Fujitsu and Accenture, provides a pluggable interoperability framework for performing transactions across disparate blockchain networks. Cactus supports connectors for Ethereum, Fabric, Corda, and others, enabling secure ledger-agnostic workflows. It is foundational for building cross-chain bridges, token swaps, and multi-ledger workflows in enterprise environments.

5.4.11 Hyperledger Caliper

Hyperledger Caliper is a blockchain benchmark tool that will allow to measure the performance of a blockchain implementation based on a predefined set of use cases. It comes with a reporting engine that will show transactions per second, network latency, resource utilization and more.[7] This project has been contributed by developers from Huawei, Hyperchain, Oracle, Bitwisr, Soramitsu, IBM and the Budapest University of Technology and Economics. Currently the solution can be used in Fabric, Sawtooth, Iroha, Burrow and even Hyperledger Composer. Ethereum and other blockchain implementations will be able to make use of the benchmark tool in the near future.

5.4.12 Hyperledger Cello

Hyperledger Cello wants to make it possible to bring an on-demand, as a service, deployment model to the world of blockchain. This would greatly reduce the current efforts necessary to create and manage blockchains. The implementation aims to be as flexible as possible, focusing on baremetal, virtual machine or other containers, multi-tenant or single, and more. This project was contributed by IBM, with sponsorship from Soramitsu, Huawei and Intel.[8] Even though this project is still in incubation, some first implementations can already be tested by developers.

5.4.13 Hyperledger Composer

Hyperledger composer is a tool developed for business professionals to quickly generate business networks with smart contracts and blockchain applications. It is based on the Hyperledger Fabric framework and can be very interesting if you want to develop proof of concepts in a quick and concise manner.[9] It allows for the modelling of your existing assets, participants and transactions so that you can create a functional project that shows the possibilities of your use case.

---

[7] https://www.hyperledger.org/projects/caliper.

[8] https://www.hyperledger.org/projects/cello.

[9] https://hyperledger.github.io/composer/latest/introduction/introduction.html.

5.4.14 Hyperledger Explorer

The Hyperledger Explorer tool functions as a deployable block explorer for the projects that you are building. It allows for querying of blocks, transactions, all associated data and network information. This implementation was contributed by IBM, Intel and DTCC.[10]

5.4.15 Hyperledger Quilt

Next in line of the tools that we are presenting, is Hyperledger Quilt. The goal of this tool is to offer interoperability between ledger systems by implementing the Interledger Protocol (or ILP) which allows for value transfers between distributed and non-distributed ledgers by implementing atomic swaps based on a single account namespace for accounts within each ledger.[11] Hyperledger Quilt was contributed by NTT Data and Ripple.

5.4.16 Hyperledger Transact

Hyperledger Transact wants to provide a standard interface for executing smart contracts so that that stands completely separate from the distributed ledger platform, thereby simplifying the efforts one has to do to actually create these distributed ledger platforms in the first place.[12] To implement these new smart contract languages, it makes use of something called 'smart contract engines'. This contribution has been made by Bitwise and Cargill. This project is still very young and has a lot of work to be done but it can already be interesting to check out the repository and test the library as far as it has been developed.

5.4.17 Hyperledger Ursa

Finally, these is also Hyperledger Ursa which provides a shared cryptographic library that enables people to increase the security of their projects and prevent duplicate work when it comes to cryptography implementations.[13] First of all, there is the base crypto library which contains a shared modular signature implementation that has several signing schemes and a common API. Secondly, there is also the Z-Mix library which offers a generic way to generate zero-knowledge proofs.

---

[10] https://github.com/hyperledger/blockchain-explorer.

[11] https://www.hyperledger.org/projects/quilt.

[12] https://www.hyperledger.org/projects/transact.

[13] https://www.hyperledger.org/projects/ursa.

5.4.18 Digital Asset

Digital Asset has positioned itself as a leader in providing enterprise-grade blockchain and smart contract solutions, with a strong emphasis on regulatory compliance, business process automation, and interoperability. At the heart of the Digital Asset ecosystem is DAML (Digital Asset Modeling Language), a high-level, open-source smart contract language purpose-built for modeling digital agreements in a safe, deterministic, and domain-specific manner. Unlike general-purpose smart contract languages such as Solidity or Rust, DAML is tailored to represent complex workflows and contractual relationships across multiple parties. It provides first-class abstractions for rights, obligations, and multi-party transactions, allowing developers to encode business logic directly without managing low-level concerns like consensus, transaction finality, or cryptographic operations. This abstraction makes DAML particularly appealing for organizations operating in regulated or high-assurance environments such as finance, insurance, and healthcare. One of DAML's standout features is its ledger-agnostic design. While originally introduced as part of the proprietary Digital Asset Platform, DAML smart contracts can now run across a wide variety of backends, including:

- Hyperledger Fabric
- Hyperledger Sawtooth
- Corda
- VMware Blockchain
- Amazon Aurora (database-backed ledger)
- PostgreSQL
- Canton—Digital Asset's own privacy-preserving distributed ledger.

This multi-platform compatibility provides architectural flexibility for enterprises, enabling them to deploy DAML contracts across public, private, or hybrid infrastructures without rewriting core business logic. It also allows for phased modernization—organizations can begin with DAML on centralized infrastructure and later migrate to DLT-based architectures when appropriate. DAML's ecosystem is thriving, bolstered by active community contributions and a rich suite of development tools, including:

- Code editors and language servers
- Integrated testing and simulation environments
- Ledger APIs for secure interaction with deployed contracts
- Enterprise SDKs for Java, Python, and JavaScript.

Digital Asset's Canton ledger, a privacy-centric distributed system built for high throughput and cryptographic confidentiality, is increasingly used in production by financial institutions to automate clearing, settlement, and custody workflows. Canton ensures that only the involved parties see the content of smart contracts, aligning with data minimization and legal requirements in finance and beyond. With its strong formal foundations, DAML is also gaining academic interest, particularly in domains like formal verification of contracts, decentralized compliance enforcement, and legal informatics. Its declarative, Haskell-inspired syntax and deterministic execution model offer a compelling balance between developer productivity and systemic correctness. By abstracting away blockchain-specific complexities while maintaining interoperability and auditability, Digital Asset and DAML offer a unique value proposition: enabling enterprises to focus on business logic and automation, not infrastructure, while retaining the option to evolve into distributed architectures as needed.

5.5 IOTA

IOTA stands out not just as an alternative to traditional blockchain systems, but as a radically distinct vision built upon a Directed Acyclic Graph (DAG) structure known as the Tangle. Originally conceived as a feeless and scalable solution for the rapidly expanding Internet of Things (IoT) ecosystem, IOTA has matured into a modular, smart contract-enabled distributed ledger platform, one that is well-positioned to serve as the infrastructural backbone for machine-to-machine interactions, digital identity, microtransactions, and secure data flows. The evolution from IOTA's early ternary-based cryptographic stack toward a binary-native infrastructure began with Chrysalis, which redefined the network's technical underpinnings. The Chrysalis update replaced the legacy Winternitz One-Time Signatures with Ed25519, leading to reusable addresses and significantly enhanced cryptographic usability. More critically, it restructured transaction formats and standardized them, enabling the ecosystem to adopt modern cryptographic libraries, dramatically improve performance, and attract developers accustomed to mainstream tools. Building upon this, Stardust was introduced as a second-generation protocol update. It ushered in native tokenization, non-fungible tokens (NFTs), and the capacity for ledger extensibility—meaning developers could define and interact with new token types or asset classes directly at the base layer, without resorting to smart contracts. This marked a crucial shift: IOTA was no longer just an IoT protocol—it had become a general-purpose ledger for value and data. A defining characteristic of early IOTA was its reliance on a Coordinator, a central node that periodically issued so-called milestone transactions to secure consensus and prevent double spending. Though pragmatic in IOTA's infancy, this approach was antithetical to the ethos of decentralization. The Coordicide roadmap addressed this head-on, proposing a fully decentralized network architecture.

Now in 2025, Coordicide is no longer theoretical. The deployment of its key components—including a reputation-based access scheme known as Mana, the Fast Probabilistic Consensus (FPC) protocol, and a modular conflict resolution mechanism based on On-Tangle Voting (OTV)—has been extensively trialed on the Shimmer network, IOTA's innovation staging ground. The result is a network architecture that eliminates the Coordinator while preserving security, and achieves a consensus mechanism that is both scalable and fault-tolerant. Unlike conventional blockchain platforms, IOTA approaches smart contracts through a multi-chain architecture. Each smart contract is deployed not on a global, monolithic ledger but on independent chains that are anchored into the Tangle via periodic state commitments. This design offers fine-grained control over execution environments, security models, and transaction fee policies. Smart contracts on IOTA are implemented using WebAssembly (Wasm), allowing developers to write decentralized applications in high-performance languages such as Rust, AssemblyScript, and TinyGo. This approach ensures deterministic execution, high compatibility across environments, and minimal overhead—key for IoT contexts where computation and memory are constrained. These smart contract chains can interact asynchronously, enabling cross-chain composability while preserving the scalability benefits of the DAG structure. IOTA's smart contract model supports fee customization, giving chain operators the flexibility to define zero-fee applications or alternative economic models. This is especially important in use cases where transaction costs could hinder adoption—such as microbilling, edge data sharing, or autonomous vehicle coordination. A core use case for IOTA lies beyond financial transactions. Through the IOTA Streams framework, the network enables authenticated and encrypted data channels, where structured data packets can be securely transmitted between devices. This is of particular relevance in supply chain traceability, industrial telemetry, and sensor networks—contexts in which data authenticity and integrity are paramount. Complementing this is IOTA Identity, a full-fledged framework for Self-Sovereign Identity (SSI) based on W3C's Decentralized Identifiers (DIDs) and Verifiable Credentials. In 2025, identity credentials are not just readable and portable—they are anchored to the Tangle and cryptographically provable. This enables privacy-preserving authentication, authorization, and access control mechanisms suitable for everything from health records to smart city infrastructure. Since 2019, IOTA has replaced the monolithic IRI (IOTA Reference Implementation) with two modern, modular node clients: Hornet, developed in Go, and Bee, written in Rust. These clients are optimized for efficiency, startup performance, and resource footprint. They support local snapshots for storage pruning, enhanced gossip layers for communication, and seamless integration with IOTA's APIs and tooling. Nodes now participate in a gossip-based consensus, sharing transaction data and state metadata through peer-to-peer communication. When a new node joins the network, it undergoes a solidification process whereby it recursively requests and validates past milestones, building a local view of the Tangle. All nodes are capable of broadcasting, validating, and referencing transactions, with synchronization guarantees ensured via milestone checkpoints. In parallel, the IOTA wallet stack has also matured. The official Firefly wallet supports multi-asset management, NFT display, Shimmer and IOTA mainnets, and secure seed storage. Enterprises and dApp developers can leverage advanced libraries and SDKs, alongside APIs that support everything from transaction broadcasting to DID management and smart contract invocation.

IOTA is being piloted and deployed in a range of real-world applications. Autonomous cars use machine-to-machine micropayments to pay for charging, parking, and tolls. Smart meters interact with energy grids through programmable data and token flows. Governments explore digital twins and national identity systems anchored on IOTA's DAG, taking advantage of its zero-fee architecture and cryptographic guarantees. The DAG model gives IOTA an edge in scalability. Unlike traditional blockchains that suffer throughput degradation with increased usage, IOTA grows stronger and faster as more transactions join the network—due to each transaction contributing to the validation process. Combined with quantum-resilient cryptographic options, such as plans for Winternitz One-Time Signatures and post-quantum secure hashing algorithms, IOTA remains forward-compatible with emerging threats. The IOTA native token remains a crucial component of the network, used not for mining fees but for value transfer, resource allocation, and staking in smart contract environments. The denomination system has been standardized:

- Peta IOTA (Pi) $= 10^{15}$ i
- Tera IOTA (Ti) $= 10^{12}$ i
- Giga IOTA (Gi) $= 10^9$ i
- Mega IOTA (Mi) $= 10^6$ i
- Kilo IOTA (Ki) $= 10^3$ i
- IOTA (i) $=$ base unit.

The Shimmer network, operating as a sibling ledger, introduces token incentives and experimentation with DeFi, NFTs, and DAO structures—all composable with IOTA's base infrastructure.

5.6   The Agreements Network

The Agreements network is a clear example of blockchain technology used for legal tech. Spearheaded by Monax, also known for developing the Hyperledger Burrow implementation, the ultimate goal is to bring technology and automation to the law profession. Not only to optimize the process for the law professional but mainly to bring the focus to the client experience. As it is stated in the white paper 'Billions of micro-transactions and low-value contracts executed in digital commerce are largely unserved by a legal profession geared towards bespoke, high-value contract creation.'[14] The modern law profession remains a paper based industry that is largely out of sync with current technological advances that currently revolutionize other industries. On top of that many lawyers are currently not active in the law profession or are under-employed while millions are still looking for affordable representation. The Agreements network aims to fill up this void by making use of blockchain technology and smart contract implementations to change

---

[14] https://agreements.network/files/an_whitepaper_v1.0.pdf.

static contracts towards living agreements that can lead to automatic execution. It also allows for easy replication of contracts which lead to cost reduction and strongly diminished review times of contractual agreements. By making use of such automatic processes and living agreements that can execute when the agreed upon terms are met, leads to legal as a service models that can service the massive amount of requests coming both from industry and households looking for legal solutions in everyday situations. So how does this actually work in practice? Because while legal professionals are necessary to create the actual product, they often do not possess the technical knowledge required to actually create it. This is where a combination of legal and IT professionals are necessary to help each other creating these new type of contracts. The engine provided by the Agreements network, consists out of a BPMN-platform (Business Process Model and Notation) which is often used by business professionals to actually map out processes and can easily be aligned with the steps that legal processes need to follow. Underlying there is the smart contract engine and the blockchain layer that actually provides data assurance. The entire network consists out of the following participants:

- **Consumers**: These are the actual end-users that make use of the living agreements
- **Producers**: The developers that create the 'Archetypes' which are legal prose combined with the smart contract workflows. These producers earn a fee when their contract implementation is being used
- **Testers**: The testers are responsible for testing new Archetypes that can be found on the network and earn a fee based upon their reputation
- **Network validators**: The network validators are the nodes as we known them from other implementations and participate in the consensus mechanism. They earn a maintenance fee for upkeep of the network
- **Service providers**: Finally, there are the actual service providers as legal products often leverage other solutions such as identity, insurance and others.

Now how do these living agreements actually look like? First of all, there is a human-readable level which contains the legal information that is necessary for starting the contract. Underlying this are the machine-readable parameters that determine the outcome of the contract and can become part of the smart contract. These parameters are linked together in workflows that determine the tasks and events necessary to both start and execute the contract. The whitepaper gives a few exciting examples where the Agreements network could actually be put to good use: equipment fleet leasing, content producers and corporate governance. With equipment fleet leasing it refers to the fact that actually buying once own fleet of certain equipment is often no longer interesting as technological advances are increasing rapidly over time and fleet management becomes more and more expensive if one chooses to buy their own equipment. This is where leasing contracts come in and where contracts come in, one can make use of the Agreements network. One could easily create a living agreement that is reusable and contains information such as ownership, maintenance, insurance and right of use. Furthermore, one could integrate interfaces for payments/micropayments and insurer integrations, storage of collected data made by the equipment and evidence of use and other implementations. For content management, the Agreements network could offer solutions regarding the ownership of intellectual property, fair payment and protection versus third-party copyright infringements lawsuits. Similarly, when we look at corporate governance, the network can be used for storage of articles of incorporation, regulatory filing, shareholder votes, bylaws and so on.

5.6.1   The Network

When we look at the more technical side of things, we know that the Agreements network is an implementation leveraging the Cosmos Hub which in turn is linked to the Ethereum network. This means smart contracts on the Ethereum network can interact with the Agreements network while at the same time, the Agreements network isn't exposed to backlogs and attacks concerning the Ethereum network. If the Agreements network is implemented as a public blockchain, the participants are forced to put up a stake in the network. This stake is called a 'bond' and requires the users to place a certain number of tokens in an escrow contract. As long as the participants adhere to the network rules, they can ask their stake back at any moment. However, whenever they break the rules, their stakes are slashed and only part of the original bond can be retrieved in case the participant wishes to leave the network. The Agreements network is another implementation under development by Monax industries so it should be no surprise that the underlying technology for the base blockchain node is Hyperledger Burrow. You can use this to build your own implementation if you want to build from source. All API documentation for the Agreements network can be found on the following website: https://docs.agreements.net work/#introduction-to-the-agreements-network. Currently the network is still in test but it can be used for testing and to create some first implementations.

5.7   Steem

Steem is another platform offering developers to work on their implementation of Blockchain technology. It offers feeless transactions and contains functions that allow building functional blockchain applications to be easy and convenient.[15] The proof of their functionality can be found in the fact that, to date, they process more transactions than Bitcoin and Ethereum combined. The idea behind the platform is that contributors and users that deliver quality content are rewarded by STEEM tokens (based on votes of the other participants). Steem wants to reward everyone that contributes to a major

---

[15] https://steem.com/developers/.

venture by ownership, payment or debt from that venture.[16] This means that participants that invest financial means into a venture are weighted equally to the participants that invest their time and intellect (proof of brain). Several types of capital contribution have been defined in the white paper: STEEM, Steem Power (SP) and Steem Dollars (SBD). STEEM is the native token of the Steem blockchain platform and all other tokens that reside within the platform derive their value from this token. This token can also be bought and sold on a number of exchanges and be used as a general means of payment. The Steem platform also wants to be an enabler for start-up companies and applications. These look for long-term capital to fund their growth and development. Only this way these companies can hope to grow and eventually become successful. The problem with the cryptocurrency market is that it is filled with short-term investors that are looking to make a quick profit after which they move on. This moves against the needs of the start-ups that exist in the same market. This is why Steem has introduced Steem Power which are STEEM tokens that have been committed to a 13-week vesting schedule. On top of that, SP isn't easily traded as it is both non-transferrable and non-divisible (an exception is the automatically recurring conversion request). So why invest in Steem Power? The investment in SP has multiple returns for the participant willing to take on Steem Power. Their votes in the system gain more influence, which in turn comes with greater rewards. On top of that SP holders gain 15% of the yearly inflation based on their stake. 'Powering down', or returning the stake from SP to STEEM, happens in 13 weeks with equal stakes. Finally, there are also Steem (Blockchain) Dollars or SBD's. Also these were invented to bring stability to the network and are the 'convertible notes' of the network, used to fund the start-ups in the network. These are used to fund short-term debt and can be easily converted based on a reliable price feed in the network. To prevent abuse, the impact of fraudulent feeds, timing and fraudulent conversions is reduced.

This is done by introducing elected 'witnesses' that have to publish price feeds (delegated proof of stake). These witnesses gain a payment for their services so remaining trustworthy is in their own interest. The median conversion price moves with every 3.5 days, so participants could try to cover the current market and make trades based on this current information. To prevent such abuse, all trades are delayed for 3.5 days, making timing attacks virtually impossible. On top of that, only conversions from SBD to STEEM are freely possible, while conversion to SBD are determined by the network, so that abuse of these conversions is mitigated. Another measure is the maximum debt-to-ownership ratio of 10%. If ever the amount of SBD would exceed the STEEM market cap, the STEEM returned from SBD would be reduced to reflect the 10% cap. Finally, also the number of rates that can be given are limited so that automation cannot be used to vote and distribute STEEM to such bots. Consensus in the STEEM network is also different from other networks. Blocks are produced in rounds where for each round 21 witnesses are selected (20 by approval voting and 1 is timeshared by every witness that wasn't selected in the top 20 based on their votes). These witnesses are shuffled every

---

[16] https://www.steem.com/steem-whitepaper.pdf.

round. Because these witnesses are known beforehand, blocks can be produced every 3 s. To allow for enough performance and scalability, Steem has borrowed some ideas from the LMAX exchange such as keeping everything in memory,[17] core business logic is a single thread, and cryptographic operations are kept out of the core business logic, use an object oriented data model and divide validation in state-dependent and state-independent checks. The database portion of the Steem network is ChainBase while the AppBase in use is the first step in creating a multi-chain fabric.[18] Different from other blockchain networks, Steem still offers a possibility to recover compromised accounts. This is not always possible but if the registrar offers these services, an account can be recovered based on a previous private key. A number of applications is currently running on the platform (324 to date) and have already established a user base of about 1 million people that actively participate in the platform. The most popular applications that currently run on top of the platform are Steemit (which is a social blogging platform), eSteem (which is a mobile app to blog, share and vote), DTube (a decentralized video platform), Utopian (Funding of open source projects) and steem Monsters (a trading card game).

5.7.1 Smart Media Tokens

Another implementation that is currently under development is 'smart media tokens' or 'SMTs'. These are tokens that can be launched on top of the Steem platform and incorporate the same concept of 'proof of brain'. This would allow even more flexibility to the developers that wish to create social media content on top of the platform. Similarly, it could reward the participants based on their voting and publishing of content. These new tokens could be used for ICO's (initial coin offerings) and would allow the issuer to determine the supply (capped or unlimited). The issuer would also be able to determine the link with for example Steem Power. The total cost for issuing such a new SMT would be $1 to prevent attacks that would abuse the system introduced by Steem.[19] This implementation is still under fully development but can proof to be very interesting in the future and become the playground of some powerful new applications.

5.8 EOS.IO

EOSIO is a blockchain platform that aims to bring a network implementation that promises usability for both private and public use cases. It offers role-based security permissions, speed and secure application processing. It uses programming languages that are already in use outside of the blockchain landscape so that developers can use the tools

---

[17] Optane from Intel.

[18] https://steem.com/steem-bluepaper.pdf.

[19] https://smt.steem.com/smt-whitepaper.pdf.

they already know.[20] It also makes use of the freemium model so that participants do not have to pay for the underlying structure. The architecture that has been implemented by the platform mimics an operating system on top of which decentralized applications can be built and it allows for the use of many CPU clusters. Millions of transactions per second can be processed by this platform and fees are eliminated, allowing scaling and many participants. The consensus algorithm that is in use by the platform is Byzantine Fault Tolerance—Delegated Proof of Stake. The block production happens every 0.5 s and for every block there is authorized 1 producer that can deliver the block. These blocks are produced in rounds of 126 with 6 blocks being processed each time and 21 producers that are involved. Several tools are being offered so that developers can easier work with their implementation. They offer libraries to work with different authentication providers, several libraries to create contracts, but also libraries to develop smart phone applications and more.[21] The major implementation has been created in C++ and also the smart contracting language being used is C++, allowing developers from all over the world to take their experience to the platform. EOS makes use of a WASM based virtual machine. The several libraries that you can easily consult are:

- Nodeos which is an implementation for the core EOS node daemon. Extra features can be implemented based on the needs of your application/network
- Cleos/keosd are the key managers
- Eosjs is the JavaScript API SDK
- Demux is a reference implementation of the backend infrastructure.

5.9   Quorum

Quorum has evolved significantly since its inception by J.P. Morgan as an Ethereum-based platform tailored for enterprise use. Now under active development and stewardship by ConsenSys, Quorum continues to provide a robust foundation for building enterprise-grade decentralized applications, with a strong emphasis on privacy, permissioning, and modular consensus mechanisms. At its core, Quorum remains fully compatible with the Ethereum ecosystem. Developers can still rely on familiar tools like MetaMask, Truffle, Remix, and OpenZeppelin libraries, which greatly accelerates development and deployment cycles. This compatibility ensures seamless integration with existing Ethereum smart contract infrastructure, while offering the enterprise-ready customizations required for private and consortium deployments. Quorum extends the Go-Ethereum (Geth) client with enterprise-centric enhancements. Most notably, it has decoupled itself from Ethereum's

---

[20] https://eos.io/why-eosio/.

[21] https://github.com/eosio.

legacy consensus mechanisms. Instead of Proof of Work (which Ethereum has since abandoned in favor of Proof of Stake via Ethereum 2.0), Quorum provides pluggable consensus options including:

- Raft—A crash fault tolerant consensus mechanism suitable for fast transaction finality in private networks.
- Istanbul BFT (IBFT)—A Byzantine Fault Tolerant protocol allowing enhanced security in adversarial environments.
- Clique (Proof of Authority)—A simpler PoA-based model for controlled, permissioned blockchain scenarios.

In terms of data privacy, Quorum's architecture integrates Tessera, a mature and secure privacy manager derived from the original Constellation project. Tessera enables the encryption and secure sharing of private transactions between specific participants in the network—an essential capability for enterprise use cases in banking, healthcare, and supply chain management. A defining aspect of Quorum in 2025 is its modularity. Enterprises can now build networks from the ground up using Quorum's comprehensive tooling suite. Deployment options range from on-premise and cloud-native environments to managed services through ConsenSys and partner infrastructure providers. This flexibility empowers organizations to tailor their blockchain networks for varying regulatory, geographic, and operational constraints. In production environments, Quorum has proven capable of supporting real-world financial applications such as tokenized assets, cross-border payments, interbank settlements, and enterprise DeFi solutions. As part of the broader Enterprise Ethereum Alliance (EEA) efforts, it continues to align with industry standards for interoperability, identity, and compliance. Quorum in 2025 represents a mature, scalable, and secure enterprise blockchain solution—one that benefits from the rapid evolution of Ethereum itself, while remaining focused on the unique needs of regulated and privacy-sensitive industries.

5.10 NEO

NEO, often referred to as the "Ethereum of China," has continued its trajectory as a robust open-source platform designed to underpin a smart economy, an ecosystem in which digital assets, digital identities, and smart contracts converge to form the basis of secure, efficient, and legally compliant decentralized applications. At the heart of NEO's vision is the notion of digital trust, achieved through the use of digital certificates. These certificates bind real-world legal identities to on-chain assets, providing a regulatory-compliant framework that bridges traditional and decentralized finance. This has positioned NEO as a prime candidate for institutional adoption, especially in jurisdictions with strong identity and compliance requirements. NEO's smart contract platform remains fully Turing complete and continues to distinguish itself with multi-language support. Developers can author contracts in familiar languages such as C#, Java, and Python, thanks to NEO's use of a stack-based virtual machine (NeoVM). This inclusivity stands in contrast to platforms that demand learning domain-specific languages like Solidity, thereby lowering the barrier to entry and enabling faster enterprise and public sector experimentation. From a consensus perspective, NEO still leverages its hallmark delegated Byzantine Fault Tolerance (dBFT) protocol. This consensus model offers high throughput, immediate finality, and fault tolerance in adversarial conditions, making it particularly well-suited for high-volume financial applications. The dBFT 2.0 update, introduced in earlier versions, improved network stability and introduced a recovery mechanism to ensure continued operation during network stalls, a crucial enhancement for mission-critical applications. In the domain of cross-chain interoperability, NEO has continued its pursuit of integrating atomic swaps and inter-chain smart contract operability. The introduction of protocols like Poly Network has allowed NEO-based applications to interact with ecosystems such as Ethereum, Binance Smart Chain, and Ontology. Although challenges in cross-chain security remain, these bridges enable the composition of multi-chain decentralized finance (DeFi) architectures and asset movement. Looking toward future-proofing, quantum resistance has not been overlooked. NEO has integrated lattice-based cryptographic schemes, positioning it as one of the few major platforms actively preparing for the advent of quantum computing. The use of post-quantum cryptography, while still in experimental stages across most blockchain platforms, reflects a proactive stance on long-term cryptographic resilience. With the NEO ecosystem expanding to include frameworks like NeoFS (a decentralized file storage system) and NeoID (a verifiable digital identity layer), the platform continues to build a comprehensive infrastructure stack. In 2025, NEO stands as a versatile and enterprise-friendly blockchain that balances regulatory compliance, developer usability, and forward-looking technical features.

5.11 BigchainDB

BigchainDB is the next distributed ledger implementation on the list of platforms that we are discussing. It has been developed for private implementations where each node is permissioned to become part of the network. This platform can already be used for some of the applications that you would like to put into production but carefulness is advised, as this is still under development and some implementations might still change over time.[22] Just like some of the other platforms we have seen before, also this network is based on Tendermint. One of the advantages of this platform is that it allows for querying of the data that has been stored in the ledger. Similarly to a lot of different other implementations, also this platform makes use of Byzantine Fault Tolerance. The database in use by the network is MongoDB, which is replicated over all the nodes in the

---

[22] https://docs.bigchaindb.com/en/latest/decentralized.html.

network, so that attackers, like in any blockchain, cannot compromise the entire network if they are able to attack one of the nodes. This MongoDB allows the querying of data but how this can be used, completely depends on how the node operator wishes to expose this data (GraphQL, HTTP and REST API's are possible). An interesting feature brought by BigchainDB is that a participant can create an asset but that all of these are signed by that participant. So it is cryptographically impossible to create an asset in name of another participant. The BigchainDB 2.0 whitepaper references use cases in supply chain, intellectual property rights management, digital twin creation, IoT, Identity management, data governance, audit trails and more. There are also references to possible connections with other decentralized systems such as IPFS, Ocean Protocol, Ethereum, Hyperledger Fabric and TrueBit.

5.12   Corda

Corda is an open-source distributed ledger platform specifically designed for enterprise environments that demand high standards of privacy, interoperability, and legal enforceability. Rather than framing itself as a traditional blockchain, Corda positions itself as a decentralized database with fine-grained access control and smart contract capabilities tailored for real-world financial and business use cases. Developed originally by R3, Corda has seen widespread adoption in regulated industries such as banking, insurance, and supply chain due to its privacy-preserving architecture and extensibility. At the architectural level, Corda distinguishes itself through its use of a notary-based consensus mechanism, enabling selective visibility of transaction data. Unlike typical blockchain networks where all transactions are broadcast to every node, Corda enforces data minimization by ensuring that only the relevant parties to a transaction have access to its details. Notaries—trusted entities in the network—are responsible for verifying transaction uniqueness and ordering, preventing double spending without exposing sensitive transaction content. Corda applications, referred to as CorDapps, are built using Kotlin or Java and compiled to run on the Java Virtual Machine (JVM). These CorDapps make use of a hybrid model that blends Ethereum's smart contract abstraction and Bitcoin's Unspent Transaction Output (UTXO) model, enabling both expressive contract logic and deterministic state management. Developers define contracts as JVM bytecode, which are verified by all involved participants, ensuring legal clarity and deterministic execution across the network. To support development and testing, Corda provides a suite of sophisticated tools. The Corda demo network allows developers to rapidly spin up a simulation environment, while the Node Explorer offers a visual interface to monitor ledger activity and inspect transaction metadata. For low-level inspection, the Blob Inspector translates binary AMQP-serialized data into a human-readable format—an invaluable tool for auditing and debugging. Moreover, the Network Bootstrapper automates the initialization of network parameters and disseminates them across nodes, facilitating consistent deployment across decentralized environments. A key innovation within Corda's ecosystem is the Token SDK, which standardizes the creation, issuance, and transfer of both fungible and non-fungible tokens. This SDK enables enterprises to manage digital representations of real-world assets with regulatory compliance, supporting use cases from central bank digital currencies (CBDCs) to corporate securities. In its current evolution, Corda continues to refine its support for confidential identities, multi-party workflows, and zero-knowledge proofs, aligning its capabilities with the stringent demands of data privacy regulations like GDPR and industry-specific compliance frameworks. Though originally targeted at financial services, the platform has gained traction across domains such as healthcare, trade finance, and digital identity management.

5.13 Æternity

The æternity network is a platform that allows for the development of æpps on top of their network. What makes this implementation different from all the other platforms we have seen before? Well, æternity comes with a built-in oracle that allows immediate use of real-world data in your applications without you having to make use of any third party to provide this data. There are also packages that can be used to create major platforms and are free to use on Github. The oracle can deliver 4 types of transactions: register, extend, query and response.[23] The first helps to register an address as an oracle by an oracle operator. The extend transaction is meant to extend the TTL of an oracle that is currently operating in the network. The query transaction is used to create an oracle interaction object in the oracle state tree. This transaction also determines the TTL of the query and how long it is open for a response from the oracle. Finally, there is the response transaction which is the reply to a query transaction and this response is signed with the oracle account's private key. The network makes use of a derived version of the Ethereum Virtual machine called 'ÆVM'. The language used within the network to create smart contracts is called 'the Sophia' and is part of the ML family. State channels are used throughout the network to allow for communication and relaying messages.

5.14 Golem

Golem is an interesting application of blockchain in practice as it focusses to bring a very specific solution in a decentralized manner: distributing computer power from those that have it to those that need it. They have created a marketplace which allows for the creation of super computers based on the needs of the users, without actually having to invest in such an infrastructure and without having to rely upon centralized providers. Several use

---

[23] http://aeternity.com/documentation-hub/protocol/oracles/oracle_transactions/.

cases have been identified for the network such as Brass Golem which allows for CGI rendering of any Blender generated scenes. Also the scientific community can rely upon the network to use computer power for their research. Finally, there are developments to make the network fit for use when it comes to machine learning projects. The underlying transaction system of the network is Ethereum-based and allows to settle payments between the participants in the network in a similar manner.

5.15   Cortex

Cortex is a blockchain platform that is used specifically for AI use cases. It is a response to the limitations that have been set upon existing EVM implementations because of the cost of running code on the world computer. Cortex on the other hand, has removed these limitations so that one can actually make use of the real possibilities with a Turing complete machine. When you read the central ideas behind Cortex, you see that the developers behind the network see blockchain networks as living networks in which the nodes represent 'life'. As long as there is life, there can be responses on external events. The current implementations are seen as primitive lifeforms because they cannot respond in an intelligent manner to these external events and impulses. With Cortex, they hope to change that and actually generate a general AI network. Several of the implementations of the network rely on the work that has been done by the Ethereum community. As such, it also makes use of the Solidity language for its smart contracts. These smart contracts underlie decentralized applications which in turn could bring recommender systems, intelligent investment bots, speech and facial predictors and more.

Data models can be uploaded to the storage layer by participants and others can make use of these models. Doing so, these participants have to pay for using these models.[24] The Cortex Virtual Machine can process the results and give an output. The payment method within the system is called 'Endorphin'. The network makes use of the Cuckoo Cycle proof of work protocol to make sure that there is a 1 machine 1 vote paradigm and all participants are to a certain extent equal.

5.16   Sui

Sui is a Layer 1 blockchain platform developed by Mysten Labs, designed to radically improve blockchain scalability, developer ergonomics, and composability by rethinking the very abstraction model underlying distributed ledgers. Instead of modeling smart contracts around account-based state as seen in Ethereum or UTXO models as in Bitcoin, Sui introduces an object-centric data model that treats all on-chain assets, including user accounts, tokens, and NFTs, as programmable objects with distinct ownership, mutability,

---

[24] https://www.cortexlabs.ai/cortex_ai_on_blockchain_en.pdf.

and interaction semantics. At the heart of the Sui design is the Move programming language, a resource-oriented smart contract language originally developed for Facebook's (now defunct) Diem project. Move provides strict guarantees around ownership, asset safety, and access control by enforcing linear types. In Sui, Move has been extended and refined into Sui Move, tailored specifically to suit the needs of Sui's object-based execution model. This ensures predictable resource management, static verification of asset transfers, and avoidance of reentrancy bugs and other common vulnerabilities. Sui's most notable architectural contribution is the decoupling of consensus from data execution—a design choice made possible by its classification of transactions into two main categories:

- Owned-object transactions: Transactions that operate on independent, non-shared objects (such as NFTs or personal tokens) and can be processed without global consensus, enabling them to be validated via simple Byzantine Consistent Broadcast. These are executed with extremely low latency and parallelism.
- Shared-object transactions: Transactions that require consensus because they involve shared mutable state (e.g., AMMs, DAOs) and are processed using Narwhal and Bullshark, Sui's high-throughput, DAG-based consensus protocol designed for high scalability and fairness.

This separation is pivotal in unlocking horizontal scaling, where throughput can grow with the number of validator cores, sidestepping many bottlenecks encountered in monolithic chain designs. Sui promises industry-leading performance benchmarks, with throughput targets in the range of hundreds of thousands of transactions per second (TPS) under optimal network conditions. The parallel execution of non-conflicting transactions, dynamic validator sharding, and DAG-based consensus underpin this performance. Benchmarks from 2023–2024 demonstrated consistent performance gains compared to other Layer 1s under high-volume transaction loads, particularly for applications with a high density of independent user actions, such as gaming, ticketing, or social platforms. Sui's architecture lends itself well to web3 gaming, digital collectibles, and DeFi applications requiring high throughput and minimal finality latency. It supports highly interactive user experiences without compromising decentralization or security. Some early standout applications include BlueMove (NFT marketplace), Sui Wallet, and DeepBook (native order book protocol for DeFi). Its ecosystem is growing with a focus on developer onboarding, aided by tools like the Sui CLI, Sui Explorer, and Sui SDKs for multiple languages. Compared to contemporaries like Solana or Aptos, Sui takes a unique stance by completely re-architecting the transaction model rather than optimizing existing paradigms. While Aptos also uses Move, it retains a more traditional account model and global consensus. Solana emphasizes monolithic, ultra-fast block production with its Sealevel runtime, but Sui's ability to completely bypass consensus for independent operations makes it more modular and arguably more future-proof in terms of composability and scalability.

5.17 Aptos

Aptos is a Layer 1 blockchain that emerged from the ashes of Meta's (formerly Facebook's) Diem initiative. Developed by former Diem engineers, Aptos aims to realize the original vision of a secure, developer-friendly, and high-throughput blockchain, drawing heavily on innovations originally conceived for Diem but expanding and refining them in a permissionless, decentralized context. At the core of Aptos is the Move programming language, designed for safety, resource management, and expressiveness. Move brings a linear type system to smart contracts, enforcing strict rules about ownership and transfer of digital assets. This makes many common vulnerabilities (e.g., reentrancy attacks, double-spends) statically impossible. Unlike Ethereum's account-centric state model, Move enables precise asset tracking at the type level and enforces invariants at compile time.

Aptos's most distinctive architectural choice lies in its support for parallel transaction execution. It introduces a novel pipeline that includes:

- BlockSTM (Software Transactional Memory)—a parallel execution engine that speculatively executes transactions concurrently, determines the correct execution order, and resolves conflicts using optimistic concurrency control.
- State Merkle Trees and accumulator-based ledger architecture, which allow for efficient verification and pruning of on-chain state.
- BFT consensus—specifically a highly optimized implementation of HotStuff, called AptosBFT, which is leader-rotation-based and supports fast finality even in partially asynchronous environments.

This approach allows Aptos to maximize hardware utilization, potentially executing tens of thousands of transactions per second, with significantly reduced latencies compared to traditional blockchains. In Aptos, Move is not just a contract language; it is deeply embedded in the runtime and transaction processing pipeline. Aptos extends the Diem Move VM with modules for:

- Upgradeable smart contracts
- Custom module governance
- Fine-grained access control
- On-chain formal verification hooks.

This modularity and safety-centric approach is intended to serve mission-critical use cases in finance, government, and infrastructure. Aptos has rapidly grown its developer and application ecosystem. Use cases range from DeFi (e.g., Aries Markets), gaming (e.g., Topaz, Aptos Arena), and NFTs, to identity and infrastructure. Developer onboarding is facilitated through comprehensive tooling: Aptos CLI, Aptos SDKs, Move Prover for formal verification, and extensive documentation. Aptos has emphasized partnerships with major players, including Google Cloud, Microsoft, and NBCUniversal, indicating ambitions for enterprise-grade infrastructure and Web2/Web3 bridging.

5.18 Algorand

Algorand represents a novel approach to blockchain architecture, conceived by Turing Award-winning cryptographer Silvio Micali. From its inception, Algorand was designed to overcome the inherent trade-offs commonly associated with the blockchain trilemma: scalability, security, and decentralization. At its core lies a powerful and elegant consensus protocol, Pure Proof-of-Stake (PPoS), that relies on cryptographic sortition and verifiable random functions (VRFs) to ensure both unpredictability and security. Unlike delegated or bonded proof-of-stake systems that concentrate validation power in the hands of a few, Algorand's PPoS allows every online token holder to participate in the consensus process. Block proposers and committee members are selected at random using VRFs, and their selection is both cryptographically verifiable and private. This structure eliminates the need for staking lockups or slashing, significantly lowering the barriers to participation and enhancing decentralization. The consensus mechanism itself unfolds in three distinct phases: block proposal, soft vote, and final vote. In each phase, a randomly selected committee performs its task, progressively narrowing the candidate blocks until a single block is confirmed. Importantly, Algorand provides instant finality, once a block is added to the chain, it cannot be reversed or forked. This design feature stands in stark contrast to many other chains where probabilistic finality is the norm. Performance-wise, Algorand achieves sub-five-second block times, high throughput exceeding 6,000 transactions per second, and near-zero transaction fees. The protocol is also hardware-efficient, allowing even modest devices to participate in consensus. Notably, since its mainnet launch in 2019, Algorand has maintained 100% uptime, a proof of the robustness of its architecture. Beyond its consensus layer, Algorand features a purpose-built virtual machine known as the Algorand Virtual Machine (AVM). Smart contracts are authored in TEAL (Transaction Execution Approval Language), a low-level, stack-based scripting language designed for predictability and formal analyzability. Developers can also use PyTEAL, a higher-level Python library that compiles down to TEAL, enabling more accessible development while preserving the platform's deterministic guarantees. Algorand supports both stateful and stateless smart contracts, and leverages features such as atomic transfers, ABI (Application Binary Interface) support, and structured inter-contract communication. Its formal, analyzable contract logic makes it a strong candidate for financial, legal, and regulatory applications that require mathematical precision and auditability. The ecosystem surrounding Algorand has matured significantly. It has been adopted in a wide array of use cases, from decentralized finance (e.g., Tinyman, Folks Finance) and NFT marketplaces (e.g., Rand Gallery), to real-world asset tokenization and central bank digital currency (CBDC) pilots. Governments such as those of El Salvador and the Marshall Islands have explored Algorand for sovereign digital currency infrastructure, while companies like Circle use it as a performant layer for USDC issuance. Enterprise players like Koibanx and Republic have built financial inclusion tools on the protocol, particularly in Latin American markets. On the research frontier, Algorand continues to push boundaries. The protocol is exploring zero-knowledge proofs, cross-chain state proofs, and post-quantum secure cryptography. Its deterministic smart contracts also provide an ideal testing ground for formal verification and model checking, appealing to academics and developers seeking high assurance applications. Algorand stands out not only for its technical sophistication but also for its commitment to practical deployment, usability, and theoretical rigor. It successfully bridges the gap between cryptographic innovation and real-world scalability, making it a compelling platform for advanced research, enterprise solutions, and decentralized application development alike.

5.19 Solana

Solana represents one of the most ambitious undertakings in blockchain scalability, positioning itself as a web-scale blockchain capable of supporting thousands of decentralized applications without compromising throughput or user experience. Developed by Solana Labs and launched in 2020, the platform is best known for its extremely high performance, achieved through a unique combination of architectural innovations, especially Proof of History (PoH) and the Sealevel parallel runtime. At the heart of Solana's value proposition is its hybrid consensus mechanism, which pairs PoH with a variant of Practical Byzantine Fault Tolerance (PBFT) via the Tower BFT protocol. Proof of History is a cryptographic timestamping protocol that generates a verifiable order of events independently of the consensus process. By pre-ordering transactions before consensus, Solana drastically reduces the overhead normally required for block validation, thereby enabling exceptional throughput. Tower BFT builds on this by introducing a lightweight, low-latency voting mechanism that locks in validated blocks while preventing forks. Validators vote on blocks and maintain a local history of their votes and those of their peers, drastically reducing communication complexity in the network. Combined, PoH and Tower BFT allow Solana to finalize blocks in under 400 ms with theoretical throughput exceeding 65,000 transactions per second (TPS) on commodity hardware. Another major innovation is Solana's Sealevel execution environment, which allows for parallel transaction processing. Unlike the serial execution model used by most blockchains (including Ethereum), Sealevel identifies non-overlapping account states in incoming transactions and executes them simultaneously. This model, coupled with a sophisticated runtime scheduler and the use of a statically defined account model, unlocks unprecedented scaling capabilities. Smart contract development on Solana is performed using Rust or C/C++, compiled to WebAssembly (WASM), and interacts with the Solana runtime via a low-level interface. This provides developers with a fine-grained, high-performance environment for writing decentralized applications. While it lacks the flexibility of EVM-compatible platforms, the explicit resource management model enables more predictable performance and avoids the typical bottlenecks of gas metering systems. From a systems design perspective, Solana is a study in vertical integration. The runtime, consensus, ledger storage, and network protocols are all tightly coupled for performance. Ledger replication is handled through Turbine, a UDP-based block propagation protocol inspired by BitTorrent, which segments and streams blocks across a tree of nodes. Gulf Stream manages the mempool and forwards transactions to leaders ahead of time to improve efficiency, while Cloudbreak manages concurrent account access via a memory-mapped file system to avoid bottlenecks. Despite occasional criticism regarding centralization (e.g., reliance on data center-grade hardware and validator concentration), Solana continues to attract a growing developer and application ecosystem. Projects like Jupiter (DeFi aggregation), Mango Markets (perpetuals), Phantom (wallets), and Helium (IoT infrastructure) leverage Solana's speed and low fees to deliver near-instantaneous, real-time user experiences. Solana has also integrated Firedancer, an upcoming validator client developed by Jump Crypto, which is expected to massively increase validator performance and network throughput. This effort also mitigates client monoculture and furthers network resilience. The network is gradually integrating Zero-Knowledge proofs, light clients, and cross-chain communication protocols, aiming to position itself as a foundational layer for high-throughput DeFi, gaming, and Web3 services. Its recently launched Solana Mobile Stack (SMS) initiative and the Saga phone aim to bring native crypto experiences to mobile devices, highlighting the team's emphasis on real-world usability and adoption.

5.20 Ripple

Ripple is a network that was brought to life to deal with payment systems. It means to modernize the current structures that are in place with their network, which they call 'RippleNet', to connect banks, payment providers and digital asset exchanges.[25] Over 200 major institutions have entered their network and makes use of the infrastructure they have put into place. The native token of their platform, XRP, can be used as source liquidity on demand and in real time. Payment settlement can be speed up and exchange costs can be reduced. Their transaction settlement takes about 4 s which is a major improvement over traditional systems that can take up to 5 days. As almost all the other platforms we are discussing, we are dealing with open source technology. Another implementation of Ripple is called Interledger and is an open source implementation which allows for payments across ledgers. The XRP ledger implementation is well-documented and provides several tutorials on its use together with the interledger protocol.

---

[25] https://www.ripple.com/use-cases/.

5.21   Stellar

Stellar is another network that focuses on the payment industry and wants to revolutionize the way of working that they currently have. Difference with Ripple is that Stellar
functions as a non-stock nonprofit organization that wishes to offer low-cost financial services in order to fight poverty. This is why there is no charge in using the network and
why the software itself is open source. The main cost is in development so that one can
integrate with the network and afterwards there are the base fees for each operation that
is linked with a transaction.[26] Stellar even offers the necessary tools for KYC and AML
restrictions with their compliance protocol and offers insight on what licenses might be
needed if one were to engage in the network. The network offers the ideal solution for
micro-payments and also has real time settlement of transactions. Stellar works as a credit
holding system for issuers. This is why trust is a key concept in the network, otherwise
participants would no longer be able to trade tokens for one another. Therefore there is
the creation of a trustline and these trustlines are entries which persist within the ledger
of the network. These must always have sufficient balance to satisfy the liabilities created
by selling. There is also the native token on the network, called 'lumens' or 'XLM'.

5.22   Hedera Hashgraph

Hedera Hashgraph is the first that is able to make use of the hashgraph technology (which
is proprietary software). In theory it is able to support over 250,000 transactions a second
so that scalability is no longer an issue. Every node in the network is able to 'gossip'
about events, which are signed pieces of information on transactions, to other nodes in the
network. This gossip protocol works very efficiently and is able to spread the information
throughout the network in a very fast manner. The history of the gossip protocol can be
seen in a directed graph.[27]

On top of the directed graph that exists within each of the nodes, they also vote
on the validity of the transactions themselves where at least 2/3 of the network is
needed as witnesses. This immediately introduces the concept of 'fairness'. It is a non-
deterministic asynchronous protocol which offers several advantages over deterministic
and synchronous protocols. Deterministic protocols assume that all honest nodes will
reach consensus by a certain round r for a priori known constant r while non-deterministic
protocols do not make this assumption. On top of that, synchronous protocols assume that
messages are delivered after a certain bound, while asynchronous protocols does not make
this assumption. When we look at this short overview of all these features, it seems to be

---

[26] https://www.stellar.org/how-it-works/stellar-basics/.

[27] Jia, Y. (November 8, 2017) Demystifying Hashgraph: benefits and challenges. *Hackernoon.*
https://hackernoon.com/demystifying-hashgraph-benefits-and-challenges-d605e5c0cee5. Accessed
on October 23, 2019.

clear that this platform can bring several advantages when it comes to private blockchain implementations, while it would still be faced with the same challenges that 'classic' blockchain implementations would have to deal with.

5.23 Fantom

Fantom is a blockchain platform that aims to the development of smart cities but also advocates its possible use for public utilities, smart living, healthcare, education, traffic management, resource management, environmental sustainability and more. This is another platform that brings with it the implementation of the directed acyclic graph technology (DAGs). The OPERA chain makes use of the Lachesis consensus protocol which makes use of asynchronous processing and thus leads to high processing rates without congestion. In theory, about 300,000 transactions per second are possible.[28] The Lachesis protocol consists out of events, Clothos, Atropos and the main chain. The event block consists out of stored data which again can be made up out of multiple data packages. Next, there is the signature of the sender of the data and finally, there is the hash of the previous event block. There is also the 'Clotho' which is an event block that contains a flag table. A flag table is a data structure that consists out of a Clotho index and 'connectivity' which indicates the connection to other Clothos. An event block is elected as a Clotho when it can see the supra-majority (more than 2/3th) of blocks created in the path of previous event blocks. Finally, the Clothos are used to elect the Atropos. The Atropos is a set of special event blocks and makes up the main chain. It is this main chain, the chain of Atropos blocks that is used to validate new event blocks. The network makes use of a register based virtual machine. The advantage of register based systems over stack based systems (which are to this day used by a majority of the platforms), is that there are no PUSH or POP instructions, which leads to less overhead when processing. Also the reuse of stored variables is a possibility. The disadvantage is that each address must be explicitly stated.

5.24 Komodo

Komodo introduces the Antara framework which is a framework that can be used for end-to-end blockchain development. The platform allows for the development of multichain networks on which you can pick for each chain a consensus mechanism, hashing algorithm, specific modules and more.[29] The chains that you can build with the platform can therefore be purpose-built and are fully programmable. The Komodo platform is linked with the Bitcoin network and makes use of delayed proof of work to harness

---

[28] https://fantom.foundation/contents/data/2018files/10/wp_fantom_v1.6.pdf.

[29] https://komodoplatform.com/antara-framework/.

the strength of the Bitcoin network for security. All of these aspects make it a fairly easy to use and deploy platform that allow for quick setup.

5.25   Tezos

The Tezos platform is an open source platform that allows for asset and application creation.[30] An interesting feature that is linked with this network is that it is allowed to 'evolve' by upgrading itself. This is done by self-amendment which involves stakeholders that have to govern the process and prevent forking of the blockchain. Smart contracting on top of the platform can be done based on 6 different languages, opening up the platform to a lot of developer communities. These contracts are later verified by mathematically proving the properties that have been implemented by the developer. (Delegated) proof of stake is used in the network to reach consensus as participants can choose to participate or divert their voting rights to other participants. The voters are called 'bakers' and 'baking' is the activity of securing the ledger by signing and publishing blocks. These blocks appear in the network with a timestamp. If this lies in the future, the block can either be buffered or rejected. The native token of the network is called 'TEZ' and enables a participant to interact with the blockchain.

5.26   Tron

Tron is a platform that focuses on entertainment and content-sharing. Its goal is to cut out the middleman (i.e. Netflix) that normally takes a large share of the payments of the users. The Tron platform promises that the major part of the payments go directly to the content creators. Several coins are supported by the platform but the native token is called 'Tronix' or 'TRX'. The network allows for launching of other tokens on top of Tron such as oCoin which supports the Singapore based oBike.[31] Modelled after the Bitcoin network, the transaction system also makes use of unspent outputs but has improved on the existing system and makes use of UTXOs. There is improved security as there is a set of rules that are sent with the UTXO and all of these need to be satisfied before the receiver can actually make use of the token. The platform is supported by the Tron foundation which is a driving force in the further development of the web 3.0 ecosystem. The platform makes use of a roadmap similar to Ethereum. The first step was called 'Exodus' and implemented the free platform for P2P distribution and storage without blockchain technology. The second phase is called 'Odessey' and will implement the actual blockchain (happened in January 2019). The next phases are called 'Great Voyage' and 'Apollo' which will be released in 2020 and 2021. These will implement more options

---

[30] https://tezos.com/.

[31] Largest bike sharing company in Southeast Asia to date.

for developers and content creators based on the platform.[32] The final stages are called 'Star Trek' and 'Eternity' that will come out in 2023 and 2025 and will lead to prediction markets and gaming releases on top of the platform. Interesting links to the Tron network are USDT which is a Tether-issued dollar pegged stablecoin token. Even more interesting is the link with BitTorrent which has launched the 'BTT' coin on top of the Tron network. This allows for payments via the Tron blockchain for content shared via this network.

5.26.1 Sun Network

There is also a side chain that is being implemented called the 'Sun network', named after the founder of the Tron network. It is focused on decentralized application development. Currently the foundation is working on the Java implementation of the network.

5.27   Lisk

Lisk is a blockchain platform that allows developers to work with JavaScript.[33] This delivers the support of a major developer community so that they can easily adapt to the blockchain world. The native coin used in the network is called 'LSK' or 'Lisk'. The blockchain platform makes use of delegated proof of stake to reach consensus.

5.28   MultiChain

The final blockchain platform we show here is MultiChain which is an interesting platform when you want to test out blockchain technology or build fully capable platforms in a production environment. Does this mean that there are no other platforms out there? Of course there are but for this book we will keep it down to the examples we have shortly discussed here. But if you are willing to explore and examine the use cases you have, you are sure to find more platforms.

5.29   2nd Layer Protocols: State Channels

Next to the many platforms that have been created and/or are being created, there are also many 2nd layer protocols which can be applied to existing platforms. These are often aimed at speeding up transactions and scalability. Here you can find a short and limited

---

[32] https://www.investopedia.com/tech/what-tron-trx/.

[33] https://lisk.io/.

overview of the currently existing projects. We have seen several examples before such as the lightning network and the liquidity network.

5.29.1 Celer Network

The Celer network is a layer-2 scaling platform that allows for secure off-chain transactions. The native token called CELR can be used for transactions on this platform. It has a layered architecture which consists out of 3 separate components: cOS, cRoute and cChannel. The first delivers the development framework, the second the transfer routing and the third the generalized state channel and sidechain suite.[34] The network brings the proof of liquidity commitment which is a mining process that allows for liquidity for the off-chain computations. There is also the Liquidity Backing Auction that allows participants to provide liquidity through crowd lending. Finally, there is also the State Guardian Network which literally guards the states when participants are actually going offline.

5.29.2 Connext

Connext focuses on the Ethereum network and wants to scale the network even faster with their implementation.[35] It makes use of state channels and enables the participants to perform many transactions before netting them, very similar to the lightning network that has been created for the Bitcoin blockchain. It is flexible and can easily be implemented with smart contracts written on top of the Ethereum network.

5.29.3 Counterfactual

Counterfactual is another application that allows of off-chain computations with state channels and a set of Ethereum smart contracts.[36]

5.29.4 Funfair

Funfair is an application that focuses on the gaming and gambling industry.[37] This application allows for honest fees so that all participants get rewarded. Developers get paid for their games, participants pay for their participation. Also this solution makes use of the

---

[34] https://www.celer.network/tech.html.

[35] https://connext.network/.

[36] https://www.counterfactual.com/technology/.

[37] https://funfair.io/how-it-works/our-solution/.

Ethereum network to verify its transactions in the end. It also comes with components that allow for participant identification to adhere to all legal requirements. The token that is part of this layer network is called 'FUN'.

5.29.5 Perun

Perun offers an open source implementation of their state channel work and has been co-developed by Bosch.

5.29.6 Raiden Network

The Raiden network is an off-chain scaling solution that enables instant, low-fee and scalable payments while at the same time being able to work with ERC20-tokens.[38] Similar to several of the other research groups and implementations, the goal is state channel technology, protocols and reference implementations on top of the Ethereum network.

5.29.7 Spankchain

Believe it or not, but the blockchain technology has also reached the adult entertainment industry. With Spankchain and SpankPay there is a standard for crypto-payments that can be used in a low-cost way for consumers of online adult content.[39] In that same line there is SpankBank which is a merchant-owned credit system with the use of the BOOTY ERC20-token.

5.29.8 Trinity

Also Trinity is an off-chain scaling solution which wants to achieve real-time payments with low transaction fees, scalability and privacy.[40] The goal is to use state channel technology, increasing transaction throughput of the underlying blockchains. Trinity wants to allow for data and value flow between multiple chains in an easy and fast manner.

---

[38] https://raiden.network/.

[39] https://spankchain.com/products.

[40] https://trinity.tech/#/.

5.29.9 Truebit Protocol

TrueBit protocol is an initiative that wants to bring scalable computation to blockchain networks.[41] Currently there are limitations on the computational power of i.e. the Ethereum network due to gas limits on smart contract computations. TrueBit wants to solve this by making use of off-blockchain computational power to verify computations. If a miner still challenges the outcome of the computation, the on-chain voting of the miners will determine the correct outcome of the computation, making sure the honest outcome always wins due to economic incentives on the participants.

5.29.10 Loom Network

The Loom network wants to provide the layer that allows for DApps to become operational on any blockchain layer (Bitcoin, Ethereum, Binance Chain, Tron, EOS and Cosmos) so that you only need to develop once and achieve maximum penetration in the decentralized market.[42]

5.29.11 Matic Network

The Matic network brings an adapted version of Plasma with proof of stake based side chains so that Ethereum can be scaled even further.[43] The goal is to reduce the gas fees of the Ethereum network and work on the slow block time. Another important goal is to reduce the complexity of the network layer for developers and others who wish to enter the blockchain world with their applications and ideas.

5.29.12 Alacris

Alacris offers a blockchain agnostic platform that allows any developer to become a blockchain developer.[44] They aim for the ease of development, speed of the market, security and flexibility so that the market for decentralized applications can be opened up even further for the world. This way everyone can enjoy the advantages brought by the decentralized world.

---

[41] https://truebit.io/.

[42] https://loomx.io/.

[43] https://matic.network/.

[44] https://alacris.io/.

5.29.13 Skale

Skale offers an elastic blockchain network for Ethereum DApp developers. It is essentially a modular cloud solution that allows developers to easily provision configurable blockchain platforms for their use cases.[45]

5.29.14 Ocean Protocol

Finally, there is the Ocean protocol which offers a decentralized data exchange for AI solutions.[46] It has of course a much broader application as it aims at freeing up data by making it accessible to everyone. Data sharing in the decentralized world becomes a lot easier by making use of this protocol, so that traceability, transparency and privacy becomes enabled for all data owners. The layer also allows for the storage and computation of the data with a set of deterministic proofs on availability and integrity of the data together with verifiable service agreements.

5.30 Some Final Remarks

I hope this second edition has served as a meaningful and thought-provoking guide in your journey through the world of blockchain technology. When I first set out to write this book, my aim was not to offer an exhaustive treatment of every concept, framework, or protocol—each of which, in truth, merits an entire volume of its own—but rather to offer a broad, accessible entry point into this complex and rapidly evolving field. My goal has always been to demystify these technologies, to provide a scaffold upon which further understanding can be built, and to inspire curiosity. If you found yourself compelled to explore certain topics further, then this book has achieved its purpose. Since the publication of the first edition, the blockchain landscape has continued to evolve at a remarkable pace. In fact, by the time I had completed that initial manuscript, certain developments—such as updates to Ethereum's future roadmap—had already shifted. This is the paradox of writing about emerging technologies: any text becomes, in some sense, a historical document the moment it is finished. I have approached this second edition with that awareness, updating and revising where possible, and correcting known inaccuracies and oversights along the way. That said, I acknowledge that this work may still contain errors—whether factual, interpretive, or simply typographical. This project began as a labor of enthusiasm, often carried out in the late hours of the day, driven by genuine passion rather than editorial perfection. I remain deeply grateful for the feedback I have received, and I welcome further suggestions to improve future versions of this book. On

---

[45] https://skale.network/

[46] https://oceanprotocol.com/.

a personal note, it is both humbling and profoundly gratifying to know that you chose to spend your time engaging with this work. Reaching this final page is not just a conclusion, but the continuation of your learning journey—and mine. Writing this book was also a form of exploration for me: a way to organize, reflect upon, and share what I had learned. At times, I realize that my writing may come across as dense, hurried, or uneven; that is a byproduct of trying to compress a vast domain into a finite number of pages. Where the presentation lacks clarity, I ask for your understanding and your feedback.

Thank you for reading. Your engagement gives this work its value, and your insights will help shape future editions. I hope this book has opened doors, answered questions, and sparked new ones. Until then—keep learning, keep questioning, and I hope to hear from you soon.

Warm regards,

Stijn.

5.31   Addendum: Blockchain—The Quick Technical Introduction

This explanation I wrote a couple of years ago but still remains highly relevant today. If you find yourself a bit lost in this book across the many different concepts, types of blockchains and how these are evolving, this can be the perfect starting point. It explains some core concepts and gives a rudimentary idea on how blockchain technology works. I hid it all the way in the back of the book, but that doesn't mean that this isn't a key text for you to understand!

First, I will have to explain in short what public key cryptography is. Public key cryptography (or asymmetric cryptography) is generally used to produce two types of keys: a private key and a public key. The public key can be shared with the public while the private key has to remain private (shocking, I know). To generate these keys a one-way function is used and came into practice to solve an age-old problem when it comes to secure communication. We all know symmetric key cryptography: you just produce a private key and use this as a password or passphrase for an account, lock, or anything else. Easy right? Imagine we want to send messages to one another, which we would like to encrypt so that we are the only people that can read it. Solution: we just share the same password, problem solved! Well, not really, because, first of all, we need to find a secure manner to share those keys with each other. This can already pose quite a problem. The second problem is the one of numbers. You might want to send secure messages to me, but I can imagine you would like to do the same with all your friends, family and colleagues. That are a lot of private keys to send and store! This would mean complete mayhem in the real world. Public key cryptography found the solution here. You can just share your public key with everyone, leave it in a public database and transmit it over insecure networks. It is meant to be shared and known by everyone. If you now use my public key to encrypt a message, I am the only person that can decrypt it with my private key.

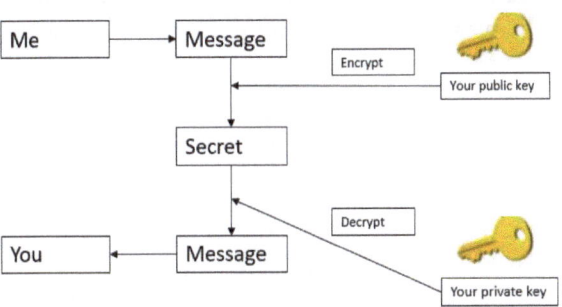

Public key cryptography

Some of you might have already made the link to blockchain and cryptocurrencies: your wallet address and the private key you use to access it. Of course, there are many more uses for public key cryptography, think about digital signatures that are used to verify the sender of a message. The way these keys are generated is more often than not based on hashing algorithms that produce a certain outcome based on entropy. There is a reason why you can no longer access your wallet when you lose your private key, these are meant to be unbreakable. Of course when the algorithm can be broken, your keys can be broken as well. Depending on the blockchain platform you are using, different types of hashing are being used to generate these keys. This is also the reason why some coins can be stored together and others cannot. Often there is also some added procedures: this is why i.e. the addresses for Ethereum and Bitcoin look so different.

Something else we use is elliptic key cryptography. This will bring us a bit out of our comfort zone (certainly if cryptography is completely new for you). To start with we have to talk about finite fields which can be defined as a finite set of numbers and 2 operations (addition and multiplication) that satisfy a specific set of rules. The next step are elliptical curves. These are of the form: $y^2 = x^3 + ax + b$.

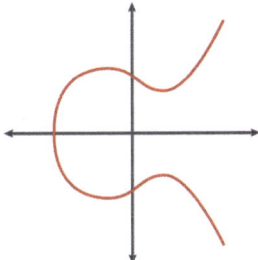

Continuous elliptic curve

These elliptical curves are used in cryptography and in blockchain implementations. For Bitcoin it is $y^2 = x^3 + 7$ or secp256k1. It is often said that this specific implementation was picked because it has the lowest probability of backdoors being implanted by the NSA. This is why many other blockchain platforms make use of the same elliptical curve.

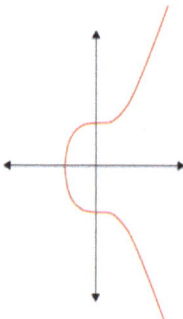

secp256k1

But now towards the why: why do we need elliptical curves? Elliptical curves are used for something very specific: point addition. Point addition is actually just as it sounds. We add two points that lie on the curve. The weird thing is that the outcome of this addition, a third point, will also be on the curve![47] This is a very interesting property that is thankfully being put to use.

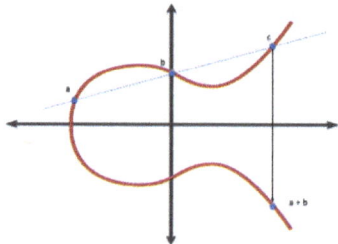

Point addition

Now we have come to the end of our journey: we will combine finite fields with elliptical curves. All of this is finally combined to come to the actual core of the business: elliptical curve cryptography for which we need finite cyclic groups. So what are groups? Groups are finite fields with only one operation, which in this case is point addition.

---

[47] Exceptions are when the intersecting line with the curve is perfectly vertical or when it is the tangent of the curve.

If you have all of this information, you can start creating your cryptographic curve which can be used in elliptical curve public key cryptography. It has many uses, but in the world of blockchain it is used for signing and verifying transactions. You can clearly see that it is crucial that these underlying curves cannot be broken by attackers, otherwise the security of the entire system would be at stake. Again, as mentioned before, secp256k1 was chosen by many blockchain platforms because it had the least chance of a backdoor being built in by the NSA. When we talk about blockchain, we talk about ledgers. In the classic way of working there is a third-party necessary to verify payments, notarize transactions, make use of escrow, allow voting and registration. With the advent of blockchain, we move away from these third parties which centralize power. In itself centralization isn't necessarily bad but it often leads to inefficiency, high cost, loss of privacy and control, corruption and more. With a distributed network this is no longer possible, as the participants decide the outcome and validity of transactions. There is a single truth that must be supported by the majority, and not by a single power in the network.

People often forget what this technology actually is, and instantly start looking at the implementations. However, to understand the possibilities, you first need to truly know and realize what this technology represents. One important part is the existence of a peer-to-peer network. People nowadays are used to a centralized way of working when it comes to the internet. When we all visit a webpage, we know that it is running on a server somewhere and that we are visiting the same location. However, this wasn't always the case. The very beginning of the internet was that of a peer-to-peer network where computers were directly communicating with one another. This technique is still used nowadays to share files over Bittorrent and other networks. A second example is the TOR-network, which is a free, open-source network that is used for anonymous communication (it does have a negative reputation as it is also used for underground activities). The problem with centralized networks such as the internet is that there are centralized providers that can provide or deny access, control what is seen and more. This third party can be hacked, fail or even become corrupt. This is why also blockchain technology moved away from centralized entities in the first place. We remove any centralized servers and allow the participant nodes to directly communicate with each other. Even more importantly is the costs that are brought by third parties. These often make processes overly expensive and rule out these services for a lot of people and (small) businesses that aren't able to afford these prices. The problem is that these costs are unnecessary for the process to function, as it is only used as a check towards compliance. With blockchain, you can automate these checks and as such reduce these costs significantly.

The final part to understand the technology is the concept of hashing. When you hash a certain dataset (this can be a word, a sentence, some numbers or even an entire book if you would want to), you receive a unique identifier of that dataset. Whatever the size of the input, the output size will always be the same. On top of that, if you only change one number, letter or symbol, the resulting hash will look completely different. And when I say completely, I mean COMPLETELY. This way you have an assurance that the data has not been modified. As you can see below, the difference between the hashes of the word 'apple' and the word 'apples' is clear.

There are many different possible hashing algorithms out there but they need some key features to be succesful. One is that they have to be collission resistant, meaning that you cannot find 2 inputs that will lead to the same output. Another is that they should be preimage resistant, meaning that you cannot guess the input based on the output hash. These algorithms are commonly used in cybersecurity for password schemes to improve the security of applications. Instead of storing passwords directly, the hashes of passwords are stored so that passwords cannot simply be stolen out of the application (even though commonly used passwords can still be extracted by attackers) In the past, several of these algorithms have been 'broken', meaning that one could revert hashes to their original inputs.

How is it applied in blockchain tehcnology? In several ways as you will see later on, but one can imagine several ways on how this could be applied in any field. You could take a hash of a document and store it somewhere safe, and if you ever wanted to proof that the document didn't change, you could simply recreate the hash of the document and compare it with the stored hash (this is actually one of the first use cases of what could be done with blockchain other than cryptocurrency).

In blockchain this technique is used so that resulting transactions can rather fast be compared with each other. When you start hashing transactions, you can also hash hashes and create from a group of hashes, eventually a single hash. This is called the Merkle tree and this can be used to compress a lot of data. The Merkle tree can be used to prove what data is held within a block.

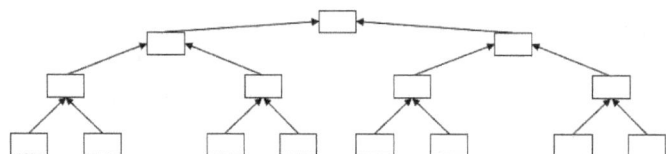

Simple Merkle tree

All of these blocks consist of sets of transactions that are chained together in one huge ledger. The blockchain, in fact, represents nothing more than a historical overview of the transactions that have taken place in the network. These techniques together help us create an append-only ledger of transactions which is distributed over all the nodes in the network. These transactions are contained in a linked list of blocks.

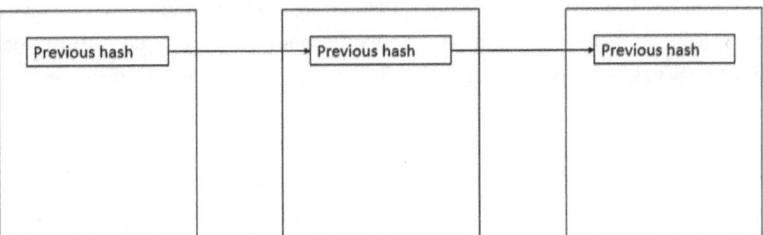

Fig. 5.1 Linking together of blocks

5.31.1 Building 'Blocks'

The term 'blockchain' refers to the very core of the technology. The data structure underlying is an ordered back-linked list of blocks which consist of transactions. These transactions represent payments between all the participants taking part in the blockchain network. The term 'payments' here should be seen quite broad. It could consist or payments as we know it via cryptocurrencies but it could also refer to any action confirmation between two parties depending on the blockchain platform. The way the blocks are linked to each other is by making use of the hash of the previous block that was last added to the chain as seen in Fig. 5.1. If you think about it, the blockchain with the transaction data is nothing more than a ledger where the data has been structured in a different way.

Because we know that each hash is a unique fingerprint, we can always know for sure that the block is part of the chain. Important to note here is that a parent block (the most recently added block) can have more than one child blocks, while a child will always have one parent. When there is more than one child, we are dealing with a fork in the system. Normally these forks will be resolved and only one of the children is used to continue the chain (and become a parent themselves). In some cases however, some of these forks stay on and we will deal with separate chains that all once started from the same parent. We always need to have a starting point, a first block, which is conveniently called the 'genesis block'. Because we could visually understand that blocks are being stacked upon each other, we refer to the most recent block as the 'tip' or 'top' and the distance to the genesis block as the 'height'.[48] The greater this 'height' becomes, the more difficult it will be to make a change to one of these earlier blocks. The longer the chain becomes from a certain block, the more computer power it will require to recalculate the information contained in all the blocks.

What else is stored in the blocks? We have two main parts between which we have to distinguish: the block itself and the block header. The hash of the previous block is one of the items that is stored in the block header. This way the chain between the blocks is

---

[48] One could try to use this height to try to identify a block but this is error prone, as the height is not a unique identifier. The hash on the other hand, will give you this unique identifier.

created. That is not the only thing though, depending on the blockchain platform you can also find the Merkle root, timestamp and nonce in there with a couple of other parameters (i.e. difficulty target, version, …). In Fig. 5.2 you can find the example for the Bitcoin blockchain.

Not all this information might be clear for now but no worries, we will explain as we go on in the book. The Merkle root gives us the digital fingerprint of the transactions that are stored in the block itself. It is a 'hash of hashes' based on the transaction IDs or 'TXIDs'. This hash is unique for the transactions in the block itself (Fig. 5.3).

Again, this is a simplified view of what can be found in the block headers. Of course, the block consists of more than only the block header. The 'bulk' of a block is made up out of the transactions themselves (Fig. 5.4).

As you can see, we are dealing with huge amounts of data, not only in the blocks, but also in the block header. It is the hash that is ultimately calculated of the entire block that

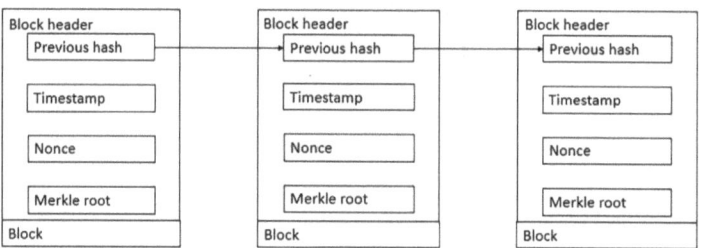

Fig. 5.2 Block header information bitcoin

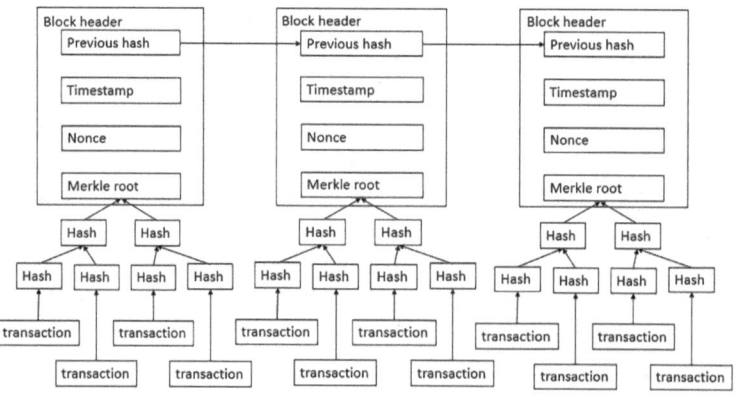

Fig. 5.3 What can be found in the Merkle root for bitcoin

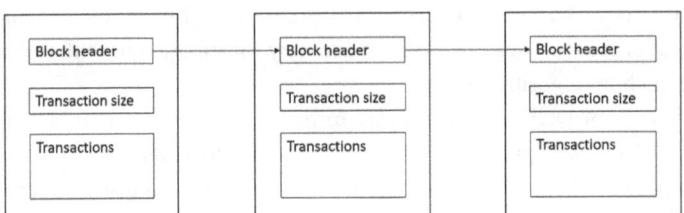

Fig. 5.4 The entire chain

can correctly and uniquely identify that block within the entire blockchain.[49] For Bitcoin, the SHA-256 algorithm combined with RIPEMD-160 is used to calculate these hashes but these algorithms can differ quite a lot depending on the platform you are looking at. Now we have an idea of how transactions are put into blocks and how everything is linked together, the main question remains: how do we perform transactions? The idea is that you can sign your transactions with your private key in such a way that it is not only clear that you are the person that are spending it, but also that you have the right to spend it and that you didn't spend the currency twice. Transactions are broadcast through the network and mined into blocks. These will only be processed if these transactions are performed based on the consensus rules that all participants agree on.

In short, the lifecycle of a transaction is as follows:

1. A transaction is created and signed by the creator. This transaction should immediately contain all information necessary to verify and execute the transaction.
2. These proposed transactions are shared with other nodes in the network which verify them.
3. If accepted, they are propagated throughout the network, otherwise they are discarded. Mining nodes can include these transactions into blocks that can be mined and eventually added to the chain of earlier accepted transactions.

5.31.2 Blockchain or Distributed Ledger?

An important note that I immediately want to make here is the distinction between blockchain and distributed ledger technology (or DLT). Often it is said that each blockchain is a distributed ledger but not every distributed ledger is a blockchain. Distributed ledgers are databases that try to share data among geographical different locations without a central actor having control over the entire network. You can see that there are some similarities in concept and what they try to achieve. A major difference between

---

[49] The hash of the genesis block within the Bitcoin network is 000000000019d6689c085ae165831e 934ff763ae46a2a6c172b3f1b60a8ce26f.

the two is how new data is appended to the platform. While in blockchain technology one makes use of a consensus algorithm to add new information, distributed ledgers don't always have such an algorithm in place.

The application of DLT's differ in many forms as you will see in this book, just as the application of blockchain platforms. The use of name "blockchain" or "distributed ledger" has many implications. Not only is the technology different but also the perception of the two names. While the first is well-known and hyped all over the world, the second remains more hidden in the shadows and seems to be more known among IT specialists. So why use one name or the other? Some companies want to ride the hype and use "blockchain" while others want to step away from the hype and show that they are really focusing on the technology itself and use "distributed ledger".

Another point one should take into account is the "types" of blockchain that currently exist. There are the public, permissionless blockchains (such as Bitcoin and Ethereum) which have no restrictions when it comes to either access or participation. We can also call them the "true" blockchains. We also have private, permissioned blockchains where only a certain group of people can gain access and participate (such as Rubix and Hyperledger platforms). You also have some platforms that exist in-between these two 'extremes'. The first are the public but permissioned blockchains which allow everyone to transact and see the transaction log while only a few can participate in the consensus mechanism (such as Ripple and private versions of Ethereum). Finally, there are also the private but permissionless blockchains where the consensus algorithm is open to everyone while transactions are limited to a specific number of participants. There is no real example available of a network that fully achieves this (the one that comes closest currently might be the Exonum network).

There are also the DAGs or directed acyclic graphs that have also entered the blockchain space with their own solutions and networks. To not further complicate the progress in this book, I will use the term blockchain and distributed ledger as synonyms (I know some of you might not agree with this approach), and will specifically refer to DAGs in case we are discussing them in more detail.

5.31.3   Blockchain Address

The next step in understanding the world of blockchain, is the blockchain address. A blockchain address[50] is one of the main concepts within blockchain and cryptocurrencies to understand. It is based on public key cryptography (also known as asymmetric cryptography) where one makes use of a private key and a public key. As you could infer from the name, public keys are keys that can be known by the public and can be seen as a bank

---

[50] In the early days of the Bitcoin network, you could pay directly to an IP address. You can imagine several problems with this, such as 'man in the middle'-attacks. This is why this system was abandoned in favor of more secure options.

account number (even though not exactly the same!). They are mainly used to identify you, while private keys should always be kept private. They function as the password of your account and are used to sign transactions or to unlock your cryptocurrencies on you 'account'. There is a wide arrange of algorithms that is able to create such public and private keys. Over time, because of security concerns, these blockchain addresses have evolved from those public keys to hashes from these public keys. This can be done in a lot of different ways so that for each cryptocurrency there are different blockchain addresses and it is often not possible to send different cryptocurrencies to the same blockchain address (differences in the algorithms prevent this). If payments are being shared over the network to blockchain addresses, these 'addresses' can only be unlocked by making use of appropriate private keys. Based on the manner that these addresses are derived, it can be possible to store altcoins (different cryptocurrencies) on the same address.

5.31.4 Blockchain Wallet

Closely related to addresses is the concept of blockchain wallets. These wallets aren't used to store cryptocurrencies but are used to interact with the network. They are used to generate the information necessary to send and receive cryptocurrency and to do this they make generate a number of private–public key sets. This can happen at random by making use of a random seed or this can be based on a passphrase, password, seed words, ... in something that is called a 'deterministic' wallet. The address (as explained before) is used to receive transactions. The private key is used to sign transactions.[51] The wallet software (if we are dealing with a digital wallet), counts the balances associated with each of the addresses in the wallets, creates the sum and shows this as your 'balance'. So once again, your cryptocurrencies aren't directly stored in the wallet itself, it is rather a more convenient way of dealing with the public–private key infrastructure.

Depending on how you make use of a wallet, they can be defined as either 'cold' or 'hot'. A hot wallet is the easiest to understand, as it is a wallet that is connected to the internet. There are several providers out there that will allow you to make a wallet. Hot wallets are also called software wallets and they come in several different kinds. There are the web wallets which can be created in a browser, another type is the desktop wallet. These can be downloaded on your machine and are therefore considered safer than web wallets. Still, you will have to keep your wallet safe and take backups if possible.

A cold wallet on the other hand has no connection to the internet, and are used to store cryptocurrencies offline. This is a much safer way of storing (keeping in mind you don't lose your cold wallet) as hot wallets can be prone to cyberattacks. A hardware wallet is a first form of cold wallet. These are physical devices that are used to store tokens for a longer time. There are also implementations that can be used similar to perform transactions. Problem here can be the firmware implementation of the wallet, which is

---

[51] Or seed phrase, depending on the wallet you are using.

not always as secure as it should be. A smartphone permanently kept offline can be seen as a hardware wallet with similar security. Finally, there are also paper wallets. As you might have imagined, this is simply a piece of paper with QR codes that contain the public and private keys. Paper wallets are very dangerous, as a piece of paper is clearly open to specific dangers. On top of that, these types of wallets can only be used once, to send the entire amount to another address.

5.31.5 Node

When we talk about blockchain and the network it represents, we also speak about nodes. Nodes are the lifeblood of the network as they are always responsible for a given set of tasks. These tasks can include the creation, receiving or transmitting of a message. Without the nodes, the network would no longer exist, even if the software would still be up to date. These nodes are distributed all over the world, across a widespread network.[52]

So what is a node? A node is any electronic device that is connected to the network and has an IP address. One of the main purposes of the network is to maintain a copy of the blockchain and process transactions (depending on the type of node). The owners of these nodes willingly use their hardware, computer power and energy to maintain the network.

We should also make a distinction between different types of nodes: full nodes, supernodes, miner nodes and SPV clients. Even though they are equal throughout the network, each type supports the network in a different manner. First of all, there is the full node which downloads a complete copy of the blockchain and checks for any new transactions based on the consensus protocol that is in use. They are responsible for the verification of transactions and blocks, using the consensus algorithm (explained later). They are also able to relay new transactions or blocks to the blockchain. When this full node is publicly visible, we talk about a 'supernode'. The owner of a full node can choose to run it either as a hidden node (not visible for others by making use of firewalls or the TOR network) or as a visible node. The advantage of a supernode for the network is that it connects to any other node that wants to make a connection and communicates with it, acting as a redistribution point, both for data stored in the node and to facilitate communication with other nodes on the network.

A light node (or SPV node) on the other hand is referencing the copy of the blockchain on a full node. It is named after the SPV method or 'Simplified Payment Verification', where users can verify if a transaction was included in a block without having to download and maintain the entire blockchain database. These nodes rely on the information provided by supernodes and sumply act as communication endpoints (we find this commonly in a lot of wallet software).

---

[52] Lisk.io.

Finally, we should highlight the difference between a client node and a miner node. While anyone can run a full node (having the necessary hardware requirements), this is not the same as a mining node. When a full node is just validating transactions, we call this a client node. If the owner is willing to invest in often expensive hardware (depending on the consensus protocol), he will also be able to mine new blocks while running his node. The concept of mining is explained next.

5.31.6 Mining

Mining is one of the key concepts within blockchain technology. It is the way new transactions are being accepted within new blocks,[53] which are added to the existing chain, as well as how new cryptocurrency is being created. It is always used as a countermeasure against fraud and makes sure that all participants within the network remain true. The mining itself is quite costly, as it requires hardware to be used for the mining process, energy to power the mining itself and time. Mining takes place in a couple of steps. First of all, the mining nodes need to collect the unconfirmed transactions that are waiting in a pool to be processed. These are forged into a block (which is the collection of the transactions with some extra metadata). Each miner can select the same or a different set of transactions (this can be due to parameters of the node or geographic location). The next step, depending on the consensus algorithm, is to sign the transaction according to the rules of the network. This can be a mathematical puzzle, a number of votes of the participants or another system. If a valid solution is found, the miner can broadcast his block and solution to the other participants which can validate the solution. If correct, this is confirmed and added to the blockchain of these nodes as long as all the transactions inside the block can be executed according to the blockchain history. This is called the 'winning' block.

As we saw above, for this, the miner should be rewarded and this is done in two ways: the miner receives the transaction fees of the transactions that are included in the block and the new coins that are being created when a new block is added. The miner can receive this reward based on the algorithm that is being used within the network, either proof of work, proof of stake or otherwise.

The mining process is not only the key to the creation of new cryptocurrency, it is also the mechanism that helps create decentralized consensus in a trustless environment. All nodes over the network receive the blocks and can consequently check its validity. This means that consensus will emerge over time as there is not an election at a specific time but by an asynchronous interaction of all the nodes in the network. You must realize that in networks such as Bitcoin, the computer power necessary to compete and mine for the next block has increased exponentially over time. This is because of the increase of entrants in the market space but also because of evolutions in hardware solutions. Over

---

[53] In the case of Bitcoin, a new block is being added every 10 min.

time mining pools saw the light of day. By working together, the pool has a higher chance to find the next winning block so that the rewards can be shared among the participants. The infrastructure of mining installations has evolved greatly over time and depending on the blockchain platform, we will go deeper into the when and why of these developments. For some of these platforms one needs quite advanced infrastructure, while others are still open for everyone.

Of course, when we are dealing with an enterprise implementation of a blockchain platform, you are not going to work with classic miner nodes. Instead you will work with a more simple consensus algorithm so that each participant can easily check and validate what is happening throughout the network. The need for competition is reduced as these participants actually know each other already so that fraudulent transactions can easily be linked back. This way participants can be removed from the network when they try to cheat their business partners in a consortium.

5.31.7 The Consensus Protocol

We quite often talk about protocols when we talk about blockchain technology. This is of course not something that is only limited to blockchain but can be found in any implementation of telecommunication technology. When we are talking about a protocol, we are talking about an entire set of rules which decide how you can connect to a system and interact with it. These rules can be really extensive as they can determine which hardware you have to use, which software is allowed and what the semantics are of messages that are being transmit over a network. Same as with other telecommunication services, this is the same for blockchain. When we talk about open-source blockchain implementations, like Bitcoin or Ethereum, there are no restrictions on hardware and the software needed is completely free. Even though, now this is also still the case for private blockchain implementations, one could see future developments where this would no longer be the case.

5.31.7.1 Proof of Work

Proof of work was the first consensus protocol to be used within a blockchain network. The first network to implement this type of consensus protocol was the Bitcoin network. The idea is that miners have to use their nodes to solve a mathematical problem. It will require a lot of work and computer power to solve, but verifying the result should be easy. This way of consensus is designed to be difficult and to require a lot of fire power. If it becomes too easy to solve, certain security issues could be introduced: mining could become too fast, leading to floating blocks and chains without a 'main' chain. An example is Bitcoin where the goal is to have a new block every 10 min. As computing power increases over time, the number of participant increases and the computer power added to the network multiplies, the difficulty of the proof of work algorithm needs to become more difficult as well. Some networks have tried to move in a different direction by creating algorithms that are resistant against mining software so that everyone can keep on mining with classic computers (leaving the network as democratic as possible). A target hash will be set by the network and the nodes have to try to compute a hash based on the block and the nonce that will be below this target number. The lower the target is set, the more difficult it will be for the participants to find a correct and acceptable hash. The proof of work protocol can help to address the issue of Byzantine fault tolerance by making use of the before mentioned nonce and by combining messages into blocks. To prevent precomputation, the nonce is unique for each node and can only be used once.

An important point of criticism on this type of protocol is the amount of energy that is being consumed by networks that apply this type of protocol. In times of climate change, scarce resources and economic crisis this is an important point to consider.

There are a lot of different proof of work consensus protocols that are currently in use by several networks.

5.31.7.2 Proof of Stake

Proof of stake was developed after the proof of work protocol and is more and more being used within blockchain networks. The first network to implement this kind of protocol was Peercoin in 2012. In the proof of stake network the miner of the next block is selected pseudo randomly as the amount of cryptocurrency held by the node influences the chances of being chosen. The probability of being chosen is thus directly linked to the stake you have in the network.

It is clearly more cost effective than the proof of work consensus protocol as miners don't have to use energy to solve a mathematical problem. Secondly, it has proven to be more secure. A common example is the 51%-attack where blockchain networks become vulnerable from the second a participant has 51% of the computing power in a network. From this second, he can validate all his own transactions, against the wishes of the other participants as they can no longer stop him. This might seems contradictory, but the stakeholders with the highest stakes are motivated to maintain the network, because if an attack would occur, this would damage the reputation of the network and hurt these participants as the value of their stakes would diminish. There is also a downside to this protocol, called the 'nothing at stake'-problem. When there is a consensus failure in the network, and the participants in the network have nothing to lose, there is nothing to stop these participants of supporting different side chains.

5.31.7.3 Delegated Proof of Stake

The delegated proof of stake protocol maintains an irrefutable agreement on the truth across the network. The protocol makes use of real-time voting combined with reputation to achieve consensus. This allows every holder of cryptocurrency to influence the network.

This network makes use of delegates which are elected in their roles and have to put a certain amount of cryptocurrency within a base account. The larger this amount is, the more influence the delegate can exert over the network. In case of malicious behavior, the money in the base account is lost. We can also call this deposit-based proof of stake. While the delegates are responsible for the validation of transaction, it is up to the participants to request regularly if the blocks mined contain all the correct transactions. This makes sure that the network is self-governed and policed. You can immediately sense that this is more democratic than the other consensus protocols.

5.31.7.4 Proof of Authority

Proof of authority (or PoA) is an alternative that is often used by private blockchain[54] networks (more related towards distributed ledger networks) where proof of work is replaced by the 'identity' of the nodes as a stake in the network. It are only these selected nodes that are allowed to mine new blocks. It are only these 'validator' nodes that are allowed to add transactions to the blocks that are consequently added to the blockchain. With proof of authority and validators, there is also the new concept of 'reputation'. The reputation of the validators is crucial for the existence of the network. If the reputation of one of the validators or the 'validator authority' is damaged, the other participants might leave the network or challenge the newly created blocks and its transactions.

This protocol brings both advantages and disadvantages if you compare this to the other protocol implementations. The main risk with PoA is that if there is only 1 validator node, you centralize the risk to a single point of failure. This is a main risk to take into consideration when we talk about distributed networks.

However, it does not require the massive computing power that is necessary for networks that make use of proof of work. PoA also has an advantage over proof of stake. With PoA the entire identity of a node is put forward. If it act maliciously it stands to lose his entire stake into the network. With proof of stake, the participant only stands to lose his current stake that he put forward. Which means that someone who has a lower overall participation in the network stands to lose less than someone who has invested heavily in the network.

5.31.7.5 Other Protocols Used in Blockchain Platforms

Several other types of protocols can be used in blockchain platforms so that one can come to a consensus. One of these protocols, strongly related to proof of stake is proof of importance. The difference with proof of stake is that in the PoI environment, also the transactions of the user are taken into account. This way the protocol tries to measure the level of trust and importance of the node in the entire network.[55] Another interesting protocol is the Proof of Activity protocol, related to both proof of work and proof of stake. It's more energy efficient than proof of work as only in the first phase this is used, as in the second the protocol makes use of proof of stake. There is also proof of capacity,

---

[54] There are also certain public networks that make use of this protocol.

[55] Used by the NEM blockchain.

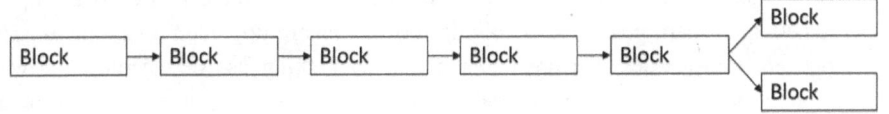

Fig. 5.5 Blockchain fork

where the main driver is the hard disk space that is still available (instead of CPU as we find with the proof of work protocol).[56]

Other protocols that you might encounter are: proof of replication, proof of burn, proof of space, proof of space–time, proof of deposit, proof of data possession and so on. You can clearly see that that a lot of different blockchain platforms are experimenting with different solutions to provide consensus in a distributed and decentralized environment, in a secure and efficient way. For each of these protocols you can give both advantages and disadvantages, depending on the goal you are trying to achieve and the way you are working with your organization.

5.31.8 Blockchain Forks

Blockchain forks are an important subject within the world of blockchain. It refers to competing or coexisting side chains within the same network. Simply because of the decentralized structure of the network, the occurrence of forks seem to be natural. Blocks are propagated through the network and arrive at different nodes at different times. This is can also be the cause of the so-called orphan blocks. Normally, the nodes will try to extend the chain with the largest cumulative difficulty.[57]

We can talk about a fork when there are two or more candidate blocks that are competing with one another to form the longest chain. If a miner discovers a 'correct' block, it is immediately sent to its neighbors. Several nodes can in time discover a different solution and broadcast this through the network. The nodes closest to the original miners of the block will start building their chain based on this block and continue working on next blocks. If a fork comes into existence this way, the issue is normally resolved within one block. The reason is that one group of miners will find a next solution first, even if the computer power within the network is evenly distributed among the several competing groups. The next solution will be shared among the network nodes, accepted and spread through the network. The competing nodes will receive this next solution, accept it and stop working on the competing solution, thereby resolving the fork (Fig. 5.5).[58]

---

[56] It is also called hard drive mining and can be found, i.e. with the Burstcoin cryptocurrency.

[57] The chain that contains the most proof of work.

[58] A fork like this might happen once a week while a fork that extends to 2 blocks is extremely rare (because of the explanation above).

There is also the occurrence of hard forks. This is when there is a software update over the network where protocols or mining procedures are upgraded. Once the upgrade has happened, transactions that are being mined by making use of the older software, will no longer be accepted by the upgraded nodes. This way a new and persistent branch comes into being. There comes a parallel set of transactions into being that take place on the different chains. A soft fork is a change in the software where only previous blocks and transactions are made invalid while still being backward-compatible going forward. Another difference between a hard and a soft fork is that for a soft fork only a majority of the miners need to upgrade while a hard fork requires all nodes to upgrade to the new version.

5.31.9 Sidechains

With the explanation of forks, you can start to imagine the existence of sidechains. These are blockchains attached to another (the 'parent' and the 'child'). Because of this connection, assets are interchangeable over the network at a fixed deterministic exchange rate while the sidechain can operate completely independently of the parent and make use of its own consensus protocol (Fig. 5.6).

This transfer is in fact nothing more than an illusion. Tokens are locked in the parent chain and the equivalent amount of tokens are unlocked in the child chain. If you want to transfer, the tokens in the child are locked while the cryptocurrencies in the parent are once again unlocked. For this to be possible, there are several assumptions that are made. The most important underlying principle that we want to reach and understand is the point of something called 'settlement finality'. The concept of settlement finality is a common one in the financial services industry. It is the moment where you can be sure that a transaction is 'final' and will no longer be reverted. In a blockchain environment where you are working with a proof of work algorithm, this can be difficult as at any given point it might be possible (even though less likely over time) that a longer chain is created that doesn't include some of the transactions. If we consider public blockchains, making use of proof of work, a standard is waiting for six confirmations (new mined blocks on top of the block that includes our transaction) before a transaction is seen as 'final'. Its practical implications mean that we have to trust in the honesty of the participants in both

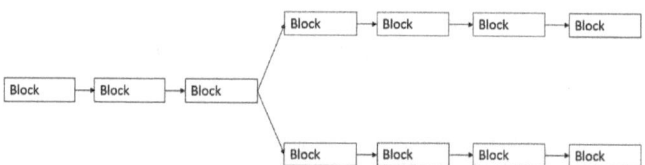

Fig. 5.6 Sidechains

chains and that they are both censorship resistant. All of this requires that the participants are honest, including those participants holding the locked tokens. Otherwise you enter a situation where locked tokens can be spent and we create a situation where double spending is once again possible.

There also exists the possibility where the child chain doesn't have settlement finality. In this case one could make use of so-called custodians that have to vote when to lock or unlock a certain amount of tokens. This voting system can be adapted to any form which suites the blockchains that are being linked the best which makes this quite a flexible system to work with. There are several ways that this system can be implemented. The first is by making use of a central exchange that enforces the 2-way peg between the 2 chains by only unlocking coins of chain 1 when an equivalent amount of tokens belonging to chain 2 are locked (Fig. 5.7).

You can clearly see that using this system goes against the very nature of blockchain. This way you are reintroducing the single point of failure and you are once again making use of centralization. You could try to set up a form of decentralization by making use of multiple parties that make use of a multi-signature approach. This is something that could perfectly work in a private setting (Fig. 5.8).

A second approach is stepping away from any centralization and linking the two chains by implementing an understanding of each chains consensus system. This way the tokens can be unlocked from the second the chain is able to verify that there has been a locking transaction. This brings several insecurities with it when you are working with a system where one of the chains doesn't have settlement finality. This is something that again could be applied in a private blockchain/distributed ledger setting, but not in the public world considering the risks that this set-up would bring in what is essentially a trustless environment. You could make use of several ways to create this specific set-up, but it would have to come down to a simplified way of acknowledging transactions and therefore

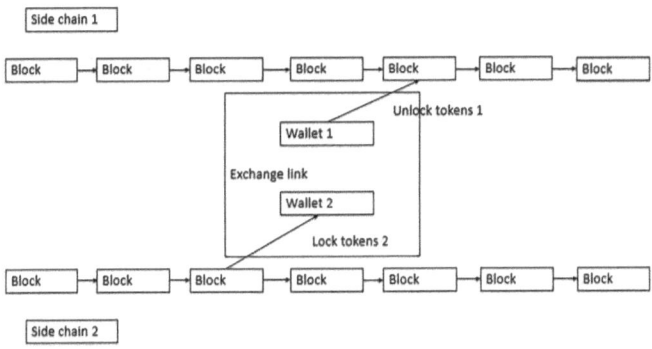

Fig. 5.7 Central exchange

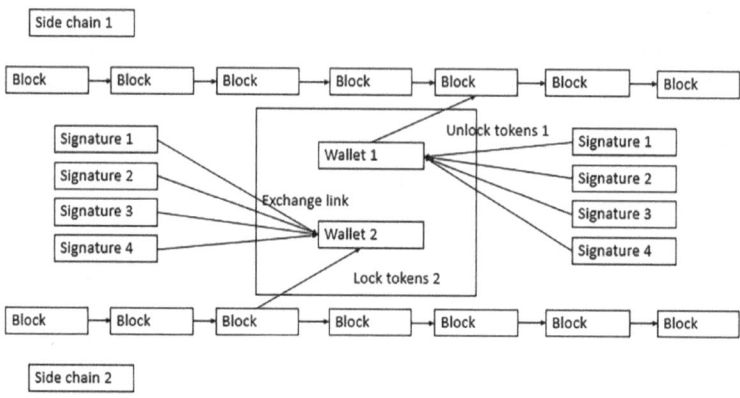

Fig. 5.8 Multi-signature approach

make use of the Merkle root that is so often used in one way or another in the blockchain world (Fig. 5.9).

Another approach that is related to the previous example is called 'entangled blockchains'. Here the relationship between the two separate chains is brought to the next level. When coins are locked in one chain, this immediately means that the equivalent amount in the other chain are released and vice versa (Fig. 5.10).

The final example we are going to give is that of 'drivechains'. Here the participants are allowed to vote on when to release the locked coins and when to send these to another chain. These votes can be locked within a certain section of the transaction information. These voters are more often than not linked to one of the chains, determining the actions that take place for the other chain as well. You can clearly see that trust in the participants is the main concern here (Fig. 5.11).

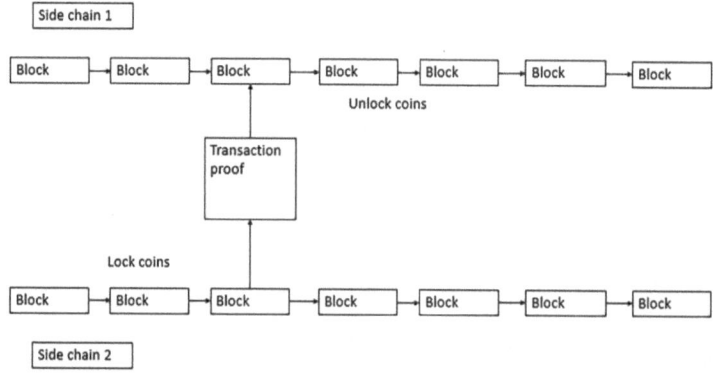

Fig. 5.9 Linked by consensus

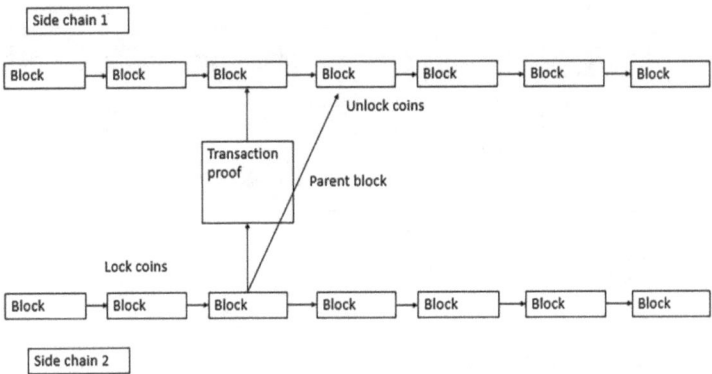

Fig. 5.10 Entangled chains

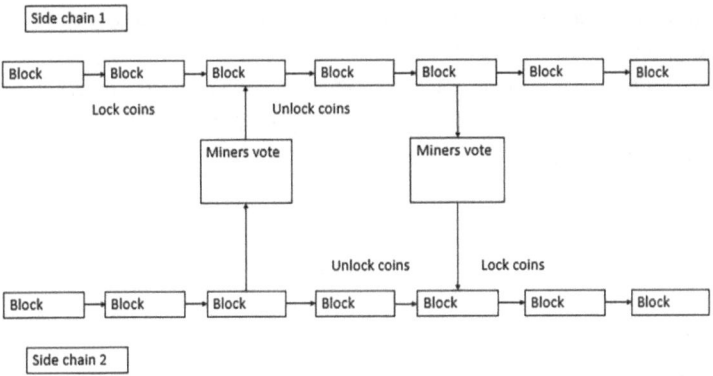

Fig. 5.11 Drivechain

Of course, these are all just clear-cut examples that can be used independently but in reality a number of combinations between these approaches is a real possibility. Depending on the use case you are working on, splitting or combining these approaches can fit your solution best. A lot depends on the private–public and permissioned- permissionless approach, combined with the expected trust in the participants.

5.31.10 The Blockchain Technology Stack

Opposite to other technology implementations, you have to consider the entire 'stack' of the technology when you would like to work with it within your organization. At the core there is decentralization and consensus that you would like to consider and so you

Layer	Description	Examples
Application	User interface	dAPP, …
Services	Interconnection of applications	Oracles, wallets, smart contracts, …
Protocol	Consensus protocol	Algorithms & side chains
Network	Transportation of information	P2P, RPLx, …
Infrastructure	Node infrastructure	Mining, tokens, nodes, storage, …

Fig. 5.12 The blockchain technology stack

have to look at your very infrastructure and ask yourself the question: are you currently prepared to step into a new way of working? You have to, in a sense, let the classic view of centralization and control go to make room for an interconnected system that no longer has a single point of failure (Fig. 5.12).

It comes with both advantages and challenges but each of these 'layers' has to be taken into consideration when you are thinking about applying blockchain. It is much more than cryptocurrencies alone, as you will soon discover.

Bibliography

Antonopoulos, A. and Wood, G. (2018) *Mastering Ethereum*. 1st ed. California: O'reilly Media.

Antonopoulos, A. (2017) *Mastering* Bitcoin: *programming the open blockchain*. 2nd ed. California: O'Reilly Media.

Asolo, B. (December 20, 2018) Bitcoin's UTXO Set Explained. *Mycryptopedia*. https://www.myc ryptopedia.com/bitcoin-utxo-unspent-transaction-output-set-explained/. Accessed on November 28, 2019.

Asolo, B. (November 1, 2018) What is Segregated Witness? *Myencryptopedia*. https://www.mycryp topedia.com/what-is-segregated-witness/. Accessed December 24, 2019.

Asolo, B. (November 1, 2018) Monero Ring Signature Explained. *Mycryptopedia*. https://www.myc ryptopedia.com/monero-ring-signature-explained/. Accessed November 26, 2019.

Asolo, B. (October 30, 2018) X11 Algorithm Explained. *Mycryptopedia*. https://www.mycryptop edia.com/x11-algorithm-explained/. Accessed November 27, 2019.

Asolo, Bisola (November 1, 2018) IOTA Explained. *Mycryptopedia*. https://www.mycryptopedia. com/iota-explained/. Accessed December 13, 2019.

Asolo, B. (February 16, 2019) Bitcoin Schnorr Signatures Explained. *Mycryptopedia*. https://www. mycryptopedia.com/bitcoin-schnorr-signatures-explained/. Accessed on November 17, 2019.

Back, A. (August 1, 2002) Hashcash—A denial of Service Counter-Measure.

Baczuk, J. (May 24, 2019) How to fork Bitcoin—Part1. *Medium*. https://medium.com/@jordan.bac zuk/how-to-fork-bitcoin-part-1-397598ef7e66. Accessed on September 19, 2019.

Batiz-Benet J. (2018) go-merkledag. *Github—ipfs*. https://github.com/ipfs/specs/tree/master/mer kledag. Accessed on August 14, 2019.

Ben-Sasson, E., Bentov, I., Hresh, Y. and Riabzev, M. (March 6, 2018) Scalable, transparent, and post-quantum secure computational integrity. *Israel Institute of Technology*. https://eprint.iacr.org/ 2018/046.pdf. Accessed November 23, 2019.

Bergmann, C. (April 29, 2017) The lightning network explained, part I: how to build a payment channel. *Btcmanager*. https://btcmanager.com/lightning-network-primer-pt-i-building-payment-channels/?q=/lightning-network-primer-pt-i-building-payment-channels/. Accessed July 25, 2019.

Bitcoin. (December 19, 2017) Satoshi Client Node Discovery. *Github—Bitcoin* https://en.bitcoin.it/ wiki/Satoshi_Client_Node_Discovery. Accessed November 4, 2019.

Bitcoin. (December 26, 2018) Protocol Documentation. *Github—Bitcoin*. https://en.bitcoin.it/wiki/ Protocol_documentation#Signatures. Accessed November 20, 2019.

Bitcoin. (December 13, 2019) Transaction. *Github—Bitcoin*. https://en.bitcoin.it/wiki/Transaction. Accessed December 26, 2019.

S. Van Hijfte, *Blockchain Platforms*, Synthesis Lectures on Computer Science,
https://doi.org/10.1007/978-3-032-00979-1

Bryk, A. (November 1, 2018) Blockchain Attack Vectors: Vulnerabilities of the Most Secure Technology. *Apriorit.* https://www.apriorit.com/dev-blog/578-blockchain-attack-vectors; Accessed on September 7, 2019.

Buterin, V. (January 28, 2015) The P + epsilon Attack. *Ethereum blog.* https://blog.ethereum.org/2015/01/28/p-epsilon-attack/. Accessed on September 2, 2019.

Buterin, V. (July 11, 2014) Toward a 12-second block time. *Ethereum blog.* https://blog.ethereum.org/2014/07/11/toward-a-12-second-block-time/#:~:text=At%2012%20seconds%20per%20block,a%20stale%20rate%20of%2050%25.. Accessed on July 11, 2019.

Buterin, V. (May 9, 2015) Olympic: Frontier pre-release. *Ethereum blog.* https://blog.ethereum.org/2015/05/09/olympic-frontier-pre-release/. Accessed on December 17, 2019.

Buterin, V. (May 9, 2016) On Settlement Finality. *Ethereum blog.* https://blog.ethereum.org/2016/05/09/on-settlement-finality/. Accessed on July 2, 2019.

Chandraker, A., Kachhela, J. and Wright, A. (2019) Digital identity, cats and why fungibility is key to blockchain's future, *PA Consulting.* https://www.paconsulting.com/insights/blockchain-fungibility-future/. Accessed June 26, 2019.

Charlon, F. (May 13, 2015) Open Assets Protocol. *Open Assets* https://github.com/OpenAssets/open-assets-protocol/blob/master/asset-definition-protocol.mediawiki. Accessed October 17, 2019.

Chen, M. (April 13, 2019) Inter exchange Client Address Protocol (ICAP). *Github—Ethereum* https://github.com/ethereum/wiki/wiki/Inter-exchange-Client-Address-Protocol-(ICAP). Accessed on July 3, 2019.

Chinchilla, c. (August 2, 2019) RLP. *Ethereum wiki.* https://github.com/ethereum/wiki/wiki/RLP. Accessed on December 13, 2019.

Cimpanu, C. (September 4, 2018) Bitcoin gold delisted from major cryptocurrency exchange after refusing to pay hack damages. *Zdnet.* https://www.zdnet.com/article/bitcoin-gold-delisted-from-major-cryptocurrency-exchange-after-refusing-to-pay-hack-damages/. Accessed December 19, 2019.

Conner, E. (July 27, 2018) A case for Ethereum block reward reduction to 2 ETH in Constantinople (EIP-1234). *Medium.* https://medium.com/@eric.conner/a-case-for-ethereum-block-reward-reduction-in-constantinople-eip-1234-25732431fc77. Accessed December 11, 2019.

Couts, A. (December 27, 2013) Such Generosity! After Dogewallet heist, Dogecoin community aims to reimburse victims. *Digital trends.* https://www.digitaltrends.com/cool-tech/dogecoin-dogewallet-hack-save-dogemas/. Accessed November 29, 2019.

Curran, B. (April 18, 2020) What is Practical Byzantine Fault Tolerance? Complete Beginner's Guide. *Blockonomi.* https://blockonomi.com/practical-byzantine-fault-tolerance/. Accessed on July 18, 2019.

Curran, B. (June 26, 2018) What is Nakamoto Consensus? Complete Beginner's Guide. *Blockonomi.* https://blockonomi.com/nakamoto-consensus/. Accessed on July 12, 2019.

Dannen, C. (2017) *Introducing Ethereum & Solidity.* 1st ed. New York, NY: Apress.

Dashjr, L. (January 19, 2017) Bip-0062. *Github—Bitcoin bips* https://github.com/bitcoin/bips/blob/master/bip-0062.mediawiki. Accessed October 14, 2019.

Davies, J. (January, 2019) secp256k1. *Github—ElementsProject.* https://github.com/ElementsProject/secp256k1-zkp/tree/secp256k1-zkp/src/modules/musig?source=post_page. Accessed January 4, 2020.

Dawson, R. and Baxter, M. (August 29, 2019) Announcing Hyperledger Besu. *Hyperledger.* https://www.hyperledger.org/blog/2019/08/29/announcing-hyperledger-besu. Accessed January 22, 2020.

Decker C. and Wattenhofer R. A Fast and Scalable Payment Network with Bitcoin Duplex Micropayment Channels. *Ethz.* https://tik-old.ee.ethz.ch/file/716b955c130e6c703fac336ea17b1670/duplex-micropayment-channels.pdf. Accessed October 13, 2019.

Decker, C. and Russell, R. eltoo: A Simple Layer2 Protocol for Bitcoin. *Blockstream.* https://blocks tream.com/eltoo.pdf. Accessed October 14, 2019.

Dexter, S. (March 11, 2018) 1% Shard Attack Explained—Ethereum Sharding (Contd..) *Mango research.* https://www.mangoresearch.co/1-shard-attack-explained-ethereum-sharding-contd/. Accessed September 5, 2019.

Donald, J.A. (November 2, 2008) Bitcoin P2P e-cash paper. https://www.metzdowd.com/pipermail/ cryptography/2008-November/014814.html. Accessed August 9, 2019.

Edmonds, R. (March 8, 2018) Best CPUs for Crypto Mining. *Windows Central.* https://www.win dowscentral.com/best-cpus-crypto-mining. Accessed December 18, 2019.

Edwin (November 15, 2017). 1983: eCash door David Chaum. https://www.bitcoinsaltcoins.nl/ 1983-ecash-david-chaum/. Accessed May 17, 2020.

erc721.org/

Eyal, I. and Sirer, E.G. Majroity is not Enough: Bitcoin Mining is Vulnerable. *Cornell.* https://www. cs.cornell.edu/~ie53/publications/btcProcFC.pdf. Accessed August 20, 2019.

Feinberg, A. (December 26, 2013) Millions of Meme-based Dogecoins stolen on Christmas day. *Gizmodo.* https://gizmodo.com/millions-of-meme-based-dogecoins-stolen-on-christmas-da-148981 9762. Accessed November 30, 2019.

Field, M. (November 12, 2018) Holographic consensus—part 1. *Medium.* https://medium.com/dao stack/holographic-consensus-part-1-116a73ba1e1c. Accessed January 12, 2020.

Frankenfield, J. (March 5, 2018) Namecoin. *Investopedia.* https://www.investopedia.com/terms/n/ namecoin.asp. Accessed November 28, 2019.

Frankenfield, J. (July 5, 2018) Peercoin. *Investopedia.* https://www.investopedia.com/terms/p/peerco in.asp. Accessed on November 30, 2019.

Friedman, W. (March 26, 2015) Drop Zone: P2P E-commerce paper. https://www.metzdowd.com/ pipermail/cryptography/2015-March/025212.html. Accessed August 4, 2019.

Gabizon, A. (September 25, 2016) Zcash Parameters and how they will be generated. *Electric coin.* https://electriccoin.co/blog/generating-zcash-parameters. Accessed November 11, 2019.

Gabizon, A. (February 28, 2017) Explaining SNARKs. *Electric coin* https://electriccoin.co/blog/ snark-explain. Accessed on December 3, 2019.

Gabizon, A. (February 28, 2017) Explaining SNARKs. *Electric coin* https://electriccoin.co/blog/ snark-explain2. Accessed on December 3, 2019.

Gabizon, A. (February 28, 2017) Explaining SNARKs. *Electric coin* https://electriccoin.co/blog/ snark-explain3. Accessed on December 3, 2019.

Gabizon, A. (February 28, 2017) Explaining SNARKs. *Electric coin* https://electriccoin.co/blog/ snark-explain5. Accessed on December 3, 2019.

Gabizon, A. (February 28, 2017) Explaining SNARKs. *Electric coin* https://electriccoin.co/blog/ snark-explain6. Accessed on December 3, 2019.

Gabizon, A. (February 28, 2017) Explaining SNARKs. *Electric coin* https://electriccoin.co/blog/ snark-explain7. Accessed on December 3, 2019.

Gennaro, R., Gentry, C., Parno, B. and Raykova, M. (2012) Quadratic Span Programs and Succinct NIZKs withpout PCPs. *IBM T.J. Watson Research Center.* https://eprint.iacr.org/2012/215.pdf. Accessed November 11, 2019.

Groth, J. (October 26, 2010) Short Pairing-based Non-interactive Zero-knowledge Arguments. *University College London.* http://www0.cs.ucl.ac.uk/staff/J.Groth/ShortNIZK.pdf. Accessed October 1, 2019.

Hinkes, A. (May 29, 2016) The Law of the DAO. *Coindesk.* https://www.coindesk.com/the-law-of- the-dao. Accessed December 28, 2019.

Hoogendoorn, R. (December 3, 2019) Easypaysy makes Bitcoin addresses much easier. *Medium.* https://medium.com/@nederob/easypaysy-makes-bitcoin-addresses-much-easier-faf40988614. Accessed on June 4, 2020.

Hopkins et al. (1984) *'The evolution of fault tolerant computing'* Springer.

How Elements works and the roles of network participants. *Blockstream.* https://elementsproject.org/how-it-works. Accessed July 13, 2019.

http://aeternity.com/documentation-hub/protocol/oracles/oracle_transactions/

http://multiformats.io/

http://blockchainlab.com/pdf/Ethereum_white_paper-a_next_generation_smart_contract_and_dec entralized_application_platform-vitalik-buterin.pdf

http://eips.ethereum.org/EIPS/eip-608

http://plasma.io/

http://primecoin.io/

http://www.asciitable.com/

https://0x.org/portal/account

https://0x.org/why#benefits

https://agreements.network/files/an_whitepaper_v1.0.pdf

https://alacris.io/

https://connext.network/

https://cosmos.network/docs/intro/sdk-design.html#baseapp

https://cosmos.network/docs/spec/ibc/

https://cosmos.network/intro

https://daml.com/features/

https://dat.foundation/

https://digitalasset.com/

https://docs.bigchaindb.com/en/latest/decentralized.html

https://docs.corda.net/_static/corda-technical-whitepaper.pdf

https://docs.iota.org/docs/iota-basics/0.1/concepts/

https://docs.iota.org/docs/iri/0.1/introduction/overview

https://docs.ipfs.io/guides/concepts/ipns/

https://eips.ethereum.org/EIPS/eip-20

https://eos.io/why-eosio/

https://ethereumclassic.org/roadmap/

https://fantom.foundation/contents/data/2018files/10/wp_fantom_v1.6.pdf

https://filecoin.io/filecoin.pdf

https://funfair.io/how-it-works/our-solution/

https://github.com/corda/corda

https://github.com/EOSIO

https://github.com/ethereum/EIPs/issues/644

https://github.com/ethereum/EIPs/issues/677

https://github.com/ethereum/eips/issues/827

https://github.com/ethersphere/swarm/wiki/IPFS-&-SWARM

https://github.com/hyperledger/blockchain-explorer

https://github.com/hyperledger/burrow/tree/master

https://github.com/hyperswarm

https://github.com/libp2p/specs

https://github.com/OpenZeppelin/openzeppelin-solidity/blob/master/contracts/token/ERC721/ERC 721.sol

https://grid.hyperledger.org/docs/grid/nightly/master/introduction.html

https://hyperledger.github.io/composer/latest/introduction/introduction.html
https://hyperledger-fabric.readthedocs.io/en/release-1.4/build_network.html#install-prerequisites
https://hyperledger-fabric.readthedocs.io/en/release-1.4/whatis.html
https://ipld.io/
https://iroha.readthedocs.io/en/latest/overview.html
https://komodoplatform.com/antara-framework/
https://lisk.io/
https://loomx.io/
https://matic.network/
https://neo.org/
https://oceanprotocol.com/
https://radarrelay.com/
https://raiden.network/
https://sawtooth.hyperledger.org/docs/core/releases/latest/introduction.html
https://skale.network/
https://smt.steem.com/smt-whitepaper.pdf
https://spankchain.com/products
https://steem.com/developers/
https://steem.com/steem-bluepaper.pdf
https://tendermint.com/docs/
https://tendermint.com/docs/spec/abci/
https://tezos.com/
https://trinity.tech/#/
https://truebit.io/
https://www.celer.network/tech.html
https://www.corda.net/get-started/
https://www.cortexlabs.ai/Cortex_AI_on_Blockchain_EN.pdf
https://www.counterfactual.com/technology/
https://www.goquorum.com/developers
https://www.hyperledger.org/projects/aries
https://www.hyperledger.org/projects/avalon
https://www.hyperledger.org/projects/caliper
https://www.hyperledger.org/projects/cello
https://www.hyperledger.org/projects/fabric
https://www.hyperledger.org/projects/hyperledger-indy
https://www.hyperledger.org/projects/iroha
https://www.hyperledger.org/projects/quilt
https://www.hyperledger.org/projects/transact
https://www.hyperledger.org/projects/ursa
https://www.investopedia.com/tech/what-tron-trx/
https://www.ripple.com/use-cases/
https://www.steem.com/steem-whitepaper.pdf
https://www.stellar.org/how-it-works/stellar-basics/
https://bitcoinclassic.com/news/closing.html
https://bitcoingold.org/
https://bitcoinsv.io/
https://blockstream.com/liquid/
https://btcprivate.org/
https://counterparty.io/platform/

https://docs.ethhub.io/ethereum-roadmap/ethereum-2.0/eth-2.0-phases/

https://dogecoin.com/

https://education.district0x.io/general-topics/understanding-ethereum/basics-state-channels/

https://education.district0x.io/general-topics/understanding-ethereum/ethereum-sharding-explai
ned/

https://education.district0x.io/general-topics/understanding-ethereum/understanding-plasma/

https://en.bitcoin.it/wiki/List_of_address_prefixes

https://en.bitcoinwiki.org/wiki/GridCoin

https://ethereum-homestead.readthedocs.io/en/latest/introduction/the-homestead-release.html

https://forkdrop.io/how-many-bitcoin-forks-are-there

https://github.com/bitcoinxt/bitcoinxt/releases

https://github.com/ethereum/devp2p/blob/master/rlpx.md

https://github.com/ethereum/wiki/wiki/Design-Rationale

https://github.com/ewasm/design

https://github.com/mimblewimble/grin/blob/master/doc/intro.md

https://github.com/w3f/messaging/

https://gridcoin.us/

https://knowyourmeme.com/memes/doge

https://litecoin.org/

https://swarm-guide.readthedocs.io/en/latest/introduction.html

https://web.getmonero.org/get-started/what-is-monero/

https://www.bitcoincash.org/

https://www.bitcoindiamond.org/

https://www.bitcoininterest.io/

https://www.bitcoinunlimited.info/

https://www.dash.org

https://www.namecoin.org/

https://www.sec.gov/news/press-release/2014-111

https://www.utf8-chartable.de/unicode-utf8-table.pl

https://z.cash/technology/

Jameson, H. (November 18, 2016) Hard Fork No. 4: Spurious Dragon. *Ethereum blog.* https://blog.
ethereum.org/2016/11/18/hard-fork-no-4-spurious-dragon/. Accessed December 18, 2019.

Jankov, T. (June 1, 2018) Ethereum messaging: explaining whisper and status.im. *Sitepoint.* https://
www.sitepoint.com/ethereum-messaging-whisper-status/. Accessed January 13, 2020.

Jedusor, T.E. (July 19, 2016) MimbleWimble. *Scaling Bitcoin.* https://scalingbitcoin.org/papers/mim
blewimble.txt. Accessed November 26, 2019.

Jia, Y. (November 8, 2017) Demystifying Hashgraph: benefits and challenges. *Hackernoon.* https://
hackernoon.com/demystifying-hashgraph-benefits-and-challenges-d605e5c0cee5. Accessed on
October 23, 2019.

Jordan, R. (January 10, 2018) How to scale Ethereum: sharding explained. *Medium.* https://med
ium.com/prysmatic-labs/how-to-scale-ethereum-sharding-explained-ba2e283b7fce.   Accessed
December 21, 2019.

Kasireddy, P. (September 27, 2017) How does Ethereum work, anyway? *Medium.* https://med
ium.com/@preethikasireddy/how-does-ethereum-work-anyway-22d1df506369.   Accessed   on
December 13, 2019.

Klein, M. and Montomery, H. (May 13, 2020) TCS ApprovesHyperledger Cactus as New project.
Hyperledger. https://www.hyperledger.org/blog/2020/05/13/tsc-approves-hyperledger-cactus-as-
new-project. Accessed June 4, 2020.

Kosba, A., Miller, A., Shi, E., Wen, Z. and Papamanthou, C. (2015) Hawk: the blockchain model of cryptography and privacy-preserving smart contracts. *University of Maryland*. https://eprint.iacr.org/2015/675.pdf. Accessed November 23, 2019.

Largest bike sharing company in Southeast Asia to date

Lerner, S.D. (November, 2014) DECOR+HOP: A Scalable Blockchain Protocol. *Semantic scholar.* https://pdfs.semanticscholar.org/141e/d5f15e791ec7a9537a7b3250f4b7524ce302.pdf. Accessed on July 27, 2019.

Liao, N. (June 9, 2017) On Settlement Finality and Distributed Ledger Technology. *Yale Journal on Regulation.* yalejreg.com/nc/on-settlement-finality-and-distributed-ledger-technology-by-nancy-liao/. Accessed June 30, 2019.

Liquid (April 15, 2019). https://blog.liquid.com/examples-of-privacy-coins-monero-zcash-dash. Accessed November 26, 2019.

Manning, L. (May 1, 2019) Percentage of CoinJoin Bitcoin Transactions Triples over past year. *Bitcoin Magazine.* https://bitcoinmagazine.com/articles/percentage-coinjoin-bitcoin-transactions-triples-over-past-year. Accessed November 6, 2019.

Maxwell, G. (January 23, 2018) Taproot: Privacy preserving switchable scripting. *Linux Foundation.* https://lists.linuxfoundation.org/pipermail/bitcoin-dev/2018-January/015614.html. Accessed October 4, 2019.

Maxwell, G. (February 5, 2018) Graftroo: Private and efficient surrogate scripts under the taproot assumption. *Linux Foundation.* https://lists.linuxfoundation.org/pipermail/bitcoin-dev/2018-February/015700.html. Accessed on October 24, 2019.

Mihov, D. (February 6, 2018) All Ledger wallets have a flaw that lets hackers steal your cryptocurrency. *The next web.* https://thenextweb.com/hardfork/2018/02/06/cryptocurrency-wallet-ledget-hardware/. Accessed September 26, 2019.

Mitra, R. (2019) Understanding Ethereum Constantinople : A hard fork. *Blockgeeks.* https://blockgeeks.com/guides/ethereum-constantinople-hard-fork/. Accessed December 20, 2019.

Monahan, T. (2017) Unprotected function. *Github—Crytic.* https://github.com/crytic/not-so-smart-contracts/tree/master/unprotected_function. Accessed on September 14, 2019.

Mullins, R. (2012) What is a Turing machine? *Department of Computer Science and Technology—University of Cambridge.* https://www.cl.cam.ac.uk/projects/raspberrypi/tutorials/turing-machine/one.html. Accessed on June 5, 2019.

Nelaturi, K. (February 5, 2018) Understanding blockchain tech—CAP theorem. *Mangosearch.com.* https://www.mangoresearch.co/understanding-blockchain-tech-cap-theorem/. Accessed June 27, 2019.

Nopara73 (April 28, 2020) ZeroLink: The Bitcoin Fungibility Framework. *Github—ZeroLink.* https://github.com/nopara73/ZeroLink?source=post_page. Accessed October 15, 2019.

Oscar, W. (March 22, 2019) WTF is Cuckoo Cycle PoW algorithm that attract projects like Cortex and Grin? *Hackernoon.* https://hackernoon.com/wtf-is-cuckoo-cycle-pow-algorithm-that-attract-projects-like-cortex-and-grin-ad1ff96effa9. Accessed on July 25, 2019.

Payment channels. *Bitcoin.* https://en.bitcoin.it/wiki/Payment_channels. Accessed October 8, 2019.

Peterson, P. (November 23, 2016) Anatomy of A Zcash Transaction. *Electric coin.* https://electriccoin.co/blog/anatomy-of-zcash/. Accessed October 4, 2019.

Poon, J. and Dryja, T. (January 14, 2016) The Bitcoin lightening network: scalable off) chain instant payments. http://lightning.network/lightning-network-paper.pdf. Accessed October 21, 2019.

Protocol labs (July 19, 2017) Filecoin: A Decentralized Storage Network. *Protocol Labs.* https://filecoin.io/filecoin.pdf. Accessed on August 28, 2019.

Ray, J. (April 2, 2019) Welcome to the Ethereum Wiki! *Github—Ethereum.* https://github.com/ethereum/wiki/wiki/Ethash & https://github.com/ethereum/wiki/wiki/Dagger-Hashimoto. Accessed on Augst 6, 2019.

Ray, J. (March 4, 2019) Sharding roadmap. *Ethereum Wiki*. https://github.com/ethereum/wiki/wiki/Sharding-roadmap. Accessed December 20, 2019.

Reiff, N. (June 25, 2019) A history of Bitcoin hard forks. *Investopedia*. https://www.investopedia.com/tech/history-bitcoin-hard-forks/

Roberts, D. (January 9, 2014) Mergen-Mining.mediawiki. *Github—Namecoin*. https://github.com/namecoin/wiki/blob/master/Merged-Mining.mediawiki. Accessed on July 6, 2019.

Robinson, D. (2018) ivy-Bitcoin. https://docs.ivy-lang.org/bitcoin/language/IvySyntax.html. Accessed on December 6, 2019.

Rootstock experts (2015) Sidechains, Drivechains, and RSK 2-Way peg Design. *Rootstock*. https://www.rsk.co/noticia/sidechains-drivechains-and-rsk-2-way-peg-design/. Accessed August 12, 2019.

Rosic, A. (2017) Blockchain Address 101: What Are Addresses on Blockchains? *Blockgeeks*. https://blockgeeks.com/guides/blockchain-address-101/. Accessed on July 4, 2019.

Rosic, A. (2017) What is Ethereum Metropolis: the ultimate guide. *Blockgeeks*. https://blockgeeks.com/guides/ethereum-metropolis/. Accessed December 18, 2019.

Rosic, A. (2017) What is Ethereum Casper Protocol? Crash Course. *Blockgeeks*. https://blockgeeks.com/guides/ethereum-casper/. Accessed December 22, 2019.

Rosic, A. (2018) What is Ethereum gas? *Bockgeeks*. https://blockgeeks.com/guides/ethereum-gas/. Accessed December 11, 2019.

Schwartz, A. (January 6, 2011) Squaring the triangle: secure, decentralized, human-readable names. https://web.archive.org/web/20170424134548/http://www.aaronsw.com/weblog/squarezooko. Accessed November 28, 2019.

Schwartz, D. (August 31, 2011) How does merged mining work? *Stackexchange* https://bitcoin.stackexchange.com/questions/273/how-does-merged-mining-work. Accessed on July 10, 2019.

ScroogeMcDuckButWithBitcoin (2016) Drop Zone. https://github.com/17Q4MX2hmktmpuUKHFuoRmS5MfB5XPbhod/dropzone_ruby. Accessed on August 3, 2019.

Sedgwick, K. (April 4, 2019) Decentralized Networks Aren't Censorship-Resistant as You Think. *News.Bitcoin.com*. https://news.bitcoin.com/decentralized-networks-arent-as-censorship-resistant-as-you-think/. Accessed on July 2, 2019.

Seigen, Jameson, M., Nieminen, T., Neocortex and Juarez A.M. (March 2013) Cryptonight Hash Function https://cryptonote.org/cns/cns008.txt. Accessed on November 12, 2019.

Sharma, R. (June 25, 2019) What is Dash Cryptocurrency? *Investopedia*. https://www.investopedia.com/tech/what-dash-cryptocurrency/. Accessed November 27, 2019.

Shead, M. (February 14, 2011) State Machines—Basics of Computer Science. *Blog.markshead.com* https://blog.markshead.com/869/state-machines-computer-science/. Accessed June 5, 2019.

Smith, N.T. SHA 256 pseuedocode? *Stackoverflow*. https://stackoverflow.com/questions/11937192/sha-256-pseuedocode/46916317#46916317. Accessed May 26, 2020.

Sompolinsky, Y. and Zohar, A. (August, 2013) Secure High-Rate Transaction Processing in Bitcoin. *IACR*. https://eprint.iacr.org/2013/881.pdf. Accessed on July 30, 2019.

Sompolinsky, Y., Lewenberg, Y. and Zohar, A. (2016) SPECTRE: Serialization of Proof-of-work Events: Confirming Transactions via Recursive Elections. *HUJI*. www.cs.huji.ac.il/~yoni_sompo/pubs/17/SPECTRE.pdf. Accessed on August 1, 2019.

Sompolinsky, Y., Wyborski, S. and Zohar, A. (February 2, 2020) PHANTOM and GHOSTDAG. A scalable generalization of Nakamoto Consensus. *IACR*. https://eprint.iacr.org/2018/104.pdf. Accessed on February 27, 2020.

Spilman, J. (April 20, 2019) Anti DoS for tx replacement. *Linux Foundation*. https://lists.linuxfoundation.org/pipermail/bitcoin-dev/2013-April/002433.html. Accessed October 8, 2019.

Stepanov, H. (July 1, 2019) bip-0143 *Github—Bitcoin*. https://github.com/bitcoin/bips/blob/master/bip-0143.mediawiki. Accessed on December 28, 2019.

Stone, D. (March 26, 2018) An overview of SPECTRE—a blockDAG consensus protocol (part 2). *Medium.* https://medium.com/@drstone/an-overview-of-spectre-a-blockdag-consensus-protocol-part-2-36d3d2bd33fc. Accessed on August 3, 2019.

Stone, D. (March 29, 2018) An overview of PHANTOM: A blockDAG consensus protocol (part 3). *Medium.* https://medium.com/@drstone/an-overview-of-phantom-a-blockdag-consensus-protocol-part-3-f28fa5d76ef7. Accessed on August 4, 2019.

Sztorc, P. (December 14, 2015) Truthcoin. *Truthcoin.* http://bitcoinhivemind.com/papers/truthcoin-whitepaper.pdf. Accessed November 18, 2019.

Thake, M. (November 9, 2018) What is DAG Distributed Ledger Technology? *Medium.* https://medium.com/nakamo-to/what-is-dag-distributed-ledger-technology-8b182a858e19. Accessed on August 14, 2019.

Towns, A. (December 14, 2018) Schnorr and taproot (etc) upgrade. *Linux Foundation* https://lists.linuxfoundation.org/pipermail/bitcoin-dev/2018-December/016556.html?source=post_page. Accessed January 8, 2020.

Towns, A. (July 13, 2018) Generalised taproot. *Linux Foundation.* https://lists.linuxfoundation.org/pipermail/bitcoin-dev/2018-July/016249.html. Accessed on October 10, 2019.

Tran, A. (May 23, 2018) An Introduction to the BlockDAG Paradigm. *Daglabs.* https://blog.daglabs.com/an-introduction-to-the-blockdag-paradigm-50027f44facb. Accessed on August 28, 2019.

Tromp, J. (November, 2019) Cuck(at)oo Cycle. *Github—cuckoo.* https://github.com/tromp/cuckoo. Accessed on July 22, 2019.

Tual, S. (August 4, 2015) Ethereum Protocol Update 1. *Ethereum blog.* https://blog.ethereum.org/2015/08/04/ethereum-protocol-update-1/. Accessed December 17, 2019.

Van Hijfte, S. (2020) *Decoding blockchain for business.* 1st ed. New York, NY: Apress.

Vu, Q.H., Lupu, M., Ooi, B.C. (2010) Peer-to-peer Computing: Principles & Applications. 1st ed. U.S.: Springer, p. 35.

Wiigo Coin (January 2, 2019) ERC223 Token Standard Pros & Cons. *Medium.* https://medium.com/@wiiggocoin/erc223-token-standard-pros-cons-93a01f0239f. Accessed January 14, 2020.

Van Wirdum, A. (January 24, 2019) Taproot is Coming: What it is, and ho wit will benefit Bitcoin. *Bitcoin Magazine.* https://bitcoinmagazine.com/articles/taproot-coming-what-it-and-how-it-will-benefit-bitcoin. Accessed October 2, 2019.

Woo Kim, S. (May 28, 2018) Safety and Liveness—Blockchain in the Point of View of FLP Impossibility. *Medium.* https://medium.com/codechain/safety-and-liveness-blockchain-in-the-point-of-view-of-flp-impossibility-182e33927ce6. Accessed June 28, 2019.

Wood, G. (2019) Ehtereum: a secure decentralized generalized transaction ledger Byzantium version. https://ethereum.github.io/yellowpaper/paper.pdf

Wuille, P. (January 16, 2020) Bip taproot. *Github—Bitcoin bips.* https://github.com/sipa/bips/blob/bip-schnorr/bip-taproot.mediawiki. Accessed on January 20, 2020.

Wuille, P., Poelstra, A. and Kanjalkar.S. (2019) Analyze a Miniscript. *Blockstream.* http://bitcoin.sipa.be/Miniscript/. Accessed December 7, 2019.

Zander, T. (November 30, 2016) Classic is back. https://web.archive.org/web/20170202055402/https://zander.github.io/posts/Classic%20is%20Back/

Zeitfracht Medien GmbH
Ferdinand-Jühlke-Straße 7
99095 Erfurt, Deutschland
produktsicherheit@kolibri360.de